# ARCTICOLOGIES

# ARCTICOLOGIES

## Early Modern Actions for Our Warmer World

Lowell Duckert

University of Minnesota Press
Minneapolis
London

The University of Minnesota Press gratefully acknowledges the generous assistance provided for the publication of this book by the College of Arts and Sciences, the Center for Material Culture, and the Department of English at the University of Delaware.

Portions of "Winterlude: Flake" are adapted from "Flake: The Shapes of Snow in Early Modern Culture," in *Water and Cognition in Early Modern English Literature,* ed. Nic Helms and Steve Mentz (Amsterdam: Amsterdam University Press, 2024). Portions of chapter 1 are adapted from "Minerals in Winter: Robert Wittie's Cold Treatment," in *Spa Culture and Literature in England, 1500–1800,* ed. Sophie Chiari and Samuel Cuisinier-Delorme, Early Modern Literature in History, 191–209 (New York: Palgrave Macmillan, 2021). Portions of "Winterlude: Err" are adapted from "Arctic-Oceanic New York," in *Oceanic New York,* ed. Steve Mentz (Brooklyn, N.Y.: punctum, 2015). Portions of chapter 2 are adapted from "Imaginary Worlds," in *A Cultural History of the Sea in the Early Modern Age,* ed. Steve Mentz (London: Bloomsbury, 2023), Bloomsbury Academic, an imprint of Bloomsbury Publishing Plc. Portions of the "Co(l)da" are adapted from "Speaking as the North," in *The Sundial,* Arizona Center for Medieval and Renaissance Studies, 2019.



Published by the University of Minnesota Press
111 Third Avenue South, Suite 290
Minneapolis, MN 55401–2520
http://www.upress.umn.edu

ISBN 978-1-5179-1357-1 (hc)
ISBN 978-1-5179-1358-8 (pb)

A Cataloging-in-Publication record for this book is available from the Library of Congress.

Printed in the United States of America on acid-free paper



UMP BmB 2025

To Erin, girl from the north country

I was following the

—Fleet Foxes, "White Winter Hymnal"

What power art thou, who from below
Hast made me rise unwillingly and slow
From beds of everlasting snow?

—Henry Purcell, "The Cold Song"

# Contents

# Preface

## *Plunge*

Thronged up with cold.

—William Shakespeare, *Pericles*

Cold seems inanimate only until it touches you. I found this out on the mid-Atlantic coast a few winters ago when contemplating the immersive experience of the "polar-bear plunge" I had just taken, seeking out the (or any) multispecies interactions between fearless humans and the furry bears for which these ceremonies are humorously named. While often touted as "invigorating," these increasingly popular plunges have taken on a new light in an era of global warming and the polar bear's iconic status as a vulnerable species forced to swim ever-widening distances for food.[1] Such plunges test tenacity, to be sure, but they do not necessarily privilege one diver's status over the other; nor do they depend on domesticating actual species.[2] Less a metaphorical trope (humans as bears) and more of a map of distant attachments (or absent presences), a "polar plunge" for many participants requires visualizing the faraway, imagining places where the largest land predators are making their precarious lives known. Such immersion might actually *re*-immerse us—phenomenologically, I suspect—in Arctic waters materially inseparable from human activity. Is there an ethics of plunging to be felt at events advertizing the chilly thrills of sudden sensation on southern beaches and in northern elsewheres, a chance to think about humans' (perhaps their own bodies') effects on the waters they anthropogenically insert themselves into and then alter?

Two such dips come to mind. The first is a trio of voyages by Dutch navigator William Barents (ca. 1550–1597) to Nova Zembla, an archipelago north of Russia, from 1594–7. For Barents, who ultimately died of scurvy-inducing exposure, what made polar bears particularly dangerous was their ability to pursue his crew across long spans of water. Observe, for example, the entry by Gerrit de Veer (fl. 1570–1598), the expeditions' narrator, on July 9, 1594: a stalking bear entered their boat unsuspected near the island of Spitsbergen, after which a crewmember "shot her into the body with a musket";[3] unbelievably, "she leapt vp, and swam in the water."[4] The terrified men tied a rope around her neck, hoping to bring her, alive, as a "strange wonder [to] Holland," but "the bear swome to the boat, and with her fore-feet got hold of the sterne thereof," heaving almost half of herself in.[5] They then rushed to the other side out of fear and in effort to counterbalance the bear's enormous weight. The rope, fortunately for them, catches on the rudder, presenting one man with the opportunity to deal a lethal blow from his "halfe-pike."[6] The fleece is ultimately brought to Amsterdam.

Being one of the earliest attacks on the frightened Dutchmen (many more would be encountered later by land and by sea), the polar bear's prowess initially inspired them to wonder at her "most wonderfull strength, which almost is not to be found in any beast, for no man euer heard the like to be done by any lyon or cruel beast whatsoeuer."[7] The marvel, and indeed paradox, is that polar bears have bodies that are penetrable and yet are (seemingly) impervious to death. Indeed, the title page of the English translation of Barents's travels published in 1609 describes polar bears as "Monsters of the Sea."[8] Similarly, de Veer portrays the surrounding ice as partaking in the she-bear's bestial cruelty: after successfully avoiding an unremitting stream of stealthy icebergs on their return home in 1597, he writes that "we had escaped out of death's clawes" (*des doots kaecken*; "the jaws of death").[9] White ice and white bear conspire to kill the human in cold blood, as do white seas. In de Veer's Arctic, then, the human may only envy the polar bear's above- and below-water endurance. "Clawes" are a murderous reminder to his readers that plunges into Arctic ecologies more broadly, and into their biting waters more particularly, magnify the already-violable northern European body at risk, an admission that often spells death for the creaturely populations it violently engages, thereby challenging contemporary hopes that the Arctic was a hospitable and cohabitable space.

The second such "plunge" is my own that took place on February 3, 2019, at Rehoboth Beach. Totaling 3,544 "bears," it raised $906 thousand for Special Olympics Delaware. At 1:00 pm the air temperature hung

FIGURE 1. Pre-plunge, Rehoboth Beach, Delaware. Photograph by Hank Stoklosa / Special Olympics Delaware.

around a crisp 43 degrees Fahrenheit, while the water temperature was officially recorded at 39. Most immersions lasted for a few seconds, ranging from waist-high run-ins to full-on body slams. Police formed a protective line about a hundred feet from shore, with scuba divers on hand to ensure that everyone who went into the water eventually exited. (The second wave was delayed, I was told, because one person went missing). The experience was as expected as it was inexplicable: the original shock of cold was followed by a burst of energy, but I did not foresee my inability to speak to the state trooper layered in his protective gear, words failing to leave my gasping mouth. Immersion affects quickly, I thought, and yet makes slow. Toweling off on the beach, I wondered where the "polar bear" part of the "plunge" was located and whether anyone else was busy inquiring, whether they even cared. Maybe it was too serious a thought, a downer certain to ruin someone's recreational good time for a charitable cause. Why not just embrace the bracing?

I was warming up by now: might my plunge be construed as an attempt to keep the "clawes" of winter at bay a little longer, despite being connected, as they are, to (real) brumal bears? Is this yet another form of hypermasculine and borean forthrightness in the face of frigid adversity, a heroic quality that Barents certainly tapped into? A quick immersion that leads to adept emersion: this is the triumphal kind of plunge I did not sign up for, but rather, dripping there, came to confront.

I am still not sure whether I am asking the "right questions" of these "animals"—paraphrasing Vinciane Despret's provocative title—although I am willing to guess what they may say to us about the potential for "plunge" to reaffirm (and further) our intimacies with polar beings.[10] What more can immersion kindle?[11] When Ursula K. Heise speaks of "multispecies justice" in "The Hug of the Polar Bear," the coda to her book *Imagining Extinction,* she posits that stories and images, in lieu of physical encounters, nevertheless negotiate the treatment of endangered others, and that "cultural, political, and economic differences shape our thinking and talking about how species should live together as much as biological and ecological differences do."[12] Cold is what mortifies, what stultifies vigor, we are told; but the phenomenological affect inherent to the plunge, I propose, can enliven ecological conditions. Decide to take the plunge: immersive experiences acknowledge the additional communities that impinge on your own. (Stories count, too.) Such overlays, like the Arctic Circle itself within the Global North and South, must afford, and subsequently address, the disparate interests of neighbors both human and nonhuman who are involuntarily plunged into evidential injustices. While the dynamic has adjusted over time (it is now the bear who flees the deathly "clawes" of anthropogenic climate change), pivoting from the late sixteenth century to today suggests that warming waterways still act as a medium, steeping a mid-Atlantic tradition in the thinning icescapes of the poles and presenting us with an opportunity to reflect on the collapse of long-distance relations that occurs at the moment of plunge.

# Introduction

## *Cold Open*

> What is north. Is it a direction or a process. A method or a place. Is it space accelerated into time, like a glacial flood. Is it time spread into space, like permafrost. Is it always further on, further north until it makes a vertical drop, like a voice that traverses, illuminates everything but will not itself be held.
> Is it trajectory or endpoint, or both.
>
> —Caroline Bergvall, *Drift*

> What is six winters? They are quickly gone.
>
> —William Shakespeare, *Richard II*

This book is a compilation of "Arcticologies," my loose term for sixteenth- and seventeenth-century stories that have an invigorating role left to play in the retelling of climate history and our fraught futures with cold. In their introduction to the single collection dedicated to "a premodern perspective" on the topic, Dolly Jørgensen and Virginia Langum write that European visions "adopt and develop or contradict and question the concept of an othered or essentialized North."[1] But unlike these editors, who note their "intent of exploring the North as an envisioned, rather than physical, space,"[2] I plumb the material forces that directed their gaze and the substantial entanglements that supported their visions. While some of my selections seek to "adopt" polarities, each of my chapters ultimately fights against the historical tendency to posit an exoticized, abstracted, looked-upon Arctic. Proclaiming human ingenuity and perception to be somehow cut-off from its northern environment also perpetuates, echoing Edward Said (1978), a longstanding "borealism."[3] Early modernity aids today's attempts to bring the Arctic into politics by contextualizing its matter as already embedded within political systems: it is not so much an "opening" for politics to enter now, but a redirection into longstanding entanglements. *Arcticologies* should not be mistaken for a comprehensive study (I will cite several of those); nor does it finally finish the story by supplying a missing temporal link (although it makes a strong case for the period's inclusion). In all, it is a meticulous curation of curious texts meant to recruit other (*your*) pursuits. The proceeding pages constellate materials engrossed in the "doings" of cold, in the fanciful and factual glimpses of the "Arctic" and of "north," and in those monikers' remaking. Delving into the *imaginatio borealis*[4] as a still-generative rather than long-exhausted site, I will outline a few characteristic features of my flitting archive before sliding into my centerpiece, which is *The Great Frost: Cold Doings in London* (1608) by Thomas Dekker (ca. 1572–1632).

- North is (a) disorientation. Most of my texts are north-looking by virtue of their setting: North America, northern Europe, and those various islands and waters fringing the Arctic Circle that connect the two continents. Metropolitan life is one stop on my longer horizonal scan of the northern hemisphere. But there are many definitions of "north": geodetic/geographical ("true"), magnetic, grid, and astronomical. To "go north" is slang for being "on the up." When something "heads south," it goes awry. But its various meanings do not recalibrate headings as much as cause the idea of "north" itself to contort. Peter Davidson remarks that "north" is a "shifting idea" because it always recedes from our attempts at encapsulation. It is better to speak of "a," not "the," north.[5] To follow his logic is to "kee[p] the twilight" that hovers between specificity and unrecognizability, be it topography or the nature of knowing altogether: "almost everything that consoles us," he confesses, "is false."[6] This sentiment does not bar discomfort from the discussion. Travelers grow anxious without secure bearings. But what is unsettling, to his point, can also be creative. The effect of low light is dizzying, which is precisely its attractive affect. When thinking about *norths,* an aesthetic of unmooring predominates. The artistic disorientation of "north" acts centripetally and fugally, pulling relations in and redistributing them out, aggregated anew. It is in this oscillating direction that I want us to set out, where cold "doings" can reach into not only traditional sites of northernness but also those less attached to the compass-bearing north, the polar high north, or axes altogether. There is cold to be discovered in seemingly incompatible places—ice in the equatorial tropics, snow in the desert—and searching for them helps to foresee the endless, un/likely permutations that changing temperatures will bring to things north and south from us.

- The volumes herein are not voiced by humans alone. I am captivated by Gretel Ehrlich's vision of a "very cold library": "at both ends of the world, the persistent undulations of snowflakes, sands, gravels, gases, and waters are stories held inside ice—recent stories, and ones from long ago."[7] Composition names an ongoing, elemental conversation that results in the vociferous matter known as "story." There is locution "inside ice"; there are garrulous "undulations" left to map. For these reasons, seemingly incompatible genres gather in my inventory as well. I analyze seminal works in the history of science, such as the *New Experiments and Observations Touching Cold* by Robert Boyle (1627–1691) in 1665, for their literary qualities. I take seriously, for example, what that inhuman "touching" entails. Similarly, Thomas James's (1592/3–1635) narrative of over-wintering on Charlton Island (1631–1632) is more than a blip on the way to the first successful navigation of the Northwest Passage in 1906 by Norwegian explorer Roald Amundsen (1872–1928). I treat its travails as a pivotal case study in "becoming ice," the process of human decomposition and recomposition with "strange" landscapes. James's talent was not singular: poets penned "Frozen Verse"[8]; printers stamped their achievements on the ice; John Webster (1580[?]–1625[?]) blamed the "dull . . . time of winter, presented in so open and black a theatre"[9] for the poor attendance at his play *The White Devil* (1612); natural philosophers cursed congealed inkpots; and artists pictured coldscapes as sprawling archipelagos (coastal glaciers) and frosted windowpanes (miniature snowflakes). Consider, for example, something so simple as a snowdrift noted by the tutor Roger Ascham (1515–1568) in *Toxophilus* (1545): "This experience made me more marvel at the nature of the wind than it made me cunning in the knowledge of the wind."[10] The mesmerizing motion of the wind on the snow is a "marvel" by itself and does not necessarily incur the seeking and unveiling ("knowing") of its beautiful inner workings. No answers to cryptic questions are blowing in this wind; instead, he is wholeheartedly content with his airy enwrapping of felt "experience." Ascham's arrest exemplifies the fluttering curation of "Arcticologies": aggregates of human–cold, "nature"–culture musings, whose foundations are made up of inventive, irresistible drifts.

- *Omne malum ab aquilone* ("out of the North / all ill comes forth"[11]). My catalogue of cold texts is an eclectic one, furnishing moments of fondness and affiliation, as well as the expected motifs of a "malevolent," "demonic north" and its "locus of evil."[12] Winter is coming both *at* and *for* you. Be "discontent" (Shakespeare, *Richard III*, 1.1.1).[13] After Dante (1265–1321), we know that there is no fate worse than to be damned to a frozen circle.[14] John Milton's Arctic hellscape in *Paradise Lost* (1667/1674), "a frozen Continent . . . dark and wild" where "cold performs th' effect of Fire,"[15] proves that he paid little mind to pagans' paradisaical myths but favored the bleakness of contemporary reports. "Gloomy" mountain glaciers were wide-ranging, too:[16] such as the Alps that were an "ocean of featherd raine"[17] to the English diarist John Evelyn (1620–1706), or the "Globes of Ice, and flakes of solid Snow"[18] mentioned in *Sophonisba: Or, Hannibal's Overthrow* (1676) by Nathaniel Lee (1653[?]–1692). But, in this "ocean" of mine, we will meet the occasional eccentric whose icy idiosyncrasies and nonnormative permutations of desire fractured the conventional and permissible. Many of the expeditions that follow, like that of the English captain James, could certainly be counted as disastrous both financially and physically. Yet frost-fair paraphernalia, for example, do not build so much on fiasco as they do on frivolity, and I include other architectural opportunities like these (like a little London literally raised on ice) to present an ampler frame of co-constructive activity with the cold. If they knew that the winter was going to get you, they eagerly awaited the chance to intermingle, and their irrepressible joys are edifying in their own right.

- I participate in an ongoing effort to craft a "long history of northern travel writing," one that leads to Erhlich, Barry Lopez, John Moss, and Sara Wheeler.[19] The phrase "travels in the north" pronounces a spacious continuum. Sir Clements Robert Markham's *The Lands of Silence* (1921), Sir Albert Hastings Markham's *Northward Ho!* (1879), and Fridtjof Nansen's *In Northern Mists* (1911) were also "Arcticologies" as I have been defining the term. All northern explorers, they inserted themselves into a renowned lineage of travel narratives that began in antiquity. Their predecessors were Richard Hakluyt (1552[?]–1616), Samuel Purchas (1577–1626), and Luke Foxe (1586–1635). But the earlier authors who navigated cold should not be judged by how well their ideas align with the "Arctic dreams" of twentieth- and twenty-first-century environmentalist writers who also tell of a tenanted, high-spirited location. At least one throughline traverses the centuries of discovery, even if previous aspirations turned out to be unrealistic: the anthologies they produced were brimming with cold's inhuman agency. I prefer to focus on the intersections within the "long history," thus disclosing recent travel writers' early modern posturing (their citational practices, for example) while also revealing how their ecological visions rejuvenate the borean imaginings of the past. These dialogical points of interest reshape the ways in which we read and story a multitemporal Arctic: where insights are to be gleaned, reviewed, and then acted upon; where the search after the boreal is a means to dwell on what is possible rather than police fact from fiction.
- This book follows the trails blazed by ecofeminist theory and feminist science discourse. My compilation gestures to illustrious scientific fathers like Francis Bacon (1561–1626), Boyle, and Thomas Browne (1605–1682), but it also emphasizes the work of women who have advanced cold's grip on cultural imaginations. Despite being a best-selling writer, Ehrlich is acutely aware that the "library" has historically

ostracized women from ice fields. "Iceolation,"[20] in her words, bespeaks the ubiquitous feeling of isolation in Arctic places, but I also think that her coinage underscores the fact that hypermasculinity remains uneasily synonymous with the cold.[21] Misogynistic tropes have persisted this way: for Shakespeare's Petruchio to "break the ice, and do this feat" (*Taming of the Shrew*, 1.2.264), he must woo the snow-queen Katherina. In winter, women were ridiculed for their willingness to "fall" down (licentiously) on the ice. While almost all of my primary sources are written by male authors, the attention I pay to gender and sexuality, especially the more affirmative configurations of desire that cold allows, is due to the insights of female artists and critics who are tackling this well-established hegemony and antifeminist analogies. "I am bodily, I am earthly, and sometimes, I feel cold (even if I am inside)," professes Stephanie D. Clare, "however, we have yet to understand how earthly, temperate existence implicates differential experiences of subjectivity and objectification."[22] Lisa Bloom's book *Gender on Ice* is essential reading on these shelves, with its interrogation of men's "passion for blankness" and "the coitus of discovery" that consummates it.[23] In a more egalitarian branch of polar studies, *The Blazing World* (1666) by Margaret Cavendish (1623[?]–1673) begins with a voyage to the North Pole[24] and exemplifies what Gina Bloom calls the female "voice in motion,"[25] one that is still running, for instance, with the Iditarod racer Blair Braverman's 2016 memoir *Welcome to the Goddamn Ice Cube*.[26] Located within these pages is an inclusive membership that assists in widening the ambit of "welcome" to those excluded too often and for too long.

- Regardless of its association with shimmering ice fields and the sparkling imagination, the Arctic has never been "white." My analysis of cold's "doings" is admittedly tied to a northern European archive to which white writers contributed and had access. But multiple Indigenous men and women at this time were trafficked, illustrated, and compelled to perform for royal and public audiences. My task is to make the wine-dark water of Adriaen Coenen's *Visboek* (1577–1579)—a bay named

FIGURE 2. The abduction of an Inuk by Martin Frobisher (1535[?]–1594) in 1576, from Adriaen Coenen's *Visboek* (1577–1579), sig. 48v, The Hague, KB, National Library of the Netherlands KW 78 E 54. The man died shortly after arriving in London.

after an Englishman who abducted the anonymous Inuk man in 1576—more multiculturally vivid. Indigenous presences are historically evident, even if their voices have been suppressed or their very existence denied, and this is true for our visits both to London and to other latitudes. The Arctic and the places touched by it are "haunted" by colonial violence, in Coll Thrush's sense, twisted with "ghosts" and vestiges of past lives.[27] To hearken to these stories is to decenter whiteness from the geopolitical Circle, meaning both its status within the spiraling hemispheric barrier and its placement inside the smaller circles of cryological relations. Provincializing early modern Europe acknowledges the campaigns of resistance happening in this day and age. The question of privatized Arctic "ownership" clashes with Indigenous rights to territorial sovereignty: claims that seek regional autonomy from exploitative administrations, not from the ecologies in which they are enmeshed. This book incorporates pre/colonial

Indigenous perspectives and incidents of transcultural exchange in order to challenge Eurocentric claims to the cold, including white supremacists' pernicious appropriation of "borealist" civilizations from Viking lore and Nazi mysticism that erase any original inhabitants they deem to be inferior.[28] Even though the "cult of the north"[29] bends toward socialism and fascism both, the latter has been on the rise. If titles like *A Negro Explorer at the North Pole* (1912), Matthew Henson's autobiography, and Tété-Michel Kpomassie's *An African in Greenland* (1981) seem outlandish, the prismatic Arctic I paint here recognizes the modern-day communities of color who continue to live with the repercussions of previous tragedies, and who, through humor, activism, and art, work hard to remediate them.[30]

- "Shall I compare thee to an Arctic day (or night)"?[31] When addressing the Arctic as "home," we should also take into account northern visions of Europe *from* Indigenous, (early) modern perspectives. This book's genesis is indebted to the voices of Indigenous writer-activists. Any imagining of a future planet via the past must engage with the communities who were, and are, part of it.[32] To try to honor what Zoe Todd has named "Indigenizing the Anthropocene,"[33] *Arcticologies* sets up an open-ended, interdisciplinary conversation between the early modern environmental humanities, polar sciences, and traditional ecological knowledges over four hundred years of contact. I am inspired by Igor Krupnik and Dyanna Jolly's collection *The Earth Is Faster Now,* which employs the concept of the "frontier" for "communicating environmental change from the perspective of indigenous arctic people."[34] When a "faster" earth *now* meets a slower earth *then,* the "frontiers" of Kalaallit Nunaat (Greenland) and Qikiqtaaluk (Baffin Island) yield more representative studies into the ontology, epistemology, and ethics of cold.[35] Sheila Watt-Cloutier passionately advocates for northern peoples' "right to be cold."[36] "Ice is life," she argues, and carbon-polluting governments have a responsibility to heed this fact and to treat "*all* ice-dependent arctic life" with dignity and respect.[37] Building on these foundational works (and more), I plan to show how early modern cold bridges Indigenous and non-Indigenous stories and practices, generating new networks for talking about, and ultimately tackling, Arctic ills. The book's antiracist and decolonizing stance is meant to amplify protesters' and policy-makers' work in progress. In doing so, it hopes to enlist additional voices too.

FIGURE 3. *The Great Frost: Cold Doings in London* (1608), Houghton Library.

## Much Ado about Cold: Thomas Dekker's *Great Frost*

The English playwright was enthralled by the agency of cold. Published at a printshop on London Bridge directly above the gelid exhilarations below, his cover page recounts the city's first-ever frost fair. It is one of the earliest visualizations of "cold doings" (the things cold does) to and in the subpolar metropolis. Bowling, beer-drinking, and back-sliding are only a few of the novel forms of leisure it allows. The pamphlet's format is dialogic: it involves a Londoner ("Citizen") describing winter's workings to an old rustic ("Country-man") who has come to walk "upon a field of glasse as it were, . . . a slippery world."[38] The latter knew the river had congealed before during Elizabeth I's reign (1564), but this year is markedly different in degrees of both temperature and festivity: "In a few cold words," he puns, "the Thames [is] frozen ouer," to which the citizen replies, "yea Father, and frozen ouer and ouer."[39] The citizen, however, in his caution, and in comparison to the title page's delights, turns into a cold killjoy: "The Frost hath made a floore upon [the river], which shewes like gray Marble, roughly hewen out: it is a very pauement of glasse, but that it is more strong. The Thames now lies in, or rather is turned (as some thinke) bankerupt, and dares not shew her head."[40] Under the bridge, "winter castles of yce, which jutting against the arches . . . and striueing (like an unruly Drunkard at a gate of the Citie in the night time) to passe through, haue there bin stayed and lodged so long, till they haue lyen in heapes and got one upon another."[41] The citizen equates the crude piling-on of ice with the lewd hordes carousing on it. He disabuses the country man of the wondrous story he had heard of fuel-delivering "wherries" operated by pullies. He also refuses to share a drink with him from one of the marvelous taverns on wheels patrolling the ice. Instead, the curious country man and abstemious citizen partake in a lesson in civic duty. After the "cakes of Ice . . . were made and baked cold in the mouth of winter, at the least a fortnight or three weekes, before they were crusted and cremēted togither; but after they once ioynd their strēghts in one, their backs held out and cold not be brokē."[42] Out of the "mouth" of winter comes a truism: "We may make this good use euen out of this watry and transformed element," expounds the older, "that . . . violent factions and combinations . . . in a Commonwealth, are not easily disolued, if once they bee suffered to grow up to a head."[43] A brumal bromide to inspire the strongest of civic solidarities: a "cold breakfast"[44] for the sanctimonious civilian, perhaps, but not for the typical commoner.

And yet, tasting the caking flakes only stokes others' desire for adventure: "Wylde youthes and boyes were the first Marchant venturers to discouer these cold Ilandes of Ise . . . trauelling into our new found Fréezeland, by those créekes."[45] Identifying ice-"trauellers" with polar explorers and merchant capitalists helps amplify the cold's attractive stakes. Indeed, "no danger could nip their bloods with feare" as they braved "that waterie wilderness," watched by thousands of onlookers who swore they would not "follow their steppes."[46] But when dared, they did; the rest of the pamphlet recalls the vast numbers of people, the victuals imbibed, and, most vividly, the resultant deaths: "It hath been a kinde of battaile for the time, for some haue fallen in up to the knées, others to the middle, others to the arme-pittes, yea and some haue been ducked ouerhear and eares, yet haue crawled out like drowned Rats, whiles others haue suncke to the bottome that neuer rose againe to the top: they had cold bed to lye in."[47] Arctic playtime is over. The hurts and harms once brought upon the discoverer's body are now visited upon the city. Commerce comes to a standstill: "It was (before) called The dead Terme, and now may wee call this, The dead Vacation, The frozen Vacation, The cold Vacation."[48] Business- and body-killer, wintering robs food, wood, and spirit: "Not onely hath this frost nipt away those comforts that should reuiue the outward parts of the body, but those that should giue strength and life to the inward."[49] A time of dearth and dark—days of the "dead"—is contrary to what the country man expected or wanted to hear. Chided by the citizens' litany of chills, wrapped up in "the wrath of Winter,"[50] his attitude warps.

The stifling cold brings the urban and rural regions, like their representatives, sympathetically closer, though stiffly so: "The same colde hand of Winter is thrust into our bosomes, the same sharpe ayre strikes woundes into our bodies: the same Sunne shines uppon us, but the same Sunne doeth not heate us no more [than] it doeth you."[51] Finding consolation in equally divided adversity delivered in Shylockian style, the two men remark on the eventual thaw (assuring themselves on the depths of its destruction); the older lectures the younger on the great frosts of the past (for which he is commended by his partner for personifying a chronicle); they disclose the knavish tricks of the lottery (compromising its integrity); and, ultimately, they settle on the consolation that other nations have it worse (undercutting the compassionate contract). "So that the calamities that haue faine upon us by this crueltie of the weather, are so much to be endured with the greater patience, and with more thankesgiuing to God, because his hand hath punished neighbors and other Nations as heauily (if not more seuerely) [than] he hath us."[52] No winter, it seems, is complete without difference from others and indifference to them (like the curious and conniving city "rats"). Cold is a "breakfast" for civic champions, a component of a healthy society when it cultivates forbearance, not actual food. The dissolute deserve literal dissolution (to be "drowned"). The men exchange gifts before departing: the country man with a "Moddell of the Country" and the citizen with a "Mappe of [the] Citie."[53] To the reader, they bestow a warning: do not seek to know the intricacies of cold's doings. To do things on the ice, such as playing the lottery, is to take a chance, most likely winning a "cold Vacation" before quickly losing your life.

Dekker later found himself writing about winter while jailed, serving time (1612–1619) in the king's bench prison, Southwark, for a debt he owed to John Webster (father of the playwright). There he revised *The Great Frost,* now seven years old, as *The Cold Yeare* (1615), dwelling anew on the doings of the "deep snow . . . in which men and cattell . . . perished"[54] a year earlier. Dekker significantly extends the dialogue from a decade before, collapsing sub/arctic climates and detailing the "accidents"[55] that it incurs, before attempting to right these errors via the citizen's espousal of hard work. Once more, he presents a dialogue between a London shopkeeper ("Cittizen") and an elderly customer ("North-Country-man"), at moments repeating his previous work in order to connect again the tribulations of city and country, creating yet another cultural trauma of national proportions. That *same* "cold hand of Winter is thrust into our bosomes,"[56] notes the elder, and when he is pressed by the younger to prognosticate what will follow "this strange Winter," the picture is apocalyptic: "When these great . . . Mountaines of Yce be digged downe, and be made leuell with the Waters; when these hard Rockes shall melt into Riuers, . . . then it is to be feared, that the swift, violent, and unresistable Land-currents . . . will beate downe Bridges, beate downe Buildings, ouer-flow our Corne-fields, ouer-run the Pastures, drowne our Cattell, and endanger the liues both of Man and Beast."[57] The snows of yesteryear are inauspicious. But, despite what looks like a casual reworking of older material, there are several differences pertaining to the particular "yeare" of 1614, the most obvious being the great snowdrifts that accompanied the frost: "The heapes of Snow in those former times, being this yeare doubled and trebled, the miserie that falles with it, must by consequence, be multiplyed."[58]

"Multiplyed!" indeed, answers the traveler who has seen the snow enfolding families "to undoe them"[59] firsthand across the country, their terror enough that one could easily mistake England for the Arctic. In 1608, only the most courageous souls walked on the water at winter, moving like intrepid captains across the "glassy" surface of "Fréezeland." But now the fabled continent comes to them from somewhere "beyond [the] Sea":

> I will tell you Sir, if you saw some plases by which I haue passed but within these three weeks, you would verily thinke, that Freezland were come ouer Sea, swimming on a cake of Ice, and that it was lodged in England. Nay you would, if you dwelt as coldly and miserably, as some poore people of our owne Nation doe, you would almost sweare, that those partes of England lay under the Frozen Zone, and scarce remember there were a Sunne in Heaven, so seldome doe his fyres cast any heate upon them.[60]

The northerner knew that his "nation" had always been on a collision course with the far/ther north, or at least with the cold it bred and brought over. When the "beyond" punctures the "plases" of home, it ceases being "beyond." England under snow is also "under the frozen zone." The "mappe" of Dekker's previous interlocutors has been effectively redrawn by these cold interlopers: once-separate climates "cake" together, transforming the entire country itself, layer by layer, into a "swimming" ice-island at sea. Wintry weather has again linked spheres both little (country and city) and large (nation and zone)—and even smaller (miserable "poore" to sufficiently "heated")—but what is left unsaid is whether this cryological conflation of cartography, climate, and class remains an aberration (the *the* of the title definitively marking the winter's singularity in the citizens' long cultural memory of cold), or if the season is to be interpreted as one very "cold year" out of an elongated and strengthening trend. The printed header "of strange accidents," not found on the title page, foregrounds this question. "I thinke you haue not seene your Cittie so whited this fourtie yeares,"[61] remarks the unnamed north-man, rendering the recent white-out as a meteorological misstep. The citizen agrees with his calculation. The "strange," in any case, has lost none of its appeal: like the wanderer of 1608, the visitor wishes to see for himself the rumors of a city turned winter wonderland, to espy a famous river frozen over, a London overrun with "white Beares, . . . Monsters . . . that . . . ran aliue in the Strees, and devoured people,"[62] drifts so deep that four men lie buried with their horses in a gaping "Pitte of Snow" and that "many more" corpses of "Men, Women, and Children" lie scattered about "that neuer will come within reach of our knowledge."[63]

The most striking insertion of Dekker's, though, is a "most lamentable"[64] tale told by the elder to the younger. Two Londoners journeying north to an unspecified town are caught in a blizzard. Blinded and trusting their horses, they "left the beaten Path (all hidden in Snow,) and forsaking the direct way to the Towne, had gotten on a suddaine into one of the Woods."[65] The accident (their "suddaine" and literal erring from the road) is costly: one dies of the "dangerous cold Feauer"[66] in the other's arms. Beleaguered and bereaved, the survivor stumbles into town, moves its populace to "pittie,"[67] and returns with help to bury his friend's body. There, "ouer grieuing at the losse of his Companion, and at so rare and vnheard-of a Calamitie, fell likewise extreamely sicke in the same Towne: And whether he did recouer or not, I have not heard."[68] The 1615 pamphlet's *mise en abyme* schematic certainly sketches an image of "the dead term," that doomsday portrait on the first page, just as its language casts the winter's "strangeness" and its "accidents" as ghastly vignettes (devouring bears, drifts, and griefs), some real and some imagined, that are best kept "rare," "vnheard-of," and hopefully not repeated.

*Cold Yeare* ends on an encouraging note, then, but only if one "digs downe" and out according to the citizen's prescriptive regimen of labor: "The tyranny of this Season, killes all trading"[69] (a familiar complaint), yet winter is not wholly liable for the death of business this time. Human lassitude is culpable as well: he chastises those tradesmen who "haue either little to doe, or else can doe little, by reason of the Weather, when they throw by their Tooles, fall . . . to slinging of Snow-bals."[70] Leisure leads only to a slump in London's economic prosperity; after all, he asserts, snow is commercially worthless, and therefore has no use: "Unless they bee Shoe-makers, . . . none can extract or melt a penny of Siluer out of all these heapes."[71] Like the respectable and savvy shopkeeper that he is, the citizen sends his guest to the freshly paved site of Smithfield, boasting of the noble enterprises he will witness there: "Whereas you shall see by the carefull prouidence, care, and industrie, of our Honorable Senators . . . much Money buried under that durtie Fielde, by the buying of hundreds of Labourers to reduce it . . . to the fairest and most famous Market-place, that is in the whole Kingdome."[72] One way to beat the winter blues is to build, bury, and buy, to outwork the "doings" of cold, even if means forgetting the untold numbers of bodies "buried" in the ground or the labor-power that sells its time but is prohibited from picking up playful pursuits, trading tools for snowballs in their downtime. No, the proscription goes: do not deviate from the "beaten path," set to work, and wait for the weather to clear, lest an "accident" tragically befall you. And look: "it hath now left snowing,"[73] announces the older man in astonishment, his final words on his way out the door, into the domesticated "durtie," now wiser for the winter.

The reader of the second pamphlet, Dekker purports, "shall finde many thinges for his profit"[74] by reexamining the overlay of English and Arctic winters that the characters (and, meta-discursively, they themselves) inhabit at the time of publication. Both texts, arguably, outline cases for overwintering, and ultimately overcoming, the cold. The admonitions of 1608 (*do not tangle with a "slippery world"*) are revised into methods for safely skirting entanglement (*the "slippery world" is your own.*) To state this shift in Dekker's vision another way: one's "cold Vacation" is no longer a choice (to go on); it is a trip one is already taking (to go through), complete with icy tales that are both inadvisable and inspiring. It is impossible to know what was behind his digression in seven short years; as the author of *The Shoemakers Holiday* (1599), we might assume that a lingering worry about the less-well-off members of the population lent itself to a pronounced valuation of handicrafts and a satirization of those high-minded citizens who would seek to denigrate them.

To round out my discussion of Dekker's journalistic series, however, I want to return to a wintry suggestion briefly touched on above in his biographical detail and left lingering in the northerner's last lines. It is unclear whether the snow will cease (it has "left" for "now"), business will bounce back (it had been "killed"), or the lonely companion will recover (from his "feauer"). These moments are all at the threshold, as they catch the conversationalist at the house's actual point of entry/exit, and are significant in their inability to resolve the chanciness of cold despite humans' attempts to corral its behaviors and overcorrect its accidents: from crashing climates (delivered by ice floe), to circuitous pathways (steering horsemen astray), to sidetracked citizens (distracted by snowballs). Even a "lotterie" could ascribe to its participants a misleading degree of control: a winner hand-picked by a master of ceremonies amidst the fluxes of fortune.

Recall that Dekker was physically confined at the time of redrafting. Upon release, he published his *Dreame* (1620). Awakening "ovt of a longe Sleepe,"[75] he is shocked to find his features nightmarishly transformed: "my cold hands had tane leaue of feare, / Yet my Heart panted, and my Haire turn'd white, / More through the Ghastly Obiects of this Night, / [Than] with the Snow of Age."[76] He is whitened, that is, by what he witnessed, metaphorically hardened by his ordeals inside a cell. The material winters of "snow"—the "cold yeare" of 1614 nested within the larger "age" of seven years—are not responsible for his accelerated "age" progression. And so, Dekker resembles the personification of winter, a trope that his country man of 1615 escalates to a pitch his predecessor of 1608 barely approached:

> I have been an old Brier, and stood many a Northerly Storme: the Windes haue often blowne bitterly in my Face, Frostes haue nipped my Blood, Ysicles (you see), hang at my Beard, and a hill of Snow couers my head. I am the Sonne of Winter, and like the Father, that as hee does, I loue to be seene in all places. I had as leise walke up to the knees in Snow, as to tread upon Turkie Carpets: And therefore my Jorney to see London once more ere I die, is as merry to mee, as if I were a Woman and went a Gossipping; For the Earth shewes now, as if shee lay inne, (All in White).[77]

To be "all in white" betrays the uneasy confusion between embodiment and seasonality that all of the aforementioned characters share: whether the human is "all in" ontologically, its blood in/fused with face-nipping "frostes," or whether part (but not "all") of the self is metamorphosed by contact. In either case, one's humanness precariously attaches to winter's "white" like an icicle dangles from a beard. Winter widens the ambiguity between snow and man. The question of transgression and corporeal integrity posed by Dekker, his fictional country man, and his fellow countrymen amount, literally, to "a hill of Snow."

The citizen, however, wants none of this speculation. The country has been scourged enough by "an Arme from Heauen": floods, fires, "killing Frostes," the intolerable fluctuations in food supplies, and "now last of all, with deepe and most dangerous Snowes."[78] But rather than amending their sinful ways after receiving these divine signs, his peers merely jest: "Wee make but a May-game, fashioning ridiculous Monsters of that, which God in vengeauce poures on our heades; when in doing so, wee mocke our owne selues, that are more monstrous and ugly in all the shapes of sinne."[79] His dense complaint is worth unpacking: the sculpting of snowmen, in other words, mocks (ridicules) God's judgment by mocking (reproducing) man's form, a shape made in the image of that same deity, transforming idealized creation into a ridiculous set of sneering creatures. To make matters worse, these monsters are made with the very material that has been sent to punish mankind. (The invective launched against snowballs seems petty in light of this compact and condemnatory sermon.) His interlocutor agrees, tersely perhaps, in order to change the topic: "You melt (Sir) out of a heape of Snow, very profitable and holsome instructions."[80] At first glance, the business owner sees at his door a sturdy Englishman, a hypermasculine sojourner and seeker of the cold set in opposition to soft or luxuriating sorts (the effeminate "Turk" and the neighboring wag, both denizens of warm places). And yet the possibility of a snow-man's existence equally confronts him. A hybridized "sonne of Winter," born from a "frost"-"father," has been invited inside. Snowmen plague the sanctimonious citizen for suggesting this cryogenic potential, and while a deeper moral might "melt" from the situation, the logic assumes that said snow will disappear, a promise that the pamphlet does not fulfill.

The desire for winter's release is real. Richard II had wished as much in Shakespeare's eponymous play: "Alack the heavy day, / That I have worn so many winters out / And know not now what name to call myself. / Oh, that I were a mockery king of snow, / Standing before the sun of Bolingbroke, / To melt myself away in water-drops" (*Richard II,* 4.1.250–55). Richard's beautiful self-reflection in the snow figuratively foreshadows his monarchical dissolution. However, read alongside Dekker's enforced confinement, one who had seen the civic body (and his own) all "couered" in white, the thawing "mockery" is a poignant fantasy of escape from winter's "heavy days," those "windes" that "dig downe" into the body. To defrost: it is a dream befitting one who had "worn so many winters" in a cold cell, a snow-man who knew becoming-winter all too well, and who meditated on the "myself," the self, suspended in a delicate state of delayed deliquescence.

## "Cold Doings" in Detail, Or, the Argument

"Sir" . . . "you melt." Dekker pictures cold's vigorous interrelationships—between climate and culture, urban and rural, body and environment—that were appealing as well as lethal. Subsequently, he helps sketch many of the "doings" that early modern cold has to offer. At a time when "the cold pole" and "the map of frigor"[81] were just beginning to be painted in (and were still unfinished[82]), Dekker dedicated part of his career to detailing, twice, humans' physical interactions with snow and ice. His entire life nearly coincided with one of the northern hemisphere's chilliest periods in recent history: the Grindelwald Fluctuation (ca. 1560–1630). For him, cold was a neighbor (like citizen and country man) with whom you necessarily negotiated, dealt *with,* down the "yeares." This social contract was a mis/adventurous one; those same crowds who strolled "upon a field of glasse," for instance, were also "trauelling into our new found Fréezeland." "Frizeland," or "Frisland," was an imaginary island located off the coast of Greenland. Published at the pinnacle of Danish, Dutch, and English endeavors to discover the Northwest and East Passages to the treasures of Cathay, Dekker's Thames becomes an elongated slide to a distant elsewhere, a chance for the less daring to reflect on their enlarging world. His diptychs are worth investigating not so much for what they tell us about cold's mechanical behaviors, but more so for the questions they pose about lives conducted below or near zero. When and why does "the frozen zone" sweep southward? What does it mean to think of the Arctic not as a region far away, but rather in and as "our" home? Whom does the "our" in- and ex-clude? How does a river become "fréeze"-"land," transforming into something "new found" between earth (land) and water (ice)? Is ice a form of "glasse"? What is cold's "thrust," and what physically happens when human "bosomes" and winter's "hand" interpenetrate? How, in short, does one safely navigate a "slippery world"?

All of these questions center on a deceivingly simple yet overarching query: what *is* cold? While the makeup of hail and snow could be described using the language of Aristotelian meteorology (fourth century BCE), as frozen water vapors, what made moist and rising air freeze and fall, for example, defied easy explanation. As we will see (chapter 1), Dekker's portrayals sit squarely within the century's increasingly heated debates over the nature of cold. Natural philosophers, explorers, and artists of the sixteenth and seventeenth centuries offered a variety of responses: cold was a material substance comprised of "frigorifick atoms";[83] it was the elemental force behind freezing, or "conglutination";[84] it pierced bodies and plugged up their pores; it was a shapeshifter that appeared as icebergs and snowflakes, spikes and sheets; it lived in "the frozen zone" of the upper globe, but it also rode the north wind and spread out across glaciers; it gave, took, or preserved life (and sometimes did all three at once); it was intensely pleasurable; it was playful stuff rolled into a ball or skated on as a "field"; it inaugurated frost fairs, participated in plays, and performed at courts; it crossed taxonomic lines (ice crystals were vegetative, waterfalls wore human faces, and calving shelves made "great rutte or noise"[85] like libidinous beasts); it thwarted colonial ambitions with every case of frostbite and with each ship scuttled or wrecked, testing cultural capacities for climatic resilience and redefining the "human" as a porous being physically inseparable from its winter-worlds.

What we now call "temperature" ultimately boils down to energy flows.[86] Unaware of thermodynamics' three laws postulated in the nineteenth century (energy cannot be created or destroyed; entropy always increases; entropy approaches a constant value as it nears absolute zero), premodern cryosophers ventured deeper into cold's ontic dimensions, far past the borders of bare surface phenomena. On a theoretical spectrum extending from the "privative" (a lack of heat) to the "positive" (an actual presence), scholars leaning to the latter followed the pre-Socratic thinker Parmenides (ca. 450 BCE), who, a century before Aristotle, pursued the tangible origin of cold: what he called the *primum frigidum* (literally "first cold" in Latin). Cold, they pondered, might not be the byproduct of an unknown chemical reaction, or the outcome of sunlight's declension and duration, but a creature of its own. Early modern authors certainly viewed cold as an empirical measure of temperature or the deprivation of heat, but they also told of its raw, invigorating animacy; they probed "thrilling region[s] of thick-ribbèd ice" (Shakespeare, *Measure for Measure,* 3.1.123) and felt their bodies bond with it for benefit and for ill. If "ice is integral to the human condition,"[87] as attested by geographer Klaus Dodds, this book reveals how "integral" cold is to post-"human conditions," how it integrates with anatomy and story to challenge one of the most obstinate tenets of human exceptionalism: the idea of existence independent from material, "regional" emplacement. They prove that the maxim of "no ice, no us"[88]—as the astronomer Tobias Owen put it in 2005—need not be an anthropocentric statement so long as that idea of "us" is a distributed one, cognizant of status and the privileges that attend to it. The illusion of integrity, of an inherent wholeness, cracks under the weight of more-than-human enmeshment with cold/er things.

Perceiving cold as both a substance and a force resists rendering its energies into predictable and repetitive phenomena. The mundanity of freezing has little traction in Dekker's age. Opposing persistent tropes of numbness, stultification, and lethality, the present book magnifies the era's chilly entanglements of in/organic matter with inhuman agencies in order to present a more robust account of human–cold connectivity. Their encounters certainly met these expectations, but they also exceeded them. The inevitability of death, paralysis, or desensitivity is a prediction too often taken for granted; it avoids the fuller possibilities of cryosocial experience. Cold manifests what Jane Bennett calls "thing-power": "the curious ability of inanimate things to animate, to act, to produce effects dramatic and subtle."[89] We still talk of "catching a cold"[90] in an epidemiological context, which denotes both the catching (of a disease) and the instance of having been caught (by a virus). "Nipping" cold, the hallmark of a tactile, in/visible agent at work, raised difficult topics of human vulnerability, such as the inadequacy of shelter. The "powerful" affect they track does not designate a force outside the material body; nor does it erase the subjective notion of observation. Instead, it confirms that any subject's liveliness (its being) depends on its interaction with the lively matter that flows through and around it, effectively reassembling the body as a site of subject–object relations. That is, environment is less a demarcation line (cleaving inside from outside) and more an ongoing act of imbrication with a malleable partner. To "get" cold announced an event, a cooperative "doing"; early modern writings directly respond to, and combat, the long-standing associations of cold with inertia and lifelessness, or worse, the myopic view of cold as an inanimate, life-stealing object.

As cold's vibrant and variable ontological properties were being discussed, a growing body of knowledge slowly accrued; and yet, the only consensus reached concerned its epistemological elusiveness. In its unidentifiable origins and its multitudinous effects, cold frustrated human attempts to grasp its vitality and chart its underlying structure. Take ice, one of cold's most ready associations and this book's recurring protagonist: its formation looks to us now like a quotidian process in which, as water cools, its molecules dutifully line up into hexagonal rows. In the sixteenth and seventeenth centuries, however, freezing was a more mysterious phenomenon; the nature of ice was a conundrum, even as its frosty collisions with culture were keenly and routinely felt. It broke bridges, cooled drinks in the summer, and carved into towns. Its slipperiness led to accidents, foiled dreams of safe passage, and fomented desires. Left to congeal for long enough, it eventually transformed into rock "crystal."[91] Ice had been circulating both onshore and offshore for centuries; it represented a quiz that could be answered but not entirely solved. "Water turned to bone" (*wæter wearð to bane*).[92] The sixty-ninth Old English riddle from the Exeter Book (tenth century CE) found a way to pose itself to new players.[93] Curious minds un/intentionally followed ice leads into uncharted territories and trajectories; they exposed themselves to smoothness's unfamiliar slides, shocks, and play; they watched liquid's softness "turn" into intractable hardness, and then they braced for sudden melt. Delicate, dangerous, and in demand: their multi-angled outlooks make a convincing case for reimagining ice's roles in the everyday lives of both the past and the present. Mariana Gosnell's extensive study of the "astonishing substance," for instance, points out that there are seventeen different types of ice (and counting).[94] There is amusement and amazement, still, in its multitude (which the adage "no two snowflakes are alike" prosaically underscores). In other words, the material histories present here do not just argue for cold's overdue complexity, but rather show how its intricacies never fully went away, even as attempts were made to resolve them or to refute their allure.

Cold always kept its secrets, even as it crept into one's "bones." The gist of it, simply put, could not be caught. Bacon, the English polymath, famously advised that "whosoeuer will be an Inquirer into Nature, let him resort to a Conseruatory of Snow and Ice."[95] For him, unlocking the mystery of cold promised to reveal how "nature" operated. Yet, instead of suturing subjects from objects—one result of the "New Science" Bacon helped inaugurate—this book argues that early modern interactions with cold forged creative, more-than-human bonds among warm-blooded bodies, brumal environments, and the lubricious imagination. Cold pursuits, in a word, were collaborative. In the impossible catching of cold, humans nevertheless learned to work with it in tandem, occasioning what Donna J. Haraway names *sympoiesis* ("making with").[96] Inquirers plunged into storehouses of "Snow and Ice" to coax "promiscuous"[97] intimacies with chatty ice blocks (chapter 1); mapped the North Pole as a turbulent whirlpool (chapter 2); dramatized air that "bites shrewdly" (Shakespeare, *Hamlet*, 1.4.1) (chapter 5); and felt in the chill wind a cause for congregation, one that cultivated a sympathy for their less resilient neighbors (chapter 3). Encouraged by the cooler climate of "the Little Ice Age"—a term now encompassing a few degrees (centigrade) drop across northern Europe ca. 1300–1850 CE, ethnographers, poets, meteorologists (and more) investigated cold's nature not to discover crystallized truths neatly arranged into interlocking patterns, but to assemble with its puzzling, palpable liveliness. To ponder cold's elusiveness was to become, in practice and experience, constructively numb and creatively inspirited, to have some senses sharpened and others dulled. Encounters with cold motivated humans' investigations into the nature of their ecological enmeshment within a global "conseruatory" delicately buttressed by poles of "Snow and Ice." Rather than explaining cold's "doings," the authors cited in this study tangibly demonstrated them. Come and be caught by cold, their texts say; there is no end to catching it.

This book is an experimental project that uncovers cold's dynamism at different degrees of intensity, traces its assortment of agential forms, and visits its vibrant transatlantic places. Its argument may be encapsulated like so: early modern cold crystallized human and nonhuman figures into interdependent arrays both dazzling and deadly; stimulated artistic imaginations and sculpted knowledges; and entangled local latitudes with the globe's far-northern lines. The nimble actor of cold effected an unprecedented series of encounters between the populous, pulsating, and interconnected spaces comprising an ever-widening cryosphere. In 1923, the Polish scientist Antoni Bolesław Dobrowolski coined the term "cryosphere" in *Historia Naturalna Lodu*

(Natural history of ice). From the Greek *kruos* ("frost, icy cold") and *sphaira* ("ball"), it "collectively describes the portions of the Earth's surface where water is in its frozen state—snow cover, glaciers, ice sheets and shelves, freshwater ice, sea ice, icebergs, permafrost, and ground ice."[98] My interpretation of "cryosphere" supports twenty-first-century textbook definitions like this one, but it also enlarges their scope to approximate what Boyle called "the sphere of Activity of Cold."[99] His phrase amasses the sundry words the first cryologists used to trail cold's pullulating properties, tracking its multidirectional vectors across vast stretches of time and distance. "Arctic" and "circle," "zone" and "winter," "north" and "wind"—all balled up under one rubric—telegraph cold's versatility, swirl dis/similar opinions about its "breath"-taking touch at scales personal and planetary (Co[l]da).

An onto-epistemological enigma, the matter of cold was nevertheless a catalyst for cooperation and a means for thinking through the challenging conjunctions of climate and culture. But I am also interested in what cold does and can do today. To my critiques of ontological and geographical divides I resist adding a temporal one. Invoking the prefix "cryo-" in these contexts might seem anachronistic at first, since its use began only around 1800,[100] but as I parse early modernity's "icy cold," it unleashed a wide range of meanings that "cryo-" would later inherit and attempt to wrangle (such as the percentage of the world with temperatures below the triple point of water [273.16 kelvins][101]). The "cryosphere," by way of Boyle, is a restless orb: the intractable stuff of "Cold" compacted into a gyrating "sphere," whose "activity" is always of the *inter-* kind, including those operations that exist outside of, close to, and in contrast with European points of view. Imperfect and oblong, its figure looks more like an undulating ring than a neatly enclosed circle, billowy rather than perfectly round. To come under its influence was to find oneself bent into and out of shapes, and often baffled for it, but also newly attuned to the unsimple process in which *kruos* is made, melted, and returned (if, when, and how). Boyle and his peers did not set the world's wobbly and outstretched cryosphere in motion, but they witnessed, wrote, and wrought its changes in startling terms. As the "sphere" regains our attention over three and a half centuries after Boyle's publication, partnering with early moderns' teeming perspectives ensures that "the dance of the white caps" remains unhalted.[102]

At its core, this book's argument is doggedly presentist as much as it is deeply historicist. The two camps might chafe; and yet, I see them as an unlikely team sledding toward the same goal. *Arcticologies* brings Dekker's four-hundred-year-old dialogue into the climate-change conversations transpiring at this very moment. By recognizing the things cold did (the elations as well as the afflictions it brought, the latter predominantly borne by the bodies of the poor), his pamphlets are educative precisely because they snap us out of modern frameworks that reassert the "disenchantment"[103] of cold and its "doings." Serenella Iovino and Serpil Oppermann invite scholars to "story" relationships with a teeming material world,[104] and the authors who constitute this study demonstrate that there are better tales to tell about cold besides its translation into three laws, the origins of the ice trade, or brave men's heroic deaths. My underlying hope is that Dekker and his contemporaries inaugurate a bracing type of interdisciplinary research, a transhistorical "cold studies" that reframes how we view its "doings" in both the past and the present.[105] By story-ing its infiltrative and intimate influence, its adherents model ways for us to scrutinize our involvements with sub/arctic, non/human neighbors right now. Their language sounds strangely familiar to us; it strikes discordant and concordant notes at once. Drawing attention to these startling moments of linguistic nearness, I intend to narrow (but not completely expunge) the historical distance between now and then. Our recurring phenomena of "polar vortices" and "bomb cyclones," for instance, are extensions of the era's "great frosts" and spiraling poles (chapter 2). The "colde hand" is not quite the "same" as it was then, of course, and yet its fingers still uncurl toward us. "Too hot, too hot" (Shakespeare, *Winter's Tale,* 1.2.108): in our warming world that is becoming less "slippery" every year, it is time to turn to previous encounters with cold.

A "cold studies" approach also compels us to meditate on what is ahead for the Arctic in the unfolding Anthropocene, especially when taking into account the ongoing aims of climate justice, particularly whether cold's oddly resonant "doings" of the past may assist the efforts of present-day communities like the Iñupiat, Inuit, Sámi, and Chukchi who are taking cryopolitical action against the precariousness thrust on them by nations to their south. Early modern characterizations of a tentacular, entangled north boost environmentalists' broader calls for reconnecting the Arctic to the greater health of the globe, and for debunking the stereotypes of a depeopled and trackless nothingness that stubbornly linger on. Extractive capitalism has managed to harness these harmful illusions to the displacement of Indigenous populations, cultures whose despoiled homes count for some of the most biodiverse sections on earth. Past responses to weathering unseasonable winters promote a vocabulary (if not immediate answers) for thinking on, and speaking to, present questions about how to weather a warming world.[106] Whether a noun, verb, or in-between (a gerund), the un/usual terms I highlight are meant, ultimately, to be actionable. Earlier accounts might not uncover cold's mysteries or reach a true or total understanding, but they will deepen a sense of its threatened powers, and in so doing, strengthen notions of human–Arctic, panhemispheric relationality advocated by activists and scientists. Solely reading centuries-old texts, unfortunately, will not "save" our vanishing ice and snow. But at a time in which popular climate studies obsess over ends (and *the* end) of a planet headed for meltdown, or a world after or without ice, the "doings" of early modern cold assist in counterapocalyptic thinking: they ask us to identify what has been lost and who is at risk in the thinning cold, but also, in their audacious "instructions" for how to winter on, they urge us to imagine alternate futures focused on ethical obligation and care instead of inevitable collapse. The rest of the introduction chips off Dekker's argumentative block. Let us pull up alongside these bergy bits for better inspection, for there is much more that needs to be done:

## "This Fourtie Yeares": Early Modern Climate Change

Does this mean that early moderns thought about "climate change"? To paraphrase the environmental historian Dagomar Degroot: possibly. "Of course, cultural responses to climate change do not require explicit awareness of climate change."[107] That being said, "limited awareness . . . may have been more widespread than surviving written sources suggest."[108] Just as "change" escapes singular definition, so does the event of "climate change" exceed the boundaries of periodization. Listen, for example, to the anonymous author of the 1684 *Great Britains Wonder*: "Though such unusual Frosts to us are strange, / Perhaps it may predict some greater Change."[109] Answering in the affirmative does not dismiss aspects of historical difference; in fact, identifying like-minded intersections as well as contrasts harnesses creative energies of the past to modern-day environmentalist efforts. "Humans have been trying to find the modes with which to know a precarious and changeable Earth for as long as they have been imagining worlds," concludes Tobias Menely in his study of "geohistorical poetics" in the long eighteenth century.[110] "Any poem can be understood, in its world making and time shaping, to offer a meditation on the enigmatic yet omnipresent nature of energy, in its planetary and social manifestations."[111] In Rebecca Laroche and Jennifer Munroe's opinion, an ecofeminist approach to Shakespeare's plays "does not idealize the language of the past, but rather sees in the past a destabilizing potential in this unthinking world."[112] Cold is just that rattling, "world remaking" blast from the past.

When the 1634 poem "On the Great Frost" by William Cartwright mentions "Green-Land's Removal" and "sudden Trump," it laments the loss of pasture ("Green-Land")—blanketed in white frost and prevented from growing back—and trumpets a climatological doomsday (the biblical Last Judgment).[113] Bearing in mind the fact that U.S. President Donald J. Trump offered to buy Greenland in the summer of 2019 (and indicated his interest again in 2025),[114] Cartwright's word choice invites two hasty misreadings of mid-seventeenth-century climate catastrophe. At the same time, his poem's final question looks shockingly similar to the dire climate predictions and deadlines (due to a disastrous political administration) that predominate today's headlines: "For whilst we suffer this, ought we not fear / The World shall not survive to a fourth year?"[115] For early moderns, cold lingers too long and penetrates too deep. Nowadays, a presence gives way to absence, where heat and thaw and city-sized ice sheets signal incontrovertibly the hazards of climate change. But there are analogies to be discovered here as well (the fear of runaway icebergs, for instance) that serve to shake up staid thinking about cold and furnish more nuanced responses to climate sensitivity and "survival." Skirting semiotic arguments about whether the phrase "early modern climate change" is an anachronism, a malaprop, or worse draws more important attention to the material conditions of imperiled communities, a cold "doing" for and with others, and the unequal capacities for adaption amidst documented atmospheric fluctuations.

Belittling early modern voices as passive chronicles of bitter years is a disservice. Casting their ideas as benighted is a sign, too, of our "unthinking" times. The pageant *Summer's Last Will and Testament* (ca. 1592–1600) by Thomas Nashe (1567–1601) personified the cold snaps that plagued the summers of 1594–1596. (Hence the "back" of Backwinter, Winter's son.) "Adieu, farewell earth's bliss," its song goes, "this world uncertain is."[116] Nashe's quip helps us remember that "climate," like "weather," like "winter" (chapter 4), lacks a fundamental order. Disequilibrium could be seen as the norm, not the deviation from it. In his famous 110-thousand-year-long history of "abrupt climate change," glaciologist Richard B. Alley uniquely compares climate to a "drunk." Ice cores reveal "wildly variable" climates and their fast-acting changes. Whenever a climate is "forced" to change, it "jumps" rather than steadily inclining or declining.[117] Climate stability, in other words, is the anomaly.

In their embodied accounts of swaggering seasonality, Elizabethan pamphleteers and those thereafter fell under cold's sway. They understood that winter was always an invariable stretch, even if those of recent years lasted longer, hit harder, came "back" suddenly, and left unpredictably. Early modern authors dwelled in the multitiered "here" of what Jeffrey J. Cohen calls "eco-temps": "composites of time and climate, ephemeral locales that through repetition endure to bequeath across history a multisensory archive."[118] They thought deeply about their delicate times. "Important as [a] biblical background may have been," stresses Sophie Chiari, "early modern scholars and writers began to question the extent and even the reality of the sky's influence upon their daily lives."[119] From speculating over a plottable, if imperfect, trajectory from warmer to cooler ("Change"); to recognizing topical, local, and short-term shifts from hot to cold ("change"); to raising fears of an overlong winter and the return of rushing spring; to atoning for the "sinnes" of the "Fallocene";[120] to yearning poignantly for warmth and wishing for balance (or even its semblance); to eyeing the icecaps' undiscovered role: all of these chattering exchanges amounted to Nashe's overarching "uncertainty" and *Wonder*'s abiding, open-ended "perhaps." While coined by Daniel Pauly in 1995 as "shifting baseline syndrome," the expectation for ecological conditions' shift over time was known by another name. The ever-evolving thinking of the pamphleteers about cold divulges an environmental consciousness in the making, especially in regard to "climate": where it was going and into what it was transforming; how "unusual" it was; whether the "strange" would ever become familiar; and, perennially, how their very lives relied on it.

Reading past texts to address climatic instability then and now might at first appear futile. Writers lacked the proper scientific tools to verify larger trends, after all. Without these instruments, it seems unlikely that they could grasp their place within the earth's much longer climate history. Robert Fotherby, however, who accompanied William Baffin (1584[?]–1621) on his 1613 voyage to Spitsbergen, ascended a glacier and then ingeniously estimated its height by dislodging pieces with his staff, "which, in their falling made a noise on each side, much like to a piece of glass thrown down the well within Dover Castle."[121] Discovering his icy perch to be made of moistened snow firmed up by frost, he judged it "like still to increase, as (I think) it hath done since the world's creation."[122] But looking back at premodern moments when ice was encroaching rather than retreating across the world does not confront the culprit, so we are told, of all our carbon-dioxide woes: the Industrial Revolution (launched ca. 1760). Indeed, nonspecialist histories of cold and of circumpolar places tend to start in the eighteenth and nineteenth centuries, briskly moving from a hapless age of exploration (redeemed only by its courage and adventure) to the post-Enlightenment epoch of expertise (with its gifts of technology and science).[123] From our side (or spike) of the Great Acceleration (1950–), this grand narrative depicts a seismic shift in broad strokes: from the north as an enemy to humans, to humans—chiefly of the neoliberal Global North—as an enemy to the northern regions. Anthropogenic global warming, the hallmark of the Anthropocene, has inverted the antagonistic spectrum. The "revenge" of the Arctic is becoming a popular catchphrase, as if speaking about ice at the pole automatically refers to another endless war.[124] Warmth, once a friend to bygone "frozen ages," is now our foe; only by becalming an angry, oceanic antagonist will we finally be able to dial down the planetary thermostat.

Such polarizing logics are unavoidable, but they are revisable. To be clear, the goal of tracing coolly connected bodies, climates, and times is not to simply conclude, with twenty-first century clarity, what was "right" and "wrong" about Fotherby's and others' beliefs. Nor is it to fantasize about unsullied affiliations with a north we have irrevocably lost. Early modern fishers, hunters, and whalers, to name a few, undeniably committed a fair share of environmental degradation abroad, turning a time of domestic distress into lucrative profits. I speak, in toto, of "creation"; I would rather build a multimile-long time and "weather machine"[125] of arcane, co-implicated workings. Debapriya Sarkar phrases a "participatory readerly ethics" like so: "Writers engage in acts of world-making with the tacit knowledge that their fictive worlds, incomplete and visionary, will be remade by various reading publics."[126] The complications of resilience (who "shall" and "shall not survive") remain in question. Both common individuals and civic authorities felt obliged to alleviate cold's drastic and disproportionate outcomes; they also found ways to welcome "strange" fellows into their "cold beds." Dekker's cold "companion" is at ecology's doorstep. Philemon Holland (1552–1637) advises in his 1601 translation of Pliny's *Historie of the World* (first century CE) that, "if the countrey or climat be hot, an house must stand into the North."[127] The north's weather (from Old English *weder,* related to "wind") comes "into" the home. Melding is as messy as it meteorologically looks, with or without open windows, and Holland's readers watched their winter "weather-world,"[128] wondering about said thresholds and whether they and who else could "stand" it. I amplify ice-inflected voices like his in order to promote declarations of Arctic interdependence. Climate changes of irregular duration, magnitude, and effect provoked cooperative forms of care in addition to skepticism and apathy, and they can continue to do so. If "ice is time solidified,"[129] according to Ehrlich, there is still some left for our warming world.

## "Shewes Like Gray Marble": How to Look (at) Cold

To mark the occasion of the 2015 United Nations Climate Change Conference (COP 21) in Paris from November 30 to December 12, the Danish-Icelandic artist Olafur Eliasson arranged twelve ice blocks into a ring outside the Place du Panthéon. *Ice Watch*'s obvious pun is that it references both time (the chunks as hours on a watch face) and the activity of watching. The message to the world's political leaders seemed crystal clear: the time of, and for, ice is running out. The open-air installation invited onlookers to engage with ice intimately. Indeed, many of the photographs depict Parisians nestled against its contours: listening, sculpting, and kissing the cold. Eliasson accordingly asks global citizens to "watch" their involvement with ice more closely. Interconnection is seen as a hopeful force of contravention. In 1611–12, nearly four hundred years before, the Dutch explorer Jan Cornelisz May (ca. 1560–1617) searched in vain for the passage from the east (Nova Zembla) and west (Nova Scotia). Returning to the Netherlands in December, he brought back bear skins, walrus teeth, and American furs. "The freight had little value," however, as something else outshone these trinkets: "as a curiosity, a huge ice block was exhibited in the Admiralty Court."[130] The political content of this surprising berg is less apprehensible than Eliasson's. What was the ice "doing" there? Why was it deemed important to haul back to Europe? Did May's compatriots do more than look at it? Did they feel cold? Did the "curiosity" kindle an embrace? How long the "block" lasted, what effects it had on the populace, and how it was physically approached escapes the record. Its intrigue lingers on, though; melted long ago, its meanings continue to proliferate. In a nod to May's idiosyncratic show, this book gets up close to cold's lasting connections across impermanent engagements (the fascination with de/frosting, the Arctic's "hugeness" rendered into art, the messages and places a piece of ice conveyed), but it also points out features that have faded over time: its liveliness, its interconnectedness, the co-creativity that comes with its presence, the ethicopolitical "doings" it inspires when confronting its absence. There is "value," after all, in watching early moderns approach ice from multiple angles.

Others have asked this question of iced productions before, of course: the disciplines of art and art history demonstrate an abiding preoccupation with cold works and realms, and my study draws steady inspiration from them. Maggie M. Cao speaks about the power of public displays of ice "to marshal entropy as a weapon against the legacies of colonialism."[131] Looking to the north, Mark A. Cheetham believes that "eco art that re-envisions the North hopes to contribute to ways of thinking and being that will redefine the Anthropocene as an epoch of cooperation rather than exploitation."[132] As for the weather, Janine Randerson's concept of "meteorological art" means that "encounters with ice in public art gives us unexpected inspiration, delight, and the opportunity to grieve. . . . The specificity of a real fragment of an iceberg stands in for the whole cryosphere: our weather world in flux."[133] In their estimations, cold is a member of the artistic process: the medium does not just passively convey the message, but is responsible for it. The malleability of ice and snow—smooth, slushy, stiff—exemplifies

John Durham Peters's elemental philosophy that "media . . . are vessels and environments, containers of possibility that anchor our existence and make what we are doing possible."[134] But cold also mediates (inserts itself) in unmooring ways: "The history of media is the history of the productive impossibility of capturing what exists."[135] Maybe May positioned his ice cube as performance art. Maybe he intended it to advertise his peers' seafaring stamina, this tiny segment of the Arctic leaving a slick trail to greater glory. Its "doings" certainly evade capture: dripping into Amsterdam's canals, it heads back out to the North Sea. Like Peters, I am interested in how these quizzical "doings" of cold make the "doing" of craft possible. (And that includes what I am currently "doing" on this page.) Not simply a flawless "vessel" offering an unbroken view into the past, ice's commingling with artists contributes to the business of entropy (when encouragements become impediments to enterprise), both precolonial and postcolonial; cracks definitions of bounded environments (when the Arctic comes to court); and ushers in fragile cooperations and frenetic creations (when it ties non/human parties in the room together). Cold's slippery vehicle, in a word, propels human "curiosity."

While the visual and media arts' robust engagement with the subject of cold has been primarily in the late twentieth and early twenty-first centuries, their insights usefully apply to early modern material culture as well. Art historian Christopher P. Heuer's pioneering *Into the White* is a perfect case in point. For him, the "Renaissance Arctic" confounded representation itself, heralding the "end of the image": "The critical work of 'Arctic' art is not making stuff (even tragic stuff) visible and *meaningful*, but is, perhaps, in interrogating the *limits* of Arctic visibility, of Arctic meaning, via practices that academia and the art world (as complicit in polar melting as any other capital-based forces today) cannot easily frame."[136] In his view, the Arctic's opacity teaches us that northern human–nonhuman relations remain incompletely limned: just as light bends as it moves through ice, so the artwork draws attention to its own constrained, occluded perspective. We are not told to see better, in other words, but to better comprehend the dimness of what is seen. To be "into the white" is to be in a whiteout, to peer into a cloudy ice block only to find yourself caught in a blizzardy, liminal space without clear outcomes. Nevertheless, these murkier shades of pale underline the crucial lesson concerning overlaid environments:

"The Arctic meant not just a new realm to draw into early modern mapping schemes. In its messy obduracy, it refused to stay cleanly 'apart' from its dwellers and describers."[137] Indeed, "there are no fortresses" when it comes to early moderns' "visual poetics" of the region.[138] As did the first Arctic pilots, I too consider the "limits" of knowledge as moveable. The artforms that organize this book treat *ne plus ultra* ("not further beyond") and *meta incognita* ("the unknown limits") as borders to be tested, and sometimes transgressed, but never fully straightened out, even if their creators declare otherwise. Their artistry likewise allows for other experiences that transcend the visual image, transmitting a wider spectrum of sensory encounters via drama, poetry, travel narrative, topical pamphlets, and scientific treatise.

At its icy heart, this book represents a cordial effort to unite with different disciplines of the environmental humanities like art history and media studies. More specifically, it also attempts to link literary periods that have drifted detrimentally apart. In his "spiritual history of ice," Eric G. Wilson differentiates between *esoteric* (hidden, internal) and *exoteric* (public, external) knowledges.[139] Romantic points of view, he argues, evolved from a premodern inability to fully inhabit the former. May's successors were finally able to beat back the *exoteric*, a "largely neutral or negative" category, to become "among the first . . . to embrace ice as a positive . . . the principle of life."[140] Valiantly, "they . . . redeem ice from its . . . past." Thus, the American nature writer Henry David Thoreau (1817–1862) could opine in his 1854 *Walden* that "ice is an interesting subject for contemplation"[141] and be applauded for his perspicacity, while the Anglo-Irish natural philosopher Boyle, who also made a famous decree about cold—that "it is so barren a subject"[142]—represents an outmoded "past" that did not dare or care to scratch beneath the surface. Thoreau's salvific, transcendental mindset elevates pond ice from the plainer externalizing and objectifying gaze of commodification.

I do not mean simply to assail Wilson's framework, however. I raise it, first, because I believe that his salvific narrative is endemic of a pattern within literary scholarship that too often skirts early modernity's ice.[143] Elizabeth Kolbert and Francis Spufford's *The Ends of the Earth: An Anthology of the Finest Writing on the Arctic and the Antarctic*, for example, begins with John Franklin (d. 1847) and Frederick A. Cook (1865–1940), as if premodernity's scruffiness is an automatic disqualifier.[144] Secondly, and more constructively, I envision the critical rewards that bridging this lacuna would bring. When drifting with the stuff of cold, the physical shell need not be discarded for an arcane core inside, nor must we instantiate a divide between an esoteric "positive" and an exoteric "negative" at all. Early modern ice-thinkers examined its "life"-like qualities both cursorily and in great detail; they asked questions about the difficult, elemental middles (nature and culture, matter and spirit) in which they lived and died; they offered up sensations less reliant on, and sometimes incompatible with, the celebrated "sublime"; they started, and extended, conversations about cold's charms that have yet to be cleared up. I am not interested in reclaiming ice's profundity back from Romanticism, then, for doing so would only (and competitively) fashion another dichotomy between intellectual sides and "firsts." As Bennett has argued in her 2011 *Vibrant Matter,* the story of modernity's *re*-enchantment is a misleading one: authors from Olaus Magnus (1490–1557) to Christopher Marlowe (1564–1593) ascribe to their cold world a magical anima of various abilities that the Enlightenment could only claim to have extinguished. I engage ideas like Wilson's throughout in an attempt to break up chronological compartments and deepen our understanding, even if dimly, of how cold inspires humans' ideas about "northern" things and their powers across times: from Mary Shelley's (1797–1851) "country of eternal light,"[145] to the glint off the open polar sea espied by American explorer Isaac Hayes (1832–1881), to the auroral fires I saw streak the Swedish skies in 2020. I witnessed "Arctic [early] modernities"[146] in the making that night. Tracing earlier "doings" resists the sharp divisions of periodization; by signaling potential points of fusion, it anticipates a truly transhistorical style of cold studies.

## "Multiplyed!": A Dictionary for Ar(c)ticulating Cold

As if responding to its rapidly changing pace, Arctic studies abound with neologisms forged to meet the moment, some of which have already made an appearance here. Ilan Kelman speaks of "Arcticness" as a mode of being,[147] while Gísli Pálsson notes the "arcticality" of things.[148] "Arctician" (n.) and "arcticize/d" (v. and adj.) are unusual but useable. Concerning the Northwest Passage, one can describe "Arctic fever,"[149] "voyages of delusion," or an "Arctic labyrinth."[150] "Delusion" comes from the Latin *deludere* ("to mock"), as if the joke is on those earlier, more teleologically minded explorers who mistakenly sought a stable east-west route across the northern hemisphere. But I prefer the ludic qualities—from *ludere* ("to play")—of the word instead, since deviation from linear trajectories can be profoundly creative. These ill-conceived voyages and ventures onto the ice are not just foolish errands culminating in eternal shame; rather, they mark an openness to trickery and a reception to being taught. Out of the coldscape's twists and turns comes language: words like "nordicity" and "winterity," two entries in Daniel Chartier's unfinished "grammar of the idea of north."[151] This verbosity bespeaks coupling rather than alterity, of linguistics tied to territory. Here, François Rabelais' (1490–1553[?]) mock-hero Pantagruel scatters crystallized words onto a frosted deck, puzzled by their garrulous pop and fizz.[152] "Topographic humanists," states Robert Macfarlane in *Landmarks,* regard "landscape" as an "active and shaping force in our imagination, our ethics, and our relations with each other and the world."[153] To be a "north-minded"[154] writer reflects a more-than-human conversation: one's words are regionally inflected by means of the author's literal participation with the "shaping forces" of cold.

The "blue humanities," and especially the subdiscipline of aquatic media studies, have been crucial in streaming the contours of our "currents" (née "fields")[155] and their associated discourses such as ecophenomenology. My attention to northern lingo is a nod to these critics' overt calls for newer terms that detail the vast assortments of human–water experience. Steve Mentz urges scholars to "move offshore" with seven "deterritorializing"[156] words, while Melody Jue's concept of "wild blue media"[157] likewise disorients the ways of understanding and inhabiting water in order to deepen humans' affinities for it. Jue cultivates the ocean's "conceptual displacement" in an effort to confront land-based biases, asking us to engage in a "milieu-specific analysis" of our own environmental contexts. "I aim to leave the critic somewhat at sea," she says, "unsettled from their habituated ways of speaking about the world."[158] So do I. In its engagement with watery forms (snow, baths, ice), this book builds on the increasing interest in "blue" and "oceanic" topics in early modern studies. I will take some ideas out to sea to observe what churns, but I will also put them on ice to look at their crust. Early modernity's unruly coldness adds important aspects of hardness, slowness, and scale to the present discussion of "wet theory."[159] Giant "Icy hills" and tiny "Atoms of Cold"[160] complement hydrocritical penchants for fluidity and flow—and they add a dab of dryness to my

FIGURE 4. Ice shelves in Jukkasjärvi, Sweden. Photograph by Erin Cassese.

elemental palette to boot. Both solid and slippy, ice's interstitiality (as earth-water) contributes a hefty "deterritorializing" push, although it results less in a complete break from foundational discourse (the swapping of "field") than in a hanging on to the weird fissures that appear within it: querying, for instance, the floating, "glasse"-like substance that once was (or is) water. My investigation is intended to supplement the swifter, though no less significant, currents of others. I contemplate what is "unsettled" when thinking through ice: whether a souvenir printed on the frozen-over Thames and a folio illustration depicting a death-defying glissade in Spitsbergen, both published in 1684, can denaturalize the biases we bring to cold airs, waters, and places, as well as teach us about how best and how else to approach them.

The kind of cold media studies I am outlining is not without precedent.[161] Hester Blum's recent study of shipboard newspapers printed during the Antarctic voyages of Robert Falcon Scott (1868–1912) and Ernest Shackleton (1874–1922) skillfully illustrates how cold media of the past crosses over into today's climatic concerns. Born from previous climatic extremes, *polar ecomedia,* according to Blum, are templates for contending with present extremes: "The evanescent printed records generated in polar extremity . . . offer conceptual and formal devices for describing, comprehending, and, most ambitiously, surviving climatic extremity."[162] While I share her penchant for presentist tactics, this study augments her perceptive use of "extreme," uplifting early modern corollaries in which story (conveyed through poem, play, and picture) espoused the intricacies of survival. Printers like Joseph Moxon (1627–1691) were hard at work in the cold London winter of 1683–1684, and as we will see, similarly and self-consciously drew attention to their subpolar labor (albeit under conditions less extreme in terms of isolation and temperature). These anecdotes reveal the ways cold inculcates a will to create as well as to persist. The manufacture of poems, ballads, and sundry keepsakes in real-time highlights the connection between the literal *cryo-* (like a Thamesian floe) and the cultural imagination I call "cryopoiesis." Not to be confused with "cryopoetics," which analyzes the ideas of cold within texts,[163] *poiesis* accentuates moments of co-making. The etchings, essays, maps (and more) located herein illustrate loquacious acts of ar(c)ticulation unique to the era: that is to say, they amplify episodes in which cold words and worlds conjoin. Cold does not just imprint on bodies forced to react against its impressions: it also stimulates that sense of "north-mindedness," physically impacting the imagination, pressing it poetically on. Blum's idea of "extreme printing," in my view, is thereby pushed to the extreme. To adopt some of her terms, the "polar imprint" traces the extent and effects of ecomaterial "arbitration," meaning the role of "the mediating element itself."[164] On these occasions, letters, numbers, and illustrations come *from,* by being nipped *by,* the cold.

The voluble products of a reciprocal, human–"cryo" craftwork that await you stress early modern makers' ties to the historical realities of cold. Their etymological excursions, to take one example, pinpoint cool's insinuation into the linguistic realms of artistic expression. But with it comes a caveat: just as I discussed Wilson's Romantic preferment, my intervention should not fuel a controversy over who (or which period) felt cold "most keenly."[165] My inclusion of pre-Edwardian (and Victorian, Georgian) voices expands the store of valuable insights culled from past societies who grappled, as we do now, with the calamities of climate. As Blum importantly suggests, the transience of polar ephemera offers "resources for futurity"[166] in our Anthropocenic times. More than mere embellishments or discardable decorations, the weather-worn and weather-borne media embossed in a cold city center like seventeenth-century London (reports that have proven perdurable so far) speak to the relentless pressures of ecological adaptation, as well as their prospective relief. Some had to travel to the "ends of the earth" (plagiarizing Blum's title) to relay this urgent message of precarity, while other types were able to deliver their thoughts on perseverance directly on the water. *Arcticologies* publicizes early moderns' signature passion for cryopoietic co-making, both near *and* far, and reprints said "news" of Arctic hopes and fears in frost-tipped fonts.

By reexamining past imprints communicating cold, I proffer a land- and water-marked vocabulary of my own. I treat cold structures (glaciers, blocks, flakes) as inventive diction devices that tackle "habituated" ways of ecologically speaking. Ice words tempt us to play with the conventional. They are tinged with "metaplasm": "a change in a word," Haraway clarifies, "by adding, omitting, inverting, or transposing its letters, syllables, or sounds." "Flesh and signifier, bodies and words, stories and worlds: these are joined in naturecultures."[167] When the poet Elizabeth Bradfield came across the phrase "ice needle" in the esteemed handbook of maritime navigation by American mathematician Nathaniel Bowditch (1773–1838)—"a long, thin ice crystal whose cross-section is typically hexagonal"—she expanded on it: "I want ice to be my mending. I want cold to stitch me."[168] An ice needle, to her, is one that both pierces and pulls together. Her innovation notices how ice interweaves: icy puncturing means slips (of the tongue) but also aggregative sutures and piecing(s) together. I repeat plasmic practices like hers throughout these pages. Words like "frigorifick" are not just antiquated terms worth adding to ecological lexicons for their historical sake alone. I highlight them in order to change how we speak, think, and act about cold.[169] They pronounce verbal, veering "doings" with which we may do meaningful things. It might seem tautological—"gerund" comes from Latin *gerere,* meaning "do"—but such is the course of unclear collisions I have planned for us: a positive feedback loop, a snowball effect of "doings" that broadcasts what cold is, does, and can do. How "getting cold" (like "warming up") can be sympathetic, when growing "colder" (like "warmer") means seizing, astray, on something, and where even the stable "Pole" of the North has spin.

In a twenty-first-century Arctic whose descriptors betoken so much loss (of cold, of habitats, of rights), there is more to say. "Our encounters and experiences [with ice] are subject to accumulation, compaction, and disruption,"[170] claims Dodds. In my previous book (2017), I focused on the composition of "hydrographies": the texts that wet human and nonhuman bodies co-create. Here, I continue "going glacial."[171] By extrapolating creative terms from the early modern archive, I propose ways for reexamining our attachments to cold's strange agency and strained places. This is why I eschew the language of "heroism" and "crusade," such as the "Arctic Grail"[172] quest, in favor of cold "incursions,"[173] "crucibles,"[174] and "blinks."[175] I am interested in different trials of mixture, humility, and inquisitiveness that do not depend on extremely dangerous acts of domination, or that dictate, per the television series *Life below Zero* (2013–), a return to, and fetishization of, (Jack) Londonian ruggedness. Talk of spiritual purity and toughness, such as "super-alpinism" and backdrops for "inner" journeys, have little purchase here.[176] Survivalist fantasies reward those who, alone, outlive a hostile Arctic, avoiding the key question of *which* habitats do, and do not, survive. Think of this book as an experimental laboratory, a "conseruatory" in the cold-making. To this end, several of my test results are rendered as one-word expressions in brief essays I call "winterludes." Each word may segue to the next chapter, reach back, or do both. Taking up early modern writers' invitation to story cold's un/fastening features, each of them stems from my own personal experience with slow things, moving along or against their speeds. My wish is for readers to depart with an open-ended glossary, and an impetus of their own for re-storying cold.

## "Cold Vacation": The Iceberg at the End of the World

I realize that that my additive tone cannot ignore the matter of cold's depletion: a lost early modern awareness of elemental integration as well as the physical loss of ice and snow. We can take anthropogenic realities into account while also conditioning cold kinds of interspecies and multispecies flourishing. It is almost impossible to talk about the poles without talking about "ends." The end of ice equals the end of human civilization, at least along the coasts, if not altogether, in which present thawing is only a slow-motion prelude to the inevitable meltdown later. The opposite forecast, "snowmageddon" or "snowpocalypse" tap into this predilection for doomsday scenarios: the famous freeze-ray effect of the 2004 film *The Day after Tomorrow,* directed by Roland Emmerich; the failed climate engineering of the 2013 *Snowpiercer* (dir. Bong Joon-ho); the folkloric "death chill" of the 2024 *Ghostbusters: Frozen Empire* (dir. Gil Kenan). The revenge of frosty Gaia will be vicious. Multiple studies of the past decade or so keep up the subject of termination: Dahr Jamail "bears witness" to "the end of ice";[177] Peter Wadhams bids it "a personal farewell";[178] Henry Pollack imagines "a world without ice";[179] and Alun Anderson considers what comes "after" it is gone.[180] (I am quoting from their titles, to be fair: the contents espouse a sincere, extensively researched, and admirable commitment to planetary health.)

At the same time, however, I believe that prepositions are rhetorically important: thinking *through* and *with* cold water promotes starting points other than an assumed "end" from which to work backwards. My worry about this end-trend is threefold: first, such projections fast forward to *a* future; instead, cold's gradual disappearance urges us to inhabit the present to pluralize possible Arctics. Second, the feared result of "without" is primarily human endangerment and/or extinction, a logic that sets up dichotomies ("the frozen zone" against "us") and invites misanthropic condemnations (enlightened humans against less conscientious "others"). The world already knows too much war(m). Third, the impulse regards time as linear rather than compacted; that is, it skips over the opportunity to reexamine cooler pasts, as if investigating how humans live with ice is suddenly a modern ecological predicament. But one does not have to wait until ice is gone to recognize its import. To quote Doug Macdougall's idea of "the once and future story"[181] of the Ice Ages, little ones make for good storytellers, too, whose writers dwelled on eschatological and seasonal ends (and some on no end in sight) and yet could detail their uncertain enmeshments through episodes of cryophilia as well as cryophobia. These are ages from which we may draw inspiration, intimacies to which we may return. The "future history of the Arctic,"[182] no longer a geographical outlier, is being written, and past histories have much to say about what will and should be told.

It is vital to recognize the estrangement and resulting grief of human–cold relations, the emotional toll that is ignored by top-down environmental policies that promise short-term fixes to ontological uncouplings. "Humans have long projected that which they most desire and fear onto the ice," Elizabeth Rush humbly admits in *The Quickening* (2023), "and I am no exception."[183] The 1584 journey inside the Froidière of Chaux ice cave by French storyteller Bénigne Poissenot (ca. 1550–1586) begins with a "burning desire" before turning "terrifying."[184] This is a kind of "desire" that signals a fervid partnership with the Jura Mountains. To be ardent is to be adjacent. The Kantian "sublime" is too reliant on human faculties and the mind's in/ability to grasp ice's awesome terrors. But the early modern "passions,"[185] tied as they were to variations in temperature and one's physical embeddedness within chilly cities, caves, and channels, underscore the infinite ways cold continues to impact our moods. Humoral theory dictated that one's personality is determined by fluid levels of black and yellow bile, phlegm, and blood. The temperaments associated with cold—melancholic (cold and dry earth, autumn) and phlegmatic (cold and wet water, winter)—surely lend themselves to modern medicine's diagnosis of seasonal affective disorder (SAD) and the association of cold places with clinical depression. As glacial bodies dissolve at alarming rates, Poissenot's frisson shows us how to mourn them in unaccustomed ways: not as outsized, indifferent influences, but as intimate companions.

This despondency, moreover, may engage with like-minded others equally troubled by their passing. Drew Daniel argues that early modern melancholy was an "assemblage": "a multiplicity, an expressive array of materials and postures and cases distributed across the social surround."[186] The friendliness of Poissenot's torrid encounter helps us work out our own unfinished feelings for and with cold life forms, to deliver a rousing "elegy for a melting planet."[187] *Elegy* (from Greek *elegos,* "mournful poem") and *eulogy* (*eulogia,* "praise") are tight-knit. On August 28, 2019, as part of their "Un-Glacier Tour II," anthropologists Cymene Howe and Dominic Boyer placed a marker atop Iceland's Ok mountain to commemorate the loss of its glacier (Okjökull) due to climate change: "the world's first monument to a glacier-that-was."[188] What they witnessed, as reported by glaciologist Oddur Sigurdsson, is "dead ice."[189] Cold's gradual retreat across the French Alps likewise memorializes an impassioned, cryopsychological connection "that was," and that still is: to speak of "dead ice" is also to remember the lives that it enclasps, the unsnuffed "desires" it inflames.

But what exactly are we mourning at these sites? Is it a life unperturbed by thoughts of vanishing glaciers, yet another anxiety about global warming? Is it, just as nostalgically, the fracturing of an indivisible bond humans and ice (fellow terraformers) once shared, only to watch it fade forevermore? What stands out to me at this stop on the "tour" is that communal sorrow tethers human existence to what M Jackson calls "the secret lives of glaciers."[190] Not simply a fanciful exercise in letting glaciers figuratively live or die, examining their unexplored "lives" poses serious questions about material liveliness, how the qualifiers of "alive" and "dead" are decided, and what the ethicopolitical repercussions of these decisions might be. Cold grounds humans in "naturecultures" in which their lives are but a part.[191] (This is a "secret" that should not be concealed.) When Mark C. Serreze, the geographer and director of the National Snow and Ice Data Center (NSIDC), speaks of the Arctic as "stirring," he spotlights its "complexity."[192] But as he pinpoints sea ice's "death spiral," he laments its recession by recognizing his personal relation to it: "Part of me," he confesses, "is also dying."[193] Most, presumably, would be hesitant to assign ice biological status, although this reluctancy becomes more complicated when we recall, for instance, that glaciers provide vast amounts of drinking water; shelter organisms like microbes and moss; and are respected as sentient beings intrinsic to Indigenous oral histories.[194] Ok's funereal ceremony honors a "stirring" far north and yet anticipates, solastalgically, further distress. In the same way, an excited early modern Arctic redirects our attention both to glacial "lives" lost and to those we are currently losing. The elegy I am composing is one that recognizes, often uncomfortably, ice and humans' mutual mortality, but its tenor is meant to whip up relational change.

Whether advancing, shrinking, or shirking, we are obliged to evaluate the trajectories we have chosen toward or away from the cold, and furthermore why these orbits are set so. Thom van Dooren's notion of "flight ways" reverberates with my attempted rerouting. As with "life," he calls us to reflect on "what extinction *is* and what it *means*."[195] Due to extinction's "dull edge," its "drawn-out and ongoing *process* of loss,"[196] he prefers to speak of bird species as reactionary movements—a "way of life"[197]—as opposed to preconfigured specimens. There is no singular event behind extinction, he argues, and that requires us to be more cognizant of the different bearings it takes and the burdens it registers. Glacial "flight ways" would move beyond the animal (avian) to the inorganic. For me, his nonteleological approach is useful for gauging the ongoingness of cold matter, tracking the "edge" of ice, meter by meter, as it splinters off into promontories and dripping spears. But, by concentrating on "regimes of violent-care" ("how intimate care for some . . . bodies, some species, sits alongside the domination, coercion, and abandonment of others"[198]), we learn "ways" for combating the sacrificial logics that dictate glacial loss for the greater human good. The dull feeling of human exceptionalism is strong, for sure; it is easier to be numb to any inkling of grief. Melting, then, points to the mourning of "the diminishment of mourning itself, the loss of the rich and varied expressions of grief that have evolved on this planet over millions of years."[199] Yet "storied-mourning," he hopes, counteracts creatures' prescribed lines of "flight" toward death: "Stories play an important role in *communicating* this loss more widely, while helping to tease out the various ways in which loss matters, sometimes drawing distant listeners into a sense of felt connection and so affective involvement in a loss."[200] To accompany ice's "flight ways" marks an effort to resensitize ourselves, to mourn more fully, with something that proves to be, paradoxically, both "dull" and inflammatory.

Borrowing from Lauren Berlant, my readings ultimately offer up a sort of "cool optimism."[201] I am not optimistic about a breezy human–cold harmony; rather, I agree that "optimism is . . . a scene of negotiated sustenance that makes life bearable as it presents itself ambivalently, unevenly, incoherently."[202] Underlining ecological interconnectivity, at face value, is not enough, but I also believe that the "doings" (the early modern *ways* of cold) show us how dwelling is never a finished process. Cold's thickening and thinning sharpened some sociopolitical thoughts and actions, blunted others, and honed them anew. Despite its smoothness, in other words, ice has the grip of friction to it; it grinds on bodies and minds. It cements as well: a cardinal feature of "emergent ecologies,"[203] Eben Kirksey notes, is their adhesiveness. Thus, the slipping and sticking that a touch of cold entails, such as "stirring" arousal and melancholic sadness, offer us new ways to eliminate obstructions to environmental justice and health while accelerating efforts already in motion to ensure their inhabitants' prosperity. Ruminate too much on "end times," I fear, and apocalyptic proclamations become self-fulfilling.

In what follows, I choose to work with others on an unforeclosed future. I would rather stay with all of the Arctic's predicaments at present while also touring its storied past. Anna Tsing's unique use of the phrase "the end of the world" references the harvest of highly prized matsutake mushrooms. Their pickers barter in secretive, short-lived markets that, along with the fungi, spring out of "capitalist ruins."[204] Instead of collapsing the end of Arctic space (its biome) with the culmination of human time (its chronology), the "end" commences alternative, and spontaneous, ecological transactions. Envisioning the iceberg at "the end of the world" might smack of Captain Nicholas Sloane's 2018 entrepreneurial bid to tow icebergs into thirsty, well-paying urban areas.[205] Like Tsing, though, I imagine a more broadly concerted effort to find "fugitive moments of entanglement in the midst of institutionalized alienation,"[206] to build a "latent commons"[207] with pieces of ice exiting either end of the imperiled world, and to embrace the cold in times of thaw, not for the sake of conservation/preservation, but to rearticulate potentiality, and some hope, via uncertain slipways and combinatory circuits. I wave "farewell" as the iceberg passes by, and then, left in its wake, I wonder what it must be like to fare *well* together.

## "Holsome Instructions": The Rediscovery of Slowness

This book has a deliberately slow structure: its methodology encourages close readings and long pauses over early modern points in time both predictably quick (a slide) and oddly prolonged (a winter's passing). Its leisurely pace helps to espy the densely packed, more-than-human assemblages that cold makes. Karen Raber has suggested that "we need a kind of 'slow posthumanism' that arises out of millions of cellular pulses across the strands of culture, the academy and individuals over a longer temporal arc."[208] *Arcticologies* takes a long look at how and where the *post-* takes place: the hardening of water into ice, the ennui of polar nights, the stiffening of limbs into statues, the welcome of carnivalesque amusement. It invites us to go with the slow, employing a "*slow*-ciological"[209] approach that inspects cold's multifaceted sides. But this unhurried language still allows for addressing climate inequity, especially as it relates to Indigenous rights and the poor: the arrest of certain bodies, the displacement of others, and the general plight of those who have been forced to adapt to the diminishment of cold. Slow justice, to be clear, is not an option. Swift equality, restitution, and a transnational resolution to mitigate global warming is precisely what the notion of "degrowth"[210] entails. Braking is also a "doing": the result is a "slow future" (as opposed to none), a true "freezing" of assets and redistribution of wealth, where the remunerations for "slow violence" are sped up while the burning of fossil fuels is decelerated.[211] Slowness is a critique of modernity, Lutz Koepnick maintains, for it supplies counternarrative dissonance to the retold story of humanity's infinitely fast-forwarding, carbon-profiteering progress.[212]

Returning to the cusp of Enlightenment revolution seems strikingly familiar to the current moment, a turning point in how humans depreciate and appreciate cold's energy and the icy ecosystems it runs. As a methodology, then, cold-infused early modern environmental humanities—"cold studies," for short—carefully rethinks the "possible," a key word in Isabelle Stengers's manifesto *Slow Science*.[213] Glacial speeds speak to the privileging of acceleration ("fast tracks") within the academy as well. I will probably make some missteps here, to be honest, and wander off where the cold takes me. I proudly count myself as one of the "slow professors."[214] As Christine Hoffmann points out in her smart study of "stupid humanism," folly, in the Erasmian sense of "copia," was once considered part of a rigorous research agenda.[215] Precision and exactitude have their places here, and so does abundance. To be devoted to cold's copious "doings" is not to get them perfectly right: it is to stumble on cracks in your preconceived notions, and, once bewildered, find them reformed. "That is hot ice and wondrous strange snow! / How shall we find the concord of this discord?" (Shakespeare, *Midsummer Night's Dream,* 5.1.59–60). Onward into labyrinthine "Arcticologies," I say to Theseus: *frostina lente.*

# Winterlude

## *Flake*

When dayes are long, this Figure may
Help you passe the time away:
And it wil breed you much delight,
To passe away the Winters night.

—D.N., *The Figure of Six*

A tiny speck of snow once arrested the famous scientist Johannes Kepler (1571–1630) on his walk through Prague. Staring at the star-shaped patterns that dabbed his coat, his pamphlet *The Six-Cornered Snowflake,* published the following year (1611), set out to explain their puzzling consistency. The astronomer's thoughts, however, only proliferated: "Why . . . six points? What is the origin of the number six? Who carved the nucleus, before it fell, into six horns of ice? What cause is it that prescribes in that surface, which is now in the very act of condensing, six points in a circle for six prongs to be welded on to them?"[1] Uncomfortable with the idea of an ordered pattern existing at random, he ultimately decided on a "formative faculty" (*facultas formatrix*) acting in accordance with "supreme reason" that had "existed from the first in the Creator's design."[2] Nearly four hundred years later, the secular "agent" behind snowflakes' hexagonal shape remains undiscovered; as science writer Philip Ball puts it, "the secret of the snowflake endures."[3] Contrary to early modern humoral theories that held that melancholia-inducing winter dulled the passions, Kepler's brain "pronged" six ways admits the acuteness of cold. In its very inception, his natural-philosophical investigation demonstrates the "welding" of cognition with the physical environment, a commingling of thought processes and atmospheric processes that fosters further inquiries into the structure of frost. Many leaflets like D.N.'s (1652) promised to keep the mind active during the cold season, sketching series of mnemonic games to be played by the thought-thawing fireside. The goal was to "passe" sanely into spring. But here the "delight" of investigation is born (or "bred") through, not despite, its meeting with the six-armed "Figure."[4] Kepler eventually concluded that it was "folly . . . to be so carried away" with "nothing."[5] But something—that is, the snow—prods him on. (The pun is on Latin *nihil, nix* ["snow"], and German *nichts.*) The "playfulness"[6] he admits between words and snow betrays the weather's creative impress: "for as I write it has begun to snow, and more thickly than a moment ago. I have been busily examining the little flakes."[7] As he meditates, words and nucleii pass from sky to sense, mind to manuscript. Let fall: his experience is an apprehension in the literal sense, a human-snow clasp ("seizure") that leads to a limited mental grasp, a flimsy understanding of his fluttery subject matter.

❋ ❋

Is it "folly," really, to follow their drift? What if the "carried" (away) is welcome? Is there a "point" to reexamining *six* in today's warming climates? The snowflake stymies the processes of inductive and deductive reasoning by which humans burrow into the heart of hexagonal matter in order to sleuth out its unerring principle. Early modern snowflakes compel us, no less, to rethink "cognition" itself. In their flittering agency and fragile form, they model how human knowledge of the cryosphere both branches out and breaks off via the observer's embodied encounters with elemental forces. Ice crystals act as more than a facile heuristic; to skim their "surface" (as Kepler did) inaugurates an exercise in un/knowing, one that radiates, across multiple directions for indeterminate duration, into nodes of variable complexity. The result is "thickly" creative. A snowflake's physics and phenomenology, then and now, exceed the limits of human knowledge, while at the same time exciting further experiments with creatures of the cold. Adding to the flake's enduring intrigue, the *Oxford English Dictionary* cites its "difficult etymology" of Middle English origin: its potential derivations are from *flaw, flaught* (meaning "a flash"), and *flay*; it is also cognate with Old Norse *flóke* ("flock of wool") and connotes "something flat" from *flaga* ("slab of stone"). The conclusion is that "possibly several distinct words have

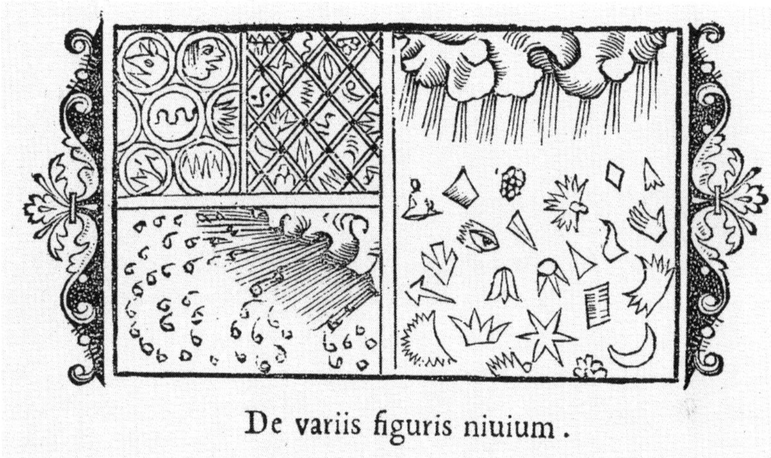


FIGURE 5. *De variis figuris niuium* (On the different shapes of snow), from Olaus Magnus, *Historia de Gentibus Septentrionalibus* (1555; English trans. as *Description of the Northern Peoples*). National Library of Norway.

coalesced," leaving "the mutual relation of the English senses . . . very uncertain."[8] As that which binds together material relations and linguistic content, *flake* announces a "difficult" coalition to ascertain (epistemologically), "uncertain" in its origin and endpoint (teleologically), and yet very real in its imbrication (ontologically). Adrian F. Ward argues that "winter wakes up your mind."[9] I think Kepler would agree.

* * *

Several prominent thinkers found themselves enchanted by water's crystalline formation. Rather than automatically assert their mastery, though, their firsthand sketches significantly extended the flake's mystery. Even a mechanistic intellect like that of René Descartes (1596–1650) recognized snowflakes' extremities as "alive and stirring,"[10] and when Robert Hooke (1635–1703) turned his microscope to "several kindes of frozen Figures" in his groundbreaking *Micrographia* (1665), he could only magnify that sextic symmetry the crystals stubbornly encrypted: "the most simple and plain operation of Nature . . . we are yet ignorant."[11] Magnus's woodcut from *A Description of the Northern Peoples* (see Figure 5, "On the different shapes of snow") stands out, however, for it implies that the "secret" should simply be admired, not decoded: "It seems more a matter for amazement than enquiry why and how so many shapes and forms, which elude the skill of any artist you choose to name, are so suddenly stamped upon such soft, tiny objects."[12] At least fifteen to twenty shapes may be seen in one day, he claims. The farther north one goes, the greater the variability in both "quality" and "quantity" of the descending "multiplicity."[13] Revealing the primary imprinter (or progenitor's "stamp") is less important than reveling in the plethora of falling "objects." While his picture is often cited as one of snowfall's earliest portrayals, the image also helpfully illustrates the art–nature kinship a flake's feathery touch makes possible. Realizing that a warm room encourages frost's craftsmanship, he is initially envious: "The cold outside and the wonderful handwork of Nature are seen to have so embroidered those panes with such different patterns that any artist you like, when he had looked at them, would be more capable of marvelling at her genius than of copying it."[14] And yet, he continues, the silversmiths and fabric makers of the north are extraordinarily talented at depicting snow's plentitude: they "are just as well taught by the most beautiful objects in Nature as are artists elsewhere in the world by the talents of a master."[15]

❄❄❄❄

By transferring the "tiny" figure of the snowflake from glass to page, he defines the artistic process ("handwork") as a shared subject–object endeavor. The "stamping," Magnus pronounces, is mutual; the published representations are fashioned because of, and not despite, human inquisitors suddenly facing the "soft" flecks of cold as he did. When one's goals are philosophical revelation (the end of "enquiry") or exact copying (a "just as" form of perfect mimesis), the amusing eccentricities of snow shapes disappears. His mode of reproducing snowflakes seeks to advance their or "her" secrets as well as creative "skill" instead. The "marvel" is right there, still, for all his readers: faint traces of cold collaboration, pictorialized on a pane of pleasures. As Magnus points to the windowsill as a natural-cultural canvas, he highlights the imperfect mixture of material forms that constituted early modern meteorological phenomena, especially the morally "pure" kind of precipitation called snow (see chapter 5). A closer inspection of his "pictures of snow on windows" exhibits a remarkable hodgepodge of forms—a flower and a grape cluster; an eye and a hand; a rabbit-eared creature adjacent to a gaping human face; a bell beside a spike—all amounting to a garden, menagerie, mine, and mirror rolled into one, a miniature gallery that runs the gamut of in/organic forms.[16]

Analogies to plants are common when describing snow's puzzling symmetry and frost's fractal patterns, of course. Hooke saw a forest of "*laminæ* . . . like so many blades of *Fern*."[17] But the simile between kind (like to like) is indebted (even if it is downplayed) to Magnus's vision that implied that these kinship classifications were physically entangled in one another. In its crisscrossed sets of animals, vegetables, and minerals, the picture both records (by being attached to a past experience) and enacts (by revealing how the witness was woven into that attachment) the interlaced structure of the snowflake, conveying its ability to forge links across kind by sending out flaky, six-branched arms that stick to other kin both inside and outside one's given taxonomic and hierarchical kingdom. Within its quadtych structure, then, Magnus's multispecies, semi-anthropomorphic conjunctions (what the snowflake gathers into its very substance) are foregrounded, emphasizing the intimacy that envelops and subtends human and nonhuman realms. Whether conceived geometrically as spheres (upper left), grids (upper middle), swirls (bottom left), or precipitating pieces (right), the viewer recreates a snowflake's radial connections. As her eye wanders from shape to shape and container to contents, passing through a series of intricate crystalline portals, they follow a flakey path that cannot be mapped beforehand, only made along the way.

❋ ❋ ❋ ❋ ❋

Flaking out with Magnus is a fitting place, finally, to branch off.[18] At this point, I will leave you with six lessons (*as expected*) from the sixteenth- and seventeenth-century snowflake. (1) The touch of the snowflake announces a mind–body–environment assemblage, the human–nonhuman sedimentation *flaga* implies that dispels snow's status as an objectified substance, a miniature item whose grand "secret" will be coaxed from it via rigorous scientific inspection. (2) Peering into ice crystals through the lenses of these authors tells us more about human desires *to* understand: an impulsive projection of pattern onto the world's messy fluidity, an inclination toward a natural order forever out of reach. (3) Linear models of causation are too brittle for flake-thinking. What emerges in place of the *how* and *why* is a creative kind of cold cognition that presumes, and even incorporates, "flaws" (errors). (4) This idea is not meant to be deliberately skeptical (at best) or unscientific or antiscientific (at worst); actually, the radiating quality of the snowflake models the sort of interdisciplinary inquisitiveness necessary for addressing today's most pressing problems, inspiring collaborations that may diverge into more-than-human modes of thinking. (5) Snowflakes' aesthetics have a crucial role to play in the conversation, too. Stomping through the snow to carve out his elaborate designs, "snowshoe artist" Simon Beck joins earlier designers like Magnus who similarly discovered the "delights" of embodied art-making.[19] (6) To "flake out," in sum, works against the exhaustive and noncommittal implications that the phrase has come to signify. In an era in which ice crystals are indisputably melting at precipitous rates, the power of kinetic accretion exhibited by a snowflake's rousing "figure" has never been more necessary.

❄ ❄ ❄ ❄ ❄ ❄

# 1 Finding Frīgus

> "If you curl up into a ball," he said, "if you defend yourself and get dressed, the enemy will penetrate down to your liver: cold is more invasive than you. No. Present yourself, uncover yourself, go toward it, make it your friend; it'll respect you. Turn the *against* into a *for.*" Yet without going beyond the lethal limit.
>
> —Michel Serres, *Biogea*

> I am cold.
>
> —René Descartes's reported last words, Stockholm

According to the Dutch extreme athlete Wim Hof, cold should be everyone's "warm friend."[1] The famous "method" that bears his name—the three "pillars" of cold therapy, the cold, breathing, and commitment (the Wim Hof Method [WHM])—promises a stronger immune system, better sleep, and increased energy. Clothing and temperature control, he claims, leave the human body under-stimulated, thereby "atrophying the age-old mechanisms related to our survival and basic function." A steadfast practitioner of WHM, the program promises, learns to unlock their "inner power, . . . the ability of our body to adapt to extreme temperature and survive within our natural environment." But this glacial guru's advice, while well-intentioned ("to a happier, healthier, and stronger you"), should give the cryocurious pause. Could this "power" be just another attempt at reasserting human resilience and control over inhabitable environments of "our" own making—an immersive practice meant to harden the permeable body, to teach it to manage the cold for the sake of self-help? In *The Way of the Iceman* (2016), Hof speaks rather unkindly of his old "friend" to boot: "You can't learn anything from the cold. But you can learn to not do some things."[2] If we cannot count on cold to set a positive example for living in the climatic "extremes" of the Anthropocene, then what *does* it teach the world's remaining icemen and icewomen, as well as those warmed societies set in their anthropogenic ways?

Early modern cryosophers, I propose, aid this inquiry. *Pace* Hof, the period's coolest students prove that there are affirmative lessons to "learn" from the cold: doings to do in addition to "things . . . to not do." Examples of the latter are ubiquitous. The satirist Thomas Nashe warns that, "when Winter reigns the water is so cold / That it is poison, present death to those / That wash or bathe their limbs in his cold streams."[3] Humoral theory, the prevalent discourse handed down by the Greek physicians Hippocrates and Galen, viewed the human body as a combination of four humors (black and yellow bile, blood, and phlegm) suspended in a delicate amalgam. Dis-ease occurred when these fluids lost their equilibrium. Many medical manuals from the last half of the seventeenth century advised against the ingestion of cold water, let alone one's (e.g., Hof's) full immersion. Reserved for unfaithful servants or penitent monks,[4] an excessive amount of cold was believed to plug the body's pores, trapping its unhealthy elements inside.[5] But the doctors did not always concur. Hermann van der Heyden (ca. 1572–1650), for example, defended cold bathing: "Neither is this our Cold Water useful onely, taken inwardly, in inward diseases; but applied Outwardly also, it cures the Outward Pains of the Body."[6] John Floyer (1649–1734) believed that, "in our Northern Climes, we must close our Pores, preserve our native Heat, and, if we will live long, and healthful, we must render our Skins dense and close, by Cold Water."[7] Even when remedying outbreaks of burning illness, specialists' cold prescriptions for correcting a patient's humoral imbalances were cautious at best. Treatments tended to question the body's innate integrity rather than uphold it. By adding the tangible matter of cold to this humoral conversation, I uncover the "things" that cool types of inhuman agency do to corporeal forms. Can one actually "friend" the cold, not just unfriend it? Where would one seek this unusual friendship, and how would they handle its "poisons"? What wisdom about human–cold relations emanates from this chill camaraderie?

This chapter fills out the faint traces of *frīgus* mentioned in the introduction. Drawing from a range of literary, remedial, and natural-philosophical texts invested in the un/healthy effects of cold contact, it spells out the central historical concepts that inform this book as a whole: the prevailing theories behind cold's origin (*primum frigidum*) and impacts ("doings") during the sixteenth and seventeenth centuries. We will tour the cold library like so: the first half scrutinizes the meteorological musings of Francis Bacon, René Descartes, and Thomas Hobbes (1598–1579). But it is Robert Boyle's massive 1665 *New Experiments and Observations Touching Cold* that best conveys the intricacies of cold encounters. His "promiscuous" experiments (from the Latin *promiscuus,* "to mix indiscriminately") effectively fuse the human observer with the nonhuman observed. By "listening" to a block of ice, he models "touching," affective-laden experiences with the cold that we may both replicate and improve on.

The second half dips into the 1660 *Scarbrough Spaw* of Robert Wittie (1613[?]–1684), an English physician who successfully managed to turn his country's exposed eastern coast into a thriving therapeutic resort. While he is persuasive in his defense of a salubrious north and the physiological benefits that come from its coldness, Wittie's most notable accomplishment, I argue, is situating the spa-going human subject in wider global–local waters, collapsing hydrospatial distance by eliminating the separation between embodiment and environment. At his spa/*Spaw,* subcutaneous and subterranean "veins" intersect. I call this permeative and interelemental exercise "cryocorporeality."[8] In their most recent collection on "the geographic nature of embodiment," Mary Floyd-Wilson and Garrett A. Sullivan Jr. "downplay reified, static conceptions of the *body* in favour of an analysis of *embodiment* as an ongoing process of engagement with (and in) the world."[9] The material–metaphorical mapping of wintry humans and minerals that occurs at the source of a local wellspring recognizes the body's degree of wellness as dependent on physical degrees of temperature; and yet, it simultaneously checks that same body's capacity to completely compose itself. In conclusion, I ask why we should reexamine past perceptions of cooling in a world that is currently warming. Returning to Boyle's curious episode of promiscuity and cold-inflected vocabulary, along with Wittie's spa-derived macrocosmic–microcosmic model, magnify the precarious water cycles of today's cryosphere, calling our attention to, and care for, its porous bodies most at risk.

## Counting *Calor*

It is useful at this early point to situate Boyle, Wittie, and their colleagues within the period's competing, contrasting, and complementary knowledges about the nature of cold. Debates at this time centered on what cold actually *was*, ontologically speaking (and not always coexistent with heat), as well as from *where* it originated: whether in the dry air of underground caves, the wetness of fast and fatal "streams," the powdery fineness of snow, or the uncrackable enormity of ice. Even at these trusted sites, however, the thing of cold could be an unreliable presence. Phenomenological quandaries only deepened its ontic and epistemic peculiarities. In its purest adjectival sense, "cold" denoted a perceptible quality that was dependent on one's physical embodiment at a given moment; thus, what felt "cold" for one individual might feel comfortable to another. Reacting to this arbitrariness (by virtue of being tied to subjective experience in the absence of objective measurement), some inquirers grew wary of tactility altogether. Well water will feel cool in the summer yet tepid in the winter. "As far as sense and touch goes," wrote Bacon, "heat is a variable and respective thing."[10] But skeptical investigations into the sensation of cold (as a property of matter) also sponsored multiple theories concerning the substance of cold (as matter proper). Bacon could speak of heat being "respective" while, at the same time, he drafted a "Table of degrees."[11] Gradations of cold were both inherently interactive and highly unique, then, and attached themselves to regional specificities and local variations. Without accurate instrumentation, the magnitude of cold was often ranked by what it did, where, and for how long, its acuteness rising incrementally from diaphanous frost on bedroom windows, to bent nails in floorboards, to burst beer barrels left outside for too long.

To counter this capriciousness, historic attempts were made to construct an empirical system of measurement. If cold was to be expressed in a universal scientific language, in a numerical form like "degrees," it needed first to be objectified, before being translated into an internationally recognized rubric. The earliest thermoscopes noted changes in temperature but lacked stable units of definition: a frustrating dilemma that would eventually lead to the invention of the thermometer and, much later, the "calorie." But the conversions between Daniel Fahrenheit (1686–1736), Anders Celsius (1701–1744), and William Thomson, First

Baron Kelvin (1824–1907) only reasserted the variable accounting of cold: what conditions the level 0 degrees signifies, for instance, or the exact mark at which freezing begins. "Measurement is only interesting when you know what you are measuring—when there is a purpose," writes physicist Gino Segrè, and "that required a better understanding of heat."[12] What was observed was not always clear or understood. Gustavus Parker's *Portable Barometer* (1699) noticed encounters between "Hemispherical Effluvia," "Eddies of Air," and "Frigorifick Saline."[13] What cooled the mixture—the "Frigorifick" component—however, remained unidentifiable. Cold's pressure, too, remained open for interpretation. In a chapter on the generation of rain and snow, Parker "prove[s] the truth of a Paradox or two, that the Air is both lighter and heavier in wet weather, and both heavier and lighter in dry weather."[14] As a "paradox," cold continued to puzzle those who sought to constrain its protean aspects (an infinitude of feeling) even as they tried to gauge it with the most innovative technologies of the day (a finite range of numbers).

Elsewhere, detailed commentaries on "artificial" and "natural" freezing, like those found in the Florentine Accademia del Cimento's 1684 *Essayes of Natural Experiments,* instructed well-off hosts how to reap the deliciously uncommon "harvests of the cold months," or how to mold bizarre tabletop spectacles by appreciating ice's malleable mystique.[15] Cornelius Drebbel cooled Westminster Abbey in the presence of James I (1566–1625) in the summer of 1620 by mixing saltpeter (also known as potassium nitrate) with snow in order to lower the freezing point of water, refrigerating the abbey's air just enough to dazzle his damped audience.[16] The incredible process had already been described as a kind of "chaos" by Giambattista della Porta (1535[?]–1615) in his 1658 *Naturall Magick* as a way to freeze wine.[17] Drebbel's "mighty cold,"[18] a conjuration that was otherwise described as "magick," "chaos," or "paradox," testifies to a long legacy of bemusement as much as bafflement, an enigma difficulty embraced rather than easily resolved. It seems that that simplest of questions (what *is* cold?) can be met only with wider speculation: of epistemology (quantifiable measurement), phenomenology (qualitative affect), and ontology (material composition).

Where would one begin such a quest? Any search for what constitutes cold necessarily broaches the question of its cause: the mythical *primum frigidum* spoken of by Parmenides. Bacon, while not the first seeker of cold's elemental basis, effectively rejuvenated this pseudo-scientific pursuit. His 1627 *Sylua Syluarum* is a frost-nipped forest, for it stipulates no less than seven "Meanes of Producing Cold": (1) the "Expiring of Cold out of the Inward Parts of the Earth in Winter"; (2) "the Contact of Cold Bodies"; (3) "the Primary Nature of all Tangible bodies"; (4) "the Density of the Body"; (5) "a Quicke Spirit inclosed in a Cold Body"; (6) "the Chasing and Driuing away of Spirits, such as haue some Degree of Heat"; and lastly, (7) "the Exhaling or Drawing out of the warme Spirits."[19] For Bacon, "[the] *Quid ipsum* of heat is motion and nothing else"[20]; yet high and low temperatures are less free-floating entities moving at different speeds, and more tethered partners: "Heat and Cold," he writes, "are Natures two Hands, whereby she chiefly worketh."[21] He, like many others, was acquainted with the ancient idea of "antiperistasis," *ἀντιπερίστασις*, from the Greek for "against a standing round, circumstance." This doctrine held that boosting one factor (such as an increase in cold) would heighten its opposing feature (a spike in body heat). The belief also explains why, while his main interest in *Novum Organum* (1620) is the nature of heat, he makes frequent comparisons to cold: "Heat and cold share many actions, though for very different reasons. For snow seems after a while to burn children's hands; and cold no less than heat keeps meat from putrefying; while heats contract bodies, just as cold bodies do."[22] Because warmth (for him) is built in to the equation, there is nothing on earth "that is extremely cold."[23] One distinction between the two, it seems, involves cold's dearth: "We lack cold other than that which can be had in winter weather, in caves, or in snow and ice houses,"[24] he admits, further complaining that "nature supplies cold so grudgingly."[25] The fact that cold must be sought suggests a learning disability: "In this connection ["namely heat and cold"] human power hobbles along on one leg."[26] A fire may be lit and its flames stoked. Cold's immediate "lack," however, figuratively lames the philosopher, humbling (or "hobbling") the human genius instead of stroking its ego.

Even though he likened cold's aloofness to a kind of mental handicap, Bacon's inductive reasoning seemingly gained strength by straying from the position of scientific certainty, an achievement interpreted here as type of able-bodiedness. The obvious challenges in pinning down the *primum frigidum* and in mapping out useable levels of "degree" only provoked greater inspection: "For Cold we must staie till it commeth; or seeeke it in deepe Caues, or high Mountaines: And when all is done, we cannot obtaine it in any great degree."[27] Highlighting the creative, ambidextrous reciprocity between hot and cold—"Nature's two hands"—it is *Sylua Syluarum*'s second cause of cold (the "Contact of Cold Bodies . . . for Cold is Actiue and Transitive into Bodies Adiacent"[28]) that etched his name into the millennia-long history of temperature: "Whosoeuer will be an Inquirer into Nature, let him resort to a Conseruatory of Snow and Ice."[29] His ardent seeking of an "actiue" cold and his pun on "degree," as both quantity and quality, establish a human–nonhuman consortium of contact that endures because of cold's recalcitrance, not despite it. To think "on one leg" adopts a nonnormative position of accruing cold data, a different way of conducting research that is at odds with the valorization of ultimate knowability. The dance of hotness and coldness, of temperatures entwined "hand" in "hand," and the patience and modesty required from the observer present a necessary check against the technoscientific, anthropocentric, and androcentric mindset that has come to define pre-Enlightenment figures of natural philosophy such as Bacon himself.[30] His opinions on mankind's dominion over nature should absolutely be interrogated; at the same time, though, his exhortation to his peers (and us) to "resort to," to "seeeke" cold (often touted as a cryophilic motto) represents an open-ended methodology that mandates subject–object inseparability and anticipates its uncertain outcomes. Bacon, ironically, died of pneumonia after stuffing a hen with snow: a reminder that the encounter always retains a lethal edge (a point to which I will return in closing). This is a fallible "conseruatory," a school of embodied knowledge temporarily conserved (literally, "kept together") without the fail-safe guarantee of preservation, one built on a foundation constantly at risk of falling apart.

## Frost's Impressions

Bacon is less known, perhaps, for a pronouncement he makes later in his monumental tome of natural history: "Whosoeuer will make Experiments of Cold, let him be prouided of . . . a Conseruatorie of Snow."[31] Simply put, to find the source of *frīgus* (Latin for "cold," as he had elsewhere named it[32]), one must interact with the stuff of snow. Let us take his advice, then. We already know how outspoken the Geneva Bible (1599) is on the subject: "Hast thou entered into the treasures of the snow? or hast thou seen the treasures of the hail?" (Job 38:22). For one seeking the genesis of snow and a clear understanding of how it and its meteoric kin (like hail) are made, Christianity offers a ready answer. Snow is evidence of God's will; his voice ushers in existence: "for he saith to the snow, Be thou upon the earth likewise to the small rain and to the great rain of his power" (Job 37:6). Similarly, freezing happens when he orders water to "be" so: "at the breath of God the frost is given, and the breadth of the waters is made narrow . . . The waters are hid as with a stone: and the face of the depth is frozen" (Job 37:10, 38:30). Despite their invitation, the verses are meant to end debate. To scrutinize God's actions is to challenge divine authority itself. A central part of patient, Job-like suffering, therefore, is wondering at his celestial works: "whether it be for punishment, or for his land, or of mercy, he causeth it to come" (Job 37:13). Justifying God's command with cruelly harsh winters sent to rebuke a seemingly repentant populace required acrobatic feats of biblical exegesis.[33]

But for those less interested in churchly didacticism (snow *is* because God literally says so), any wise entry point into the "treasures" of snow began with the base layer of knowledge Aristotle set down in the *Meteorologica* (ca. 340 BCE). Craig Martin demonstrates the vast influence that the classical text had on early modern authors by citing one such inheritor, the German professor Marcus Frytsche (1598): "a *meteoron* is a body imperfectly mixed, generated out of vapor or exhalation in the region of air by the force and heat of the heavenly rays."[34] Those thinkers who looked to the cold skies would have contemplated "meteors" as a merger of the four elements in motion, a sublunar braiding of hot and dry (fiery) and vaporous (watery) exhalations. Like most "aqueous phenomena" classified this way, such as rain, dew, and frost, snow was the product of evaporation (*diakrisis*) undergoing a series of transformations (*sunkrisis*) that did not result in an entirely new form. (A "perfect" mixture, on the other hand, was its own substance, distinct from the elements that composed it.) Clouds condensed as water vapor (*atmis*) rose into the middle region of the atmosphere, the air temperature dictating the hardness of their precipitation.[35] Prognostication (the precursor of "forecasting") was typically separated from these scholarly investigations; indeed, notes Martin, "the predictive side of meteorology rarely combined with causal explorations."[36] As authors debated over topics like telos, they added to a growing body of meteorological literature bound together by indeterminacy instead of answers: "[They] recognized that understandings . . . should be flexible and limited and that knowledge of the causes of the weather was inherently uncertain."[37] Distinctions between hail and snow were blurry, for example, even if the former fell more frequently in the summer.

The snowy skies were intrinsically un/predictable, foreseeable only to a dim extent, their ir/regular drifts exacerbated by a centuries-long period of prolonged cooling. The accelerated production of meteorological epistemologies meant that the words of Job were not always taken at rhetorical face value. As providence became a prominent rationale for catastrophic events, "natural philosophical understandings of meteorology became intertwined with the religious meaning and significance of weather itself."[38] In sum, and in keeping with the widespread terminology of exhalations supplied by Aristotle, snowy "meteors," contra sacred instruction, amassed a proliferation of natural-philosophical (sometimes theological) explanations that avoided both mundane description and clear-cut comprehension. At this momentously cold time in history, snow floated from the heavens only to flout the idea of an omniscient (godly) maker or academic (human) mind: its meaningful "treasures" too many to exhaust, engendering a heap too high to house but also too sparkling to ignore.

*A Goodly Gallerye* (1563), by the Puritan divine William Fulke (1538–1589), is a fine place for sussing out the complicated origin of snow. An amalgamation of Aristotle, Pliny, and Seneca, it marks the first time "meteorology" entered the English language, and it appeared in nine different editions in the span of a century. Fulke's anti-Romanist polemics led to his appointment as master of Pembroke Hall, Cambridge, in 1578. But he is best remembered for his earlier work of rational investigation into "Impressiones, named of ther height, Meteora,"[39] which was meant to counter astrological readings. Fulke found the practice of prognostication antithetical to the truer science of astronomy. Dutifully Aristotelian, he divides meteors into "vnperfectly" and "perfectly mixed" (un/resistant to change, respectively), made up of either moist "vapores" or dry "exhalations."[40] "Snowe," he says, "is a cloude congeled by greate colde, before it be perfectlye resolued from vapors into water."[41] This basic understanding of cold would predominate discussions. Poor Robin, whose *Almanack* was first printed in 1664 and went through annual publications from 1669 to 1700, writes in the

*Book of Knowledge* (1688) that "snow is ingendred of Rain, the Cloud congealing through extremity of Cold,"[42] and John Tulley, observing "the Natural Causes of Watry Meteors, as Snow, Hail, Rain &c."[43] from Boston, repeated the same almost verbatim over one hundred years later in his 1693 *Almanack*: "You must first Understand, that all Watery Meteors, as Rain, Snow, or such like, is but a moist Vapour drawn up by the Vertue of the Sun, and the rest of the Planets into the middle Region of the air, where being congealed or dissolved, upon the earth, as hail or rain."[44] Snow seems to a simple meteor, by this summary, the known components of its material composition handed down (or up) through the ages.

Fulke's account proves snow is less easily "understand[able]," however, when he turns to what snow does in addition to what it is. If "hore froste," which is "nothing els but dewe congeled by ouermuche cold . . . [that] doth often stynke" because it is drawn from fetid places like lakes full of "stinking" mud,[45] the cold cloud gains a sensory quality as much as it collapses spatial differences between lower, middle, and high regions of the atmosphere. Noisome "matter"[46] that falls to earth might have its formation in the waters at your very feet. Even without a definitive grasp of the water cycle, of which melting ice and snow play a major part (a theory that would later be proven by the findings of Pierre Perrault [ca. 1608–1680]), the *cryo-* factor of the hydrological cycle widens to include a number of snowy "impressiones" of which we are unfamiliar. For Fulke, fluctuations from "vnperfectly" to "perfectly mixed" meant that snow could take on both mineral and vegetable aspects: the stone "Christal," he maintains, comes from snowmelt freezing again on high hills, and, contrary to its associations with barren landscapes, it "causeth thinges growing to be fruictfull, and increase, because the cold dryueth heate vnto the rootes, and so cherysheth the plantes."[47] With its vegetative agency—from the Latin *vegetat* ("enlivening")—snow embraces life forms; its impress fructifies, makes fertile. In its mineralogical makeup, it keeps open the possibilities of metamorphosis; it channels heat, conducts change. Early modern meteorologists described snow in ways that highlighted its vibrancy, and the influential energy it carried was called "cold."

In "Of the Nature of Terrestrial Bodies," the first discourse of his 1637 *Meteorology,* Descartes argues that all bodies are composed of small particles of varying shapes, sizes, and regularities, their forms roughly matching the durability of the object that they compose: water's, for instance, are "long, smooth, and slippery, like little eels,"[48] and thereby easily breakable. These bodies, in turn, are surrounded by a "very fine material,"[49] itself composed of parts of various sizes (the larger they are, the stronger their force), that moves at differing speeds according to the time of day and season, proximity to the equator, and distance from the earth's surface. This "material" is both highly agitable and capable of agitating other particles. Stirring depends on the size of a body's "pores"[50] as it comes into contact with said forces. These pores act like portals, determining the degree of agitation, and thus, he argues, the temperature, since only that which is "subtle"[51] (smaller) than the doorway may enter. Ice forms from the absence of agitation: "When [water] is no more agitated, or no less fine, than it normally is [i.e., when its particles' pores cannot admit the "less fine" or larger material that has the strength to knock others about], . . . it does not have enough force to bend and agitate [the particles] in this way; this is the reason they come to a stop, haphazardly joined to and lying upon one another, and thus form a hard body, namely ice."[52]

In short, freezing signals a pore blockage: "Water freezes only when the finer material among its particles does not have the force to agitate them."[53] (For a teaching aid, Descartes provides a morbid tableau: eels can survive in a holey fishing boat that permits water to pass through; eels on the shore, however, will perish with cold.) Ice proves especially hard to thaw because the fineness (smallness) of its pores lets little inside. Marble and metal feel colder than wood, he explains, because, like ice, they have trouble admitting finer parts into their already-narrow passageways. The human nervous system detects heat or cold based on the amount of particulate excitement: "as regards heat and cold, we need to consider nothing except that the small particles of the bodies we touch, being agitated more or less strongly than usual—either by the small particles of this very fine material or by whatever other cause there may be—also agitate more or less the small threads of those our nerves which are the organs of touch."[54] Although it makes mention of imperviousness and stoppages, Descartes's meteorological take on the cause of freezing affords a remarkable glimpse into the business of cryocorporeal exchange; that is, he magnifies the porous, interpenetrative process behind cold.

If the absence of perturbation generates the sensation of cold, the matter of ice would demonstrate the cessation of particulate movement. Hypotheses about frozen states risked downplaying, in the language of Fulke, the "cherysheth" dimension of cold, leaving little room for talk of "increase." Fortunately, other theories offset cold's negative valences (as a decrease) by espousing its quickening, commingling qualities. The sixth "dialogue" of Hobbes's *Decameron Physiologicum* (1678), "Of the Causes and Effects of Heat and Cold," advances ideas of cold that account for freezing *as* movement. For him, humans cannot infer heat from simply feeling any shift; it takes a certain type. "For not every Motion causeth Heat, but this agitation onely, which we call compounded motion."[55] From the Latin for "put together" (*componere*), "compounded" matter comes close to Descartes's infiltrated bodies, and yet one can also discern a departure: cold is made *by* contact (the act of being compounded) rather than encounter's deprivation (by virtue of being "no more agitated"). Cold, in brief, is not the privation of heat, but the manufacture of a specific movement: "For seeing the Motion that begets Heat, tendeth to the separation of the parts of the Body whereon it acteth, it stands with reason, that the Motion which maketh Cold, should be such as sets them closer together."[56] On a tactile level, this observation is understandable: up close, ice appears like super-condensed (smashed) water. In Hobbes's words, it is "nothing else but the smallest imaginable parts of Air and Water mixt; which is made hard by this compounded Motion, that keeps the parts so close together, as not to be separated in one place without disordering the Motion of them all."[57] Ice, compounded by a compounding force, must necessarily maintain this motion: not only does matter commingle leading up to the moment of freezing (Descartes's position), but it does so in the event, and furthermore must maintain its movement thereafter. Frozen matter moves, to the extent that it aggregates under pressure, "puts," and pieces "together."

But why, one of his imaginary interlocutors (*A*) asks, "is not Ice as well made in a moved as in a still water?"[58] As Descartes did with his punctured vessel, Hobbes turns to a river to illustrate his thinking. He guesses at iceberg formation amidst the "agitation"[59] of northern seas by watching ice spread over the Thames: "Part (being too great to pass [London] Bridge) stoppeth there and sustains that which follows."[60] Growing as they do not go past, carried "one against another"[61] by currents and tides, the river's flows enable a process of compound accumulation. The cold crafting of "great Bodies"[62] takes place through motions that occur no matter how "moved" or "still" water appears at first glance. In his riparian reflection, Hobbes may have hit on the Deleuzoguattarian "speed"[63] of ice: its penchant for congregating in seemingly motionless conditions, for gaining intensity in what looks like transfixed spots.

His overarching emphasis on motion importantly extends to human anatomy as well. Persons *A* and *B* discuss an "Experiment" that has already become "common": watching cold as it "communicate[s] it self" via "Wind" from a vessel of snow to another of water, "the ice in the Pail by its dissolution transfer[ing] its Hardness."[64] The operation, *A* opines, is not that unusual: "The Greeks have the word *φρίκη* [*fríki*] (whence the Latins have their word *Frigus*) to signifie the curling of water by the Wind; and use the same also for Horrour, which is the passion of one that cometh suddenly into a cold Air, or is put into a sudden affright, whereby he shrinks, and his hair stands upright. Which manifestly shews that the Motion which causeth Cold, is that which pressing the Superficies of a Body, sets the parts of it closer together."[65] Hobbes's etymological point is a bit specious,[66] but he is correct in an assigning a feeling to the force of *frigus,* positing a cryocorporeal connection, and thereby a nondistinction, among a body's "superficies," its environment, and the organs of emotion. The question remains, however, whether this corporeal and compounding motion of cold is necessarily restricted to a single "passion" such as fright—that is, whether piloerection might stem from titillation as well as terror, whether one might curl up to cold rather than shirk its sudden coming.

## Touching the "Frigorifick"

No one more eagerly accepted Bacon's invitation to "make experiments of cold" than Boyle. Descartes's and Hobbes's motion-based theories of cold had failed to put the *primum* matter to rest. Epitomizing the "experimental," Boyle brilliantly filled this epistemological vacuum. The feeling of *frīgus* is palpable throughout his *New Experiments and Observations,* a massive compendium of almost every cryological study that had been made theretofore. Although he begins his treatise with the infamous dictum that "cold is so barren a subject,"[67] he nonetheless devotes nearly nine hundred pages to its fruitfulness. Because of its sheer size, I will focus less on the minutiae of his experiments, the accuracy of his arguments (his own and others'), or where his exhaustive investigation fits into the longer history and sociology of science.[68] Instead, his hands-on methods intrigue me more: how he conducts his experimental research and thereby constructs meaning. Boyle's "touching" approach is avowedly painstaking, and he avoids rushing to conclusions; its tempo is cautious: "I found the framing of an Universal and unexceptionable Hypothesis of Cold, to be a work of greater difficulty, [than] every Body would imagine. . . . That Hypotheses hastily pitch'd upon, do seldom keep their Reputation long; and divers of them that are highly Applauded at the first, come after a while to be Forsaken, even by those that devised them" (4:221–22). Since the title page espouses "newness," his readers might expect him "to have begun the natural History of Cold" where others could not; and yet he modestly admits, "I think fit to intimate, that I look upon what I have done but as a Beginning" (4:222). In other words, his tests are borderless "beginnings," rather than trials with starts and ends that can be pinpointed, promising trajectories in place of predictable results. This type of open-ended excursion typifies what Anna Tsing calls "radical curiosity."[69] Experiments, once implemented, conceive additional tries. The word "pitch'd" best encapsulates his nonteleological intention to enter instead of conquer the Baconian "conseruatory." Meaning "to thrust in, fix in, set in place," but also "to cast, throw, or fall forwards,"[70] Boyle's lab is set up like a slide, a slope to "pitch" conjectures: that is, the perfect place for un/grasping the cold.

Where to begin, then, after offering an incomplete study about something whose origins are so mystifying that a verb like "pitch'd" is the first to come to mind? Similar to those before him, ascertaining cold via subjective experience is not convincing enough: "By reason of the various and unheeded predispositions of our Bodies, the single and immediate informations of our senses are not always to be trusted" (4:252). Believing the senses would be solipsistic, indeed; the "body" of Boyle would stand in for a universal one. What can be safely established, however, is that coldness is a "Tactile Quality" relative to "our Organs of Feeling," with "Operations on divers other Bodies besides ours" (4:229). Cold, in sum, affects diverse bodies differently. But Boyle knows this notion is self-evident; so, in order to submit anything truly "new" in response to the long-pondered question, he must first vet the theories that have already been proposed. Most of the heft of *New Experiments and Observations,* in fact, is an examination of others' observations. His "experimental history" (4:265) essentially tests the veracity of ancient and contemporary opinions in a patient, orderly fashion. Page upon page offers the reader various exercises in disproof, with Boyle systematically ruling out posited reasons for *primum frigidum*: from the element of water (Aristotle) to the atomic swarms of Epicurus (fourth century BCE), from privation to antiperistasis—a "vulgar conceit very unconsonant to the nature of inanimate beings" (4:469)—on up to "Winds" and the "indeavour inwards" by the body's "exterior parts" (4:505) postulated by Hobbes a decade earlier in *De Corpore* (1655).

A telling example of Boyle's critical work ethic may be found in the sixth section of his history, titled the "Preservation and Destruction of Bodies by Cold" (4:288), a topic that allows him to check "the ingress of frigorifick Atoms," or "Corpuscles," endorsed by atomists (4:293). The quandary to be considered is how "a moderate degree of Cold preserves many Bodies, and that glaciation destroys, or at least prejudices most others (probably by discomposing or vitiating their Texture) when they come to be thaw'd" (4:294). To freeze, in short, is not always to preserve. Frostbite alone is proof enough that bodies are penetrable when frozen, and thus their inviolability cannot be guaranteed. Something must get in, and what actually accounts for cold's modest corporeal maintenance or its prejudicial vitiation hangs on the dubiousness of "probably." He phrases the conundrum this way: whether to suppose that "in Glaciation the moist and fluid parts are wedg'd in by intruding swarms of frigorifick Atomes, or that those restless particles, that were wont to keep the Body fluid or soft, are called forth of it, be the cause of glaciation; which soever of these two ways we pitch upon, we must in frozen Bodies conceive an unwonted rest to be produced of those movable particles, whose internal commotions, and disorderly coalitions and Avolations [flying away], are either the Causes, or the necessary Concomitants of Corruption" (4:295). The slow "pitch" here, more to Boyle's prefatory point, allows for multiple possibilities to happen at once: a "disorderly coalition," an "avolation," and a "rest," an "unwonted" virtuality. Cold is a conjectural space of thought where the "hastily" (the coming to conclusion) has little credibility after one recognizes the various stages of particle speed, tempos of the "wedged" and the "restless."

By speaking about the cause of cold in explicitly ambivalent and multivalent ways, Boyle's academic series of appraisals skirts the need to supply, at the finish of *New Experiments and Observations,* a syllogistic rationale or a chemical reaction translated into replicable, stoichiometric formulas. Rather than reach the entire truth behind cold, which would be a fitting close to his "begun," he repeatedly underscores dispute as an integral part of scientific inquiry. "Experiments about the Measure of the Expansion and the Contraction of Liquors by Cold" (4:319), for example, investigate the mundane occurrence of frozen containers bursting under pressure. If Descartes's attribution of cold to "a privation of Heat" was correct, he wonders, then "how these little Eels should by that recess acquire as strong an endeavor outwards" is inexplicable (4:329), but on the other hand, and according to the Epicurean way of comprehending cold, if "these Corpuscles stealing insensibly into the Liquors they insinuate themselves into, without any shew of boisterousness or violence, 'tis not so easie to conceive how they should display so strange a force against the sides of those strong vessels that they break" (4:329). After evaluating the atomists' theory yet again, this time through "Experiments touching the weight of Bodies frozen and unfrozen" (4:410), like eggs, which showing their masses to be equal, the only predictable outcome is equivocation: "I doubt whether it may, on the contrary, be safely concluded, that the Atomists Theory of Cold is false" (4:415).

This inconclusiveness does not mean that Boyle judges all theories equally (Hobbes, his fierce competitor, is an expected target [4:503]), but that a degree of uncertainty necessarily lingers in his pronouncements. "My design," he confesses, "in playing the Sceptick on this subject, is not so much to reject other mens probable opinions, of a *primum frigidum,* as absolutely false, as 'tis to give an account, why I look upon them, as doubtful" (4:381). Taking on this role could be an ingenious strategy for pretending to know the "subject" of cold, a pretentious demonstration of one's pseudomastery or encyclopedic erudition meant to endlessly defer the question. But another motivation might be to inhabit cold's dubiousness deliberately, to *deliberate* in order to "pitch" into its ambiguities. The "sceptick," one who expresses doubt, is also one who proposes (further) inquiry, finds impetus in the not-quite-"false." Boyle fails to crack the cold not simply from lack of philosophical fitness (a shortcoming to be blamed on an insufficient angle of intellectual "pitch"), but owing to the unknowable, freezing-while-fleeting *frīgus* itself.

If the riddling *primum* refuses to be solved, it also becomes harder to "reject" premises as either right or wrong. What if this epistemic openness was actively desired in addition to being dispassionately observed? Could this indeterminacy, merely noted or tolerated at first, grow into a predilection for cold's impactful agency? Boyle's book has more to say to this onto-epistemological question. Despite his deductive logic that appears to operate only by subtraction—his methodical mind moving down a list of authoritative hypotheses, checking off feature by frosty feature, cross-referencing cold ideas across times, authors, and geographies, all amounting to a grandly "doubtful" conclusion—I glimpse in Boyle's experiments the hallmark of those Bruno Latour calls "additive empiricists."[71] They, he says, are "interested in objective facts and grounded claims, but they like to add, to complicate, to specify, and, whenever possible to slow down and, above all, hesitate so as to multiply the voices that can be heard."[72] Latour's sobriquet also raises an important point for modern-day readers acquainted with the bad-faith arguments of "climate change denial," "alternative facts," and "fake science." To "pitch" is not the same as to deny. Instead, a good "sceptick" recognizes that scientific facts are produced, disseminated, and tested over time (this is a given), but she also asks whether the issues of cold are valued, and which, and why (not). Boyle's approach, "slowed down," helps maintain cold's status as a "matter of concern," or in Latourian parlance, a "state of affairs" that resists sliding into a neat, noiseless category of the "object" supported by an uncritical empiricism.[73]

The keyword I follow here is "frigorifick," a term attributed to him (albeit in 1668), and one out of several expressions invented in the seventeenth century that stem from the Latinate *frīgus* ("cold"), starting with *frigid* (adj.) in 1622 and extending to *frigidate* (v.) in 1691.[74] (Parker's "Frigorifick Saline" from 1699 is at the tail end of this idiomatic influx.) *Frigor* (n.), "extreme coldness," had only recently entered the English language in 1599. But "frigorifick" is more than just a clever inflection that turns a nounal state into an adjectival trait. Lodged in Boyle's "frigorifick" vocabulary are depictions of the cold (*frīgus*) as a lab partner at work. He initially balks at the suggestion. One reason why he will not subscribe to the principle of antiperistasis, for example, is that he is reluctant to grant heat and cold any volition, quoting the 1653 *Cursus Philosophicus* of the French natural philosopher Emanuel Maignan (1601[?]–1676) in calling it a notion that "I confess I cannot approve, (since to ascribe, as he does, a *fuga Contrarii* to Cold and Hot spirits, is in my apprehension to turn inanimate Bodies into intelligent and designing Beings)" (4:496–97). The theory of antiperistasis could encourage mechanical definitions of "cold and hot," conceiving them as rote qualities that automatically intensify via contact with their opposite (*contrarii*).

Yet the veering *fuga* ("flight") of their "spirits" also bespeaks a mercurial agency that routinely evades their viewer. The capriciousness of cold leads Boyle to confront "a certain inexplicable self invigoration, which is commonly propos'd in such a way as invests inanimate bodies with the prerogatives of free Agents" (4:493). The fugal seems at odds with human intelligence at times; admittedly, Boyle's lab looks less and less Latourian in these pronouncements. As we will soon see, however, while actants are not "free" in the purest sense, since they receive their motility through attachment, they are still "agents" capable of "designing," or collaborating, with their colleagues, challenging the label of "inanimate." Recall Boyle's analysis of frostbitten tissue: "frigorifick Atomes," be they "wedg'd" in, or in flight from "fluid parts," filter through a body that is both susceptible to "corruption" and corrupted by said cold "swarms." Boyle's standing in the history of cryogenics, the early-twentieth-century branch of physics that studies the production and effects of cold, is worth reappraising: not as one who vaingloriously pursued the genesis ("generation, creation") *of* cold, but as a remarkable witness to, and participant *in*, cold's generative creations.[75] Cold's enclasp is where human–nonhuman coproduction vigorously takes place. Exposure to cold exposes the body as a site violable and violated, a composite "texture" of frenetic and "frigorifick" parts temporarily held together only by its propensity to become "discompos'd" (4:296).

In Boyle's touching case, one watches the "frigorifick" shift from adjective to verb whenever *frigidum* physically enters his body. His practice relies more on risky personal insertions than on technoscientific calculations. In the introduction, he acknowledges that he is "unable to produce or intend Cold as we can do Heat, nor command the Experiments that concern Congelation" (4:223). Without matter to command, cold is something he must cooperate with, and occasionally be afflicted by: "I shall lose no reputation by this History (as incompleat as it comes forth) I think, if Ingenious Men knew, how much Trouble and Exercise of my patience it has cost me, they would, peradventure, vouchsafe me some of their thanks, if not for what I have done, yet for what I have suffer'd for their sakes" (4:223–42). His preface, then, in its praise of the "noble" and "troublesome" enterprise of the inductive method (4:224), characterizes Boyle as a scientific martyr; at the same time, the memory of his aches and pains through rigorous exercises that eventually resulted in an "incompleat" explanation foregrounds an embodied mode of exploration that refuses to separate subject from object. Although his is a "tender Constitution of Body" more prone to "oftentimes reduce me to be more concern'd to Shun the Effects of Cold, [than] Observe the *Phænomena* of It" (4:223), the touch of skin to ice is the prerequisite for *Touching* to take place. In order to observe, one must touch and be willing to be touched, shun the "shun" in favor of embrace.

"Tender" as he is, he dwells on the range of cold's influence. Since "the sphere of Activity of Cold, or . . . the space, to whose extremities every way the action of a Cold body is able to reach, is a thing very well worth the enquiring after, but more difficult to find, then at first one would imagine" (4:335), Boyle must go "after" it: here (the thirteenth title) and in each subsection of his book outlining the "experiments" and "observations" that incorporate cold's touch. The "sphere" is a tight span of intimacy that "reaches" up and through the cryocurious scientist. Compared to the spacious spread afforded to "heat in fire" or to the atmosphere's "many odorous Bodies" in general, "in such small parcels of Ice it self, as in our Experiments we are wont to deal with, we have found the sphere . . . exceeding narrow" (4:336), leading him to question "whether the sense could discern a cold Body, otherwise [than] by immediate Contact" (4:336). Trials are not simply "made my self" (4:336); rather, they are made *to* and *on* a nonsingular, more-than-human "self." The circling "sphere" of cold requires the observer to enter its orbit of activity, submitting the body to experiential–experimental transgress.

## Feeling (the) "Promiscuous"

For Boyle, these "self"-transformations often occur through tangible "contact" with cold matter, "bodies" in which the secret essence of cold—its central "spirit"—may or may not be implanted. Even though Boyle's repetitive, analytical approach mandates a strict regimen of tests and results, he will occasionally supply an "appendix" (4:418) as well: a catch-all section set aside for anything he deems "promiscuous," like reflections that "are not so readily reducible to the . . . foregoing heads" (4:355). *Promiscuous* (ca. 1570) comes from the Latin *promiscuus* ("indiscriminate") and *miscere* ("to mix").[76] (The association with sexual relations arose several centuries later.) His final title, reserved for "Promiscuous Experiments and Observations concerning Cold" (4:418), for example, is a hodgepodge of disorderly experiences that do not fit neatly into his (or any) system of organization.

It is in these unsortable and unknowable encounters that Boyle's intimacies with cold are made most manifest. Timing ice's dissolution, he and his assistants huddled around fragments dusted with salt, listening intently for "a little crackling noise," holding it "betwixt a candle and the eye" to look for "a steam or smoak" (4:349). But cold drew him even closer: to better understand "adhæsion," for instance, he "held a nail betwixt my lips in the open air a very little space, which stuck so firmly to them, that I could not pull it thence without difficulty and pain" (4:534). In the months of December and January, he gathered flowers out in "frosty weather" (4:419); unable to detect a scent, he considered whether the cold "had some undiscerned influence upon the Organ of smelling, which made the sense more dull" (4:419). His first-hand mix-ups with the "frigorifick" blend the theoretical object of cold (the observed) with the human subject of the scientist (the observer). Here he is "touching cold" by sound, taste, and smell, caught up in a sticky "promiscuous"-ness of randomly affective events, where the "organs" of detection meet the cold in pain, insensitivity, and perhaps pleasure. In his hesitancy to pinpoint coldness too "hastily," he slows down to smell the "Primrose" (4:419). Boyle desires to be in cold's exciting, never-"dull" presence; he demonstrates a bias *for* undiscriminating relations at moments like these, even if he cannot completely master the mix. Melding with him through the animate "body" of ice, nail, weather, and flower, cold scrambles ontological forms of "being" comprised of discrete, independent "agents."

Cold's laboratory life comes in many shapes and sizes throughout Boyle's countless observations; that said, ice clearly predominates his opus's "promiscuous" assignations. His entire fifteenth title, for instance, is devoted to "touching Ice" in action (4:346). Checking its remarkable "cohesion," he applies weights "of differing Diameters and lengths" to frozen cylinders and watches a man stomp on a hefty slab (4:347). Marveling over ice's ability to withstand such immense pressures, he here points out that its hardness can easily be cut with glass and "common Knives" nonetheless. One especially sensual scene from his catalogue stands out, however: "I once caused divers pieces of thick ice to be brought out of a cool place into a somewhat warm room, and listening, observ'd a noise to come from them, as if it had been produced by store of little cracks made in them, but somewhat or other prevented me from repeating the Experiment, and satisfying my self about the Conjecture" (4:356–57). What prevents him (the "somewhat or other") is unclear. Is it sympathy for (one more) ice block forced to sustain a torturously "crackling" fate? Boredom? A mundane need to proceed to the next opinion?

For a compendious philosopher, someone who inveighs against "self invigoration," these lively "little" cracks must have been startling. The crevices sound a lack of "cohesion," exhibiting fractures that the (supposedly) individual mind and autonomous self can neither sufficiently comprehend nor explain. But for a literal "frigot" like Boyle ("a person of frigid temperament") these breaches present additional opportunities for cold commingling, seams at which the mixed-up self may adhere, and once there, touchingly and promiscuously linger. On the one hand, what is "satisfying" might be the conclusion of study and the confirmation of one's proposed "conjecture"; on the other hand, the undisclosed "somewhat" defers that moment of completion indefinitely. The latter interpretation helps explain why Boyle abruptly moves on to the next title in his titanic tome of cold's effects. "The strangeness and variety of the Theme," he claims, "has [been] made so prolix already" (4:357). Thus marks an unfortunate end to the ice affair—but only for now. His ambivalence keeps open the recrudescent promise of future experiments, those onto-epistemological fissures insinuated in the preface, a "beginning" to be "begun," to be "pitch'd upon," at another date.

As cold noises its influence on his reassembling body, Boyle enters into brilliant co-"designing" modes that blur the ontological differentiation between cold "beings." But they also create: to his lab he attaches a studio. It is the "prolix," in fact, that reifies as art: *pro-*, ("outward") and *liquere* ("be liquid"). "Strangeness" turns out to be cool in aesthetic terms. Once, he showed to the Royal Society "very pretty shapes of Trees" by steaming turpentine inside glass (4:451). He can paint with cold, too: "To these I could add divers other instances of the like tendency, to make it still the more probable, that though oftentimes one may happen to find pretty Idæas's, or Apparitions in ice; yet the like, or as fine, may be produc'd by chance" (4:451). The ephemerality of ice is what grants it an ethereal appearance, a ghostly quality that applies to the airy and eerie realm of ideas while still tethered to (solid) liquid things. What is more, the "chance" occurrence of these patterns accentuates cold's abiding spectrality. This perception often rings true in the annals of long-lost ice art, and Boyle himself implies the many occasions he had to pro- and interactively craft with cold stuff: "I have sometimes obtained by freezing . . . figures that were so pretty, but withal so unconstantly produc'd, and so easily variable by circumstances, that it would fill a Book particularly to describe them." Milk is particularly effective, he claims, although something as quotidian as "common water" will also do (4:452).

Cold's inherent spontaneity (the act of being surprised *into* "producing" by its in/visible presence) is what affords Boyle the "chance" to cofashion in the first place. Anticipating the modern vogue for whole books dedicated to snowflakes' beauty, and repeating the adage that no one should "expect to find them every time the same" (4:452), he accepts the reality that the snowflake's infinite variation exceeds the scientist's apprehension, proving that their "pretty" outlook depends on the aleatory, agitated cold. When assessing whether a solution, when frozen, reflects the object from which it was derived (on the contrary, he declares, for ice definitively diffracts), he becomes affixed to the ice crystals nevertheless: "I found more [than] once, that by putting hot water into a somewhat slender Cylinder of glass, and agitating it in a frigorifick mixture, consisting of beaten ice, salt, and water, so that it was very speedily frozen thereby, it was congeal'd into an ice much more regularly and prettily figur'd, [than] I have seen it in divers of the waters impregnated with the fix'd salts of Plants, though of *these* we are told such wonders" (4:449). Not only does he defend "frigorifick" aesthetics in his sarcastic tone ("*these* we are told"), but the moment inspires him to try out little "wonders" and eccentric "idæas," tiny tasks of cryopoiesis that might result in arboreal-like figures, but that also might take on novel shapes that do not easily conform to "the vegetable" or "the animal Kingdom," cold chimerical blends of something in-between (4:451).

The "prolixity" of ice announces a merger between storytellers. Boyle's account is as much a conversation *with* cold and between verbose interlocutors as it is a concordance of classical and contemporary references made *about* it. What makes Boyle's essay unique in the long history of cold studies, besides the prominence he gives to firsthand experimentation, is his inclusion of travel narratives from the undiscovered countries of the northwest and northeast Arctic, as well as from subarctic North America: Gerrit de Veer's account of William Barents's three voyages to Nova Zembla from 1594–1597, published in 1598, translated into English in 1609, and included in Samuel Purchas's 1625 *Pilgrimes*; Olaus Magnus's rich descriptions of the Scandinavian regions surrounding the North Sea; and Thomas James's journal of overwintering in southern Hudson Bay from 1631 to 1632, appearing in 1633 as *The Strange and Dangerous Voyage.* (James's account is the subject of chapter 4.) Boyle defends their inclusion in his preface on the basis that their writings, while not expressly scientific in a hard mechanical sense, do aid philosophical inquiry. They too provide tantalizing topics to contemplate, test, and even corroborate: "I did not only decline the mention of divers things, with which I fear many Writers would have adorned a History of Cold, but even of those that I my self have inserted, I would have left out divers, were it not, that many of the Relations, that may appear so wonderful, seem not to me to be repugnant to the nature of things, but only suppose a far greater degree of Cold, [than] we have in these parts, and yet the familiar effects of the Cold we have here, would perhaps be looked on as incredible, by one that were born and bred in the Kingdom of Congo" (4:220). By not dismissing their claims outright, Boyle links the idea of the experimental lab from his to theirs. He also proves to be a calculating researcher when it comes to literature, choosing carefully from the archive of "cold" the examples that de-"familiarize" it: not only through shifts in perspective—ice is more valuable than gold in Africa; any amount of frost is "wonderful" in Jamaica (4:220)—but also by asserting that the "incredible" still lurks in something that northern climes take for granted.

And the "prolixity" *in* the text between human and nonhuman respondents leaves behind a legacy of storied scientific matter, modeling an innovative brand of critical Arcticology that intentionally mixes disparate fields of study and motivates additional encounters. The insertion of these stories works to his advantage, in that they keep the "strangeness" nearer, not at bay. On the "bigness" of ice, for instance, he can only work with others' words: he pulls from "out of the best Journals . . . a few more Testimonies to keep them by their mutual support, from being entertain'd with a Disbelief, which their strangeness would else tempt men to" (4:352). Boyle is effectively expanding his evidentiary archive, incorporating travel narratives into his scientific enterprise. In this sense, *New Experiments and Observations* itself is a "promiscuous" experiment in mixed-genre interdisciplinary work, drawing from first-person eyewitnesses who happened to pen compelling forms of "strangeness" as "entertainment," providing information that was not designed simply to mollify their worried financial investors or merchant companies back home. (James, we will see, is the epitome of this style now called "nonfiction.") Boyle's second major contribution, then, is a form of scientifically "storied matter."[77] When art and science intersect via the materiality of cold, different ways of apprehending the world's ice stor(i)es open up. Able to marvel at the cold vicariously through written accounts ("testimonies"), he casts what is known about his subject into ambiguity, neither belief nor "disbelief," extending to the reader his own feeling of polar provocation. Such acknowledgments, he admits, "may better embolden Travellers, [than] satisfie Philosophers" (4:350). The point, again, has never been to "satisfie": the scientific investigation (then) and the narrative imagination (now) are equally expedited by the pursuit of the elusive cold.

The interdisciplinary structure of *New Experiments and Observations* is one reason that the work is esteemed by historians of science. But that science, it turns out, was also shaped by one of the Little Ice Age's sharpest moments: the Maunder Minimum (ca. 1645–1715). Boyle's touching (and being touched) spurs the collection of cold impresses, known as *Touching,* to press, engendering a tactile example of the more-than-human natural-philosophical archive. His chilled, literary body testifies to this coauthorship, but so does the text's literal, "promiscuous" manufacture. Henry Oldenburg, Boyle's publisher, notes in his opening missive to the reader that the chemist waited unduly long for winter to arrive so he might "perfect an Experiment he was desirous to insert" (4:206). The preface arrived at the Royal Society in parts in the winter of 1664–1665 because, "when the Frost began, which was late in the season, the Coldness did within a while arrive at that degree, that by its operation upon the moisten'd paper, it long put a stop to the Proceedings of the Press" (4:206). The degree of cold is always significant: too much cold stymies "moisten'd" paper; too little cold prevents ideas gathered from interactive experiments to be impressed on it. Like "disbelief," cold both disables and enables writing. Cold is the material genesis behind *New Experiments and Observations*; cold threatens the means of re/production. If Boyle's previously "pretty" moments had illustrated for us how to make a cold observation (entering into one by virtue of being "promiscuous"), this practical realization underscores how stories are actually fabricated. Cast this way, compositions and their "frigorifick" contents are capable of snapping together in print only under fickle conditions, ever-susceptible to cold's fits, "stops," and starts.

The inconclusiveness of Boyle's survey can indeed feel frustrating, but only if the reason for embarking was to reach an achievable end, an ultimate "hypothesis of cold." To hold him accountable for "why I suffer so Unfinished a piece" (4:223) configures his efforts as insatiable, and somewhat sadistic, adventures in exasperation. My framing of his experiments, however, stresses Oldenburg's reference to the "desirous." Boyle, I suggest, was someone who delighted in the "wonders" of promiscuity, finding enjoyment in personal exposure instead of detached indifference and "perfect" trials, even while working within the strict parameters of inductive and deductive methods that point to a singular answer. Despite the weather delays, "[Boyle] hopes the Publication may not be yet too late for diligent Readers, to make some use of the season for examining his Experiments, or trying some of the New ones" (4:206). From the beginning, his book has been a pitch to *pitch* further. At its conclusion, at least in terms of the pages' limit, he reasserts that his indecisiveness has always been an invitation: "The notion of cold in general is not so obvious a thing to be rightly pitch'd upon" (4:507). The less "obvious" cold becomes, the more it enjoins "new" attempts at "insertion."[78] For Boyle, a second edition followed in 1683, bookended by three additional studies: *New Experiments Touching the Condensation of the Air by Meer Cold* (1671); *A Sceptical Dialogue about the Positive or Privative Nature of Cold* (1674/1690); and *Of the Mechanical Origine of Heat and Cold* (1675/1690). An encouragement to conjoin with cold's "unfinished" business has ostensibly been Boyle's mission from page 1: posing the question of how best to pick up these "pieces" (if at all), he "pitches" this prospect forward from his cooler age, throwing it to us to answer.

Boyle's model for approaching his subject matter, as I see it (to story on storied matter; employing twinned propensities for scientific and literary analysis; checking systems of "belief" against facts), can usefully recalibrate our own cryocritical endeavors. Perhaps the model has been lost for those living outside the Little Ice Age, but Boyle's experiments, I have been arguing, depend on nonhuman "designs," including climate. His lab is weather-dependent, after all. Compiling his data during a usually warm winter, he laments that "I was fain to Wait for, and make Use of a Fit of frosty weather (which has very long been a rarity) as solicitously as Pilots watch for, and improve a Wind" (4:223). His statement about unexpected postponement approximates Bacon's grievance about cold's scarcity—an artificially cooled, climate-controlled lab was still a long way from being invented—yet it also mirrors a pronounced sympathetic strain in contemporary glaciology. In eras of climate change, whether cooling or warming, one may "wait" indefinitely for the object of study to come and/or return. Better technology has brought more accurate predictions, and yet the anticipation (and sometimes impatience) linger out in the field. The ability to work with an ephemeral medium like "frosty weather" remains compulsory. An obligation (being "fain") to the cold persists, lending an *ubi sunt* ("where are") quality to the examiner's tone, one whose methods explicitly yearn for "the snows of yesteryear."[79] It might seem obvious to point out that actual degrees of cold are necessary for conducting cold experiments. The lesson, however, can be instructive in what it tells us about the researcher's interdependent relationship with her findings, results made even more exigent by understanding their precariousness. To study cold, especially now, is to reflect on the provisional and impermanent: such are the demands of "ice time" and "water time," the "materiality of duration."[80]

## Drinking Cold

"Listening" preserves the prolificness of cold, even if the "divers pieces of thick ice" that initially enabled said exchange cannot last in perpetuity. But, like a cold block thrust into a "warm room," what happens to the human interlocutor's body once its shaking flesh carries the record of their little talks? Keeping in mind Hof's dictum about cold's negative instruction, I now turn from chatt(er)ing *with,* to taking *in,* cold waters. I trade the noisy lab for the nourishing clinic, Wittie's *Scarbrough Spaw,* in order to "learn" some "things" about cold's medicinal and emotional powers. When explaining how an object's temperature stays the same and yet feels more or less cold to bodies' "sensitive parts," Boyle referred, tellingly, to bathers (4:230). I engage the onto-epistemological puzzle of *frīgus* from a different set of sensory phenomena: not just when ice is "brought out of a cool place" to be accompanied, but also when immersion and ingestion are explicitly prescribed, when *frīgus* transfuses with physiology. Before we plunge into the operations of cryocorporeality at microcosmic and macrocosmic scales, however, we should prepare ourselves with the proper medical-historical context.

Writers following Fulke grew interested in cold's impressive impacts on human bodies. How "cold dryueth" into humans, in some ways more "fruictfull" and in some less, was a popular subject of conversation in remedial circles. The Spanish physician Nicolás Monardes (ca. 1512–1588) defends the "properties & vertues" of "the faire Ladie Snow" in *Historia Medicinal de las Cosas Que Se Traen de Nuestras Indias Occidentales* (completed 1574; translated as *Ioyfull Newes out of the Newfound World* by John Frampton in 1577/80), particularly "the good that drinking colde doeth."[81] For Monardes (citing a maxim by the Latin grammarian Aulus Gellius [ca. 125–1280]): "The yeere of Snow, the yeere of Fertility"), snow destroys "euil hearbes, and doth fructifie and increase them which are good."[82] He wishes to know how a human body, like a "good" herb, reacts to the ingestion of cold water and thereby "increases" its health. Noting that Galen "doth counsell to drinke colde,"[83] a hot fever would logically abate with a direct dose. (More on allopathic remedies later.) He goes on to enumerate four different ways of making cold: air, wells, saltpeter, and snow. Out of the four, "the colde which dooth proceede of Snowe, dooth not offend as other colde dooth."[84] Cold water made with snow is, in a word, the healthiest. For testament to this fact, he cites the example of "many being sicke, and hauing great occassions of sicknes, after that they drinke cold, are whole straight way: and when they have geuen ouer the use of it, they become sicke agayne."[85] The "fruictfull" force identified by Fulke that flows through the diagnosed febrile body turns into a treatment.

Like a good doctor, Monardes advises moderation in all things. Too much cold sends one into a steep decline: "it [will] appeareth," he cautions, "howe euill the use of the sayde snowe is, and the water which doeth come out of it, if it bee not by the way of medicine onely."[86] In Robert Barclay's (1582–1621) bestselling romance *Argenis* (1621; translated from Latin by Kingesmill Long in 1625), Arsidas, feted in Mauritania by the governor Iuba, nearly dies after consuming frozen apples in summer, washed down with beverages served in "Cups of Ice," the unseasonable delicacy and aesthetic delight too rare to pass over: "But after they were risen from Dinner, and Arsidas was iestingly discommending the vse of hot drinkes, hee felt all his sinewes, by little and little, to faint with extremity of cold; insomuch, as casting vp his meat, his life had almost followed."[87] A physician must handle cold with care, lest the patient, like a gluttonous Arsidas, imbibe "too freely." Even if "euill" (but only if misused), the benefits outweigh the risks when taken properly: "There is no price to bee esteemed too it, nor understanding that can expounde it."[88] Despite Monardes's acknowledgment that cold's gastrological magic remains a mystery, its inexplicability leads to a ringing endorsement at the end of his short treatise: "Those which are accustomed to drink it herein, let euery man drink cold."[89] If one is willing to stomach the snow (literally), this cold courage will be rewarded. Soon after, the poet Richard James (1592–1638) hailed hot water as "thow drinke of death."[90]

As a palatable element within the "ecology of the passions,"[91] cold's physiological effects were entwined with its psychological impacts. Chilled humors, simply put, altered moods. In his voluminous 1621 *Anatomy of Melancholy,* Robert Burton (1577–1640) attributes "bad air" as one cause of the mental condition, especially temperatures at opposite ends of the spectrum: "cold air in the other extreme is almost as bad as hot."[92] His anthology underscores "the geographic nature of embodiment"[93] by arguing that northerners' emotions are tied to their sub/arctic enmeshment: "In those . . . countries, the people are therefore generally dull, heavy, and many witches, which . . . Saxo Grammaticus, Olaus [Magnus], Baptista Porta ascribe to melancholy."[94] The north had long been linked to witchcraft,[95] although Burton is careful to attribute the cause of melancholia to the hexing icescape itself: "But these cold climes are more subject to natural melancholy (not this artificial) which is cold and dry[,] for which cause Mercurius Britannicus belike puts melancholy men to inhabit just under the Pole."[96] Burton is referring to *Mundus Alter et Idem* (1605), the fantastical satire by Joseph Hall (1574–1656), also known as "an English Mercury" (*Mercurius Britannicus*). The land of "Fooliana the Craggy," which "lieth iust vnder the pole: the farthest of all the Land Southward . . . is a Mountaynous, stony, and eternally frosty country, lying in an ayre extreamely cold, and as extreamely dry."[97] In the dutchy of "Solitaria the Sad" sits the country's main wonder, "Cholly-melans caue."[98] There is no supernatural spell at work here besides the environment's "cold and dry" qualities that transfix the subject. Melancholy was supposed to proliferate under these conditions: on the early modern calendar, that meant either during the season of winter (associated with earth, the "cold and dry") or autumn (related to water, the cold and wet), two climatic dyads common in the higher latitudes. A person susceptible to cold air, would, as a result of that encounter, boost their bodily stores of black bile and phlegm, assuming a melancholic or phlegmatic aspect (respectively). In compiling these sundry ascriptions, Burton lends credibility to sources that would otherwise seem "artificial" (because poetic and fanciful). For him, the "natural" workings of "cold air" are evinced in the humanistic record. Imaginative cartographies like Hall's could display, or anatomize, melancholy's cold cause. Just as his counterparts in medicine were uncovering the influence that "air" exerts on bodies and minds alike, Burton helps pinpoint the place where cold takes hold: one's very anatomy.

Returning to these authors unlocks a more complicated story of cryocorporeality than is typically afforded to the matter of cold. In Bacon's early foray into the physical properties of temperature—a short fragment titled "*Calor et Frigus*" (ca. 1608)—he repeats the more conventional wisdom about cold's insalubrious absorption: "Cold maketh bones of living creatures more fragile"; it "maketh . . . the blood to clot and turn more blue"; it "causes rheums and distillations by compressing the brain, and laxes by like reason"; and, in the end, "those parts which are voidest of blood, as the nose, the ears, the toes, the fingers," will "mortify and rot."[99] Yet he also differentiates between healthy and hurtful types of cold: "The frost dew which we see in hoar frost and in the rymes upon trees or the like accounted more mortifying cold than snow, for snow cherisheth the ground and any thing sowed in it, the other biteth and killeth."[100] Bacon's cold "biteth" *and* cureth, ails and ills; it is not surprising that the enlightened citizens of his *New Atlantis* (1627) dig tunnels three miles deep into the island of Bensalem, "for all Coagulations, Indurations, Refrigerations, and Conseruations of Bodies."[101] The erudite inhabitants also use them "sometimes, (which may seeme strange,) for Curing of some Diseases, and for Prolongation of Life, in some Hermits that choose to liue ther."[102] "Salomon's

House,"[103] the model for his scientific utopia, and a tropical one at that ("wee sayled from Peru"[104]), must make room for the cold. Bacon's vocabulary of "cherisheth" echoes Fulke's "cherysheth" of vegetable enrapture. He insinuates a life-prolonging principle of cold, contributing to a centuries-long conversation over its therapeutic powers to advance life, not just suspend it. Was cold a vital, "living creature" enfolded with other life forms, and prone to "mortifying," like everything else, or did life restart only at the moment of thaw, at the reentry of warmth? The ambivalent "bite" of cold was a question seemingly designed for northern physicians, medical authorities who wondered whether "refrigeration" could foster as well as preserve, enliven and elongate at once.

## Minerals in Winter

Wittie first took the waters of Scarborough in 1637–1638, after settling in nearby Hull. As one of the dedicatory poems to *Scarbrough Spaw* insinuates, however, drawing distempered patients to a town on the North Sea coast was not an easy task. His grand therapeutic plan faced an ancient grudge held against the world's northern places: "All ill from th'North? nay, that's not so, / For here the wholesome waters flow."[105] (The reference is to the Book of Jeremiah: "*Omne malum ab Aquilone.*") The first two thirds of *Scarbrough Spaw* lays out an argument worth the poet's ("R. W.") admiration, culling together an erudite collection of Greek, Latin, and biblical authorities who noted the benefits of drinking water. "There is nothing more necessary unto nourishment" (22), especially when it is cold: "It is most healthfull being taken inwardly, and is prescribed by Physicians in many cases, both to prevent and cure diseases, and tends much to preserve us in our well being" (40–41). It is an oft-repeated sentiment obviously intended for the reader's edification: "The principall token of good and wholesome water is, that it be simple or unmixed, and then it loads not the stomach, and easily passes through the Hypochondres, being also soon hot and soon cold" (160).

The remaining sections essentially tout the extraordinary virtues of mineral springs. To sell his particular brand of "wholesome" water, Wittie had to describe both the "nature" and "operation" of the substance his potential patrons would ingest. As a physician steeped in the humoral tradition, Wittie believed that bodily imbalances were properly cared for allopathically (as in, by opposites). A cold and moist illness, for instance, required a hot and dry treatment. Scarborough's water could, "by due and daily use thereof, . . . correct cold & moist bodies, and cure such diseases as proceed from the excess of cold and moysture" (192). His prescription appears to have a glaring problem, though, since cold cannot combat cold. (He does not subscribe, in a word, to the theory of "counteraction," or antiperistasis). Fortunately, the spa's proprietary minerals are ushered in at this critical juncture. The intrinsic heat of salt, iron, and nitre (inorganic compounds he had personally identified in his laboratory) adds the key ingredient of wellness: "impregnated with the qualities and natures of the said Minerals," the water "consequently is hot and dry in operation" (192). He persists: "Nor let any startle at this assertion, that I affirm this *Spaw* water to be cold and moist, and also hot & dry, which are contrary qualities, since it is cold & moist actually in the instantaneous use of it, but doth heat and dry virtually, & in process of time" (192–93). In other words, spa water goes down cold but slowly burns once inside.

As the beneficiary of a prestigious education—receiving an MD from King's College, Cambridge in 1647—Wittie cites plenty of historical anecdotes and paraphrases hosts of near-contemporary colleagues like Monardes: melted snow should not "be drunk alone," for example, "because of its exceeding coldnesse" (64–65), even if it "preserves the earth" (66–67) from putrefaction; the spa is "strongest" in the winter, so drinkers must first expose the water to air to avoid "paralytick and convulsive motions" (245). Yet his *Scarbrough Spaw* also makes significant contributions to hydrotherapy scholarship. Any generic kind of cold water will drop a body's temperature, and "no man need go to Scarbrough for these intentions" (194), but the minerals' latent heat in his spa is what causes it to "peirc[e] into the most narrow and secret passages of the body, & is excellent in opening obstructions, which are the causes of most diseases" (195). As previously mentioned, early modern medical practitioners agreed that an "exceeding" amount of cold effectively contracted these pores (the narrowing of blood vessels now known as vasoconstriction), either preventing previous sickness from escaping or incubating novel illnesses entirely. Wittie's waters emend this accepted logic: "Minerals in Winter," the coldest conceivable, actually clear rather than close the body's blocked pathways. He outlines the purgative and diuretic effects in detail ("casting forth plentifully both it selfe and the excrementitious humours" [196]), even conducting a successful experiment on himself.

Three pints in the morning resulted in "an evacuation both ways" (197). The waters both rectify and reinforce: lest one fears being weakened by this flowing process, with it comes "a corroberating or strengthening quality, whereby it fortifies the parts, and so arms nature with new strength to the preventing of relapses" (199).

Visiting his spa even improves the mood. In his expert opinion, low temperatures maintain a healthy temperament. Cold and moist waters literally keep the dark materials at bay, in the bowels: "It is a most Soveraign remedy against Hypochondriack Melancholly and Windiness, suppressing the vapours which fly up to the head, and cheering the heart, as I might instance at large" (205). He claims to have cured two ministers this way, pointing out that "Mr. L." travels one hundred and fifty miles annually for a drink (205–6). Wittie's most convincing evidence is, again, his own body: "I have sometimes drunk of it not for necessity but company, or to make some little evacuation from flegmatick humours, being of an athletick constitution, when within three days I found so great an agility and cheerfulness of body and mind [than] I had before, as I have wondred at it, that if I had stayed a fortnight, I could not have expected more benefit" (230). Come on into the *Spaw* and get cold, he gestures to his readers; let the water redefine *you*, deep down, on the anatomical and subsequently psychological level.

With all four properties ("cold and moist . . . hot & dry") swirling around at once, Wittie could advertise a glass of his spa water, ingeniously, as an elemental and alimentary cure-all. For "hot and sharp humours," he advises an immediate application by "incession" or "injection." In this case, the initial dose of coldness will be "more cleansing and healing" (208). Those who suffer from intestinal blockages such as "Colick" should drink it "a little warm, and the patient should also bathe in it" (206); here, the traditional cold-water cleanse ("in process of time") is best served tepid, slightly sped up via immersion. Either dunked in or drunk down, delivered lukewarm or straight up from the cool source, hot- or cold-, wet- or dry-induced maladies are guaranteed to disappear. His pitch amounts to an early modern eco-touristic brochure, and is worth reading in full: "In a word if any intentions be to be performed in a medicinall way, by allaying or mitigating some hot distemper, opening obstructions, evacuating morbifick humours by Urine or Seige, and strengthening the inward parts of the body, it may be fully and compleatly effected by this water, wherein it operates so safely, as I have very rarely observed any ill Symptomes to arise: nor have I scarce named any distemper, of which I have not made particular observation, and most of them many times over, or been certainly informed by credible Authors" (209–10). A potable tonic that can be transported to London and "found good" (246) or "carryed abroad" (247) and decanted: Wittie managed to package (in words) Scarborough's water as a wondrous elixir, thereby reserving a unique place for cold in the wider history of spa culture.

## Blue Bloods

Still, the popularity of "the Germane Spaws" (8) and hot(ter) spots like them elsewhere compelled Wittie to contend with his continental competition and improve on his own. Besides promoting the healthy components of the town's water, Wittie's ancillary aim in *Scarbrough Spaw* was showcasing his country's balneological virtues in comparison to other regions' famous mineral springs. Essentially valorizing the local cold for an international clientele, he penned a series of careful objections to refute the rumour that "because of the coldness of our climate, the water is not so well concocted with the heat of the Sun, and so is hard of digestion" (33). The sun's warming rays could not penetrate far enough into the earth's interior (a maximum depth of ten feet, which had recently been mathematically determined) meaning that other factors were responsible for his water's virtuous "concoction." He conjectures: some unspecified planetary "influence" on the minerals within (34); the earth being warmer in winter than in summer, as the natural philosophers say, because of the heat-trapping "frosts . . . that shut the pores of it" (35); and the fact that God would not unequally distribute healing waters to southern countries alone (35–36). Yet, even without an ascertainable cause, England simply "doth abound more" (36) in medicinal waters that meet the highest standards ("tokens") of sight, taste, and smell set by trusted ancient authorities (37). In short, while "there is no Country but it affords wholesome water, even the most frozen Country of Greenland, . . . the waters of England are good" (32), if not equal, to the rest. To his detractors in "Spain, France, and the hot Countries," he believes that "our waters are as wholesome for our bodies, as theirs are for them in those hot climates, and much more [than] theirs would be for us" (36). It is "good" enough, that is, to drink at home; one need not binge abroad.

Despite its ostensible subject matter (the "Nature and Vertues of the Spaw at Scarbrough" [sig. A1r.], the two topics I have investigated thus far), Wittie's study also engages one of the most contentious hydrographical debates of his era: "the Original of Springs" (sig. A1r.). Springs originate, he opines, from rain and snow entering secret passages in the earth, "which are like unto small fibres of veins, not discernible by the eye, terminating in the skin in all the parts of our bodies" (127). By referring to a popular metaphor of the human body as a geological system[106]—here, a subterranean tangle of mineral and sanguine "veins," soily and cutaneous "skin"—Wittie locates the spa-goer in a microcosmic and macrocosmic overlay presciently known as the water cycle, while carefully distinguishing the site-specific efficacy of Scarborough's water from similar springs around the world. A willing body materially taking in the waters of Scarborough does just that: waters infiltrate via ingestion or immersion and reach to the nerve endings ("terminat[ions]") with their restorative strength. Although "wholesome" waters exist globally, England's (not Greenland's) are "good" precisely because of the local terroir. The mineralogical image allows him to expand on his ecumenical and cosmopolitan argument made earlier ("whether it runs East, West, North, or South, they [are] all indifferently good and wholesome" [162]), but in a slightly more nationalistic "vein."

By coldly equating his countrymen's vascular makeup with the countryside's vaunted mineral networks, Wittie's spa and *Scarbrough Spaw* are conversant with Floyd-Wilson's notion of "geohumoralism," or "regionally framed humoralism."[107] Following the logic of humoral theory, a cold, windy, and wet island like England should render its citizens prone to melancholic and phlegmatic characteristics. "The infirmities subject to man in [winter]," are, after all, "cold and phlegmatick diseases," wrote Thomas Willsford in *Natures Secrets* (1658).[108] Some northern authors attempted to reframe this dynamic in their favor, drawing on Aristotle instead of Hippocrates (ca. 460–377 BCE) and Galen (129–199 CE) to argue that cool climates in fact *removed* these dullish humors instead of compounding them: leaving one hot-dry (choleric) or hot-moist (sanguine) as a result, and presumably primed for colonialist action. Wittie, to be fair, did not have this kind of "strengthening" in mind for Scarborough ("cheerfulness" appears to be his private goal) yet the *Scarbrough Spaw*'s nationalistic undertone intimates, nevertheless, the far-from-"good" racial and ethnic repurposing of cold. (I will return to that malpractice in the co[l]da.) His wintery minerals, for now, may steel the body's constitution in healthful, less harmful ways.

Our tasting would probably end here. But while musing on river water, one of the several "sorts" (46) he eruditely describes, Wittie worries that he has "wade[d] too far into this stream, least I lose my self and my Subject" (169). Contrary to his talk of ends, their progress would not terminate in an overheated body, at least, but perspire back out through the "secret passages" (195), or pores, that he once revealed: an evaporative cooling process more commonly known as "sweating." Wittie in the water, remarkably, starts to "lose [his] self." A corollary of "geohumoralism," Floyd-Wilson argues, was the dissolution of an integral, place-based identity: "The environment necessarily produced and destabilized early modern . . . selves."[109] In Wittie's case, the cryo- and hydro-components of his spa's seaside environment loosened the borders of somatic integrity as well. His overlay of "veins" regulated *via* that body's specific environment advances on Monardes's prescription, for it helps us to see the body's temperance, its "wholesome"-ness, as reliant on regimens of minute temperature adjustments. At the same time, it puts a strain on that same body's ability to stabilize itself, since it displays the ecological pressures of cold airs and waters constantly exerting themselves on its porous boundaries, checking that idea of "wholeness" that a holistic spa, especially, would guarantee to its soundest, most cryophilic customers. Confining mineral waters within any perimeter is an impossible task. With either a sip or a soak, in sum, the self (the "subject") becomes outspread. Inadvertently or not, *Scarbrough Spaw*'s regional advocacy offers a bracing lesson in ecological attachment: the transnational currents of cold. We depart along similar "streams" of thought, wondering about (and thereby enlarging) rather than resolving (and thereby constraining) the incompletion of interconnectivity, dwelling on parts not wholes, drinking to new possibilities rather than "corroborating" what came before.

## Feeling "Exquisete" in the "Extream"

Any imaginative possibilities nevertheless met sizable intellectual resistance from medical experts well-versed in cryogenesis: both the creation of cold and the engendering of its ills. Cold's fruitive nature, I have suggested, existed on a physiological spectrum somewhere between "good" and "euill," sickness and health, internal and external, regional and universal, life and death. A modicum of cold (as with heat) could be prescribed every now and then for righting lopsided humors; yet contact with snow and ice, for the most part, was to be avoided, leaving meteors' "impressiones" unwelcome and unwanted. Wittie's methods, simply put, were unorthodox, and so his cryotherapeutic insights, rendered dubious, could be roundly ignored.

Surveying early modern climate history, it is not hard to see why *Scarbrough Spaw*'s instructions proved difficult to swallow. A year after Wittie's death, John Peter, a physician, penned *A Philosophical Account of This Hard Frost* (1684), one of the most graphic descriptions of overexposure available at the time. Airborne "Particles of Cold," "Corpuscles of Cold," and "Atomes of Cold," being "conceived in the Frozen Womb of the Earth," coagulate into ice and snow after colliding with "Liquid Watery Bodies."[110] Like Fulke, his foremost concern is the "Impressions"[111] these "atomes" have made on himself and his fellow Londoners. Severe temperature swings from freezing to thawing (and back again) are unhealthy because fluctuations weaken the body's fortifications: "What quarter then can we expect should be given to the various Juices of our Bodies? Can any Extream be Friendly to Nature? Can such sudden Alteration of the Weather prove otherwise, than mightily prejudicial to our Healths? Those Passages of our Bodies which were so long so closely lock'd up, will now be laid open, and become laxe and penetrable, liable to receive such Exotick putrefactive Ferments."[112] The aftershock of cold, to put it another way, is profoundly dangerous. "Exotick" (meaning exogenous) invaders can more easily seize someone whose pores *were* so strongly "lock'd up." Once inside these widened routes, and "having undoubtedly imprinted on our Bodies such Morbisick predispositions (like seeds of various Diseases),"[113] the returning frost effectively shuts in the attacker. Peter's logic, then, helps explain why seemingly sealed-off bodies can still become unwell in the depths of an unrelentingly "hard" season like his own: "In Cold,

Raw, Thawing Weather," particles "insinuat[e] themselves into our gaping Pores," where "they there stagnate."[114] Without adequate evaporation, in sum, the sickness ferments. It should be said that all parts of his prognosis—exposure to "extream" shifts in weather; unrestrained fermentation and unreplenished "juices"; the cultivation of previously deposited spores—are in addition to the detriments that cold "particles" already pose on their own. The only remedy, in the end, is to see what sort of disease sprouts. There is no "quarter," indeed, in Peter's estimation: one does not come in from the cold, the cold comes into you. The vulnerable body in and out (again) of winter awaits an inescapable fate: becoming a parasitical "womb" of fermentation and fomentation, a breeding ground for alien things eager to break forth on first thaw and attach on others. Catching a cold has never sounded so "putrefactive," nor so terrifying.

As Peter's hostile and horrific imagery demonstrates, cold's animus became more acute in the seventeenth century, all but securing its irredeemable association with "extream" affliction. Wittie's *Scarbrough Spaw* had to contend, rightly, with this ecocatastrophic feeling, and professional allies were hard to find. Chapters on "cold, an enemy to the Nerves and bones" in studies of natural philosophy, like *The Secret Miracles of Nature* (1658) divulged by the Dutch doctor Levinus Lemnius (1505–1568), remained commonplace.[115] Cryophobic proclamations like his are echoed in claims (like Peter's) that the "enemy" eventually gets in: "it hapneth sometimes,"[116] so one should, presumably, be ready for it. To "help lims oppressed with cold," for example, Lemnius advises (poorly) that one should soak and scrub the member with cold water, believing that "snow and cold water raise up heat."[117] For an adherent of antiperistasis like himself, combating cold with cold thereby makes sound medicinal sense, "for by . . . *contrarietie,* the heat comes in the cold being driven away: which every man may make proof of, by handling Snow or Ice, for his hands will presently grow hot, and look very red."[118] Lemnius could count on the benumbing experience being ubiquitous enough to state: "I think there is no man but hath sometimes proved in himself, what bitter pains the joynts endure by reason of the nerves, that have a most exquisete feeling, when they grow stiffe with a more intense and peircing cold, the blood being either extinguished, or running inward into the inmost parts; so that at the first coming of cold, the hands will wax red, and by and by, as the blood grows cold, they will grow wan and dead, being deprived of the vitall blood and Spirits."[119] It seems unlikely that Lemnius would describe the painful "peircing" of cold as "exquisete" with the connotations of beautiful and delicate. Instead, the "exquisete" notes a heightened period of sensitivity that he accurately ascribes to a decrease in circulation ("running inward") or a complete evacuation ("extinguished").

Lemnius's word choice introduces two physiophenomenological aspects at once: it proves that to be "benummed with cold," is, on the contrary, *to feel,* perhaps to feel an intensification of feeling itself. Un/comfortably numbed like so, what is marginal (the extremities) moves to the center (the core) and vice versa, the body bravely adapting to the onslaught of cold stabs. Cold does not just reveal the body to be porous, but makes it more so. Lemnius agrees with Peter and Wittie on this somatic point, but his message, importantly, is a little less antagonistic; his outlook aligns, unexpectedly, with the latter. By using the literal meaning of the word "sought out"—from the Latin *ex-* ("out") and *quaerere* ("seek")—he insinuates a different route for others to take (Wittie, and now us): those who proactively, not just defensively, "sought" the cause of cold, who had the nerve to find its origin after feeling its "exquisete" touch. One reaction to this secretive, shivery, and sometimes-vicious realm of open/ing "passages" and snarled "veins" is to stay in it, soaking with the trouble.[120]

## Take It to the "Limit"

Wittie's *Scarbrough Spaw,* far from an outlier, sits squarely within the seventeenth century's heated debates over the nature of cold. *Spaw*-seeking, or seeking *through* spas, is ultimately why Wittie's mineral winters matter still: not only was he conversant with the contentious cohorts of cryologists who took part in a larger climatological dialogue about their changing world, but he does so by locating the subject in inter/national waters, "peircing" coldness that collapses hydrospatial distance and human–nonhuman distinctions at the place of the skin. What an "exquisete" feeling that was, *and that could be.* In *Biogea,* the late French polymath Michel Serres remembers the advice his mountain guide once gave him about the cold: "'If you curl up into a ball,' he said, 'if you defend yourself and get dressed, the enemy will penetrate down to your liver: cold is more invasive than you. No. Present yourself, uncover yourself, go toward it, make it your friend; it'll respect you. Turn the *against* into a *for,* but without going beyond the lethal limit."[121] This advice might seem useless to someone stuck in the ice, alone, waiting to die. Glaciers crumble, of course, and crises do happen. But Serres' point is that the cold keeps producing more. Here, it births a sense of belonging: not how to live in a harsh world in which humans do not belong, and certainly not that the world belongs to us, but a belonging that means cohabiting the world with mineralogical beings that we cannot control, nor possess, nor objectify. Try *feel,* or, better yet, *touch* and *listen, drink,* and *bathe.* Serres' "lethal limit," his "edge," is in dialogue with these early modern cryosophers. While more alpine than aquatic, his epiphany is due to an immersive experience within a cold atmosphere, one of Wittean proportions. To spa in this spot is to observe the union of life with death, the curls and furls of pain and pleasure. The question becomes how to "'make [cold] your friend,'" how to take the "extream" along with the "exquisete," how to make "good." Here are chancy, accident-prone waters. What is left to test remains up for meditation; the experiment and the promise of nondivision are ours to try.

Conspicuously, I have yet to identify the cause of *frīgus.* But it should be clear by this point that such a cause is necessarily a *fugitive* one. Instead, I have found cold's imprints across an impressive catalogue of early modern disciplines and genres (medical textbook, romance narrative, utopian travelogue, ethnographic history, scientific essay, and tourist brochure) and highlighted their relevant terms for interrogating the limits of our Arcticological inquiries today. Boyle's legacy has been the most vociferous: "pitch'd," "sceptick," "frigorifick," "sphere," "promiscuous," and "prolix" all recalibrate human–cold questions concerning knowledge, inquiry, agency, influence, intimacy, and creation. Cold stomachs and skin extend the "veins" (Wittie) to "extream" (Peter) and "exquisite" (Lemnius) lengths. So, too, does Bacon's fervid "seeeke" belong in this cryological lexicon. And yet, it should be remembered that the viscount perished for his finding. In March 1626, traveling in a carriage through the snow to meet the newly coronated king Charles I (1600–1649), "it came into [Bacon's] thoughts" to ascertain, right then and there, "why flesh might not be preserved in snow, as in salt."[122] After stuffing a freshly cleaned chicken, "the snow so chilled him,"[123] wrote his secretary, that he became ill, his condition deteriorated, and he died a few days later. One of his final letters was to Thomas Howard

(1585–1646), fourteenth Earl of Arundel, claiming that he had "succeeded excellently well."[124]

Bacon's fate acknowledges that death may result from the "suffering" of seeking abovementioned by Boyle: a cautionary tale about measuring trials by their "success" and the acquisition of (posthumous) fame. It is also true that testing cold can embolden post-Enlightenment attempts at subject–object segregation. When Boyle peruses an old law of congelation, for instance—"the Schools define cold by the property, they ascribe to it, of congregating both Heterogeneous and Homogeneous things"—he is persuaded to "mak[e] some separations in bodies by the force of Cold" (443). But what if "strangeness" is what we desire to detect, to be frigid without an originary cause or causation, promiscuously mixing, experimenting in experiential ice-intimacies, stuck in the middle of a Scientific Revolution that (supposedly) split nature from culture, here, on the eve of the 1666 Great Fire of London, caught between flames and frost, *Touching,* feeling "somewhat warm"?

In "beginning" as much as closing, this chapter has claimed that there is *something* to be learned by listening to an ice cube and dipping into a cold *Spaw,* both in terms of what else to do and what to resist. One parting "impressione" with which to leave you is this: the point ("limit") of lethality is crucial to consider, especially the question of *who* and *what* is more penetrable than others.[125] Arctic communities, whose diets depend on marine mammals like whale and seal, are some of the most contaminated bodies on the planet. PCBs (polychlorinated biphenyls), pesticides, mercury, and other pollutants travel from south to north, where they sink and stay within food chains and flesh. The "Arctic Paradox" appears permanent.[126] And while cold kills, so does the loss of it. Feeling cold in a seventeenth-century *Spaw* might not be the most relaxing experience, admittedly, because Wittie's wide-ranging "veins" oblige us to face our warming waters, and their lethal tang, today. Emersion, in short, is not an option. There has never been an exit. As the historian of medicine Roy Porter, puts it: "The histories of the spa and of its surrounding balneological disciplines can serve as illuminating epitomes of medicine itself in the world we have lost."[127] So can the histories of cryogenics: screeching ice, thus far, conducts the way to noisy death. Yet touching *frīgus,* while not fully deciphering it, bespeaks "a deep cold that all life . . . depend on in order to remain healthy and vibrant."[128] Resensitizing serves as a recourse, a means to be-"friend." A cold world is one that primarily Indigenous communities are losing at present, which is precisely why a return to feeling *with* wet and dry wintry others of the recent past offers a valuable lesson right now. By coldly blending climate, history, and ideas under the atmospheric conditions imparted by the Maunder Minimum, Boyle's and Wittie's bold treatises deserve greater recognition for the experimental "proceedings" they provide. It is in these brisk waters and warm rooms that we might learn how to brace ourselves for balmier futures, to build company better than before, and to soak in, take on, and speak of the uncertain "beyond."

# Winterlude

## *Err*

> Hudson achieved in 1609 nothing memorable,
> even by this new way.
>
> —Hessel Gerritz

In the summer of 1609, under orders from the Dutch East India Company to venture north by northeast toward Nova Zembla, the English navigator Henry Hudson (d. 1611) erred. Thwarted by icepack, and unwilling to return so soon to his Dutch patrons, he sailed west instead, journeying down the North American coast that his friend John Smith (1580–1631) had described to him. Entering what we now know as New York Harbor in September 1609, he sailed up the North River, a waterway that Italian explorer Giovanni da Verrazano (1485–1528) sighted in 1524 but never explored. Traveling as far north as modern-day Albany before the shallow waters forced him to turn back, Hudson's journey helped establish the city of New Amsterdam for the Dutch, making him, arguably, the founder of New York City and the face behind the Hudson River. But Hudson was not looking for the isle of Manhattan or interested in the economic potential of the river valley. First mate Robert Juet's drab descriptions of the landscape prove this point: "The land grew very high and mountainous. The river is full of fish. . . . The mountaynes look as if some metall or minerall were in them."[1] Juet's cursoriness belies Hudson's true intention, however: he had hoped to find the Northwest Passage. This river, so Hudson thought, would finally make his country a great global power.

Thus, a city that often emphasizes its ties to the Atlantic Ocean owes its inception in part to another ocean: the Arctic. New York City is a city, we might say, that began because of Hudson's geographical error upriver. I purposefully use this word in its etymological sense of the Latin *errare,* "to stray, err."[2] His geographical errancy would negatively affect his image for years to come. Consider the Dutch publisher Hessel Gerritz's (1612) dismissive summation,[3] for example, or fellow passage-seeker Luke Foxe's slanderous estimation in *North-West Fox* (1635). Recalling a moment in which Hudson sent home a "Master Coolbrand" on his fourth voyage of 1610–1611, Foxe held the latter to be in "every way . . . a better man than [Hudson]," for Coolbrand was the one who "devised [the] course" into the vast saltwater bay in northern America.[4] For these two early modern critics, navigation implies a course and an endpoint. Any "error" is that which "strays" from the *correct* path or does not reach the *right* end: it is a teleology fit for the straight lines of ecological imperialism, a valiant act of hitting one's mark. Errors cost dearly to them, and it would be errors that ultimately claimed Hudson's life: he died on the fourth voyage in that body of water that now bears his name, Hudson Bay, a victim of mutiny, set adrift by his men who deviated from their captain's orders, never to be seen again after 1611. His expressed wish to Richard Hakluyt came true: "I would that my name be carved on the tablets of the sea."[5] But I believe Hudson's errancy suggests a kind of erring that does not demand an endpoint (and certainly not the recognition of his ownership over river, strait, and bay.) What would it mean to stray without something to stray *from,* to wish *for* accidents rather than militate *against* them? Erroneousness comes to be appreciated for its endless change in direction.[6] "Carved" by the ice of an inland "sea," his body went missing.[7] "Hudson" and Hudson are errors both, and still *erring.*

During the last Ice Age, 1.5 million through 10 thousand years ago, the Wisconsin ice sheet stretched from present-day Montana to Massachusetts. About fifty thousand years ago, this mobile mass of ice entered the current New York metropolitan area, sculpting places like Long Island and speckling the landscape with glacial till and moraines we call city parks: Inwood Hill, Wolfe's Pond, and Van Cortlandt.[8] Nowadays the river barely changes in elevation from where it begins at Lake Tear of the Clouds on the slope of Mount Marcy in the Adirondacks, shifting only about 5 feet in its 145-mile trip to the ocean.[9] Around 13.5 thousand years ago, however, the river was not as consistent. When "The Great Flood of New York" occurred, Iroquois Lake (now Lake Ontario) burst through its ice dam, sending a torrent of freshwater sluicing south down

FIGURE 6. Erraticism, Central Park, New York City. Photograph by the author.

the glacial river valley where it emptied into the North Atlantic and initiated a global climate change. The valley still extends below water, in fact, and for this reason the Hudson is sometimes referred to as the "drowned river." The topography of New York City, in short, is glacial. In addition to the parks previously mentioned, other Arctic remnants are more obvious. Inner-city rocks in Central Park are what geologists call "glacial erratics," boulders deposited at sites in which they conspicuously stand out from native rocks, straying from their proper place amongst mineralogical kind, and in this case, from their rightful rural setting. As geological erratics, they remind us of an ice age supposedly past, static objects around which we recreate ourselves in the present. The stuff of a transhistorical continuum, their surprising out-of-placeness acknowledges them as arrivals that still arrive. Matter agentic and mobile, rocky erratics remind us of our cryocorporeality, of the Arctic's touch.

The first peoples of the river, those nations like the Mohican residing in the region Hudson intruded upon, have another name for the Hudson River: Mahicannittuk, "the river that flows both ways." Reconceiving the Hudson as a north-south river marks an icy interchange—a circulating eddy of freeze and flood, past and future, Arctic and Atlantic—that may help citizens rise to the challenges of a cold waterworld differently: be it by freeze (vortex), flood (sea level rise), and even "snow no-show."[10] When John Playse recounted Hudson's first voyage of 1607 in search of the Northwest Passage, he included the captain's own notes. On the evening of July 11, Hudson complains, "we had the company of our troublesome neighbours, ice with fogge."[11] While noting such dangers is commonplace for travel writers of the north, calling ice a "neighbor" is not. "Neighbor" is a composite word from the Old English *nēahgebūr,* from *nēah* ("nigh, near") and *gebūr* ("inhabitant, peasant, farmer").[12] Contrary to Gerritz's disparagement, Hudson helps us realize what we have forgotten: we exist *because* of our relationship to ice, by being "nigh" to the icy ocean. In Arctic Oceanic New York, proximity shapes ontology.

It is through such a networked interchange that neighbors interact, co-constitute, coexist. Yet Hudson reminds us of historically displaced "neighbors," those who have been pushed out but have left their traces nonetheless: such as the tribes he combated on his trip upriver, whose violent deaths gave Juet place-names like "Manna-hata."[13] And who persist. As a way of "exploring the story of the theft and usurpation of Lenape lands in 1624," the Harmattan Theater first performed *Henry Hudson's Forgotten Maps* on Governors Island in 2009, part of the company's "oceanic praxis" committed to "ecoaesthetic concerns that are decolonial at their core."[14] We should not remember Hudson's journey for its "nothing," but as a reminder of our everyday Arcticality, and act on its impulse to create ethical erratics for co-"inhabitants," good neighbors, to follow. Remember 1609 not for being a failure, but for it sponsoring other ways to be, "new ways" to go, chances to stray without reaching a destination—or even positing one.

This may be a "new way," perhaps, into the geopolitics of our time in which "neighboring" nations in the Arctic look north, just as their forebears did, to metallically rich places like Greenland. Will the receding ice lead to another Manhattan project against "troublesome" non/human neighbors? No: and this is precisely the point. There is no "proper" course in this eddy of reality within we live. The city's unofficial anthem might yearn to "be a part of it,"[15] but we should all be glacial erratics when it comes to the fantasy of being *apart from* the Arctic. We are already part *of* it. This requires the "Empire City" to shed its imperialistic title and reject the tenets of white settler colonialism and the behaviors of territorializing neighbors. For here is the cold corollary of refusing ecological and ontological sovereignty: letting go of the dream of a permanently placid Hudson Valley. This does not mean we should stop erring with the world, however, but rather rethink errors as something other than the failure to "get right" or to "find" the singular object of a given search. The ice (the Ice Age) is coming at us, but for Hudson, the North River was also an invitation into another oceanic world rather than its foreclosure. Erraticism still is a time to *try*. Ultimately, envisioning an Arctic Oceanic New York assures us that passages do not terminate upstream or downstream: they proliferate relations and take into collectives; they passage us into newer ethical and geopolitical realms that make room in their parliaments for icier subjects. Arcticizing New York City's oceanic history can redefine its future not just as inevitable catastrophe, but also of cryocoexistence, polar possibilities, dreams as well as obsessions.[16] (And the same may be said about wherever you are, too.) Beginnings, not just ends, are *nigh*. We are in the neighborhood of turbulent floes, but we are all Hudson's heirs as well.

# 2 The North Portals

> Maybe they did not want to be the men who would disenchant the world, kill everyone's dream of Eden or Hollow Earth, dry the fountain from which so many utopias were pouring forth—the very same reveries that, in some ways, had attracted them to the pole.
>
> —Jean-Christophe Valtat, *Aurorarama*

> It may seeme needlesse to make any mention of *Scandia,* which is that whole *peninsula* of huge circuit, which is almost incompassed with the waues of the sea, and abutteth northward and eastward vppon the *German* and *Sarmatian* coastes, because it is as it weere scituated in another world.
>
> —Giovanni Botero, *Relations of the Most Famous Kingdoms*

In their unflagging attempts to find the fabled Asiatic otherworld of Cathay in the late sixteenth and early seventeenth centuries, English navigators depended on a specific geographical point to help them travel north by northwest: Cape Farewell (Nunap Isua), Greenland's southernmost tip. John Davis (ca. 1550–1605) named the cape on his first (1585) of three voyages because he was forced to follow the land's western coast after facing impassible ice on the opposite side. This spot, strangely enough, could be recognized hydrologically as well as terrestrially, as John Janes points out in his account of the voyage: "The water about this coast was very blacke and thicke, like to a filthy standing poole."[1] A similar sentiment is repeated by George Weymouth (ca. 1587–1611) in 1602: "This day sometimes we came into blacke water as thicke as puddle, . . . then we sounded, and could fetch no ground in one hundred and twenty fathomes."[2] The English pilot James Hall (d. 1612), too, "came in blacke water, as thicke as though it had beene puddle water" in 1605.[3] While the puzzling and puddly phenomena they witnessed is probably white summer ice melting and exposing the darker ocean water underneath, their swampy characterization of the Arctic Ocean reveals it to be a simultaneously frigid and fecund place. According to the Aristotelian tenets of spontaneous generation, "standing" water was insalubrious because it bred. Olaus Magnus lists "Northern marvels" like the savvy drinkers who save pieces of ice to cool their drinks in the summer but carefully avoid the snow "for it has hidden worms innate in it."[4] It should not be surprising, then, that Janes pictures the icebergs as bedeviling insects when he complains about the incessant "pester of yce."[5] For him, "the yrksome noyse . . . seemed to be the true patterne of desolation," a phrase that came to define eastern Greenland as "the land of Desolation."[6] But something pestilent escapes the "patterne": the small circles spotlighting stirring creatures who populate a sprawling Arctic Circle *undersea*, those weird pools passed over but not fully occluded.

"How come I to digresse to such a dull, Lenten Northern Clyme?,"[7] Thomas Nashe rhetorically asks, before bidding "farewell frost: as much to say, as farewell Island, for I haue no more to say to thee."[8] Some expected a lifeless void up north, it is true. Thomas Heywood (ca. 1573–1641) could simply dismiss "miserable and wretched cold countries."[9] Jacob Segersz van der Brugge (fl. 1634), sailing to Spitsbergen on behalf of the Dutch Noordsche Company, cited classical authorities. The surrounding ocean deserves the appellation "Mare Cronium," he believed, "because Saturn, a cold planet, is said to rule in these places. For the same reason it is also called Concretum and Amalchim, which formerly meant frozen in the language of that people, and Morimarusa (signifying a dead sea), on account of the long darkness and the exiled aspect of milder constellations."[10] His peers, however, dreamt differently: "Hyperboreans," shielded from the north wind ("Boreas"), sat atop the world in a supratropical Eden;[11] competing tales from mythology and folklore told of pygmies, giants, and cranes at war;[12] and the freshly printed narratives of Davis's immediate predecessors like Martin Frobisher (1535[?]–1594) recounted increased contact with local Inuit communities. (Van der Brugge's journal, ironically, is wholly occupied with a slew of polar-bear attacks that harassed his overwintering.) Nothing in the northern ocean was, or had ever been, "concrete."[13] It was "sea-lung," after all, that ultimately thwarted Pytheas of Marseille's northern progress in the fourth century BCE. Famous for discovering the land of "Thule" after six days' sail from Britain, this gelatinous (not gelid) mixture of elements stymied the Greek geographer. When they did see blank space on the map, this "heart of whiteness"[14] helped perpetuate colonializing projects of erasure, supersession, or both, each constituting a brazen act of "cartographic silence."[15] The cryosphere's given title of "desolation," as a hollow emptiness utterly devoid of worth and of life, is, in fact, inaccurate; in reality, it bespeaks an act of avoidance (from *desolare,* "to abandon"), a silencing of the cape's flourishing (even if "filthy") creatures.

Plumbing the opaque paths of the frozen sea was, and still is, an opportunity worth considering. Published approximately seventy-five years after Janes's account, the French theologian Isaac de la Peyrère (1596–1676) gathered a compilation of contemporary visitors to the region, the *Relation du Groenland* (1663), depicting the cape and its inky waters as a traveler's trusty point of departure (a valuable, measurable, midway point between England and Newfoundland), but it also mentions it as a place that significantly points past known horizons: "Doubtless it is thus called because those who go beyond this cape seem to be going into another world, and to be taking a long leave of their friends."[16] The cape consequently takes on the power of otherworldly transportation; its impulse to embark offers the ability not only to traverse the boundaries of this world, but to exceed its perceivable limits. It escapes definition: "It would be difficult to represent its form, on account of the snow and ice, which vary, and on account of their whiteness, which dazzles the eyes."[17] All that dazzles is not white, either; peering into ice's wondrously shifty "difference of colour" on a sled route from Elsinore to Copenhagen, from "very white" to "beautiful azure," reminds him of the phrase Virgil uses in the *Georgics* (first century BCE) to describe "the black and dark countries" that compose the opposing poles: *cærulea glacie,* or "blue ice."[18] Seen with Peyrère's prismatic vision, the cape begins to looks tricolored: blue, black, and white all over. The changes in color shift to scale as well: in the seas off Spitzbergen "there are places . . . where the water is frozen from the bottom to the top, and on the surface of this are blocks of ice as high above as the sea is deep below."[19] Parroting Weymouth's observation about the unfathomable ice pool, Peyrère cites Virgil again, this time to underscore the "immense" size of ice: "*quæ tantum vertice ad auras Aerias, / Quantum radice ad Tartara tendunt.*"[20] The oak tree extends equally above and below ground: "As far as it lifts its top to the airs of heaven, so far it strikes its roots down towards hell."[21] And so do the icebergs.

But to underscore does not necessarily mean to understand. These ice pillars, somehow arboreal in their vegetal metaphor but rhizomatic in their flight-lines capable of launching bodies past the Greenlandic "beyond," touch the depths of Tartarus (*Tartara*) and act as vertical (*vertice*) ice bridges that lead to an elsewhere, an "other" under/world. (Peyrère might be punning here on Greenland's unfortunate misnomer as a verdant country as well as the written resemblance between Tartary and Tartarus.[22]) In their multidimensional ability to usher in another world-within-world, Farewell's pools are also portals. What was a clearly delineated "frozen zone" according to classical and medieval science, which split the globe latitudinally into five circular segments, is now, conversely, an entryway that impinges on and propels forward. If it must keep a "pole," then, the far north encompasses the Greek *polos* ("pivot, axis, sky") rather than the stolid *palus* ("stake") of Latin. Containing vectors instead of points, its environs slingshot ships; it causes turns. Peyrère's catapulting cape asks us to bid farewell to telos, to take a "leave" of current friendships by stretching our journeys and imaginations "long" in an effort to accrue new Arctic relations and fare *well* together.

It is important to note that Peyrère personally saw these portals as lethal: "Dead bodies keep well," he warns the erstwhile Arctic explorer, "but the living always fare ill."[23] Although he did not dare "fare" forth himself, there are those who tried. To the German naturalist Frederick Martens (1635–1699), for example, the Spitsbergen cold sea performs a kind of carpentry. Physically skimming these "places" in 1671, he espied "round and four square tables, with round and blew pillars underneath: the tables was very plain and smooth at the top, and white with the snow; at the sides hung down a great many ickles close to one another, like a fringed table cloth."[24] Martens, who speaks of ice's "taste,"[25] including some "frozen quite curled, it look'd just like sugar-candy,"[26] views the sweet matter around him as a potential Harawayian "messmate."[27] He then fantasizes further, placing himself under the variegated table: "you shall commonly see the water look blew or yellow, if you walk under water with your eyes open and look upwards."[28]

The "if" is entirely speculative, of course, yet his beautiful ice banquet nevertheless allows him to visit the ocean floor in his imagination, inverting spatial orientations by rendering the sea below as the "blew"-yellow sky above. The communal "tables" represent a deep-water daydream of a habitable north for humans, but they are a vision, at the very least, of the waters' untold vivaciousness. A living sea creative and companionate because of, and not despite, its quickening "close"-ness: in Martens's mind, the sharpness of "icikles" can seem keenly inviting. It is interesting to think of Shakespeare's Prospero's chilling lines to Ariel through this bluer lens of enchantment: "thou . . . think'st it much . . . To run upon the sharp wind of the north, / To do me business in the veins o'th' earth / When it is baked with frost" (*Tempest*, 1.2.252–56). Remember, too, the "several strange shapes, bringing a banquet" to the beleaguered Italians at the end of 3.3.[29] Eschewing southern locales "baked" by the sun—images that the "New World" usually conjures and with which Shakespeare's play is commonly associated[30]—Martens conceives of a friendlier world "fringed" with frost instead.

What if we entered these pools today? What would they tell us about the northern worlds we think we have plotted? Contrary to Giovanni Botero's 1608 casual dismissal of historical material "scituated in another world,"[31] I find it necessary to "make . . . mention" of frigid feasts (and more) that have led to otherworldly multispecies Arctic kinships. To rephrase what Peyrère already knew from his "poole"-side precursors: *the Arctic is a portal, not a pole.* Cool-water accompaniment, in fact, has been the intended "business" of modern-day onlookers who share Martens's sapid fascination with delectable oceans. The Russian photographer Viktor Lyagushkin tellingly calls his pictures of the warming White Sea (its sea angels, its skeleton shrimp, its comb jellies) "otherworldly."[32] Going out of the blue and into the black (and back) of human–nonhuman creaturely interconnectivity entails suspending our ontological differences, whether or not by aesthetic means. Stacy Alaimo, for one, writes about the "trans-corporeal" exposure these at-risk beings living and dying in the "violet-black" illustrate for us: "A fleshy posthumanist vulnerability that denies the possibility of any living creature existing in a state of separation from its environs."[33] In their association with opaque circles of private trading, "dark pools" may also prognosticate petrocultures' hostile takeover of the oil-dark seas.[34] While elite circles of the "Capitalocene" commingle proximate (not quite "alien") bodies in poisonous and profit-driven cases, these pitchy ("blacke") not-dead pools also raise the broader specter of Timothy Morton's "dark ecology," replete with "strange strangers": unanticipated,

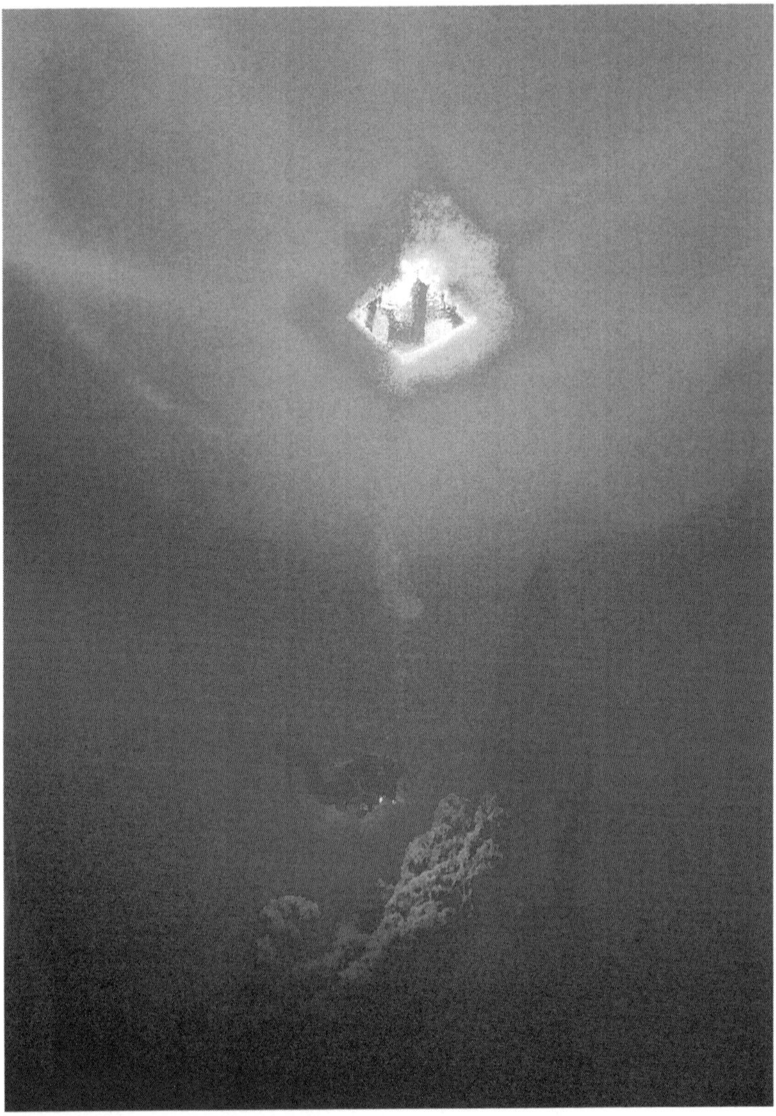

FIGURE 7. Other worlds. Photograph by Viktor Lyagushkin.

uncanny, and ever-intimate "others" that "appea[r] in this world, not beyond it," figures to what (or to whom) we are "always-already responsible."[35] These shapes haunt, Hades-like, the phrase "other worlds." The otherness I wish to evoke is one of enfolded intimacy rather than outsourced distancing, an incident to "brea[k] the cycle of sameness"[36] mandated by anthropogenic climate change and its harms. It happens at the pivotal moment you recognize you are "always-already" encircled by the Arctic portal, caught up in the cryosocial circles of recrudescent life both above and below, prompted into redefining your ways of knowing and being by gazing into its pools. (And we know that a proper plunge inspires questions.)

This chapter examines early modern portrayals of northern seascapes in order to rethink the political-ecological stakes of climate crisis at present and what the thawing of "relations" might hold in future. In my view, the Arctic's interpretative and free-flowing configurations, more so than its continental counterpart,[37] constructively unmoor our onto-epistemological and ethical bearings. While the impulse to survey one's surroundings accurately and exhaustively was pervasive at this time of discovery, Chris Barrett reminds us that "cartography's uses, logics, and strategies have troubled, as much as they have fascinated and allured."[38] Such historical "anxieties," in my mind, can be productive. If "the Arctic is no place for pragmatists,"[39] it still houses many of the world's most unwavering problems. Global warming is responsible for a host of ancillary issues ranging from species loss, to the erosion of traditional Indigenous knowledges, to neocolonial extractivism (and the coalescence of parties opposed to it). As resilience strains under the pressure of rising temperatures and sustainability seems increasingly impractical alongside positive feedback loops (ice's exponential melt), adaptation and accommodation appear to be more viable, if not logical, strategies for survival in current "cryopolitical" circles. Such methods, according to Joanna Radin and Emma Kowal, "invit[e] us to reconsider the futures we are actually creating, instead of submitting to the instinct to defer and preserve."[40]

In what follows, I focus on the efforts of those who chose to explore and expand rather than restrain and remove the "trouble" the region caused for them. Stealing a phrase from the renowned English physician Thomas Browne, I introduce the early modern imaginations of "septentrionally excited"[41] thinkers who pictured the Arctic less as a complete and single circle (Circle), and more as a series of swirling portals (circles) in overlay, of un/locking archipelagos of islands veering in and out of sequence, of passages orienting in their geographical and scalar specificity as well as dizzying in their collapses of distance. At the same time, their narratives demonstrate that to inhabit an "other" faraway world that oddly connects with your own, and is strangely similar to it, is dependent on who the "your" is at the moment of speaking. As the perspectives of Inuit "others" will attest, the oceanic dynamics of encounter change when the European orbit unwillingly extends into yours. My outlook might seem facile at first, perhaps affording an amusing kaleidoscope effect or supporting the conspiracy theories of a "Hollow Earth" (or both), but the Danish, Dutch, and English multifaceted views of the "otherworldly" north as a coruscating and encroaching whirl/pool, archipelago, and passage, as we will see, usefully distort our perceptions about this supposedly remote marine world. Their disorienting Arctics, purposefully plural and pluralizing, allow us, I maintain, to imagine our world in other ways, and in doing so, move us to create different, more proximate, ones right now.

My overarching argument, therefore, is to critique not so much the idea of a "pure" or "pristine" Arctic Ocean,[42] but rather the persistent trope of an uncreaturely (vacant) and uninspiring (insipid) rime realm, an endangered "nature" set apart from the world of "culture." Bruno Latour has linked the three phenomena of globalization/deregulation, inequality/injustice, and the denial of climate change to identify the "attractor" (or "pole") known as the "Out-of-This-World: the horizon of people who no longer belong to the realities of an earth that would react to their actions."[43] To combat its pull, "we need something like a *map* of the positions imposed by the new landscape within which not only the *affects* of public life but also its *stakes* are being redefined."[44] He advocates coming "down to earth" to touch the "Terrestrial" instead. More *aqua* than *firma,* in my opinion, *the Arctic is of this world, not out-of-it*: not a background of iced land, but a politically participatory agent. In outlining the real nautical "stakes," and by showcasing the material "affects" that enable ideational norths, I hope to complement the ongoing fact-based conversations in climate-change activism that envisage alternate (though no less impacted and entangled) worlds to challenge the dominant narrative of accelerated industrialization, a story of marginalization that relies on depopulating the cryospherical "New World" in order to advance modernity's aims. In sum: if we are to realize, for politically gainful reasons, that any position on the planet does not exist apart from the Arctic, we should pay attention to how early moderns regarded these other maritime worlds of the high north as conjoined with their own, and how they came "down to [water]" in their stunning hydrographical visions, in addition to how (well) they treated their others. As a result, other worlds may be not only visualized but also actualized. In keeping with Martens's companionate model and Peyrère's pivotal portrait, I will present the rest of this chapter as a map of portals, six routes limned with a motto of my own (*I have already inscribed two*) that serve to highlight the energetic qualities of the "yce"-y seas seen beyond.

## The Arctic Is Alive

Think back on Thomas Dekker's 1608 likening of the Thames to a "waterie wilderness": a statement belied by the "wylde youthes and boyes" running amok, and later (1615) by the "white beares" and "monsters" following in their foot-"steppes." A raucous frost fair, too, certainly clashes with the depiction of the river as an inhospitable waste/water/land. Englanders were not the only ones who "lodged" in "the frozen zone," however; for some of the most prominent geographers of the north, the higher latitudes were suitable for thriving societies. The Italian historian Peter Martyr d'Anghiera's (1457–1526) *Decades of the New World* (translated by Richard Eden in 1555/1577) became a seminal work for would-be cryonauts and wishful imperialists. Under the employment of Spain, he wrote primarily about the fertility of Central and South America. But d'Anghiera also regarded "the moderate and continvall heate in coulde regions."[45] In his treatise on "Schondia" (Scandinavia), Jacob Ziegler (ca. 1470/1–1549) chastises the ancient authorities who, "with one consente, . . . affirmed that in these north regions the could zone or clime, was condemned to perpetuall snowe intollerable to all lyuynge creatures."[46] The celebrated German cartographer and cosmographer Sebastian Münster (1489–1552) reiterated the popular claim from Jordanes's *Getica* (sixth century CE) that the north is where the Goths, the vanquishers of Rome, historically originated. Only countries as "fruitefull" as Swedland, Gotland, and Finland—based on George North's 1561 translation—could breed "people so mighty and valiaunt."[47] A cold zone, in short, could also be a cultivated one.

No one demonstrated the formidability of northern populations in greater detail, arguably, than Olaus Magnus, the Archbishop of Uppsala. His fabulous *Historia de Gentibus Septentrionalibus,* printed in Rome in 1555, was quickly translated into multiple languages, and eventually into

FIGURE 8. *De glacierum varietate.* From Olaus Magnus, *Historia de Gentibus Septentrionalibus* (1555), National Library of Norway.

English as *A Description of the Northern Peoples.* Twenty-two books and a bevy of woodcuts exponentially expanded the list of "northern marvels" initiated by Jordanes and extended by Saxo Grammaticus (ca. 1160–1220) in *Gesta Danorum.* It supplemented Adam of Bremen's (fl. 1075) notes on supernaturalism as well.[48] Due to its encyclopedic breadth and its entertaining details, the *Description* was considered by many to be an invaluable resource not just on Swedish customs but also on the broader Scandinavian region. Any serious research into the conjunction of human civilizations and rimy realms started here. In his section detailing *de glacierum varietate* ("the different kinds of ice"),[49] for example, Magnus fuses snowscape and society. An alpine house sits embedded in a glaciated rock, flanked by a frozen waterfall and riverine icebergs bearing vaguely humanoid faces. While a small fire burns inside the hut, its open-doored resemblance on the hillside above is striped with icicles. Each dwelling depicts the brutal Nordic winters as expected visitors: architecture is but one brumal instance of "the magnitude and fierceness of the cold in binding earth and water and other moist objects."[50] His magisterial collection recounted, in hundreds of chapters, the extensive interlocking of northern cultures with their icy environments.

Magnus's interest in northern vitality raises a startling preposition that William Fulke and Francis Bacon felt in the previous chapter: cold's ability to simultaneously protect, impede, and precipitate life. (The snow that "cherysheth"/"cherisheth," respectively.) The Arctic was lively in that it housed alive non/human things, but its coldness also espoused a generativity of its own. As an ordained Catholic, Magnus's epigraph is unsurprisingly ecclesiastical: "Out of the north cometh golden splendour"[51] is from the biblical book of Job (37:22). He also quotes Psalm 147:16–17: "The Lord giveth snow like wool: He scattereth the hoarfrost like ashes. He casteth forth his ice [*crystallum*] like morsels: who can stand before his cold?"[52] In its ability to provide divine "splendour" and unopposable "morsels," Magnus's north contains the literal matter of life and death. Cold has fertilizing, life-giving powers: "Huge masses of snow hanging down from trees" signify that "plentiful crops are forthcoming in the year ahead when the ground will be more fertile for fostering the seeds because of the protracted cold."[53] But one of frozen Lake Vättern's "amazing properties" is its breakup: "The waters begin to bubble and stir up from the bottom with a powerful rumbling noise.... Then, under the impact of the elements above, the whole surface of the ice separates into many fragments, and travellers who are stranded on these can hardly manage to reach the shores unless God preserves them."[54]

In other places, he thinks of cold straddling the line between the two, where resurrection effectively collapses stable distinctions between life and death.[55] In the winter, "it quite happens that fishermen will drag swallows pressed together in a mass out of the water."[56] While avian migration to warmer climes was surmised, it was not totally understood; hence, Magnus's note on "swallows hid[ing] in the water during winter"[57] became a perennial observation. Robert Burton cites the *Historia* when addressing birds' spontaneous resurgence during spring. "How comes it to pass?" he asks: "Do they sleep in winter, like [Conrad] Gesner's Alpine mice; or do they lie hid (as Olaus affirms) 'in the bottom of lakes and rivers, *spiritum continentes* [keeping in their breath]? often so found by fishermen in Poland and Scandia, two together, mouth to mouth, wing to wing; and when the spring comes they revive again, or if they be brought into a stove, or to the fire-side.'"[58] Magnus's vignette, reframed by Burton, ponders whether ice contains within it an animating principle of life—a cold *spiritus* ("breath, spirit") that infuses the warm-blooded "winged" things it enwraps—or, incredibly, whether the birds are able to hold the vital "breath" of life in their lungs for several months while surrounded by inanimate, spiritless, and breathtakingly ice-cold waters. Both possibilities may "pass" simultaneously. (Hibernation names just this interstitial state of slow, death-like life.) Magnus probably had two more verses from Job in mind when describing how cold harbors these flocks: "Hast thou entered into the treasures of the snow?" (38:22); and "Out of whose womb came the ice?" (38:28). The gelid "womb" need be neither heteronormative nor organic, but marks, in Astrida Neimanis's estimation, the "gestational,"[59] a wintry co-creativity that nets bird, fisher, and water. The "apparitions of drowned men"[60] elsewhere stalk the intermediate, purgatorial space of the not-dead and heaven-hell, depicting a "spectral Arctic"[61] that intrigued contemporaries like Nashe and that endures to this day. Glimpsed through north portals, cold's baffling fecundity entices and terrifies. Death was not ignored when testifying to living cold, but it was not all that was there.

Given his work's pervasiveness, Magnus's extraordinary visions of hibernacles and more would reappear centuries thereafter; and yet, while he catalogues questions of living with cold, and a life *of* cold, he stops short of making a complete turn to what Katherine Behar has labeled "vivophilia": "loving objects for their liveliness."[62] He contemplates the *bio-* and the *necro-* as inseparably entwined. Magnus knew his share of strife and decay: he told of "northern wars unceasing"[63] and devoted an entire book to "warfare on ice";[64] a "snowy abyss" is useful for "drowning [one's] enemies"; and small birds drop "little balls of snow"[65] that demolish unsuspecting towns downhill.[66] When discussing "burials in ice" and "men's dying in cold," he cites Vincent of Beauvais's twelfth-century *Mirror of History*: "'nor is it wonderful'" (that is, "Nature triumphs").[67] Cold, of course, kills. It also sets up, in Radin and Kowal's words, "a seemingly paradoxical conjunction . . . suspended animation and action . . . that produces a zone of existence where beings are made to live and are *not allowed to die.*"[68] "Cryopolitics," as "a politics of the liminal,"[69] is not about the policing of "life" itself (in the traditional Foucauldian definition of "biopower"), they aver, but the avoidance of death. Their landmark term adds important complications to the question of living (with) cold. Thinking about cold-power leads us places in addition to a deadly "abyss." "Cryonics" holds out the science-fiction promise of eternal life and extended time travel: an iceman found in the Arctic (or Cicely, or Encino) and miraculously restored.[70] The political dimension of "cryogenics" (the physics of low temperatures), on the other hand, asks what is being preserved, why, and what else is worth preserving. Magnus's deathless submarine swallows comport with the idea of hypothermia as a kind of sleep, a painless demise. In reality, transmutation torments the victim and distresses the chronicler, embedding their traumas in collective memory (chapter 4). The "heapes" of Dekker's uncounted countrymen "nipt away" prove im/perishability to be a chronic issue. Early modern blends of life and death are meant to be productive rather than corrective: the firn-like "compost"[71] they describe adds complexity to cold's raw range. To conceive of an Arctic like this is to tell a full-bodied story about the bone-chilling *and* fortifying, for all its gooseflesh.

## The Arctic Arrives

Peculiarly, southerners could go north by staying put: as Dekker perceived it, "Freezland" had "come ouer sea" in 1608. When answering questions about where cold came *from,* authors habitually consulted the classical conception of "climate." Coming from the Greek *klima* ("inclination, slope") and *klinein* ("to slope, lean"), "climate" referred to the division of the earth's surface into regions defined, roughly, by latitude.[72] The strength and the angle of sunlight also played a part. The "torrid" zone stretched along the equator, two "temperate" bands flanked it, and lastly, two "frozen" spans sat at the poles. Thus, William Strachey (1572[?]–1621) thought the cold weather "Virginia Britannia" experienced in 1607 was indicative of "the extraordinary frost . . . felt in most parts of Europe."[73] While it is tempting to find security in this compartmentalization, climates' borders were clear-cut only on maps. Writers grappled with a northern region that impressed an oversized amount of influence upon them, breaking down climatic distances between the "frozen zone" and their more "temperate" European homes farther south. While the earliest cryosophers did not claim to be in what is now called the Little Ice Age, peeking northward confronted them with unyielding questions about their age: specifically, why weather conditions at equal latitudes were different, and furthermore, how the frigid atmosphere of Thule could possibly stretch across the sea and enter supposedly subarctic England. Robert Boyle, for instance, intrigued by travelers' strange weather reports from other parts of the hemisphere, thought it worthwhile to determine "the coldness of differing places of equal latitude."[74] When the circles of the boreal and the urban coincided, their conjunction illustrated not only the complexities of climate but also the complicated idea of "climate" itself.

Descartes's opinion in the *Meteorology,* for instance, that "the north wind is cold because it brings with it toward the south the very fine material that was in the north, on which cold primarily depends"[75] was not only popular but also perspicacious: he observes the Arctic Circle overlapping with his own (social) circle. As the perception of a far-off, insipid land of ice and snow came under question, "frozen"–"temperate" junctions continued to prime the imagination. Michael Bravo has described the North Pole as "lively," its magnetic "hold" fashioning a "polar consciousness."[76] And expeditions skirting the top of the globe did not necessarily arrest the creative process or dull the perception, slowly replacing fiction with fact, but furthered it instead. Even the trendy theme of the Arctic as a split-off "otherworld" could mature into an analysis of how ecotones impinge as a series of interlinked circles, rather than reinforce ideas of "otherness" or antipodal mirroring, ideas that assist only in polar distantiation. On the contrary, their expanding "consciousness" denies north–south dichotomies altogether, a suture that many critics have shown to uphold cultural hegemonies and socioeconomic hierarchies.[77] By highlighting their imperfect grasp of Arctic intersectionality, early modern authors express a "historically oriented eco-cosmopolitanism,"[78] in Ursula K. Heise's words, and their imaginations still "hold" potential for melting hard divides and the structures of power that subtend them.

Consider the case of Raphael Thorius (d. 1625), a London physician who poeticized his bitter encounter with the undulating "zone." "Far from" his "native soil" of Flanders, he composed his 1651 *Cheimonopegnion,* or *A Winter Song,* in "frozen verse."[79] When the north wind moves south, it burrows deep into urban bodies:

> Congealed Icicles hang on the beard,
> With wind the eyes do weep, the teeth are heard
> To chatter in the mouth, and raging cold
> In such sad pain the fingers ends doth hold
> That though hot gales the breath upon them blows,
> They dare not higher mount to cleanse the nose.[80]

This seasonal congestion afflicts all snow-men and snow-women: even as the nose refuses to run, the eyes still "weep," providing enough lubrication for facial stalactites (dangling "icicles") to grow.

But Thorius's "beardcicles" (as they are now known) and his dreaded "snotcicles" extend, somewhat grotesquely, beyond the local. His condition causes him to linger on the northbound "Hollander," who at that very moment,

> to the North Pole his steddy stern he guides,
> While rands of ice do thwack the vessels sides;
> And all the tedious night the ice he wounds,
> Endeavouring to remove great natures bounds:
> Thus while he hews his passage through the deep,
> The penetrating cold begins to creep
> Close to his heart.[81]

As the anonymous voyager moves north, and presumably east or west in search of the Passage, an interchange develops: the cold voyages through the navigator, threading the labyrinthine veins and arteries (tinier passages) on its laborious journey inward to the anatomical core. In "creeping" so, the corporeal and cartographic maps overlap further, bringing the "North Pole" home as well. A simple sojourn outside one's home resembles a race to the pole; after all, he says, that same wind does not stop at the Dutchman's skin on its "steddy" way south:

> Who now can travell? scarcely in the town
> A man can walk with safety up and down,
> So furious doth the North-wind swagger,
> The wals, unless I reel, do seem to stagger.
> . . . In a sad case is he that opes his dore,
> Unless the whirlwinds wings be clipt before.[82]

Thorius sings the song of a mighty wind from the north that nevertheless lives in London's streets and its citizens. Here, convergence (humans and cold *never* in twain) is an opportunity to muse about future fusing.

"The melting of the Arctic will come to haunt us all."[83] Just as climate scientists these days point to the melting icecaps' direct role in rising global temperatures and severe weather events, early modern sketches of impactful "northscapes"[84] and "coldscapes"[85] help relay one of the most urgent arguments of earth system science. As the unattributed motto goes, "what happens in the Arctic does not stay in the Arctic."[86] This adage certainly resonated with Western science's predecessors. But at the same time, cold thinkers who ruminated on "a" north complicate what has turned into a oversimplified phrase: "what" the "Arctic" is and "what" is "in" there; what "happens," "stays," and ventures out; and the extent of the Circle's sway, how far it expands (or "does not"). A twenty-first-century Arctic is warming four times faster than the worldwide average, which causes sweeping disruptions: sea levels climb; climate patterns shift; land- and sea-animal migrations reroute. The Arctic's essential role has been compared to the earth's "circulatory system," an anatomical metaphor that early moderns (like Robert Wittie) emphasized and utilized. North-ness cryocorporeally crossed margins, moved into and across bodies. "Boreas," the north wind, was literally the breath. Thorius's song reconfigures the *where* of "the Arctic" as geographical place as well as bodily invader (under the skin). These embodied representations sponsor visions of an effective, interconnected realm: a "meteorophysiological"[87] canopy that stitched together disparate creatures, one that could suddenly inspread and outspread. Both poets and physicians (and more) were not merely prescient in their outlook regarding human–Arctic overlay, as if the blurrier Circle they sketched eventually came into sharper focus over time, only after enlightened minds could solve their intractable questions. Their polar picture imperfectly, and importantly, overlaps with ours, and they weird out the Circle in ways useful for their unusualness. As it bends and swerves, as it "swaggers" and "staggers," the Arctic also becomes *you.*

As the Arctic widened at its edges, moreover, it sponsored a widening sense of cryodependency. When the English polymath Gabriel Plattes (ca. 1600–1644) spoke of "Islands of Ice" in his 1639 work on metallurgy, *A Discovery of Subterranean Treasure,* he speculated about the necessity of the North and South Poles. As water in the "burning Zones"[88] evaporates, the more northern and southern regions must supply condensation as a counterbalance: "the new Accretion" of snow and hail "doth press down still with its weight the said Islands of Ice towards the Centre, where the central heat melteth it off continually, by which means the spherical form of both Earth and Water are perpetually preserved."[89]

Without ice, the "Centre" cannot hold: an inkling of what is now known as "geoclimatic equilibrium," an astute point Todd Borlik makes in his recent anthology of primary sources.[90] Plattes's nascent understanding of the hydrological cycle (to be determined later that century) also hinges on polar places. Ice makes the planet's "spherical form" possible by literally pressing it into shape. While he and his colleagues did not face our precise set of icy issues, the general cooling they experienced led them to breathtaking insights about humanity's embeddedness within larger cryosystems. Revisiting their thoughts about the interplay between climate and culture unpacks their co-constitutive complexities for us. Forswearing an instance of what Haraway calls the "god trick"—the viewer looking down on the North Pole from an illusory, universal perspective—thought experiments like Plattes's re-"situate" readers, knowledges, and practices in locations that are distant from daily life, although not detached from it.[91]

It is tempting to find security in Platte's cool cosmography. Yet the maxim about long-distance Arctic attachments is one with which early modern populations struggled, troubles that significantly refute detached modes of thinking today. Although "zones" might interregulate each other, their affixations could come undone and *undo*. Weather forecasting (relegated to "prognostication") was primarily an astrological affair, while meteorology was useful for describing the hot and cold, moist and dry contents of different precipitations. The aleatory and disorderly tugged at harmony and symmetry to become the philosophical nature of things. Attuned to the growing cold, artists reacted to the abrupt and persistent changes in weather that consequently altered their notions of climate.[92] Again, the word "climate" is instructive here. While it evolved to designate a specific region (a northern country) as well as the prevalent pattern of weather of a given area (climates of the north),[93] these neat demarcations could unexpectedly slope, tilting the intemperate blend of zones toward a temporal "frozen age": a term for hard(ening) times used by "the Water Poet," John Taylor (1578–1653).[94] On the other hand, Henry Coventry (1617/18–1686), responding to the Great Frost of 1634–1635, as if drought suddenly reversed a larger cooling trend, opened his 1636 "On the Dry Summer" cynically: "Where is the cold you quaked at, you that be / Shook with two palsies, Age and Poverty?"[95] (The "quaky" cold continued throughout the century.) Authors marveled at cold's ability to puncture latitudinal delineations, and they debated over both the nature and the timespan of its spell, whether they were "frozen" in a cold loop or just temporarily locked into a bad back-winter. Their ruminations suggest that stalwart distinctions between climate as a long-term pattern and weather as a short-term aberration were harder to shore up in reality: when it came to cold, either designation harbored inconstancy.

Ultimately, these interests evince not just what happens *in* or *to* "the Arctic": they also tell of its residents forcibly trafficked, for example, and of the countless damages done by human actions. The "empty" Arctic has unfortunately become an entrenched truism of late. But a little historical contextualization proves that its liveliness has been strategically *evacuated* in order to suit capitalistic schemes of easy-to-access enrichment. Rather than filling in a "blank" Arctic, the stories that earlier author-explorers told of cold waters and lands (Hudson Bay, Greenland, Spitsbergen) displayed diverse, occupied, and vivacious dwellings. If the "Arctic region as both apocalyptic portent and planetary dreamchild"[96] presents somewhat of a binary decision, early moderns could think of eschatological and utopic scenarios at once, most notably the idea of the paradisaical, of a "hyperborean" civilization shielded from the chilly blasts they inherited from Greek mythology. (The moniker derives from *hyper,* "beyond," and *boreas,* "the north wind.") Ancient geography told of beings at the borders of the *oikoumenē* ("the inhabited") and of "ultima Thule."[97] The "Arctic," therefore, was a drifty idea. As Dolly Jørgensen and Sverker Sörlin assert, concepts of "northness" are constantly being "made," its cartographical lines redrawn and its cultural meanings reproduced. Since antiquity, it has been the critic's task to "mak[e] the action visible."[98] The sixteenth- and seventeenth-century "Arctic" was multiple and multifaceted, brimming with life and mixtures of in/human elements. "To be alive," writes Bathsheba Demuth in her beautiful history of Beringia, "is to take a place in a chain of conversions."[99] Environmental sagas of Arctic energy flows find their parallels in an earlier upper world whose bustle, while less quantifiably calculable, was no less riveting. There is no going back to an untouched "wilderness," "waterie" or no.[100] Regularly recreated as animated, beguiling, and infringing, their cold configurations were not always without inner contradictions and tensions. But their "many norths"[101] assist in longstanding campaigns that debunk the "Arctic" as a place purely barren or desolate; as a consequence, they draw attention to how cryological

FIGURE 9. *Septentrionalium Terrarum Descriptio* (1606). Courtesy of Geographicus Rare Antique Maps.

knowledge is made, what purpose it serves, and whom it benefits. Looking *up* (zone, sky) and *in* (body), we find the north dipping *down* and *into,* and we wonder what "comes ouer" next.

## The Arctic Is a Spiral, Not a Circle

When the Flemish cartographer Gerhardus Mercator (1512–1594) published his 1569 world map that boasts his famous "projection," he added a smaller window on the bottom left considered to be the first map of the Arctic Circle. Jodocus Hondius (1563–1612) updated his predecessor's depiction in 1606 as the *Septentrionalium Terrarum Descriptio.* What immediately strikes the viewer is the black rock (*rupus nigra et altissima*) situated at the exact center of the *Polus Arcticus,* or North Pole, surrounded by four islands cut by four channels. What was peripheral is now central: this tricky god's-eye view looking straight down on the spherical globe provides a geometric, somewhat becalmed symmetry. In the land to the bottom left reside the fabled "pygmies, at most 4 feet tall, who are like those in Greenland called Scraelings," (probably, and derogatively, people of Inuit descent), while adjacent to them sits "the best and healthiest [island] of the whole north." Partitioned and preserved as if in crystal, its placid stillness is nevertheless betrayed by the other Latin inscriptions therein. Although the centrical black rock is a permanent fixture on the map, the waters around it are on the move. As written on the island slightly above the cliffs, the Arctic pulls the southern waters into its gluttonous orbit: "The Ocean rushes in between these islands by 19 mouths and makes 4 channels by which it is incessantly carried northwards & there disappears into the bowels of the earth."[102] And as it sucks, the pole incredibly spins. In a letter sent to the English polymath John Dee (1527–1609) on April 20, 1577, Mercator explains his rationale: "In the midst of the four countries is a Whirl-pool . . . into which there empty these four Indrawing Seas which divide the North. And the water rushes round and descends into the earth just as if one were pouring it through a filter funnel."[103]

Mercator's four-part display repeats, he insists, the reports of one Jacob Cnoyen, a traveler who referenced the lost *Inventio fortunata* (Fortunate discoveries) from the fourteenth century, a fabulous work whose anonymous author's testimony lent the map its idiosyncratic structure: "In the yeere 1360, a certaine English Frier, a Franciscan, and a Mathematician of Oxford, came into those Islands, who leaving them, & passing further by his magical Arte, described all those places that he sawe."[104] But the whirled waters at world's top break this tidy system; in fact, so does the element of earth. Unlike his contemporaries, Mercator did not believe this black mountain attracted the compass needle: the magnetic pole, *polus magnetis,* is actually up and to the right.[105] What we now know to be the changeable geomagnetic pole as opposed to plottable geographic one was anticipated by this maneuver. The "pole," according to his projection, is a moveable marker (*magnetis*) and a place (*Arcticus*) of mobility. Any center, then, is always a little off. Whatever solidity can be discerned sits in the middle of a ravenous vortex. The pullulating pools with their elements in tow are stops along a spiral whose point is perpetually unfixed. Mercator's portal, at last, has us focus on the asymmetrical propensity to go off-balance contained within any configuration of symmetrical ecological order. Here is where the "magical Arte" of science meets that "arte" of the imagination. The circle is broken because the maelstrom remains incomplete.[106] We are unsure into what worlds the brumal "bowels" lead, if they terminate at all.

At the same time that its disequilibrium jars with familiar arrangements of concentric circles aligned in neat cartographic form, the swirling Arctic also helps to overlay parallel sites of nature and culture in the real world to the south it purports to preside over. In other words, the "whirl-pool" of/as Arctic flux is not a disorder that needs to be set aright, but a realization of living in a world whose spatial symmetries are ephemeral (at best) and divisive (at worst). It means deserting the sturdiness of Robert Recorde's 1556 *The Castle of Knowledge,* for instance, and eschewing the clean curves of William Cuningham's 1559 *Cosmographical Glass,* in order to rethink subject–object symmetry, not as a measurable proportion of equanimity (at a distance), but as an ontological pairing (in proximity). Remember Mercator's channels that both "divide" and "round" at once; pressing up to the glass that "filters" as it "funnels" is what the French theorist Michel Serres has in mind when he describes the passage of time as "percolation," noting that *passoir* ("sieve") should be closer to *pass*: "One flux passes through while another does not."[107] But, in his temporal musings, he also makes a messier Mercatorial map: "It's better to paint a sort of fluctuating picture of relations and rapports—like the percolating basin of a glacial river, unceasingly changing its bed and showing an admirable network of forks, some of which freeze or silt up, while others open up."[108] Within the mixtures of turbulence, things pass and do not pass along passages that are frequently being un/made, their sifts obeying the liminal physics of a glacial rock.

Glimpsed through a gelid glass differently, the "pivot, axis, sky" otherwise known as the "pole" should feel familiar to us in these funnel-shaped ways. But its work should not cease to surprise us, either. "He had better cool his hot blood i'the frozen / Sea, and rise thence a rock of Adamant / To draw more wonder to the North," boasts Don Carlos in James Shirley's 1652 play *The Brothers.*[109] Despite the reintroduction of the term into North American vocabularies in 2013–2014, the "polar vortex"—the band of low pressure and cold that sits at the earth's two poles—is not a climatic aberration, but a chronic condition that, like all weather, is susceptible to extremes. True to its spiraling form, the vorticular pole may constrict (by its "indrawing") as well as expand. It always connects, and vexingly so. Beware the "whirlwind," Thorius had warned. Nevertheless, the temperature of the north from where these boreal blasts originated remained hotly contested. The Flemish astronomer-cartographer Petrus Plancius (1552–1622), for example, argued that the degree of cold actually decreases as the pole is neared, corroborated by Hudson's experience at the high latitudes of Greenland and Nova Zembla from 1607 to 1608: "[He] confirms this by scientific reasons, and says, that near the pole the sun shines for five months continually; and, although his rays are weak, yet on account of the long time they continue, they have sufficient strength to warm the ground, to render it temperate."[110] But, even without a causal explanation, it is clear that the "whirlwind" from the "whirl-pool" carried both fears and fascinations; its "wings" could not "be clipt." While Mercator's mercurial map at first glance might make his insights seem outmoded or unscientific in our era of greater meteorological understanding,[111] upon closer inspection it underscores a still-swirling Arctic (the air and water currents called the atmosphere), guaranteeing that, while the oceanic vortex has been historically reconfigured, its whirring has never truly halted. *And yet it spins.*

## The Arctic Is an Archipelago of Stories

Sometime between 1390 and 1400, two Venetian brothers named Nicolò (ca. 1326–1402) and Antonio Zeno (d. ca. 1403) supposedly skirted the Arctic Circle. Under the patronage of Zichmi of Frislanda (whom some have postulated as Henry Sinclair of Scotland), Antonio, if it is to be believed, ventured as far as America ("Estotiland" and "Drogeo"). A descendent of his, also named Nicolò Zeno, published the brothers' letters in 1558 along with a map of the various places they visited. The authenticity of their account has been controversial amongst scholars since the mid-nineteenth century, to say the least, and the debate has never really ceased.[112] The island of "Icaria" does not exist, which is most damning to their credibility, and court records locate Nicolò in Venice at the time of their legendary expedition. Whether or not one completely spurns the Zeni family as frauds putting on an elaborate hoax or finds faint (because inaccurate) traces of truth in their north Atlantic adventures, one aspect of their legacy cannot be contested: the seascape they portrayed remained influential for centuries thereafter. Their notoriety far succeeded them; explorers expected "Frislanda" (Faroe), "Eslanda" (Shetland), "Engronelanda," "Estotilanda," and "Icaria" to come into view on the journey west. ("Frislanda" sits in the sphere to the upper-left in Hondius's chart.) Rather than as an object of debate or for merely deploring the inauthenticity of their travels, the Zeni map is better appraised for purposefully letting its surveyors drift into the realm of fabrication. By not striving to convey the Arctic perfectly as it is or was, by favoring Arctics of various perspectives, and thereby underscoring the impossible verifiability of premodern Arctic maps, the brothers sketch for us the phenomenon of redesigning possible worlds. Being "the last imaginary place,"[113] as Robert McGhee believes it is, the Arctic's creative powers endure for those who wish to express them.

In his 1873 edition for the Hakluyt Society, Richard Henry Major appears sympathetic to the Venetians' inventiveness. One of his reasons for supplying a hundred-page introduction is the "vindication" of an imaginative man who "indulged in the glowing fancies and diction of his sunny country,"[114] defending topological poesy ("diction") as much as it does of the younger Nicolò's skills at compiling. Even though "the book," he assures us, "which has been declared to be 'one of the most puzzling in the whole circle of literature' will henceforth be no puzzle at all,"[115] the "puzzle" of the Circle remains perplexing. As it was centuries before, the Arctic seafloor, "the last new land,"[116] constitutes one of the few uncharted territories left on the planet, even as its surveyable swaths are either claimed or coveted by intergovernmental group members who make up the Arctic Council. What is more, northern worlds are constantly being remapped on the shores of advancing and withdrawing land and sea ice. Due to the mutable quality of the ice-filled waters, any line separating land from ocean, by nature of its liminality, is necessarily being redrawn by both hands (humans) and oceanic bodies (ice). The Circle, broken and remade in these ways, is what the far-fetched Zeni map of 1558 ultimately pictures: an archipelago of fragments without a whole, splintered lands and seaways that are not just multiple but multiplying, that grow as the "glowing" vision goes. John Gillis, "correct[ing] history's continental bias," diagnoses this mind-altering propensity "islomania."[117] Rhizomatic in nature, having neither boundaries nor center, the Arctic has both indulged and engendered "fancies," even as its areas have never been completely circumscribed, its puzzles pieced together, or its problems solved: it is an insular but never isolated world at risk in uncertain outline, and, in its unfinished composition, it stays a catalyst for experimental ways of environmental being, knowing, and doing.

Back to "the book": the worlding process in which the Zeni participate reveals the archipelago's propensity to story Arctics on the page in words as much as they illustrate them on the map in pictures. Its seas crispen characters; they invite (not stultify) tales. In her study of the "spatial, social, and material specifics" of Arctic disasters of the Victorian era, Adriana Craciun takes a "recursive" approach to accounts penned around John Franklin's 1845 expedition. Following Latour (via Michel de Certeau), she identifies "the complexity of interpretive and imaginative work within cycles of knowledge accumulation," a metanarrative she envisions as "a line of circles."[118] As it accrues knowledge in the present while also retroactively retracing the archives of the past, a given exploration moves forward in nonteleological space and time. By evaluating process over progress, we may glimpse the writing process physically at work while at sea: "Fictional and nonfictional voyages and their texts are promiscuously entangled in the model, where the cultural turn in history and the historicist turn in literature meet in the commons of the ocean."[119]

I want to linger on the transtemporal approach to the networked "commons" Craciun crucially lays out. Confronting the "epistemological delirium" that the "New Climatic Regime" generates on a daily basis, professes Latour, "is not a matter of learning how to repair cognitive deficiencies, but rather how to live in the same world, share the same culture, face up to the same stakes, perceive a landscape that can be explored in concert."[120] A concerted effort to plumb the public pools ("commons") labeled "Arctic" means looking for the nonhuman actors who challenge anthropocentric claims to the Circle by loosening humanity's authoritarian grip over its aqueous realms. If it is true that, "when you enter Arctic narrative, you enter every narrative of the Arctic ever written,"[121] to quote John Moss, the combined effort for which I am advocating becomes clearer on the basis of bibliography. Nonetheless, Craciun's remarks on the "archipelagic Arctic" of early modernity differ slightly from mine in that I seek to address the active role the oceanic environment plays in the Arctic Circle's spiraling "line" (lines) of stories, how it spins sagas across an ice-"field of dispersion" and a liquid "landscape of forking paths."[122] The Zeno brothers, indeed, obey a "fractal logic" inherent to the "archipelagic fluidity"[123] of the time, one that subtended and fueled a "culture of chaotic empiricism,"[124] a "culture" that I will wager is fed by archipelagic entities of northern seas no matter how spurious their reports may be. A material mixing that manifests in the imagination and pours onto maps—such messy matrices host ontological hybridity as well as harbor epistemological mishap, rendering the authorship of other worlds as a more-than-human endeavor.

Fractious encounters with the cold, calamitous or not, both compel the creativity necessary for world-making and resist the author's world-controlling urges. The presence of "uncolonizable" space,[125] whether provided on the map or insinuated at its margins, can also counter empiricist impulses that too often stem the flow of storying. Siobhan Carroll calls these spots "atopias: 'real' natural regions falling within the theoretical scope of contemporary human mobility, which, because of their intangibility, inhospitality, or inaccessibility, cannot be converted into the locations of affective habitation known as 'place.'"[126] Predictably, the random acts of *poiesis* that a fractured seascape occasioned were seldom seen as imperative to a country's imperialist agenda. When considering the "probabilitie of a passage" to the northwest in 1625, Samuel Purchas laments that "painters and poets are not alwayes the best oracles" before lambasting the "learned-unlearned Mariner and Mathematician"[127] William Baffin (1584[?]–1621), who had failed to produce a navigable route in the previous decade. Sir Dudley Digges (1582/3–1639), politician and shareholder in the Virginia Company and the East India Company, compounded this insult leveled at the untutored in his short treatise from 1611, *Of the Circumference of the Earth*: "*Geographye* depends on the reports of Trauellours (which Ptolomey calls *Historiam Peregrinationis*) and Trauellours be seldome *Mathematicians*, but Merchants, Saylours, Souldiers, men that may vse common Rules and Instruments, not subtilties of nice and curious practice."[128] (Paint and letters, we may assume, are not included in the list of acceptable "practices.") The mathematician Henry Briggs (1561–1630) wrote in 1616 that "Gerardus Mercator, a very industrious and excellent geographer, was abused by a map sent unto him, of four Euripi meeting about the North Pole."[129] All in all, "it is not our business to write or repeat Romances,"[130] an anonymous Arcticologist concluded in 1694.

We cannot blame the likes of Briggs for his desire to supply facts and correct faults (his meaning of "abused"), just as long as we do not give in to the myopias of Purchas and Digges that banish uneducated inquisitiveness. The realms of fact and mystery may productively coincide (even in our present "post-truth" moment) when we realize that what we know is grounded in institutions and produced by scientific practice. Others could be more hospitable: William Goodlad (ca. 1576–1639), an English whaler, wrote in 1623 that one Arctic journey transitioned into a kind of writing retreat along Spitsbergen's "uncouth Coast, whereto our English Neptunes are now so wonted, that there they have found not onely Venison but Pernassus and Helicon; and have melted a Musæan Fountain out of the Greenland Snowes and Icie Rockes. Whole Elaborate Poems have I seene of Master Heley, as also of James Presson, there composed: but we have harsher Discoveries in hand."[131] What vistas melted onto the pages of Heley and Presson? What coastal and "uncouth" world piqued their interests enough to give them pause, and greater still to poeticize? Perhaps that is the power of the Arctic font: a muse to "elaborate" upon, whose circumstances "nice" and "harsh" sponsor further speculation and "subtilties" waiting to be penned, put into "practice." An "arcticpelagic"[132] puzzle.

## The Arctic Is a Passage, Not a Destination

While the mythic qualities of the Northwest Passage and Northeast Passage summon plottable courses or emplaced things—traceable routes to be traversed and rare prizes, like a "grail,"[133] awaiting acquisition—the northern ocean was a passage (from the Latin verb *passus,* "pace") through which things multidirectionally passed, a trip that rejects teleological paths running from commencement to terminus: an Arctic "actor-network"[134] whereby things transition in transit. En route: "whales with English and Dutch Harping Irons in them" littering the Korean coast; Greenlandic driftwood nibbled by the tropical "Sea-Worm"; two walruses brought into England, where the male lived for ten weeks and "where they taught it many things"; two polar bear cubs who joined them there shortly thereafter, "no bigger than young Lambs, very gamesome and lusty."[135] Accidental discoveries of sea routes through the Arctic Ocean to Europe were widely known. In his 1625 *Pilgrimes,* Purchas printed Thomas Cowle's 1579 testimony concerning

Martin Chacke of Lisbon's successful navigation from the Portuguese East Indies to northwestern Ireland across the North American continent in 1567, separated from his company after being "driven . . . with a Westerly winde . . . through a gulfe of the New found land."[136] Hopes for finding this "fretum Anian" that set North America apart from Asia were emboldened shortly thereafter by the Greek pilot Juan de Fuca's 1596 discovery, as reported by the investor Michael Lok, of a strait just above California and Nova Spania that now bears his name.[137]

The most famous account, perhaps, is of "Indians" arriving on the shores of Roman France, set down by Pliny the Elder in his *Naturalis Historiae* (first century CE). Martyr repeats the account: "To sayle from India to Caliz by the other parte of the north by a clime and regions of extreme coulde, shulde bee doubtlesse a difficult and dangerous thynge, whereof is no memory amonge the owlde autours sauynge onely of one shyppe as Plinie and Mela doo wryte, rehersynge the testimony of Cornelius Nepos who affirmed that the kynge of Sueuia presented to Quintus Metellus Celer Lieuetenaunt of Fraunce, certeyne Indians dryuen by tempest into the sea of Germanie."[138] Something similar happened "in the days of the Emperoure Fredericus Barbarossa, [when] certeyne Indians were browght in a Canoa from the citie of Lubec."[139] Inadvertently or not (note the language of "driven," again, this time by a storm), Asiatic peoples were imagined to have completed a northerly route from east to west centuries before Chacke's achievement (or blusterous blunder) in the opposite direction.

Regardless of the above-mentioned mammals', plants', and pilots' historical veracity, the Arctic had been considered a passage linking disparate cultures for a millennium. Moreover, if Pliny's unverifiable account is taken at face value, Europe was actually the *first* "otherworld" met at the opposite side of the Arctic Ocean. To these "certeyne Indians," we may surmise, the German court represented the "New found land" before upper North America assumed the moniker of "New World" for Martyr's readers, prior to John Cabot's 1497 expedition under Henry VII to Newfoundland and Labrador, and even earlier than the eleventh-century Norse settlements in Vinland. Their accomplishment tested the patience of Europeans who wished to similarly pass years later. If "Indians" could manage a feat "difficult and dangerous," so could they. Dwelling on the "Indians . . . fortune" and the Portuguese success, for instance, the ambassador to Moscow, "restynge a whyle in maner astonysshed in his secreate phantasie, he toke great pleasure therin, and sayde . . . why shulde wee not certeinely thynke that the lyke maye bee done abowt this parte of the north withowt feare of coulde, especially to men borne and brought vp in that clime?"[140] In essence, the earlier encounter was held out with the promise of newer, more fortunate (fortune-filled) ones for those were climatically disposed to conquer. Few writers evince this logic better than the English captain Sir Humphrey Gilbert (1537–1583), whose *Discourse of a Discoverie for a New Passage to Cataia* (written 1566 and printed 1576) dedicates three of its ten chapters to the famous landing: "So that it plainly appeareth, that those Indians (which, as you have heard, in sundrie ages were driven by tempest, upon the shore of Germanic) came onely through our Northwest passage."[141] "Our" is arresting: the seeds of Arctic colonialism were no "phantasie"; the arduous passage across the ocean and (they hoped) beyond it could be possessed and protected, its original inhabitants, if necessary, kidnapped or expunged.

If my reinterpretation of the far-northern Atlantic Ocean as "passage" evokes the Middle Passage of the succeeding centuries' slave trade, I do so on purpose. Where hierarchies of race, gender, and ethnicity enter the passage, the intersectional flows are restricted. The "other" who lived in "other worlds," in short, could too easily be used as a pejorative accusation and a pernicious instantiation of difference. Review the mottoes of The Company of the Merchants Discoverers of the Northwest Passage (chartered 1612): "*juuat ire per altum*" ("he delights to go on the deep") and "*tibj seruiat ultima Thule*" ("the uttermost Thule shall serve thee").[142] Or one of the "motiues Inducing a Proiect" (presumably enumerated by Digges) that configure "the North pole terrestriall a Magnificent and pure Virgine yet vndiscouered."[143] For whom does the Arctic serve and whom does it delight? Regimes of power protect the Arctic actor-network, but only for some passengers. Enslavement had always been a lucrative option since the earliest expeditions. Portuguese captain Gaspar Corte-Real (1450–1501), who had reached "Terra Verde" in 1500, sent home "seven natives, men and women and children" the year after, "and in the other caravel, which is expected from hour to hour are coming fifty others."[144] As I insinuated earlier with "certeyne" East Asian visitors, the Arctic is not the "other" world to Indigenous others (warmer Europe provided that), but a home. What Jace Weaver calls the "red Atlantic,"[145] then, certainly applies to its polar waters. Confronting this masculinist obsession with obsequious, "virginal" hues that persists to this day—roving the premodern to the modern passage of time[146]—demands returning to the early modern experiences of Indigenous peoples of color.[147]

A public desire for novel forms of amusement helped ensure that others' oceans became "ours." Published portraits of the Inuit date as far back as 1567, the year when a woman and child were put on display in Augsburg. (I will return to them at book's end.) The first Inuk transported under English command came from Frobisher's forays into Baffin Island (Nunavut). A man ("Calichough"), woman ("Ignorth"), and child ("Nutiok") from his second voyage of 1577 were famously painted by John White (fl. 1577–1593). (All three soon died of disease.) James Hall, who sailed for Christian IV of Denmark three times from 1605 to 1607, was sent to reestablish contact with the old Norse colonies of Greenland (which had been lost, unbeknownst to the king, in the fifteenth century). His captain, John Cunningham, seized three Inuit in 1605, which he "vsed with all kindnesse"[148] on the *Trost.* Captain Godske Lindenow of the *Røde Løve* took two. The following year, Lindenow, now in command, took five more "with their Boates, and stowed them in our ships, to bring them into *Denmarke,* to enforme our selues better, by their meenes, of the state of their Countrie of *Groineland.*"[149] One of these kayaks currently resides at the Schiffer-Gesellschaft in Lubeck.[150] And on Hall's own voyage of 1612, Andrew Barker seized a man whose kayak is now showcased at the Trinity House in Hull.[151] Magnus noticed two kayaks from Greenland in an Oslo cathedral (which were used to bore holes into enemies' ships, he deduced).[152] These souvenirs of boats and human beings render the boreal seas as sites of controlled curiosity, its strangers carefully curated and their lives crafted in objectified ways that reinforce northern European hegemony. The two captives Lindenow took in 1605 exemplify the consequences of becoming better "enformed," as the Danish diplomat and editor of the excursion, C. C. A. Gosch contends: he "succeeded in taming them to some extent, and taught them to run about the ship in obedience to signs from him."[153] Domesticated wonders: the pool of the unknown becomes a display case, the whirlpool is put to rest, its story told, its bestial citizens made tractable.

Tasked with finding old worlds anew, at least in Denmark's case, the voyage from east to west incurs an oceanic time travel as the past (old/Old) is brought into the present (new/New). But who was "bettered" by the European–Inuit exchange, as we just observed, was too often lopsided in the former's favor. Nonetheless, they were startling possibilities for seeing the "other" in/as the "self" in the other worlds of the Arctic, and, in so doing, checking the colonial logic that depends on situating these spheres of identification as utterly separate. The circles may conjoin "better." Misrecognition, even if immediately disavowed, is one instance of Arctic anxiety of fungible difference. According to Robert Fabyan's 1516 *Chronicle*, three men from Newfoundland were brought to England in 1501–1502, probably its capital's first Indigenous visitors: "I sawe ij of theym apparaylyd afftyr Inglysh men In westmynstyr paleys, which at that tyme I cowde not dyscern ffrom Inglysh men."[154] Being able to "dyscern" is essential, of course, to the process of essentializing otherness: becoming the "other" of the "other world" must be avoided. The gaze, too, could reverse and work on English and not just Inuit identity. In his catastrophic quest for the Northwest Passage through Hudson Bay in 1619–1620 (published in Danish in 1624) in which sixty-three of his sixty-five-member crew perished, Jens Munk (1579–1628) notes that one of his men, "who had very swarthy complexion, and black hair" is mistaken by the Inuit as "one of their nation and countrymen," and is embraced, incredibly, because of it.[155]

Attempts at mutual "enforme-ing" did exist, at least on the surface. In 1617, before Spitsbergen was deemed valuable for its seas of whale oil, the Muscovy Company (chartered 1555), unable to make reliably profitable inroads in the area, conjured up a co-colonizing enterprise that included the Indigenous peoples of Russia. Sir John Merrick, ambassador to the czar, was granted a license "for certaine of his subiects called Lappes [Sámi], a people lyveinge in a very cold clymate and a barraine soyle" to dwell with the English there.[156] While miscegenetic aspirations like these could always be stymied by the language barrier, what often hindered the remapping of kinships were southern governments' desires to commercially exploit septentrional worlds. Those aforementioned five Inuit brought to Copenhagen in 1605, for example, were abducted so that "friendly relations [may] be permanently established"[157] between communities—imprisoned ambassadors urged (ironically) to make a deal for peace.

A few cracks can be discerned in this dichotomous logic, however, moments when the icy other/sea/world conjoins with your own in less segregated, more intersectional, terms. Strong winds carried penetrating cold as well as Inuit visitors southeastward to European shores. Reverend James Wallace sighted Inuit kayakers in Orkney two separate times (1682 and 1684), and one person supposedly made it to the mouth of the River Don near Aberdeen around 1700.[158] Consider the activity of "Calichough," Frobisher's detainee, on the River Avon: the chronicler William Adams writes that, on October 9, 1577, "he rode in a little bote made of skinne in the water at the backe, where he killed 2 duckes with a dart, and when he had done carried his bote through the marsh upon his back. The like he did at the weare and other places, where many beheld him."[159] For the Bristolian onlookers in attendance, "Calichough" kayaking on the Avon at their mayor's delight bends into spectacle, providing a local artist with an image that would become a template for illustrating Inuit life (and which adorned the narrative account of his captor). Would any have noticed, in his relative ease of hunting and transition from one waterway ("backe") to another ("marshe"), the man's almost uncanny familiarity with their own local "places"? If so, the distant and formerly distantiated bays of Frobisher and Bristol transpose onto one another. What happens when the Arctic turns out to be in your own "backe"-yard? We cannot be certain; we can only speculate, for he and "Ignorth" died "within a month."[160]

The Danish annals are less laconic. The two "natives" Lindenow "trained" in 1605 performed for the Danish king and queen after the *Røde Løve* entered Copenhagen. According to C. C. Lyschander's 1608 *Den Gronlandske Chronica,* he "made the Greenlanders show their prowess in propelling their *kayaks,* on which occasion they held their own in a race against a boat of sixteen oars."[161] Cunningham's three also managed to join in to outpace the Danes. The Spanish ambassador, who had just happened to arrive, was especially taken aback: "Three of them, in their boats, performed a kind of dance, cutting figures with their *kayaks* in a wonderful manner,"[162] after which he rewarded them handsomely with money and the fashions of a Danish gentleman (feathers, swords, and spurs). Peyrère's relation is a bit more startling; as with their kinsmen who kayaked the Avon, he sees more than merely wonder here. He caps a lengthy description of the kayak's composition and proportions with hypnotic prose: "They crossed and interlaced with each other with such rapidity, that the eye grew quote confused with looking; and so skillfully was it done, that not one of them touched each other."[163] Noting, perhaps, the dangers of "confusion" and the inability to discern the strange from the familiar, they are festooned in a mocking manner and "marched up to the Castle 'like Greenland Grandees.'"[164] The king was so impressed that he ordered a two-man kayak constructed "on the Greenland pattern."[165]

Regardless of these political tokens of appreciation and attempts at recreational assimilation or appropriation, not everything is right in the state of Denmark: the kayakers, most obviously, are still confined. Thus, in the spring of 1606, some of them tried to escape, reaching as far as "Skaane" (Skåneland, or the southern Scandinavian peninsula) before they were apprehended "by the peasants."[166] For Gosch, the flight of the Inuit "runaways" spelled the beginning of the end of the Danish strategy of reintroduction in order to smooth over any hostile retaliations: "None of the captives returning could not but be very prejudicial to the intercourse between the expedition and the natives."[167] Several of these hopeful intermediaries died on the second voyage that embarked that year, and the third voyage in 1607 (if any were aboard) never reached its destination. Denmark was a literal prison for these Inuit inmates, their oceanic passage a one-way trip terminating in death, but not before their outlandish habits can bemuse others. The "dance" is scripted; the actors' "choreography" set for diplomatic means. They may become European nobility ("grandees"), but only for play.

Although written almost fifty years later and criticized for its speciousness, Peyrère's account adds significant emotional details to the fugitives' plight. Seeing from the other's perspective has the power, he proves, to meld supposedly antithetical worlds. Those who fled in 1606 "often looked towards the north, and sighed with so much regret after their own country that their guards, being lenient, those who could seized their little boats and oars and put out to sea to try the passage."[168] The Inuit solicit actual sympathy from their caretakers. Gosch is taciturn about their fate; for Peyrère, however, those who made the attempt died of illness brought on by their further loss of "liberty." (The exact number is unclear here, as is so often the case when comparing various accounts. Presumably, the four abductees who survived Hall's return trip enlarged the group.) After their costumed parade to the castle, moreover—Peyrère places the initial escape before the ambassadors' arrival—two of those on the foiled mission of 1606 "who were less suspected than the others, because it seemed unlikely that they would expose themselves a second time to the perils they had encountered, seized their boats and succeeded in regaining the north."[169] Their motives were clear: after their pageant was over, "they relapsed into their usual melancholy; . . . they thought of nothing but how they might return to Greenland."[170]

To "try the passage" is an indefatigable feat. To "regain" the north is an endless enterprise, a passage that exists just out of reach. Peyrère allows us to see their north receding before them from their Danish cell. One "escaped, or, rather, was lost[,] for it does not seem probable that he ever could have arrived in Greenland."[171] The other is recaptured. For this man now thrice abducted, the sight of children and their mothers or nurses causes him to "burst into tears,"[172] because, his jailors rightly infer, he aches for his faraway family. Being guarded "still more strictly than before" simultaneously squashes and stimulates his and his remaining peers' hopes for free passage, "only increase[s] their desire of returning to their country, and their despair of ever doing so."[173] Almost all, save two, die of this "regret."[174] Each of them lives about ten years: the first, recruited as a pearl diver in Kolding on the Jutland peninsula, succumbs to exposure after he is forced to go "under the water like a dog"[175] in winter. The second takes flight, and it unsure whether it is the same sorrowful individual from earlier (which would then mark his third try). In any case, he swiftly made it approximately thirty of forty leagues out of the sound and into the open ocean (an astonishing 100–130 miles). Once they overtake him, his pursuers "make him understand by signs that he would never have known where to find Greenland, and that undoubtedly the waves would have swallowed him up."[176]

To the Danes, the hydrographical distance between oceans proved the best way to suppress Inuit "desires" for going. Hence the improbability of the "lost" man's return: their ignorant internees' lack of mappable knowledge epistemologically shackled them. The boat race will eventually be won if your opponent has superior speed but no sense of direction. Yet this man surprisingly responds with a cosmography of his own: "He answered by signs, that he should have followed the coast of Norway to a certain point, whence he would have crossed, and have been guided by the stars to his country."[177] The chasers might have been chastened; a retort, tragically, is not given. The man sickens and dies back in Copenhagen soon after. Peyrère's sympathy, one could say, goes only so far: sometimes naming these Indigenous passengers "unhappy Greenlanders," he primarily names them "savages," and while not outright condemning his fellow Europeans' behaviors, he is keen on exonerating them, demonstrating that "the Danes did all in their power to keep them [the last two] alive, and gave them understanding that they would be treated like their friends and fellow-countrymen."[178] Ineffective conversion to Christianity proves an impediment. But the possibilities of a mesmerizing fusion are perceivable, like Peyrère's "confused" eyeball-absorbing "patterns" of global–local, Inuit–Danish interweave. He might be reluctant to fuse diametrically opposed worlds too closely, but his enthralled attention invites the imagination to wander into other, potentially "touching" passages. Much hangs on the ambivalent "or" of the "lost" kayaker. What unsegmented horizons did those paddlers espy, slipping farther away from Copenhagen with every stroke, and what shores might the one who "escaped" have possibly attained? What sea did the pearl fisher of Kolding contact when he dove, over a decade, for a foreign government's bidding, and could he have felt the waters of the far north as he plunged?

## The Arctic Is for Visionaries

"The problem of London's Indigenous history," Coll Thrush insists, "is an enforced silence, not the hidden-ness of past events."[179] The same might be said for Copenhagen and elsewhere. Their strains are apparent: some make the passage back, while others do not; some are afforded the choice to partake in "islomania," others' efforts at percolation are policed. Such stories of guarded filtration to-and-fro do not require exposure, only greater attention. "It is not an act of discovery; rather it is an act of *re*covery, of acknowledging the deep entanglements of London's places, people, and histories with Indigenous places, people, and histories, and vice versa."[180] The enmeshment of urban with Indigenous histories creates "domains of entanglement,"[181] in his words, and they also provoke opportunities for ecological thought by widening the scope of ensnarement. A seventeenth-century Inuit spear point was found on the same Thames riverbank where frost fairs were once held.[182] Pondering these transoceanic moments allows us to escape the traps of competition ("uttermost"), condescension ("serve"), and ownership ("thee"), terms championed by the first merchant companies that have hampered conceptions of Arctic sovereignty. Kalaallit Nunaat

(Greenland) fights for increased autonomy (or separation) from the Danish monarchy to this day.[183]

We may "try" to make "the passage" freer and more negotiable[184] by learning from these worlds that *were* and facing the worlds *to be.* As binaries regarding both difference (self and other) and distance (north and south) disintegrate, the burdens borne unequally by affected cultures, however, do not simply disappear.[185] When Watt-Cloutier argues that "our home is a barometer for what is happening to our entire planet," she means that "the future of the Inuit is the future of the rest of the world."[186] But facing the populous Arctic need not pertain solely to people, she explains: "It refers to the circumpolar environment, the Arctic land and the way of life that depends on ice and snow."[187] The Arctic is one of "the best oracles," to borrow from Purchas, for predicting the planet's fate, and for Watt-Cloutier, recognizing the overlay of worlds (the result of which is causing the archipelago's rapid unraveling due to rising temperatures) proves that "fundamental change is not just sound policy but also an *ethical* imperative."[188] Far from framing groups like the Inuit Circumpolar Council (ICC) as hapless victims of corporate whims, the message is meant to be politically empowering on a universal scale: "We all have the right to be protected from climate change."[189] For Craciun, too, the predication is dire and the realities are disastrous, but it is precisely because of the future's uncertainty that rights-based policies are required: "The ethos of the unknown is worth preserving."[190]

And yet, the question of how we are to make the world common again remains the same. Preempting this dis/comforting pronouncement by several centuries, and not reluctant to liken his quest across Hudson Bay in the summer of 1631 to an old wives' tale, Luke Foxe's introduction to his 1635 *North-West Fox* compares the interminable, because undiscoverable, stretch of the Passage to the endless, because accretional, passages of story: "But for that the most desire to know what I have done, and how farre I have bin, I answer, as the Old women tells tales, *Further and further than I can tell.*"[191] I have hitherto argued that the Arctic Circle was a foreseeable horizon for some early modern icy ocean-goers. The far northern "horizon"—from the Greek *horizōn* (*kuklos*), "limiting (circle)"—certainly delimited their world. But I have also argued that the Circle expanded, spiraled, and spun for others. From pivoting portals (Peyrère) to maelstroms on maps (Mercator), and from literary circles (the Zeni) to the near-circular returns of Indigenous peoples (Inuit kayakers), these configurations of a veering and vibrant Circle help us reconceptualize the Arctic as a populated, unmappable place, a sea of inhabited and inscrutable ice islands that challenge cryopolitical strategies that assume the opposite (as trackless wasteland, as indefinitely understood, as continentally bound). Ultima Thule is ultimately unknowable, and so it is infinitely storying. Two songs for a winter's night will wind up this chapter and send us *fair*-wards to the next.

The poet Richard Niccols (1583/4–1616) added "A Winter Nights Vision" to his 1610 edition of the widely read *Mirour for Magistrates.* In it, the writer in winter, affected by the season's characteristic inflictions ("My limbes benumb'd with unkind cold, my life bloodwaxing chill"), decides to stretch his legs to warm up: "As was my wont I walked forth to ease me of such ill."[192] What he happens upon is a veritable wasteland: "Nought else upon the grasselesse ground, but winters waste was seene."[193] Winterscapes are deserted in a dual sense: as "waste," they are "unoccupied, uncultivated" (from the Latin *vastus*); they also make deserted, lay waste to the land. Spirits sink like roots out here, providing a lesson in mutability: "All which, as I grieu'd at such sight, the fields alone did range, / Did teach me know all things on earth were subject unto change."[194] The surrounding decay depressingly probes him into thinking of what else (if anything) truly lasts: "In things on earth of most auaile assurance there was none."[195] It is an assuredly melancholic reflection, fitting for a wanderer communing with cold and dry soil. Niccols cannot stop meditating on the morbid thought: "When home I came, nipt with sharpe cold of Boreas bitter aire, / After repast to my warme bed forthwith I made repaire, / Where, for the nights were tedious growen, and I disturb'd in mind / With thoughts of that daies obiect seene, not unto sleepe inclin'd."[196] Winter is in his head, and it works upon his imagination: both the vision (the "obiect" he saw) and the *Vision,* the "obiect" he produced from the recollection of that "daies" experience. The vision, according to him, is the "dreame" he had *after* finally falling asleep. The muses of "Memory" and "Fame" round out the section by supplying him with a thorough English history lesson beginning with King Arthur and ending with Richard III. The "vision" is unsurprisingly exemplary for a historian. The manifest content, we might say, is to remember that kingdoms come and go (decay), and yet, within this unavoidable fact of fickle nature, as with the changing of the seasons, greener reigns cheerily grow. On a latent level, manipulating his grand narrative quietly underneath the surface, however, are those "bitter aires" of winter that propelled his transhistorical thought process. The cold collapse of vision–*Vision* escapes him at moments, but the subliminal messaging, for us at least, is noticeable.

James Howell (1594[?]–1666), another historian, understood such influence consciously in *A Winter Dreame* (1648) of his own. He thought himself sufficiently girded against the incursions of "Boreas," comparing his five senses to a confederation of shut-in English harbors: "It was in the dead of a long Winter night," he begins, "when no eyes were open but Watchmen, and Centinell's, that I was fallen soundly asleep, the Cinq out-Ports were shut up closer [than] usually, and my sences so treble lock'd."[197] Despite feeling insensible, winter's "sharpe"-ness proves pervasive: "Though the Cousin german of Death [winter] had so strongly seiz'd thus upon the exterior parts of this poore Tabernacle of flesh, my inward were never more actif, and fuller of employments [than] they were that night."[198] While cognizant of its outward infiltration (skin's seizure), Howell seems loathe to suggest an inner breach. (If so, according to his logic, the mind-numbing cold would render his thoughts, and hence his legible memoir, in-"actif"). As someone who saw himself as a moderate during the English Civil War (1642–1651), and who penned his *Dreame* from imprisonment, the resulting story is a Faustian flight to various European countries in order to evaluate their political conditions. His final stop, "a large Island"[199] (England), allows him to remark on the contemporary strife between royalists and roundheads. "Among other things that strangers report of this Iland," he complains to a "reverend Bishop," "they say that Winter here hath too many teares in his eyes,"[200] a direct comment on the lachrymose state of affairs, as well as an image of the weepiness that winter winds induce. One's eyes, in other words, are "open" even while ostensibly closed. The transgression of bodily boundaries turns "shut up" ports (pores, sockets) into portals. Yet this permeation remains rigidly allegorical, an image of parliamentary factions "lock'd" in combat; it sponsors a dream of northern and southern worlds at war: "Out of the North / All ill comes forth."[201] Howell not only appropriates the "old saying"[202] of the evil "north" for his own political purposes (here, in censure of

Scotland's role in island affairs): he robs its material content by reducing its powers (virtues) to a pretty (virtuous) moral.

Ironically, the adage admits to an act of environmental entry that Howell himself is unwilling to accept. Of the four types of dreams he identifies—"divine, diabolicall, naturall, or humane"[203]—he believes the *Dreame* to be a result of the last kind, "relat[ive] to the actions of the day past."[204] An analyst better attuned to the emotive and somatic imprints of winter would challenge his self-diagnosis, though, for the "naturall" sort owe their genesis to "the humor which predominates" inside the body, so that "if Melancholy sway, we dream of black darksom devious places."[205] To envision the words "woe be to the bloody City"[206] hovering over an oneiric London arguably bespeaks such "sway." The dream and *Dreame* are eager, nonetheless, to capitalize on their cold, irrepressible content. Howell's penultimate paragraph boasts that, despite his incarceration, his nocturnal reverie has traveled farther than Sir John Mandeville (fl. 1357) and Thomas Coryate (ca. 1577–1617), two legendary peregrinators: proudly "you see what nimble Postillions the Animal Spirits are; and with what incredible celerity the imagination can crosse the Line, cut the Tropiques, and passe to the other Hemisphere of the world; which shewes that humane soules . . . have a kind of ubiquitary freedom, though the body be never so under restraint, as the Authors is."[207] What a poignant dream Howell had: one of liberty in the depths of a "darksom" place of season and cell; and yet, as a dream, it prefers a form of movement that fancifully leaves winter behind, even as he suggests that it is a period in which a northern climate can, and does "cut" latitudinal lines, "passe" into cellular structures with "Animal . . . celerity," and sprint the author's imagination a-"crosse" compositional worlds. His take on "freedom" divulges a "white way of thinking"[208] to boot, for unfettered Arctic passage, as the historical evidence shows (be it by body, soul, mind, or all three) has been far from "ubiquitary."

In the end, both Niccols and Howell are reluctant winterers. But to shun winter's "sharpe"-ness or meditate at length upon its "waste" are just two responses. Following their dream-visions fosters a different style of dreaming: one that abandons the Pole of singular transmission, brought to you by an oceanic "other" world ontologically opposite from your own. Mutability sparks an impulse to portray alternate pictures; to limn pools around a portable pole; to question how (and whose) stories are put in motion or are immobilized; to try to speak a different "language of future Arctic opportunism," in Craciun's words, telling legacies other than those we have inherited, thereby revealing how those prevailing narratives were historically constructed and their contingencies subsequently forgotten. "The more carefully we consider earlier cultures of exploration, the more unpredictable become our histories of Arctic exploration."[209] I would also add, for our consideration, *futures*. Appropriating the biogeographical term "Nearctic" (the realm that covers most of North America), this chapter constitutes my own attempt at articulating additional "Nearctics" (from *neo-*, "new") in order to provide *further* and *further* opportunities for others to *tell*.[210] As uncertain and imperfect cartography urges our imaginations onward, it is my hope that it furthers arcticpelagic communities as well. I have come this "farre" for now: the Arctic is a portal that spins, a passage in which worlds are imagined and their stories exchanged. *Further,* it importantly reminds us that, just as no world can be fully known, neither can its fate be truly determined.

# Winterlude

## *Ask*

What if we motivated change not through fear and loss, but through beauty and possibility? Through mutual transformation?

—M Jackson, *The Secret Lives of Glaciers*

It gives me goosebumps every time: Shakespeare's King Lear, "bareheaded" (*King Lear,* 3.2.60),[1] spent after railing against the storm, is enjoined by Kent to enter a "hovel." His "wits" have started to "turn" (3.2.67). He faces his Fool on the heath: "come on, my boy. How dost, my boy? Art cold? / I am cold myself" (3.2.68–69). It is a simple question, perhaps, and easily missed. Maybe it is even a little startling, coming from a hot-headed "dragon" (1.1.119) of a monarch, as if the "realm of Albion" has reached rare sympathy (3.2.91). But let us sit with this phrase for a spell before moving inside, contra Kent's command, for within its casual tone are insights into cold's remarkable social powers.

The mutual sensation of cold draws the "boy" and the king closer by operating at the ontological level, not just phenomenological: "I am cold myself." What physically constitutes cold is not fully known, or where it geographically comes from, but it nonetheless becomes a tangible part of the "self." Not to be dismissed, it tenderly illustrates a triangulation: "I am cold," you "art cold," and therefore I *am* like *you.* I *am* cold and I *feel* cold collapse, and deepen, in this weather-dependent moment. The "I am" is a becoming, a getting cold(er), a shifting marker of a physiological continuum of bodies, environment, and selves. As such, it is a prelude to Lear's grander sentiment in 3.4, where the cold pushes him to imagine "poor naked wretches, wheresoe'er you are, / That bide the pelting of this pitiless storm" with their "houseless heads and unfed sides," assaulted by "seasons such as these" (3.4.29–33). Cold on kingly skin scales up: from a home (hovel), to the homeless (*oikos*), and on to the weather. It causes him to deliver another fulmination, famously against pride: "Take physic, pomp; / Expose thyself to feel what wretches feel, / That thou mayest shake the superflux to them / And show the heavens more just" (3.4.34–37). Now, higher up, he has entered the ethereal space of un/godly "justice." Exposure to the cold, at its core, acts as a connector, for "to feel" it is to feel the suffering of others, level classes, and call the "superflux" of "pomp" and its privilege into question. It is a political catalyst, a sympathetic forger at work in mythical northern Britain. It leads to talk of shelter and "straw." It opens, not contracts: "I have one part in my heart / That's sorry yet for thee" (3.2.73).

"*Tom's a-cold.*" Lear's cold conversion is tested immediately after his rant on the "just" by the entrance of "poor" Edgar from within the place of supposed refuge, all "a-cold" (3.4.55), a phrase repeated four times in their exchange, in chattering rhythm (76, 132, 158), punctuating the 170-line scene with snapping consistency. "Cold" is mentioned fifteen times in *King Lear,* the most of any play in Shakespeare's oeuvre, and eight of those are compressed in scene 4 of act III. His first lines are about insecurity: "Away, the foul fiend follows me! / Through the sharp hawthorn blows the cold wind. Go to thy cold bed and / warm thee" (3.4.45).[2] Edgar, more so than Lear, has visions of warmth on his mind. Remaining outside, Lear seizes this opportunity to make a friend, utilizes the informal "thou" reserved for intimate occasions: "Thou wert better in a grave than to answer thy / uncovered body this extremity of the skies. Is man no more than this? . . . Thou art the thing itself" (3.4.93–94).

Confronted by an actual "wretch" he had just conjured up in his lofty speech, Tom's cold inspires him to flatten human stations once again, but this time to go even further to the stripped-down position of "thing"-hood. Lear's thoughts have grown ontologically wider than just two scenes before; he transgresses species lines as well as class divides, prioritizing the lifestyle of unadorned "man" over the "worm" with its "silk," the "beast" with its "hide," the "sheep" with its "wool," and the "cat" with its "perfume" (3.4.94–95). If cold touches us all, he realizes, then some of us are "un"-"covered" differently—and for him, the more denuded, the more desirable. "Unaccommodated man is no more but such a poor, / bare, forked animal as thou art" (3.4.97–98). With an "off, / off, you lendings" (3.4.98–99), he can claim he has felt the cold, like Tom, a "bare . . . animal." Cold compels us to peel back both the layers of regality and humanity. Paradoxically, in doing so, the "I" becomes "more than"; it joins in a multispecies collective of sky-bound things, rather than reduces "man" to "nothing."[3] To accommodate, one must first un-accommodate. Has it come to "confusion" (3.2.91)? Indeed, in its commingling sense.[4] His Fool once counseled him: "Thou / canst not smile as the wind sits, thou'lt catch cold shortly" (1.4.91–2). Exposure itself is taken to "extremity." Lear wants to be as close to the cold as possible, to be caught, willingly, in cold chains of being and bonding. He has gone, in a word, elemental.

Or at least he thinks he has: he is not fully "unbuttoned" (3.4.99) yet. Part of the play's tragedy is that it holds out this promise of cold as an empathetic aggregator, only to trap itself in the difficulties that arise. Praising the pluck of the "poor, bare, [and] forked," of course, is not the same as alleviating the "bare" conditions of a "life" that is "a-cold" in front of you. Lear's "undressing" risks portraying a cosplay of the unfortunate. It can be a step to acknowledging, if not understanding, the real lives inside and outside of the theater, and here it is important to remember the real-life evocations of "Poor Tom" in a bitterly cold seventeenth-century England. As Simon Palfrey writes in his book-long study of the character, they, "also called 'Abraham-men' [named after the ward in London's psychiatric hospital] thronged the countryside, announcing themselves by their whoop and holler and alarming stare, a byword for reviled fraudulence."[5] The cold cry might have fallen on unsympathetic ears, or on listeners already attuned to the subject matter, immured, the talk of hawthorns "probably a floating quotation from a popular ballad."[6] So too does the language of "wretches" sit uncomfortably aside emetic "flux," and above all, the patronizing language of lowering one's mighty stature to another's debased station—"myself" to "the thing itself"—be it human or nonhuman. Or of dehumanizing the impoverished by equating them with un-boarded beasts. The horizontal grates against the vertical. His response may also be tied with attempts at shoring up "natural" human sovereignty-superiority over animals, the "poor, bare, forked" creatures who were not as vulnerable to the cold and thereby a source of anxiety, envy, or both.[7] Hierarchies, in short, find a way in. Nude Lear's later diatribe against clothing, "against robes and furred gowns" (4.6.159) as stand-ins for his daughters, is coded with misogyny. The mad emperor is eventually enrobed, re-ennobled.

And yet, as Palfrey also points out, "Tom speaks the poor creature of earth. . . . Feel the flesh quiver from the cold. . . . The weather is alive. Place feels."[8] The scene absolutely shudders. "Art cold?" is a question that takes Lear a while to warm up to; for us, it provokes more questioning, richer asking. American poet Randall Jarrell (1914–1965) poses it, Lear-like, in "90 North": "the world—my world spins on this final point / Of cold and wretchedness: all lines, all winds / End in this whirlpool I at last discover / . . . nothing comes from nothing."[9] As cold art, the play exposes the difficulties of connecting via vulnerability and underscores its impasses and potentialities. While there is no single way for signing these social contracts,[10] and no single answer to holes in security (of fuel, "hovel" walls, and pores), it shows how there will always be an urge, a need, for doing *something* when we are feeling and being "a-cold."

# 3 Slippery Things

> "Those things," she said once, interrupting our awkward chat while we sat politely in her living room, standing up suddenly apropos of nothing and opening her front door so we could see that one of the bergs was indeed approaching. When she sat back down she said, "Life in a polynia, eh?" She smiled, watching our reaction to the word.
>
> —China Miéville, "Polynia"

> The World, and the pleasures it brings,
> Are made up of brittle and slippery things.
>
> —Anonymous, *Blanket-Fair*

In a letter dated February 9, 1684, Richard Freebody wrote to his cousin about the "Islands of Ice" that had arrived at Lydd, Kent, on the southeastern coast of England.[1] From the top of a steeple, he espied several out at sea, and one "many miles long."[2] The next day, balancing himself with a boat hook, he bravely walked off shore for the length of "2 rods" (roughly eleven yards).[3] A friend named Thomas Smith guessed there was "3 faddom" (about eighteen feet) of water beneath him.[4] Poking at the cracks in the flakes, and gauging at the bergs' hidden girth below, Freebody boasted that he might have gone farther out with a fuller tide—perhaps "a mile."[5] Their span is stunning: "it seemed to be at least 3 leagues [approximately ten miles] in length; . . . it was as far as I could see from East to West, and 'tis verily believed was the same from Dover to Lands End."[6] Another observer named "old Quick" told him that the ice visitors came from the east about a fortnight prior; as the tide fell, they commenced their journey westward, prevented from turning around by the wind. Standing on his little archipelago for almost two hours, Freebody walked, then ran, on the water: "When the wind and tide went together, . . . all the ice moved as fast as I could ride foot pace along by the side of it," at which point he "judged it must come from Holland or other eastern parts, which by reason of a continued easterly wind was brought this way."[7] The ice had therefore emigrated from Europe. Freebody's conclusion, humorous as it is, was a reasonable guess. The icy immigrants he met at his side of the English Channel were more likely blown south into the North Sea by a norther- or northwesterly wind out of the Arctic.

Still, such eyewitness accounts of strange encounters indicate the public's growing interest in the winds and currents of ocean climates. (And they are helpful for climate historians' reconstructions.) Freebody is a prototype of today's citizen scientist, passing along firsthand data, probing into fissures, eyeballing measurements, surfing the rimy skein. Rather than marking his account as simply wrong (or incorrectly "pitch'd upon," borrowing Robert Boyle's term and echoing his concern from chapter 1), I propose that his polar tale is useful in another way: it underscores how any appearance of ice, be it walkable or un/welcome, may stymie discourses of human dominion, spur on curiosities and desires, and cultivate neighborliness with non/human others. Channel-crossing icebergs act as letters, too, read on arrival by watchful coastguards, decoded for the meanings they must contain. But as material middles of solid and slush, they are carriers that ferry mystery as much as they inspire communication. More than mere mechanical transports for human correspondence, icebergs permit correspondence of unsure duration, keeping and secreting their secrets at once. Freebody jots down a message he believes he has decrypted from foreign matter dotting the English seacoast, messengers who will have melted by the time the letter reaches his cousin's hand: "Holland is here." Yet somehow we manage to amble buoyantly, if briefly, beside him. A vanished vessel arrives (yet again) centuries later, this time to far-distant shores, farther than what Freebody perceived to be "Lands End"—our own. Chattery tête-à-têtes extant in ephemerality only, the unanchored "islands" of Lydd transmit an elemental philosophy that finds its way to us. To study ice of the past is to open a line of communication across times, channels (or Channel), and directions (from west to east).

## Cold (at) Play

Freebody's story promotes ways of viewing city life as encrusted with polar spheres. The previous chapter explored the vortical, vibrant places from which cold came, and it examined the crossings that its variegated populations made (some by force) through unfolding "northscapes" whose hard, hemispherical borders were starting to fade. As I have suggested, early modern natural philosophers who inhabited the Little Ice Age were adept at overlaying insular, continental, and oceanic spaces, balling up disparate geographies into a burgeoning "frozen zone." Descartes's maxim that "the north wind is cold because it brings with it toward the south the very fine material that was in the north, on which cold primarily depends"[8] highlights the Arctic's sweeping mobility at this time, yet it also speaks directly to cold's ingressive and transgressive reach, the kind that stopped-up Raphael Thorius's nose. I want to push his statement from the *Meteorology* further: what actually happens when cold from "the north" arrives at one's "southern" home? Writers understood that winter is not just coming *at* you; winter's cold, in fact, constituted a part of themselves.

This chapter magnifies the "very fine" incoming "material" of "the north" in order to investigate what cold did once it entered into the body politic of seventeenth-century London. As the poet John Taylor penned it in 1621, it "conglutinated" with the entire metropolis.[9] What follows focuses on the pains, pleasures, and policies of gluing together. The Little Ice Age (LIA) pinpoints polar–subpolar criss-crossings from which to learn. Looking at life and death in the depths of extreme winters is informative precisely because of the attention they call to temporal messiness (in and out of season) and embodied endurance (intemperate survivance). As geographer Rudolf Brázdil (and colleagues) phrases it in his outlook on the "state" of European historical climatology, "by documenting the responses of past societes [*sic*] to perceptions and realities of climate change, useful strategies may be discovered for improving the ability of present-day innovative networks to deal with this issue."[10] My wintry stroll wends like so, unlocking said "strategies" by speaking of its cold:

- Little or not, an ice age is labile. In dialogue with recent studies in environmental history devoted to the LIA, I consider the ways early modern Londoners perceived, and engaged, the changing climate. The "cryo-history"[11] that appears below, in fact, fuels some of the field's most vigorous debates: such as a healthy skepticism over the *longue durée,* "climatic determinism," and reductive understandings of cause and effect.[12] Whether budding meteorologists dubbed their country's cooling "climate change" is less salient for me, as I have already admitted, than how human societies imagined their imbrication with changing weather inside their sloping section of the globe they called "climate." Reconstructing climate patterns in the past from records made without the benefit of modern instrumentation and standardized measurements is a Herculean task, if not impossible. Nevertheless, historical climatologists have turned to a vast array of "human" and "natural" archives to piece together accurate descriptions of sixteenth- and seventeenth-century life in the cold: narratives, data, pictures, and archaeology; ice cores, pollen spores, tree rings, and stalactite composition.[13] When the "cool sun of reason"[14] finally dawned on these bitter days, Wolfgang Behringer famously argued, it helped inaugurate the scientific revolution. Yet I am not as interested as he is in enlightened, salvific responses to climate crises (of any age); instead, I am keen on the social, political, artistic, and sexual relations that were (and may be) engendered by London's historic cold. Throwing "sun" on the cold is only one way to encounter it; the "cool sun," after all, became a fireball in the engines of fossil-fueled progress. Sam White, who tracks the unfamiliar winters of North America that impeded colonial ambitions in the late sixteenth and early seventeenth centuries, makes a convincing case for complicating the ways historians piece together climatic experience: "Complexities do not alter the reality of early modern global cooling, but they do warn against facile definitions."[15]

As we will see, they treated their little age as an elastic one, as singular neither in scope nor in consequence. In their words, they named a climate of various and tempestuous effects, one that emphasized winter weather's inherent variability and humans' and nonhumans' vulnerability to it. In their avoidance of framing a ubiquitous phenomenon uniform in time, space, and impact, they prove that the epoch's very "definition" deserves greater scrutiny. The Grindelwald Fluctuation and the Maunder Minimum periods, for example, were punctuated by relatively warmer conditions in between. Even so, Samuel Collins (1619–1670), physician to Tsar Alexis Romanov, wrote that it was only "mild[ly]" cold almost three hundred miles north of Moscow in the winter of 1664.[16] "The Cold, which is so much talk'd of in Books, hath been rare in these late years; for some English which have liv'd there [Vologda] thirty years since, have observed such an alteration in the Climate."[17] There is ample evidence, in short, to contradict any hint of meteorological unanimity. As Brian Fagan puts it in his plainly titled *The Little Ice Age* (2000), "there was never a monolithic deep freeze, rather a climatic seesaw that swung constantly backwards and forwards, in volatile and sometimes disastrous shifts. . . . Human relationships to the natural environment and short-term climate change have always been in a complex state of flux."[18] In his model, "an endless zigzag of climatic shifts, few lasting more than a quarter century"[19] replaces a consistent, linear line of temperature declension. Once we break off from the berg of an inflexible and monolithic "Age," we may reparse the LIA slightly differently: as a time (an "age") that expresses turbulence culturally recognizable (but not entirely), where laminar flows of steady increments ("little" drops in degree) cannot hide the much more labile forces at work (the sizable "ice" and the larger doings of cold).

- Unequal accommodation inspires action. Local authors, in addition to Thomas Dekker, articulated their indefinitely prolonged winters in assorted ways, and never more fervently than during the famous "frost fairs" that bookended the century (1608 and 1683–1684). The "frigorifick," I argue, stimulated an irrepressible desire to frolic. Nearly a score of anonymous pamphlets, some of them published directly on the Thames, confirm cold's communalizing powers. But not all fairgoers were equally entertained, and certain bonds were prone to break, especially when they transgressed class, gender, and sexual norms. Reviewing this playful literature is more instructive than nostalgic: they are a reminder that successful adaptation to a fluctuating climate requires asking which citizens are not afforded the same luxury (and why not). Not all inhabitants of the LIA flourished equally, and some not at all: an inequity that has become too predictable in the annals of environmental history. *Climatic adaptation is never uniform.* "Arkives" deliver a blunt reality: "The very idea of sealing up a privileged inside from a theoretically disposable outside is a tragic and self-interested myth. It does not work. It will not work."[20] Coming to terms with this fact in the past makes it that much more imperative to interrogate and contextualize further in the present.[21] Cold, once reconfigured as an empathetic agent, may still inspire the "doings" of cryopolitical action. Attending to discounted voices—the poor, the nonhuman, the affirmatively queer and carnivalesque "freak"—is a matter of climate justice, in my view, for it magnifies the imbalanced effects that climate and weather, from global warming to polar vortices, make on members of all ages: today, before, and after. One's cold "creation story from hell"[22] is another's cool advantage, and often cruelly so.

- Breaking apart coincides with coming together. Writers of the period typically portrayed themselves struggling against an obdurate foe lethal in both freeze and flood, situating their various contributions on a timeline of past and future crises known succinctly as "the frozen age." City slippers were quick to designate their frost as the hardest, shifting the baseline for what counts as unusual in each iteration. When John Evelyn writes on March 7, 1658, that "this had ben the severest Winter, that man alive had knowne in England: The Crowes feete were frozen to their prey: Ilands of Ice inclosd both fish & foule frozen, & some persons in their boates,"[23] he opens up the title of "severest" to debate. The contact could be nightmarish. Sixteen years later, travelers nearing Evelyn's flash-frozen city found themselves socked-in with snow. The author "L. W." describes their gruesome approach: "Some to my knowledge, how strange you may think it to be, what with Snow and frost were froze to their Saddles, and could not be got off by any means til they ungrated the Saddle, and so took them both of together."[24] "On that same day," he writes, "was a Post-Boy, froze to Death on his Horse, before he got to his Stage in Southwark."[25] One could compare these glaciated centaurs and doomsday scenarios to the apocalyptic vision of Giovanni Domenico Cassini (1625–1712), astrologer to King Louis XIV of France, in 1697: "I very much fear that the Crust which has so long been over the Suns Body, will now be doubly coated with Ice, so that the little remaining Light will be so intercepted, that we shall not have so much benefit of it as to see truly the Hour of the Day."[26] To quote Shakespeare's *Winter's Tale,* a play that self-consciously draws attention to its seasonal association, it seems "a sad tale's best" (2.1.26).[27]

As the seventeenth century progressed, the cold reasserted its affiliation with John Peter's "extream,"[28] all but securing its chronic association with the terrors of eco-catastrophe. A precipitous decline in temperature was the perfect partner for tragedy, a marriage that "the funeral baked meats / Did coldly furnish" (*Hamlet,* 1.2.180–81). And yet, urban winterers told more tales. In 1684, the people of Deal, Kent, and neighboring coastal counties demonstrated community-*building* to be a viable option for enduring atmospheric variability on large (climate) and small (weather) scales.[29] (We will oversee their communal efforts to deal/ live with cold's incessant surprises in conclusion.) Intense pleasure, too, managed to compete with the ubiquitous trope of terror. A charming phrase helps us think through this phenomenon of thrill, chill, and the experiential in-between: "frost fair." Although the Thames completely froze over on a dozen separate occasions or thereabouts in the sixteenth and seventeenth centuries, fairs did not always emerge. My portfolio picks up where Dekker left off (ca. 1608–1615), spanning the middle of the century before settling in "the coldest winter in the English meteorological record": 1683–1684.[30] That winter sponsored a mass proliferation of poetry, prose, and portraits; musical scores and maps; prophecies and proclamations. Pamphlets were capable of crystallizing several of these voices and points of view at once.[31]

- Feeling cold expands the limits of care. When rough and rowdy winters stacked up in seventeenth-century London, responses to the cold's unequal effects on the citizenry varied considerably. Evelyn (again) captures this cool oscillation perfectly in his entry for January 24, 1684: a "triumph of Carnoval on the Water, whilst it was a severe Judgement upon the Land."[32] Much hangs on the word "whilst," for it brings matters of survivability into relief, and with them the political imperative and the obligation to aid. Understanding past complexities proves crucial for navigating life in the uncertain Anthropocene. Revisiting mercurial events of the past and the actions they promoted, from the ludic (playtime) to the moral (charity), invites us to take similar positions in our thinner ice-world. As Fagan points out, and as Freebody's tale suggests, "the Little Ice Age is the story of Europeans' struggle against the most fundamental of all human vulnerabilities,"[33] their exposure to climatic vicissitudes. It is simply unreasonable and injurious to imply either that humans may opt out of the process—climate will have its (s)way without us—or that interglacial periods are naturally occurring processes that take place despite our voluminous emissions. Premodern cultures certainly created long-term environmental problems on the continent and abroad (coal mining, deforestation, and fen-draining, to list a few[34]), even if their anthropogenic activity was nowhere near the magnitude of fossil-fueled, large-scale industrialization that exacerbates climate change today. It is imperative to gauge the climate–culture relationship historically, as dual but though mutually driving forces, so that we may accurately predict, and perhaps alter, the ways in which that dynamic plays out in future. London's ice may be lost, but its stories are not.

## "Furious Boreas"

Whenever ice invades premodern London, the outcome admittedly tends to be more catastrophic than exploratory. Ice in the city was a destructive force with which to be reckoned. From the earliest municipal records onward, shards of river ice were especially dangerous.[35] John Stow (1525[?]–1605) lists damages beginning in 1092: "In England fell a wonderfull aboundance raine, and after insued so great frost, that Horses and Carts passed commonly ouer great Riuers, which when it thawed, the Ice brake downe many great bridges."[36] Similarly, in 1281, "there was such a frost that 5. arches of London bridge, and all Rochester bridge was borne down and carried away, with many bridges more."[37] Arches and architecture were not the only structures at risk: human and nonhuman bodies were also susceptible. Ice bridges were only temporary, of course, and predicting their inevitable break-up was always dicey. In 1564, perhaps the first season that citizens took to the ice for sport (some "plaied at the football," others "shot at pricks"[38]), the ice started to melt on January 3. Two days later, the "sudden thaw caused great floods and high waters that bare downe bridges and houses, and drowned many people in England, especially in Yorkshire, Owes bridge was born away."[39] In February 1579, rising waters resulting from ferocious snowdrifts deposited "fishes" around Westminster.[40] These piscine deaths, unfortunately, were part of a larger multispecies die-off effected by the cold. That same winter, somewhere between two and four and a half feet of snow (up to "an ell") accumulated, and "in the countries, . . . many cattell, and some men and women were ouer-whelmed and lost."[41] In 1607–1608, the winter of the frost fair, the "fréeze" came so "violently" that all the cities "hartichokes" perished in their gardens, and "many bridges were spoiled by this frost, and much fowle perished, especially smal birds which in many places were found frozen to death."[42] The same was said for the "great frost" and occasion for fairing in 1614, the subject of Dekker's second pamphlet.[43] Ice could appear and disappear all of a sudden, and with a violence. Its reach effectively bridged the English Channel. Bookseller and newsman Nathaniel Butter (1583–1664) reported in his February 24, 1624, edition of *The Affaires and Generall Businesse of Europe* that the iced "Rhine hath done great hurt."[44] Writing from Antwerp, the send-off to his readers is meant to be a warm one: "Farwell in the coldest weather, that euer I writ Letter."[45] It is the cold, as always, that tests both sides of his sentiment: getting by, being well.

Although predictable to a certain extent, as all floes eventually turn into flows, these annals prepare for, but cannot protect against, the winter woes. Repeating cold weather's ruination became almost routine. A pamphlet from 1674 notes, "there is scarce a County in *England* but may bring in several Indictments against [snow] for damages susteyned to a considerable value, not to speak of the mischiefs occasioned by great Floods when melted by the Thaw."[46] Severity crystallized in cultural memory on an annual basis. L. W.'s 1674 *Strange and True News* thought it necessary to "giv[e] you an Account of Gods Judgments by Water, for these 4 hundred Years."[47] And as Stow's perishable "hartichokes" attest, when cold invaded civic space, it penetrated both household walls and the warm skins within. The English politician Arthur Hall (1539–1605) sketched a disgusting picture of the northern countries in a 1576 letter to his friend in Italy: "What of that penetrating cold that boring out the inhabitants eyes giues them the sauce of hunger . . . and smal soppes to their dinner, flées their skinnes of without edged toole, makes them blowe away their noses in their napkins, and yet plages them with catars rewmes, and will you haue the English worde truely, the playne snotte and sniuil, so as though the nose be gon, they must wipe where it was, or else some vnsauerly matter will runne in their mouthes."[48] The famished frost-body is a rigid one susceptible to fracture; revoltingly, to Hall it could also melt away. (No "nose" might be Thorius's worst winter nightmare.) Households buckled, too. In 1674, poor English cottagers in the northwestern region of Langsdale found "themselves buried alive in Snow."[49] Unable to exit, they resorted to cannibalism. The tenacious neighbors who finally burrowed inside discovered them with "raw meat in their mouths."[50] Another unfortunate family in Bath died soon after their rescue: they simply ate too much for their famished bodies to digest. The "superabundant snow" led to utterly lachrymose lines: "a Feather'd Rain, came in abundance down, / And with dry Inundations did us Drown."[51]

With or without these barriers' doubtful assurances, when victims euphemistically "froze to Death" (e.g., the "Post-Boy's" demise), they often perished in more spectacular ways than the headlines proclaimed or the poets eulogized. Carriage passengers surprised by a snowstorm near Salisbury on December 23, 1684 were "forced to wander" aimlessly about the blanketed countryside, later to be discovered "starv'd with cold"[52] in various contortions. Some were "found dead foot to foot;"[53] others were simply "smoothered in the Snow."[54] The peaceful, pietà-like repose of unlucky couples dying side by side is disturbed by the knowledge of their asphyxiating fate: the sign of a painful death from "dry Inundations" above. Indeed, to be "starv'd" is no less tranquil than being "buried alive." (They operate in tandem in Langsdale, and terrifyingly so.) The word "starv'd" is a curious one to employ in this case. Derived from Old English *steorfan,* "to die," related to German *sterben,* from a base meaning of "be rigid," it could connote both the specific malady of malnourishment (ca. 1420) and that of cold's withering afflictions (ca. 1400).[55] To "starve"—to be glutted with "the sauce of hunger"—eventually became shorthand for "to die of cold" (1574).[56] The situation in Salisbury was not unique, and that was precisely what made it so "fearful." What is spectacular is not just the sight of the deceased, but the haste in which prior wellness deteriorates. Any "hearty and healthful"[57] creature, whether plant, animal, or human, could quickly succumb in a "superabundant," avalanching instant. "This sad time I never shall forget," writes the anonymous author of *Sad News from Salisbury* in 1685, setting survivors' eyewitness testimony to the recallable tune of "Aim Not Too High." Remember: few things are hardy enough to withstand winter's "great"-ness, indoors or outdoors, for even the shelled artichoke *chokes* in the suffocating cold. It is hard to take "heart" in repetitive, lamentable lessons like these.

Forecasting attempted to reset this balance of power and reestablish elemental domesticity. As we saw in chapter 1, early modern meteorologists vacillated between two sorts of description: prognostication (astrological prediction) and natural philosophy (causal explanation). The lingering cold of the long seventeenth century borrowed from both. In his 1684 *Diurnal Speculum,* Richard Kirby (b. 1649) proudly announced that he had "fore-told, in *Decemb.* 1683. the late and unheard of *Frost;* with the Events that may probably and suddenly ensue thereon."[58] (His excuse was that his "predictions and prognostications" were at the press in August but that their publication was withheld "by the *Printers* Temerity."[59]) *New Prophecy* (1678), by William Lilly (1602–1681), less defensively and yet just as confidently, promised that he had "reasons in Art to judge, that the approaching Winter will in general be kind and seasonable" and can anticipate which commodities (under the influence of "Oriental" or "Occidental" planets) will be prosperous.[60] Some, in a classic case of climatic determinism, explained the course of history as cold-caused. "It is observable," as "Icedore Frostiface" later (1740) declared, "that when any Frost has happened remarkably severe, it hath soon been followed by some extraordinary Revolution, Change, or Event."[61] On the ice, one may even find conspiracy theories afoot: "King Charles II [b. 1630] . . . was taken out of the World in a very suspicious Manner," he believed, in 1685.[62]

But to have the gift of prophecy! An ability to foresee the weather promised, albeit tenuously, that the "hideous" monstrosities of the recent meteorological past would never return. While some estimations served a more pragmatic utility, such as the lists of "Prognosticks of . . . Heat, Cold" done by John Worlidge (fl. 1660–1698) for subsistence purposes in his 1669 *Systema Agriculturae*,[63] the primary goal of the tracts was to assert human skill, not stewardship. Pinpointing weather back (Kirby) and forward (Lilly) in time was meant to sap its freezing strength. Their "Art" (conjuring Prospero's vanity in Shakespeare's *Tempest*) was illusory, even as the threat of interminable winter was very real. A less egotistical approach, though no more assuring, perceived humankind as part of a grander meteorological and cosmological system. John Flamsteed (1646–1719) cast his *Prophecy* (1695) from within "this Present Frost, and Great Snow"[64] in order to foretell a break in the pattern. Winter, it seems, is simple enough to understand: "This fourth, last, and worst Quarter of all the Year, commenced with the Sun's entrance into the first Scruple of the Tropick of Capricorn; at which time the Inhabitants of this Earthly Globe, receive the least Portion of the Sun's Rays and Light, which is one main Reason of Frost and Snow, and other extremity of Weather."[65] The prophecy, so far, is not that new ("what more can Reason expect?"[66]), but its insights are harder to harness. The "extremity" of cold, from his vantage point, stems from influences literally outside human orbit: "He who truly studies the Works of God, will find that Frost and Snow, Hail, Rain, and Wind, &c. come not by Chance, or from any unaccountable Motion of Matter, but at set and determinate periods and Revolations of the Planitary Bodies."[67] Winters come around like clockwork, with actions set to a predetermined plan, and yet humankind revolves in a misery-go-round of a divine making. In February, the month in which Flamsteed reports, "circling winds" are already arriving from the north: "So that from Cold Greenland, and Estoniland, Furious Boreas, threatens to bring Frost and Snow on his broad spread Wings, and throw them over these Parts of the World."[68] The fury will hopefully abate, giving way to the warm south wind of spring; until then, he prays that "we shall not have such another Frost, and Snow as in the Year 1683."[69] A pathetic sound from the flurry: our fates, prophetically, are simultaneously fixed and unknown.

The persistent need to recount annual winter hardships underscores English citizens' realization that their climate had chilled over time, even if the technical language and data of "global cooling" were unavailable to them. As the cold consistently wreaked havoc on "tender Bodies less accustomed thereunto,"[70] it became clear that the city and countryside were in the grips of climatic change for the colder, especially during the coldest winter in English history from 1683 to 1684. *Wonders on the Deep* (1684), for instance, one of many broadsheets famous for depicting entertainments on the frozen Thames, included a roughly six-hundred-year "Chronology of all the Memorable (Strong) Frosts."[71] Of the eleven frosts enumerated (starting in 1068), nearly half had occurred in the previous seventy-five years. Brief climate histories like these made the increasing frequency of deep-cold phenomena legible to the public. Without fail, *Wonders on the Deep* and many other pamphlets like it expressed a quintessential statement: this year's frost has historical precedent, but it does not have an equal.[72] "It may be remembred how mild and gentle the Winters, for several Years past, have proved in our Climate," opened one, before launching into a description of the "late" (1676) and "extraordinary frost and snow" whose "great damages" covered the "destruction" of children and cattle.[73] "They never knew it freeze in *England* more fiercely in their lives, than now it did for the time."[74] A single winter's catalogue of wonders ultimately snaps into a temporal grid known as the LIA, but only in hindsight. While bad winters had been recorded for over half a millennium, writers and fairgoers alike found themselves thrust into a dimly lit era of climatic turbulence; even so, they recognized that they were witnessing the making of history—that is, the breaking of records—right under their soles.

As the anonymous author of the "extraordinary" snowfall from 1676 suggests, self-preservation was paramount. Extra snow upped the "ordinary"; as a result, early moderns' baselines shifted. What was once "extraordinary" (even if just of "late") risked becoming the new normal. In response, questions about resilience took precedence over exact causes: "We are not now writing an Astrological Discourse," the author insists, "but a Relation, and therefore hasten to matter of Fact."[75] One issue with this factual move is that, like the weather, meteorological knowledge was variable: "And yet to render it more remarkable, 'twas observed that this rigid Frost began, the Wind being at South, generally reckon'd the warmest of any point of the Compass."[76] (Cold winds supposedly came down from the north, not up from the south.) As the title for the "worst" on record was awarded, two problems presented themselves: proving the veracity of "the true account" and recognizing that "facts" were being remade in the process. *Sad News from Salisbury* listed several names of those "who have sufficiently tasted of the bitterness, . . . for the better satisfaction of the Incredulous."[77] A different "true and perfect narrative" a decade earlier (1674) gathered its information about the "late extraordinary snows" from "letters lately sent from Persons of Good Credit and Quality in all those parts."[78]

The century's crisis of cold was thus one concerning historical representation as well as daily perseverance. Determining how to prove, or make credible, the severity of the climate also meant asking how to report it. Wintry writers did not necessarily offer a solution to this twinned dilemma, but they did propose different ways of thinking through the sharp "taste" of "bitter" contrasts. By focusing on "relations" between humans and cold, by piecing together the "facts" that make up the social age of ice, readers are encouraged to identify, and perhaps ameliorate, their puzzling ecological changes both little and big. A "loving friend" in Brigg, Lincolnshire, penned a letter to his "love" on December 18, 1676, apologizing for its delay: "We have had such a Snow, that oldest Man alive cannot remember the like."[79] It lamentably proceeds here: "I hear some poor People up higher in the Countrey, venturing abroad, lost their Lives in the great Drifts of Snow, &c." The storying of past relations, at its heart, is a means of engaging persistence anew.

## Walking on Glass

The authors cited so far attest to cold's penchant for thwarting knowledge structures and infiltrating physiological systems. Ascertaining what cold *does* proves more important than discerning what it absolutely *is* (according to, say, unassailable "astrological discourse"). Its doings impelled imperiled populaces to ponder the limits of corporate resilience (civic and corporeal), producing a view of climatic history that accounted for humanity's uncertain place within it. Fortunately, there were those who realized that winter's burden was also, in fact, what stoked the body's liberty. To meet them, we must step onto the petrified Thames. (For this, Olaus Magnus recommends "felt shoes" [*lanei calcei*], since "the power of the cold instantly turns anything greasy to an icy slipperiness."[80] I will follow his instructions.) Poetic commemorations and folio-size illustrations of the seventeenth-century frost fairs furnish a window into cold's corporeal doings on a series of enfolded scales and across a spectrum of physical-emotional reactions, engaging the municipality's fancies and fears at once. Dekker's unnamed citizen from 1608 had plenty to say about "the hurt that the Citie hath receiued by this Frost."[81] Yet recall that other Londoners preferred to take their chances in the "waterie wildernesse,"[82] and finding amusement in the frost, tempered the didactic opinions of their more wary neighbors. It is difficult to say whether the shopkeeper's cautious viewpoint was Dekker's own, but in any case, his discourse provides a snapshot into the winter-strapped mentalities of early modern residents: how they were attracted to or appalled by the ice hardening around them (or both), planting their feet in the powdery "steppes"[83] leading to and from the river and its rimy entertainment.

Risk remained omnipresent. As many of the above-mentioned narratives illustrate, snowy dangers did not suddenly disappear between the famous fairs of 1608 and 1683–1684. Iced-over rivers were always treacherous places to traverse: from the century's two tremendous gatherings, to the smaller, more impromptu congregations and trades that popped up infrequently across English history. (Transactions on the Thames were recorded as far back as 250 CE.[84]) A letter from "Bourn" in Cambridgeshire dated December 26, 1676, for example, reminds readers "not to expose themselves . . . as some very imprudently have done during this Frost, by venturing too soon or too far upon the Ice,"[85] specifically, like the twenty-five boys in Wisbich who drowned after breaking through (presumably) the River Nene during a soccer game. The stories of fatal slip-ups off and on the ice are innumerable: a "poor Creature kill'd by an unlucky fall" and "divers sad Examples" of those who "broke their legs, arms, and other parts of their bodies."[86] Focusing primarily on these examples—the infinite ways "the violence of the Ice"[87] repeats itself—comes with its own set of narratological risks: namely, skewing the human–ice ecological record so that it predominantly reflects splits and fractures, "hurt" feelings, urban menaces.

How might we heed the hazards of the 1676 match, remembering its juvenile victims, while also commemorating hard winters' chances for play? "The badness of walking"[88] is a hard spell to break. Parts of Thorius's *Song*, for instance, are prohibitive: "Boy, leave thy sliding, lest thy slippery flower / Deceive thy feet."[89] I turn now to the wide variety of frost-fair literature printed seventy-five years after Dekker's dual dialogues (his 1608 *The Great Frost* and its 1615 revision as *The Cold Yeare*). Authors who commemorated the enormous fair of 1683–1684 voiced their own concerns over collapsing cryographical circles, the same predicament that previous poets and chroniclers had fretted about; in doing so, they anticipated Frostiface's collisional verse a half century later. But the richness of this archive also indicates that London society's crash course with the cold was not inherently destructive. (T)reading carefully with the doctor's scrip in hand, we can rediscover a more vivid spectrum of human–ice interactions.

Trepidation, unsurprisingly, was often the first reaction to the river's reliable ebbs and tides coming to a halt. In *A Winter Wonder, Or, the Thames Frozen Over* (1684), Neptune laughs at the useless bridges of the city, for "ice has made one continued Shore."[90] Compounding his mockery of human engineering is the cold, configured as an infiltrator: "Greenland, Muscovy, sure their Cold have lent, / And all their Frigid Blasts have hither sent, / Whilst Boreas with his keenest Breath has blown, / To make our Winter cold, as is their own."[91] Just as Dekker's nuanced interpretation of "bosome"[92] predicted, "their" and "our" cannot hold as the Arctic creeps down the globe. Indeed, it is a bit chilling (in the frightened sense of the word) to see fires on ice ("Vulcan" has taken "Neptunes Bed"[93]) and drunk men wobbling on water: "Many Tuns of Ale and Brandy flow / Above the Ice as Waters do below."[94] The frozen world is also an inverted one, a confusing situation where both the elements and the imbibers of oxygen and "ale" appear disordered. "All things do move upon this *Element,* / As if on *Terra ferma* their feet went,"[95] while, inches down, ghoulish fish "look like dry'd Skeletons."[96]

"Blasts" southward "sent" were nearly tyrannical. According to *Wonders on the Deep,* "God . . . lock'd up the Wavy Thames, / And under Rocks of Ice confin'd her Streams."[97] Neptune "durst scarcely breath[e]" in "his strange Captivity," and despite the boisterous "trading mart" that his shackling allows, the river resembles a coffin: "The harden'd Waves . . . Marble like the Watery World Intomb."[98] All is in chains: "Strong North-Winds, with unrelenting cold, / Imprison'd Nature did in Fetters hold."[99] A "Chronology of all the Memorable (Strong) Frosts"—starting in 1068 and ending in 1676—suggests that history will eventually repeat itself, exacerbating the inmates' anxiety. The figurative language of cold's clasps had literal precedent: several of these Dantean souls, like "the Maid that fell in at Black-Fryers,"[100] can be seen in several bird's-eye views of the fair. Cold's confinement drives the people cagey; some were even condemned to watch a supernatural battle play out between bitter titans at the top of the world. *A Wonderfull Fair, Or, a Fair of Wonders* (1684) begins with an outspokenly disgruntled Winter: "In long subjection to the Southern Wind / To Groynland Nights had Winter been confin'd; / At length, quoth he, thus pent to the North Pole, / Shall I be under Punie Zephyrus controul?"[101] Lodging his complaint with the northeast wind, the "Monarch of the North" is triumphant: "Let the South my Terrors feel."[102] In all of these cases, nervous citizens are caught cold, in the middle of petty arguments between pagan gods, personified waterways, God's will, and even the ice itself, waiting either to be freed from their frosty prison or for winter to be unleashed. Any self-titled "wonders," then, are undercut with wariness, imbued with apprehension over the Thames's "terrors," even if the depths of central London (about ten meters) are not-so-terribly "deep."

Both fairs, 1608 and 1683–1684, are typically remembered as extraordinary business opportunities in London's socioeconomic history. Joseph P. Ward, for example, observes a gradual "taming" of the river in roughly one hundred years: "the decline of providentialist readings of the Thames (or perhaps more accurately, the growing number of works that took a skeptical view of such interpretations) coincided with the increasing significance of river-borne trade in London's economy and society during the later seventeenth century."[103] Obviously, warning signs like Thorius's did not prevent brave vendors from opening up their shops off-shore. It is clear from the sheer number of illustrations and poetic retellings that multitudes flocked to the "Raree-Show"[104] of the second frost fair (broken up February 8, 1684). The gloomy tone of *Wonders on the Deep* or the "blasts" of winter could not shut down the littoral carnival. "Being the Wonder of this present Age," *and* "a great consternation to all the Spectators,"[105] as one subtitle put it, buyers and sellers saw unparalleled opportunities in the ice. "What is't you lack, what is't you buy?"[106] Almost every contemporary account enumerates the fair's tantalizing goods and services. A merchant's empty speech bubble on the front page of *News from Frost-Fair upon the River of Thames* (1683) alludes to the insatiable appetite that the "innumerable crowd's of resorters"[107] brought with them. The city-in-a-city represents a one-of-a-kind, one-stop shopping spree: "On the Ice is a Town / Which till now was never known."[108] And its cries rival the summertime tumult of Bartholomew Fair: "Walk in, kind Sir, this Booth it is the chief, / We'l entertain you with a slice of Beef, / And what you please to Eat or Drink, 'tis here, / No Booth, like mine, affords such dainty cheer."[109] Lists like these go on and on.

For good reason, such "affordances" have undergirded historians' treatment of the first frost fairs.[110] Others, however, have been wary of rendering the Thames as "*only* a river,"[111] locked in commercial time. While insights into cold's unconventional modes of business are certainly important, what is patently momentous about the exhibitions, I believe, is their effective re-sorting of the boundaries between city and icescape, and between temperature and identity. Alvin Snider notes the lasting impress of Hippocratic theory at century's end: "Those who recorded the neo-boreal trend in 1684 and reported on its effects borrowed a key principle from ancient biometeorology, that embodiment is a dynamic process, not the static experience of a singular autonomous subject but an unsettled relation of balance and imbalance with surrounding conditions."[112] In other words, in addition to featuring the cryocorporeal unions that constituted "English body worlds,"[113] seventeenth-century winter fests also showcase the bank-side as a space of natural–cultural transaction. When the anonymous poet of *Great Britains Wonder* (1684) notes that "before the *Temple* there a Street is made, / And there is one almost of every Trade,"[114] it is possible to imagine the city of London temporarily extending *into* the river. A new community arises from the merger: "Here's the first Tavern built in Freezeland-street."[115] Similar to the "Fréezeland"[116] Dekker once visited, this newer community of "Freezeland" is not merely an incursion of culture into nature, an existing city transplanted onto the ice, or a watery mirror that briefly reflects the urban settings around its banks. Like Magnus's descriptions of boreal civilizations for which he is known, "Freezeland" names the threading of ice and city (and [v]ice versa), a union of the aqueous (in "freeze") and the terrestrial ("land"). Severe winter reveals the Thames and London to be coextensive.

It is worth returning, then, to the notion of "business" and its exceptional arena. *God's Works Is the Worlds Wonder* (1684) claims that it represents "the most Remarkable Passages that was acted and performed upon that spacious River of Thames,"[117] calling attention to the pop-up theaters (such as "a show booth" observable in the picture of *A Wonderfull Fair*) and the dramatic "passages" voiced therein. The miniature ice stages are not unique in this regard; almost all earthbound activities could be advertised as novelties once transported onto the ice. But

*Great Britains Wonder* expands the ideas of "action" and "performance" to include human as well as nonhuman actors at work, shifting the transactional stakes from the anomalous pleasure of merely conducting business "on" ice to interacting *with* its busy doings and the potential buyers it brings: "Behold the Wonder of this present Age, / A Famous River now become a Stage."[118] In the *New Climate Regime,* as Bruno Latour puts it, "the physical framework that the Moderns had taken for granted, the ground on which their history had always been played out, has become unstable. As if the décor had gotten up on stage to share the drama with the actors."[119] The "neo-boreal" winter of 1683–1684 truly seems "new"; it asks us to explore the preposition "on" at a moment in climate history that refused to thrust the doings of cold behind the curtain of culture. Indeed, the watercourse was a busy "stage" in this earlier "age": one that trafficked in "terrors" and trades, whose pinioning and profit-laden floor was disposed to shift with little warning, breaking sets apart as it abruptly transitioned between acts. "Though such unusual Frosts to us are strange, / Perhaps it may predict some greater Change," writes the same author of *Great Britains Wonder,* settling on an insecure yet expansive "perhaps," pondering what (if any) ecological and economic "regime" changes would come to London. Worries, wares, and what else: if all the frozen river's a stage, the unstable Thames crucially stayed open for dramatic redecorating through it all.

## Strangers in "Paradice"

It was this exact mercantile openness that extended to early modern cryophiles a vector for pleasure and Boylean promiscuity. Anticipating the conflation of sexual and commercial satisfaction by Christina Rossetti (1830–94) in her 1862 "Goblin Market" ("come buy, come buy"),[120] the "frigorifick" force that presented barkers with unique business dealings also activated desires for frolicking elemental relations. Departing from the literature's well-meaning preoccupation with "terror," I now turn to ice's playful "affordances," tracking the interstitial and interpersonal titillations that flourished on frozen tides. The second part of the neologism "frost fair" obviously invokes features of the carnivalesque as much as the undertakings of cold-blooded entrepreneurs. A "show booth" was but one of a multitude of entertainments (not just vendible commodities) that these brumal bacchanalias marketed to a bored citizenry. *An Exact and Lively Mapp* (1684), for instance, faithfully represents "the varieties of shows and Humours"[121] that took place. As Robert A. Beddard pithily states, "on the ice life was lived fast and loose."[122] But, while "the Frost Fair boom was as much a tribute to the commercial instincts of Restoration London as it was proof of its love of amusement,"[123] desires for the ice life should not be seen as secondary on the list of Londoners' exploits. "There is such Whimsies on the Frozen Ice, / Makes some believe the Thames a Paradice," proclaims *Great Britains Wonder,* the pun pointing up the pleasures (a pair of gambling dice) and the plenty (an idyllic paradise) awaiting ice walkers, many of whom welcomed its whirls on stilt, sled, sail, and skate.[124]

Winter's cold could prove both a valuable business partner and a devious playmate, icy otium admirable for "amusement's" sake. *Wonders on the Deep* lists no fewer than thirty-five possible forms of fun, with many others "not Figured."[125] True to the ephemerality of spectacle, when "strange inventions for pastime is made,"[126] these same enjoyments had to be updated in order to prolong their appeal: "It was exceeding strange at first to see / Both men and Women so adventurous be / And yet at last is grew so very common / 'Twas not admir'd, it seemed strange to no man."[127] The fair, in other words, had to be occasionally refreshed, lest the "strange" turn monotonous. Booths burgeoned—ox-roasting and fox-hunting, bull-baiting and the "Dutch Chear Sliding round"[128]—in order to banish the risk of mundanity. Recounted by nearly every broadside, these recreations became legendary both for their originality (being the first of their kind) and their remarkable degree of creativity that readily integrated wintry conditions. Just as the shopkeepers had cleverly discovered, strollers were eager to witness the history of entertainment in the (cold) making. *A True Description of Blanket Fair* (1683), for example, displays bear-baiting on the ice, "which sport to see hundreds did repair, / And I believe since the Worlds first Creation / The like was never seen in this our Nation,"[129] capitalizing on the Thames's aforementioned moniker as an "Icy stage."[130] For the anonymous composer of the tune *Blanket-Fair* (1684), human–ice innovations are delightful: the "wondrous conjunction of Water and Fire" is to be admired.[131] The poet sings of the "merry Pranks played on the River,"[132] seemingly envious of pickpockets' stealthy tricks. "Here all things like fate / Are in a slippery state" is a pretty moral for the polar age, if there ever was one, one that slowly morphs into a memento mori: "The World, and the pleasures it brings, / Are made up of brittle and slippery things."[133] Frolic while you may, in other words, for all flesh is *glass*.

What is incredible, revisiting *Blanket-Fair* and other leaflets from this period, is that careful contact with brittleness proves attractive. The cold river could claim not merely to host hot desires, but to cultivate them, becoming both an attraction and attractor in its own right. Smoothness, in short, was coveted. Brochures promoted as well as documented the feeling of frangibility, blanketing a curious citizenship with slippery thrills. The song *Freezland-Fair* (1684) states that "very strange things have bin done this strange Season," including the disappearance of the Thames: "Ye know there's a Brook, / No, no, I mistook."[134] Yet the lyrics take comfort in the oncoming spring: "I do not question, for all these odd freaks, / We shall find it agen when-e're the Frost breaks."[135] The balladeer's word choice is telling. The noun "freak," first recorded in 1563, denotes "a sudden change or turn of the mind; a capricious humour, notion, whim, or vagary."[136] As a verb (1638), it meant to "fleck or streak whimsically or capriciously; to variegate."[137] Sliding takes on a deviant sense in this song: ice's materiality has a veering streak to it, and so its "season" gladly incorporates diverse (variegated) wanderings and winter wanderers (vagrants) that may pivot at a moment's notice. The image of figure skating is entirely appropriate in this respect: probably dialectal, "freak" is cognate with Old English *frícian,* "to dance, move briskly" (ca. 1000). To this day, however, the phrase "freak of nature" (1847) is often used in a pejorative sense,[138] conjuring up an ice dancer who streaks off-script, a "brook" that suspiciously vanishes, or the satisfaction of one's unnatural, non-normative cravings. After all, the songwriter rhetorically asks in *News from Frost-Fair,* "when the Season's warm, / Who wishes for a Storm, / Or desires to be Frozen with Cold[?]"[139]

But ice's "odd" and zigzagging propulsion, repulsive to some, generates joys for others. On a cold bed lie "strange" desires and a desire for the strange(r). Jokes about the populace's propensity for backsliding (falling on the back, slang for sexual intercourse) were as rampant as they were rote. *Blanket-Fair* issues a "warning for better or worse": "slippery things have been done on the Ice," it claims, for "maids there have bin said / To lose Maiden-head."[140] If only "their Brains and their Bodies had not bin too warm," it seems, the parties would have slid away unscathed.[141] The "looseness" of ice life certainly allowed for rails against sexual licentiousness, with much of the sanctimonious ire, not surprisingly, directed toward women: "'Tis ten to one," *A Winter Wonder* wages in a long misogynist censure, "you tumble in a Trice; / For you are apt to fall, where there's no Ice."[142] (*Blanket-Fair,* too, poking fun at a damsel's hot "Buttocks," decidedly settles on "harm" in the end.[143])

The "better" part of the potential bargain, though, glimpses possibilities of consensual sexual encounters, or what could be more broadly conceived as cold's erotic charge. "Listen. Do you hear the wind moaning, the ice groaning beneath us as it strains?" asks Elizabeth Bradfield in her poem "Against Solitude" (2010).[144] Although the verb "frig" (to masturbate)—extant since the late sixteenth century (1598), and used interchangeably with "fuck" and "fool around (*with*)" since the early twentieth (1905/1933)—bears no etymological relation to "frigid" (1622), which comes from the Latin frīgus, "cold," it is nevertheless rewarding to speculate on its libidinous beginnings.[145] "Frig" is probably an onomatopoeic alteration of "frike," from *frícian,* which lent "frig" the additional meanings of "to move about restlessly; to agitate the body or limbs" (ca. 1500) and "to rub, chafe" (ca. 1529).[146] ("It's friggin' cold!" summarizes this lesson.) The "frigorifick" Thames, in so many words, is also where the "freak" of fancy *itself* was fancied, where cryophilic "freaks" could congregate freely (if not totally safely) in numbers, seeking shelter from society's hot-headed castigations, discovering the ways in which numbing leads to the nearness (and enjoyment) of others rather than unconditional pain, their agitated bodies rubbing (and maybe even frigging) to stay warm.

Consider *An Historical Account of the Late Great Frost* (1684), a collection of "the several Amours, Intreagues, Cheats, and Humours carried on and managed upon the said River during this Season."[147] Not only is the Thames a setting for these stories, but it is also a participant within them, frequently and hilariously interacting with a wide swath of characters: two suburban squires are gulled by a lady who "feign[s] a stumble";[148] a sudden break in the ice gives two pickpockets a chance to escape "just" before their capture;[149] a wife, dunked by her husband to "cool [her] courage," cuckolds him in revenge;[150] good Samaritans rescue half-submerged "Passengers" from holes they had intentionally carved and covered in snow, robbing them of their "Booty";[151] and impatient duelists worry about "the catching of a Cold in staying a minute beyond the hour."[152] The foremost danger of the frost fair is the commingling of classes and the resultant cultural confusion, a concern that supersedes doubts about the ice's variable thickness: "Where the Lord to his Lacky, and the Lady to her Maid, downwards in all degrees, were every day intermixt, together with Bawds, Whores, Pick-pockets, Jilts, and Cheats undistinguisht."[153]

Couched within this classist rhetoric, however, is an amorous anecdote. At least a few festival-goers, it seems, were aroused by the indistinguishability that attended said "intermixture." Two kinswomen from Chelsea, who had secretly "been used to Slide on a Private Pond" owned by their uncle, became so adept at it that they believed they "could not be out-done by the other Sex."[154] They devise a plan to test their hypothesis: they will put on "a Suit of Mans Apparel, and walk out amongst the Gentlemen to Practice their new gained Art."[155] Unbeknown to these sly skaters, a neighbor overhears their plot, after which he and his friend hatch a similar scheme: dressing as women, they will wait to "be Picked up by" the cross-dressed women.[156] Their ingratiation is successful, although their "intentions," it is said, could not be "more different . . . [than] any four upon the whole River besides: The Gentleman intended Mirth with them as Ladies, the Ladies with them as Jilts of their Sex, to Pledge, or leave them for a Reckoning, when they had tried how far their Impudence would extend" (34). Without a clearly established goal, the women casually let the game play out. Their capriciousness, according to the narrator, borders on "impudence." But an elaborate wooing ensues nonetheless, one that is tricky to straighten out, even for the speaker: "Let me call our Ladies Gentlemen, and Gentlemen Ladies, for so they were at least in the opinion of our Heroines, and were by them accordingly Courted, and all of them as Amorous and Complaisant as the most agreed" (34). Though cross-dressed, both couples somehow manage to play by the gendered rules of courting: the gentlemen are lady-like enough; the ladies, likewise, appear as true gallants. Retiring into a private booth, where they discourse on the topics of "Love and Happiness,"[157] each lady, emboldened by drink, eventually proves the "lawfulness of his [her] Desires" to "his [her] supposed Mistress."[158] Wanting "Tools" to "finish the work," the women decide to take their tryst "as far as it would bear."[159] They are in for a surprise: "They gave Liberty to their hands to wander under their Ladies Petticoats, thinking to seize on the Naked Altar of Love, when alas, instead thereof, they met the Sacrifice prepared thereon, ready to offer to the said Deity, in its full Glories."[160]

The discovery of hard male genitalia (an erection "in its full glories") catches the women off guard; they had expected smoother ("naked") skin beneath the undergarments. Both parties are deeply embarrassed—how will they explain their risqué behavior, and what will become of their reputations?—but the women cannot help blushing at the ruse: "Desire [was not] absolutely a Stranger to their Breast, which they could not dissemble."[161] The abashed lovers, once taken aback, now quickly arrive at a solution: they will simply stay paired with their now gender-revealed partners. Unlike before, the storyteller describes the affair (and ends the escapade) with sparser details: "I will not precisely Swear the said Ladies lost their Virginities, but leave the Readers imagination to supply what my Pen must be Silent in."[162] It is a silence mandated for modesty's sake, perhaps: the off-scene sex being the anticipated outcome of a heterosexual coupling achieved by unconventional means. And yet this taciturnity also betrays, as much as it tries to conveniently brush away, the homoerotic sparks the lovers left behind.

On the cold river, ice makes queer companions. It is unclear whether the "desire" they initially feel once undisguised speaks to same-sex or opposite-sex attraction (or both), and whether or not the "condemning Blush"[163] is meant to repress those feelings or highlight their abiding presence (being no "stranger to their breast"). But keeping in mind that the women originally "picked up" the men dressed as women (otherwise they would not be so shocked by their anatomical discovery) at least opens up their "desire" to lesbian (at first) and bisexual (later) trajectories. The presumptive exchange of clothes is also missing from the account, leaving even more non-normative couplings to the "reader's imagination." It is uncertain whether "tools" (penises) are necessary for "finishing" the job, either; if so, the women's sexual advances (by lacking the essential accoutrement) would have halted "far" before they did. In this provocative vignette, an exploratory form of "desire" slides to an unforeseeable limit, and it is the frost that arouses it. To all the "amours" and "intreagues" for which the fairs are in/famous, the storying, and re-storying, of icy assignations continue to fit stereotypically straight molds.[164] Yet historical accounts like this one importantly add a queer register to the doings of cold. Slipping from the confines of gender-class-sexuality policing, they prove how desire skates a much more elaborate figure, recasting "freaks" and "streaks" in an affirmative sense. Such frigs may reclaim, and indeed celebrate, the frolicking energy behind "freak."

## Oh! You Brittle Things

Cold's "doings" thus far expose the marriage of the country and the city, the occasionally "odd freaks," and queer desires. Abundant possibilities seemingly abound on London's ice. Would that the winters' tales of 1683–1684 could end on this contented note, for striations appear on the river's smoothest of spaces. As Ward points out, "when the river froze, . . . the metropolis was physically united for a short while, but in a way that at the same time made abundantly evident the divisions within London's society."[165] The broadsheets examined here almost universally raise this caution about the disadvantaged. *True Description* closes its celebrations with a reminder: "Yet was it hard and grievous to the poor / Who many hungry bellies did endure: / Sad spectacles a now you might behold / Who felt th'effect of this prodigious cold."[166] When *A Winter Wonder* asserts that it will "remark" on the "resort" there, the word "resort" indicates both a place of recreation (a destination for the well-off) and the action of resorting to something (the less-warm attempting to remedy a difficult situation).[167] "One spacious street of Ice" did not prove spacious enough, nor could everyone afford the river's marked-up wares.[168] "In this Fair upon the Rock of Ice, / All things were sold at an excessive price," notes *God's Works Is the Worlds Wonder,* "and during this great prodigious Frost, / Though some did get, yet many hundreds lost."[169] The frost fair, in other words, raises the specter of socioeconomic unfairness: the question of who is able to weather extreme situations, who is not, and why this is the case. A "paradice" built for some, but not all, the floating market sheltered the privileged while drawing attention to the impoverished who wandered within, and struggled outside, its frozen steps. *God's Works* witnesses the life-threatening kind of body–ice correlation: "Some people were in great Extremity; / With Care and Cold, their very Cheeks lookt blue, / For then, *behold!* they had no Work to do."[170] Printers' "blue" hands, meanwhile, could conduct business ("Press"). The hard winter allowed certain trades to flourish while putting others out of work.

Blame could land on supernatural or political causes, and sometimes both. Because "each Land-man is now become free of the Thames," pronounces *Blanket-Fair,* ferrymen will feel the pinch of cold the hardest: "'Tis some Lapland Acquaintance of Conjurer Oates, / That has ty'd up your Hands & imprison'd your Boats."[171] "Lapland" sorcerers were believed to be responsible for the tempestuous weather of the Scandinavian north,[172] while "Oates" names Titus Oates (1649–1705), the infamous fabricator of the "Popish Plot" (1678) that had stirred up anti-Catholic sentiment a few years before. Broadsides, of course, were more condemnatory in their approach, identifying a section of the populace to explicitly attack rather than assist. The eight stanzas of the tune *The Whigs Hard Hearts* (1684) battle the "Monster" known as the "Presbyterian," the "cause of this great frost": "Poor Thames! thou maist curse the foul Lake of Geneva, / For whose faults Thou dost penance, sans hope of Reprieve-a."[173] Indeed, the lake creatures, like the "great Leviathan,"[174] have sailed to England, thereby over-saturating the oil market. "Leave off," merchants of Greenland, "there is no fear of your Merchandise failing, / Since the Whales, I'm afraid, mean to give us a visit."[175] The times are unlikely to turn as their zealotry runs cold, not hot: "Y'are plagu'd now with Ice, 'cause ye love to back-slide / Methinks it should warn ye to alter your station, / For y'ave hitherto built on a slipp'ry Foundation."[176] A return (slide back) to popish/papist polar ways is impossible, though; it amounts to, in the end, just more religious slip-ups. "Was ever a Vengeance so wonderful shewn, / That a River so great should be turn'd to a Town?"[177] The song's lyrics establish the river as the suffering one, a political-ecological metaphor that essentially bypasses the town's palpable socioeconomic griefs.

Conspiracies and occultism, poorly rhymed hyperbole and bloated anthropomorphism, could not provide the succor that was so desperately needed. Passing observances or platitudes would not avail the populace, either; Thorius somewhat smugly (and snuggly) noted that "afflicted goes the poor man to his rest, / But you whom plenty hath from cares releast, / Enjoy your fires, warm beds, and merry friends, / He fears not cold who thus the Winter spends."[178] The puritanical song *Londons Wonder* (1685) thanks God for breaking up the ice and thereby dissolving winter's rage at its hedonistic source: "But yet I was troubled those pleasures to see / For fear that our Lord he should angry be."[179] Prayer is an unreliable cure for the "pleasures" of cold, however, and abstemiousness may take a "good time" to work: "Then let us be thankful and praise God therefore, / For he in good time heard the cry of the Poor."[180] As the rich glacially "grind and gripe the poor in their Extremity," and as the chorus gives "thanks" (up to eight times), the effectiveness of mere observation is tested.[181] Most pamphlets documenting the frost fair stick to a conventional structure, outlining its many pleasures and tricks before tacking on a parting segment devoted to the misery of others. "Extremity" was hard to ignore; in reality, it proved harder to tackle. To this fact of unequal adaptability came, first, a variety of complaints, and second, a range of cryopolitical responses. Writers gauged the level of cold dis/comfort around them, and in doing so, inspired an ethics of care that accounted for the brittle nature of (so-called) civic solidarity.

Perhaps no writer spotlights the penuries of cold periods better than Taylor, "The Water Poet." While not recounting one of the century's frost fairs, *The Cold Tearme, Or, the Frozen Age, Or, the Metamorphosis of the Riuer of Thames* (1621) documents the many paucities that water's morphing brings. From the second line, cold is a killer: "It was the time when men wore liquor'd bootes, / When rugged Winter, murdred hearbes & rootes: / When as the Heauens, the Earth did all attire / With plashes, puddles, pooles, blacke dirt & mire."[182] Some citizens, remembering the fabulousness of the first-ever fair thirteen years earlier, return to play; Taylor is "witnesse" to them "slipping in betwixt two Cakes of Ice." As a ferryman himself, he was particularly attentive to his fellow workers' predicament: "Then at that time (to poore mens care and costs) / A Christmas came to Towne, betwixt two Frosts."[183] His tone is often bitter, first reproaching the brazenness of pedestrians—"some there were (which I almost forgot) / That thought the frozen streames were too too hot, / 'Twas safer for them (they did vnderstand) / To walke vpon the water [than] the land"—before deriding the wider "running whirling time" unleashed by coaches and carriage-goers.[184] While the "frozen age" appears to "run" right along, nearly twenty thousand workers and their families, he claims, have been seasonally affected. Taylor frames this professional disaster in monetary terms: "I dare affirme, that Water-men this Frost / (Amongst them) twenty thousand pounds haue lost. . . . Thus was this Tearme, worse then the worst vacation, / To those that vse a watry Occupation."[185] Incredibly, "though for two mon'ths time, that fell together, / Of Windes, Raine,

Snow, and bitter Frosty wether," the hapless watermen maintained their equanimity. Through it all, not one ferrier sank to thievery, which is a commendable feat. "I doubt not but a many Trades there bee, / That hold their heads more higher farre then we."[186] Cold tests the watermen's endurance as well as their character.

But before his applause translates into a fable of morally righteous resilience, Taylor reminds readers of his theme: "The *conglutinated* Frozen streame."[187] Like "frigorifick," this nearly obsolete word (from Latin *con-*, "with," and *glūten*, "glue"[188]), names one of cold's crucial doings: its liquid ability to adhere, and in this case specifically, to bond water molecules together into ice. Conglutination trumpets the "metamorphosis" found in Taylor's title. As human and nonhuman bodies gradually fuse, as the civic (culture) slowly amalgamates with the riverine (nature), they reveal a transformation that does not totally finish, but that redefines the terms' very boundaries. Ice's precise refusal to settle between fluid and solid, its actual *preference* for staying *between* those states, is what lent its morphological multiplicity a "hideous aspect," in the words of John Chamberlain (1553–1628).[189] Given Ward's observation about the cultural dis/unity that the iced-over Thames helped to foreground historically, drawing attention to cold's un/binding public dimensions is to Taylor's advantage. "This gnashing age of Snow and Ice,"[190] if not a new epoch in geological time, allows him to explore the timeless obstacle of stinginess. "Charity is cold," as the saying goes, and so a "thinly clad" personification of said virtue "quiuers" on the ice.[191] A parson, lawyer, and broker all ignore her: "a world of people more did thrust and throng, / Yet none Relieu'd her as they past along."[192] Charity's treatment, being given the proverbial cold shoulder, does not amount to any warmth, and thus leads metaphorically to a lack of compassion for his and his cold-bound brethren's situation. The poem's final lines are pitiful: "So farewell Frost, if Charity be liuing, / Poore men shall finde it, by the rich mens giuing."[193] Taylor's censure significantly checks the wide-eyed optimism of "the conglutinated": in its gluey conglomerates of classes and its coalitions of enjoyment, London is nevertheless a cold place susceptible to social disparities, an "age" where only certain groupings prosper. The close-fisted "tearme" seems interminable, even as it is far from static. A grand metamorphosis from miserliness into largesse, while wished for, is not to be found.

Lamenting the deficiency of his countrymen's charity certainly strikes a lachrymose chord. Despite his poignant act of protest, Taylor's message risks reinforcing the divisions he seeks to replace. Turning from effects and their alleviation to causes reveals a punitive providentialism at work: "Th'adulterate Earth, long hauing play'd the whore, / In bearing and in breeding bastards store, / As Drunkards, swearers, leachers, Cheating knaues, / Punkes, Panders, base extortionizing slaues," the litany continues, "for which foule whordome, Heauen did think it meet, / To make the Earth doe pennance in a sheet."[194] The year's big freeze (ice), pelting "earthly" sinners, sits alongside the biblical catastrophes of the Flood (water) and Sodom and Gomorrah (fire). The focus on "whoredome," a transgression that the poem leaves unspecified, certainly comports with a more salacious interpretation of "conglutinated"; it is an obsession, at least, that returns in the poem's conclusion. Taylor cites one frigging way of generating warmth: "Amongst the Whores there were hot commings in, / Who euer lost, they still were sure to win. / They in one houre so strangely did heat men, / That all the Frost they scare were coole agen."[195]

Gender on Taylor's ice leaves little to be desired: either women are downtrodden (see Charity, "in poore distresled state") or they are denigrated as adulterous "earth" and her "whores."[196] The earth's feminization results not in the image of a nurturing mother, but of an irresponsible parent: "Straight a Colde freeze coate she did put on. / Which (though herselfe were senceles, what she ayles) / It made her poorest bastards blowe their nayles. / Whilst many of her Rich broode did agree, / To make their stony hearts as hard as shee."[197] Since she did not soften her bastards' cold hearts when she had the chance, the earth is to blame for her brood's behavior, thereby self-perpetuating the cycle of poorness. Perhaps Taylor was envious of the hot "whores'" trade, or he was eager to prove a point about the watermen's Job-like patience, believing that the Christian virtue of charity can be counted on only when it comes from the divine source rather than "rich mens" munificence: "Onely the Water-men iust nothing got, / And yet (by Gods good helpe) they wanted not."[198] But raising this problem of underlying misogyny in Taylor's oft-cited poem in the annals of early modern environmental history is a concerted push for charitable (more-inclusive and less-demeaning) responses to climate disasters. Authors could, and did, do better than excoriate "fallen" women prone to "fall." They reacted more creatively to cold's doings than by calling "whore."[199]

This type of coldness was too often doubled down on, its social stigmas cemented. London's mayor issued a proclamation in 1654 about "loose and vagrant persons" stalking the streets, "especially towards Winter the Evenings growing dark."[200] *Lillie's Invitation* (1668), being the same Lilly previously mentioned, does not allow anyone with "coughs" or "colds" to dine with him on Christmas.[201] And while Rowland Vaughan's 1610 *Water-Workes* and the 1675 *High-Ways of England* by Thomas Mace (1709[?]) discuss improvements to be made during and in regard to winter, they are not centered specifically on the season; nor do they confront the challenges to popular opinion and sympathy the frost poses.[202] And yet, as the "tearme" continued down one of the coldest corridors of the LIA, others devised realistic plans for conducting the charitable work to which Taylor alludes but unfortunately blunts. Thomas Tryon's (1684) "modest observations" in the next winterlude ("Sympathize") are exceptional, really, for they lay out a detailed and protosocialist agenda, setting him apart from most of his contemporaries' reports. That being said, he was not alone in his legislative line of questioning. Evelyn, whose servant had died from smallpox exacerbated by the cold air, petitioned Charles II twice for needy residents' relief.[203] In his eyes, "the River of Thames was become a Camp, ten thousands of people, Coaches, Carts, & all manner of sports continuing & increasing: miserable were the wants of poore people, Deare universaly perished in most of the parks thro-out England, & very much Cattell."[204] Here, hapless multispecies "thousands" worried about the "resort" of recourse, of a way out, and whether it would be their last.

The king, parliament, and city magistrates, it seems, were predisposed to listen; if not, then they were persuaded to do so. *God's Works* noted the royal generosity: "Of this their Sorrows, there appear'd a Sence / Upon the Heart of our Renowned Prince."[205] Acting with the Church of England, Charles II was able to soften winter's blows, according to diarist Narcissus Luttrell (1657–1732): "During this hard frost all provisions were at an excessive rate, and fireing very dear; so that it pleased his majestie, out of his goodnesse, to order a collection about the town for the poor, and he gave himself 2000l. (as is said) for an example, and large contributions were made by diver persons."[206] The London Court of Aldermen heard the watermen's petition in 1683.[207] Even if these donations constituted a power play of "Stuart paternalism" (Beddard reminds us that suffering "could not be abolished at a single stroke of the pen"[208]), even if they were performed in part to "allow monarchs and magistrates to demonstrate benevolence,"[209] the gluey cryopolitical collaboration between secular, religious, and material forces convened by the winter of 1683–1684 remains historically significant. "The decline of providentialist readings of the Thames"[210] left a vacuum to be filled by some of the meanest diatribes listed above, invectives launched against Whigs and women, witches and whales. But it also made room for the theories of cold's agency recently articulated by Hobbes and Boyle. It carved a space for charity amidst extreme circumstances so that a phrase like "farewell Frost" may be subsequently reframed. This early moment in cryopolitics marks a public awareness campaign that delivered benefits to the beings who could hardly adapt: not by abolishing the cold (or "driving" it away), but by considering how to fare well with frost, and by asking how to help others do the same. In the complicated, "conglutinated" actions of the seventeenth century lies a mode of environmental welfare that far outlasts its fairs, that speaks to our warmer age.

## Cold, Cold Heart

For historian William M. Cavert, the frosts' hardships were politically opportunistic: "both the winters of 1607–8 and 1683–4 were met with token charity from those in power and a collective shrug of the shoulders regarding weather's impact on high politics."[211] In his view, links between dearth and rebellion have been oversimplified; rather than foment revolt, the seventeenth century's "crisis" of cold actually concretized royalist authority. State-led and sponsored regimes of care, in other words, allowed governments to avoid accusations of neglect. Feeling the pain of others became a powerful political tool for self-preservation. But what if this historical "shrug" was not so hastily shrugged off? Cold citizens could demand compensation, as we just heard, without advocating for a full-scale revolution. Matthew O'Brien's reading of Dekker's 1608 *The Great Frost* concurs: "The text ultimately asserts the value of pushing for manageable reforms rather than take on the political establishment. . . . Thus, we see that the nature of the text, at least, partially is didactic."[212] Cold certainly inculcated ambivalence, especially amongst those who could afford to shrug it off; yet others were more reluctant to give a cold shoulder to the more vulnerable members of society. Anomalies in temperature enlarged the cultural inequalities already lurking within municipalities like London.

In response to bouts of extraordinary cooling, authors turned their attention to the disproportionate abilities of non/humans to weather (or not) the cold. While they often described doomed attempts at survival in excruciating detail, they also reported on the novel and sometimes entertaining approaches to navigating an uncertain space and time, and they called upon their respective authorities (their mayors and kings) to be munificent in the face of unmitigated calamity. Neither the cementing of cynical passivity nor the stoking of outright panic, in other words, were inevitable outcomes. "Whether the present unparraleld Frost, may be Attributed to the effects of Natural Causes, or not rather to the Scourging Hand of an Offended God, I shall not Determine," announces the 1684 *A Strange and Wonderfull Relation of Many Remarkable Damages Sustained Both at Sea and Land by the Present Unparraleld Frost.*[213] Providentialist readings were still prevalent (one possible cause: human inequity), as were attributions of random disaster: literally, the result of an "ill-starred event." But even without an identifiable point of origin, "unparraleld frost" sparked robust debates concerning the spread of cold—natural-philosophical, political, theological—and fostered historic efforts to remediate its "remarkable damages." There are simply too many "Lazarus's in the Streets" whose "wants calls upon the Dives's [devices] of this Age to consider [their] Conditions."[214] "The frozen zone," in Sophie Lemercier-Goddard's opinion, is a "critical" one: "In spite of its harshness, a cold climate tests not only physical resilience but also the bonding of the community."[215] The doings of cold conveyed a doing for others: the permission to collectively revel, to be sure, but also an obligation to reexamine what "resilience" entails and to redress its shortcomings.

The two frost fairs might look like fabulous bookends at opposite sides of "the frozen age," but they in fact detail the many hardships that occurred between and during the festivities on the Thames and in different parts of the iced-over isle. Returning to these more obscure (because less glamourous) travails helps to magnify the historical endeavors that were launched in order to alleviate them. Incredibly, these spur-of-the-moment "dives's" could account for future contingencies (the phenomena known as weather) while addressing the immediate difficulties of the present. Meteorological accidents became part of the planning process, rendering a form of environmental readiness that incorporated "strange" events rather than ignoring them. It was because of, and not despite, this open-ended perspective that a shared, transnational ordeal like the LIA's drop in temperature was able to spur direct action on both local and regional levels. *Strange and Wonderfull Relation,* for example, published the same year that Freebody penned his letter, documents several ships stuck in the ice immediately off England's shores. A German crew near Deal (about thirty miles northeast of Lydd) signaled their distress, after which multiple rescue attempts were launched. "All Industry [was] Inefectuall," unfortunately, for "the Vessell being Congealed too, and Environ'd with a Massy substance of Ice; so that it is all together Inaccessible; and now no farther Attempts can be made for their Relief, because the Sea, for above a Mile from the Shore, is so hard Frozen; beyond our apprehentions to Imagine, or Chronologies to Paralell."[216] The effort of providing "relief" here is laudable, even if the mission ultimately failed.

Coastal townsfolk would be given another chance, however, to welcome neighbors in need past their "marine borders."[217] "Vast sollid Cakes of Ice, of some Miles in Circuit" from "Flanders and Holland, &c."[218] piled up in Essex, Suffolk, and Norfolk (likely the same "Islands of Ice" Freebody spotted). One of them brought along bewildered company with it: "some Skeet-slyders, upon one of those large Icie plains, were unawares driven to Sea, and arived Living (though almost perished with Cold and Hungar) upon the Sea-coast of Essex."[219] It is admittedly hard to believe this story of flummoxed skaters from the Low Countries figuratively "slyding" across the English Channel on a floating rink. The uncertain outcome of the men (did they recover, and if so, who took these strangers in after they landed on the "sea-coast"?) raises a larger, though no less critical, question: how will people respond to the strange occurrences—a locked-in ship, a lost skater—that take place between ice and society, in Essex and elsewhere?

Whether or not these near-"living" skaters actually existed, their predicament nevertheless applies pressure to the idea of humans' effortless adaption to a treacherous environment. Ice-skating, perfected by the Dutch, presented an ingenious solution to wintertime immobility. Supplied with a "skate," one could slide across previously impassible straits with ease. While the noun (1662) originates with Samuel Pepys (1633–1703),[220] many in the *Strange and Wonderfull Relation* decade of the 1680s (Evelyn included) took note of this effective tool. "The Rotterdam Dutchman with fleet cutting Scates," observed *Blanket-Fair,* "to pleasure the crowd shews his tricks and his feats."[221] Yet the cutting-edge technology of skating, embraced by famished men, takes them farther than they wished, for the ice has taken them "unawares." Their "plain" of freedom is suddenly a prison. The floating "Dutchman" similarly digs into his surface material instead of evading it; his agility grants the illusion of gliding above (not on) the frozenness below. The pamphlet's skater poetics ("a very pretty art," as the celebrated diarist put it[222]) holds out this marvelous possibility at first: with "fleet" (nimble) flicks of the feet, the world's underlying hardness may be left, briefly, behind. "His Brains and activity lie in his Heels,"[223] and such wits may be used to out-maneuver his wobbly environment.

Be that as it may, the unnamed author of *Blanket-Fair* knows this logic is merely fanciful. Remember: no one is ever "free of the Thames." When ice bridges the river's opposite banks, it reminds "land-men" and women that water is, and has always been, part of the city's business in moments of both thickness and thaw. Images of the fairs' trademark booths raise yet another bridge, a zigzagging bazaar of sellers and buyers that affords economic prosperity (for some) and the chance to partake in unique recreational enjoyment (for many others). Though infrequent, these crafted fairs symbolize invitations to frolic with a riverine world, ephemeral events built of fleeting ice and time that expose the material impacts humans and nonhumans mutually make upon the other. Historical encounters like these slow down the collaborative process for us. By reducing the Thames's flow and stretching the Channel's shores, the delicateness of natural–cultural impingement, the fluctuations of weather, season, and climate, and the fragility of ecological relations become sharper. Recall the motto of *Blanket-Fair* once more: "The World, and the pleasures it brings, / Are made up of brittle and slippery things." The LIA admonishes: *learn to tread carefully,* as if upon "glasse," for you negotiate a slick "flower" that furnishes "the World" and its "pleasures" while fracturing under humanity's massive weight. In total, an act of cold conglutination simultaneously forges new bonds *and* tests the strength of preexisting ones. If it "is needless to inform London . . . what unheard of Rendevouz is daily kept upon the Frozen face of her Navigable River,"[224] as the author of *Strange and Wonderfull Relation* opines, it remains necessary to address who is (and who is not) present at the meeting.[225] "The Arctic is coming for you," argues Christopher P. Heuer.[226] As the ominous image of the Circle drooping ever-southward enters the cultural imagination, the issue of whom it takes, or who is the subject of that susceptible "you," is worth pausing over.

Dekker characteristically models this type of meditation for us. When a heart melts, it is usually one waxing sympathetic. A cold heart, contrarily, belongs to the obdurate miser. What Dekker's 1608 and 1615 dialogues suggest is no less than a rearranging and repurposing of this language of hard- and cold-heartedness. While charity is often construed as warmth ("trust me, your tidings warmes my heart, as cold as the weather is"[227]), its heat could emerge from a touch of cold. Midway through *The Cold Yeare,* the citizen listens to the countryman's tale of animal suffering: "Wee grieve as much to beholde the miserie of our poore Cattell (in this frozen-hearted season) as it doth to looke upon our owne Affliction. . . . Alas then! . . . [It] would almost breake his owne heartstringes with sighing, to see those pine and mourne, as they doe. Nay, to see Flockes of Sheepe strangled in the Snow."[228] By placing himself in the situation of his (b)ovine as well as human neighbors to the north, the citizen is able to feel what these exposed others felt: "The Story you haue told . . . makes my heart bleed, to thinke upon the calamity of my poore Countreymen."[229] Other authors contemplated the plight of animals; *Strange and Wonderfull Relation,* for instance, noted that cattle "with Pitty, have been Observed to Lick the Ice, to abate their Thirst,"[230] and worried about the struggles of different species: in the "overwhelming" snowdrifts plaguing Scotland, "Man, and Beast, though not Equally, are too sensible of the Affliction."[231] Such ruminations are commendable, since several, but not many, sources take up animals' anguish. The forlorn letter writer from Brigg, for example, "used all the care I could to preserve [half a dozen young Lambs]" trapped in three feet of snow.[232] Even so, livestock were often reduced to numbers on a bill of mortality. Dekker's distinctive kind of care, however, cuts across species lines amounting to a nonanthropocentric form of citizenship ("poor Countreymen" encompasses "cattle," "sheepe," and their human attendants) where "kine" (cows) may be treated kindly and *as* kin.[233]

The relationship could quickly tilt in the direction of dominion. Cattle, for example, were used to plow London's streets, as the countryman points out: "I see your Gyants, and tirrable heardes of Beastes, haue done your Cittie good seruice; for in stead of Grasse, they haue had cold Prouander, and helped to rid away the greater part of your Snow."[234] Erica Fudge has argued that these labor dynamics in which farmers and cows act as "co-workers" open up a space of "conversation" between companionate species and, in Dekker's case particularly, reveal a "declaration of shared sentience and partnership."[235] It is true that the speaker calls the colossal city-sweepers "our faythfull Seruants" minutes later, yet they are also "our Nurses . . . our Guides . . . our Partners . . . yea, they are the very Upholders of a poore Farmers Lands and Liuings."[236] The "beastes" are not mastered or merely employed, then, but are recognized as mutual (and essential) comrades in thriving; one's livelihood literally depends on the other "upholder." Even the perspective of the poor leek is taken into account, the courageous vegetable who "nowe by the violence and cruelty of this Weather, beaten into the earth, being rotted, dead, disgraced and trode upon."[237] Dekker's regard for multispecies welfare, like his two contributions to the annals of the LIA at large, is consequential. Charity (as a capitalized virtue), seen before on the ice, was certainly motivated by Christian doctrine as a heaven-sending act,[238] but it may also be committed by beholding the unfairness of "affliction" in general, a grief that touches on all kinds of beings. It is by beholding the "frozen-hearted" and downtrodden that blood and doings begin to flow: such stories stimulate emotions, and coldly so.

"You melt (Sir) out of a heape of Snow, very profitable and holsome instructions."[239] Dekker's diptych exemplifies the idea that cold imparts action and not stultification, that the stuff of cold is kinetic anima, community-creating, and a catalyst of/for compassion. There is no single message to be delivered out of this chapter's "heape" of early modern climate history—cold's work is more complicated than that—only suggestions for weathering well together. (Dekker himself would know, especially if we take his "all in white" status seriously.[240]) While not exactly "holsome," it has become increasingly clear over the last four hundred years that everything below the ninetieth parallel north ultimately has a "rendevouz" to make with the Arctic: if not with icebergs that spontaneously present themselves in choked shipping lanes, then most likely with rising sea levels caused by the melting of ice and "Snow."

It is worth remembering that early modern poets and printers, in the midst of what they knew to be a calamity that was both unparalleled (a passing strangeness), and yet becoming more normal (a lasting accident), toiled with frozen inkpots and warped presses to get their stories across. Anthony Wood's bottle, for example, "froze at the fier side," and "the quil would not run" until February 4, 1684.[241] Their extant writings about adaptation demonstrate the undue exertions that adaptation requires. Penning lines in extreme conditions might have conditioned them better for the cold skies that lay ahead, but not fully. The young and the old are struck alike (1608 and 1615). A legible spectrum of tinier ice ages (1683–1684) is not totally reassuring. Yet they knew that chronicling the lability of their age might impact the ways readers interacted with their own ice worlds. The slip goes, and glues, on. At their core, these freaky forays into ice significantly raise the question about how societies do or do not adapt to a fluctuating climate, particularly those urban spaces in which the privilege of adaptation is not equally shared between its human and nonhuman citizens. Speaking of frost across cold years is a conversation worth having in a world where "great" snows are growing smaller; where "cold yeares" are dwindling, and being taken, away; where lives can too easily disappear into the shivery vortex. "It hath now left snowing,"[242] says the countryman as he exits the citizen's shop. We may be losing the cold, Dekker and his contemporaries tell us, but its doings are not done.

# Winterlude

## *Sympathize*

The source of the greatest song is sympathy.

—Halldór Laxness, *Independent People*

In his 1684 *Modest Observations on the Present Extraordinary Frost,* the health guru and early proponent of vegetarianism Thomas Tryon (1634–1703) pitches an idea for aiding citizens who had experienced the worst. Hearing "the Cries of the Poor," his proposal is truly modest: "How there may be Twenty Thousand Pounds a Week, at least, raised for their Relief."[1] Inadequate access to fuel and shelter made the poor particularly prone. As the body's heat becomes more centralized, this stimulates hunger: a "great Appetite and Drought, whence follows much and excessive Eating and Drinking of gross, fatt-succulent Foods" (4). To those who are already hungry, the cold sharpens their stomach pain and symptoms of starvation. His diagnosis: the cold is a symptom, not the cause, of an entrenched societal problem known as economic inequality. Cold exacerbates already-unequal, imbalanced, dis-eased cultural conditions. The rich are to practice sobriety and temperance, while the hungry are to partake of Tryon's special recipe: a pint of milk mixed with a quarter-pint of water and a spoonful of flour, brought to a boil, and then sprinkled with some breadcrumbs. A sparse diet of protein and carbohydrates begs improvement: "I mention not this to prevent Benevolences towards the Poor, which all that are able are bound to Afford, but only to Advise them how to supply themselves when they meet not with other Accommodations but find Rich Men's Charity more Frozen than the Thames" (4). The goal, then, is not a temporary stop-gap measure that will disappear as soon as the ice melts—a transient act of charity—but to enact lasting change. Tryon is attempting to turn the well-worn axiom *omne malum ab aquilone* (Jeremiah 1:14) into *bonum,* to translate the trying circumstances into perceivable acts of northern hospitality.

In his learned opinion, cold air breeds pestilence because it traps particles like the notorious pollutants that linger in London's atmosphere: "This Excessive Frost Condenses the Air, and renders it Sulphurous and Unhealthy, especially . . . where Sea coals are generally used for Firing, and most People (especially Women) creep close to those fulsome Fires without using themselves to proper Exercises, whereby their Blood stagnates" (4). *Who* receives injury crucially ranges in scale: from the general ("most People") to the particular (domestic "Women"). It is precisely those responsible for thwarting the cold in the first place who are "especially" punished, either by noxious warmth or by the cold-air induced diseases themselves. Naming the "their" of "their Blood" magnifies those who require the most help due to unfair degrees of exposure. To readers who would attribute the acute sense of want to an aberration in the climate, Tryon is quick to prove them otherwise by pointing out the violence of winters past. Noting that "many dyed for cold" (3) in these occasions, he connects them to the many who died before and who will die thereafter unless necessary provisions (his) be taken up. Lack, in short, is insufferably long-lasting; he hopes that it "may check that Vulgar Cry of Ignorance, That Never, O Never was known the Like" (2). The cry of penurious victims should supersede the silence of plentiful obliviousness. Tryon wishes the frost to be less prodigious, to be sure; his is a climate history that intentionally incorporates calamity so that the chronic pattern of destitution may become attenuated over time by sustained civic action.

Tryon's response to the gendered and classist distribution of weathered harm accords with his underlying argument that extreme winters and resultant climatic hardships are not entirely predictable. Because of this built-in uncertainty, any measure of preparedness (the precarious stakes of self-preservation) is wholly dependent upon the strength and limits of social bonds. Indeed, astrologers could not foretell the great frost of 1683–1684 because "our Annual Prognosticators are generally Men of little Learning, and less Philosophy, and (what is worse) many times very irregular in their lives" (2), with "irregularity" serving as a byword for immorality: debauchery, flattery, and cozening. Setting aside a common explanation at the time (divine intervention), he hesitates to assign catastrophic weather to mankind's sinful practices. His worldview is based on a belief in overall balance and order, the universe being "intire, Harmonical, and Sympathetical" in sum (3). Thus, the comets seen overhead in 1682 presaged colder weather to come: as "hot and dry Exhalations drawn up from the Earth," he surmises, "it would not be difficult to Judge that Severe Colds should ensue here below: For Extreams in Nature, if they are not Causes, are at least Fore-Runners of their Contraries" (2). Meteors can be portended only imperfectly. While his use of "sympathetical" here applies to the act of working in mutual support and coordination (hot flames need cold blasts for celestial consonance to be restored), his galactic perspective is in sync with the feelings of actionable pity that are elicited by encountering another's plight: *sun-* ("with") and *pathos* ("feeling"), a sympathy for the cold(er) commoner.

*Take physic.* "Sympathetical" echoes Lear's dramatic gestures in Shakespeare's *King Lear* (3.4),[2] of course; but unlike the king's speech about the nonhuman animal *via* the trope of "unaccommodated man," Tryon's mention of those without "accommodations" expressly involves them. "For as the Innocent Inhabitants of the Air, or expanded Suburbs of Heaven, viz. Birds and Fowls, are endangered by the Elements denying their usual Benefits and Provisions, . . . so . . . man, taking advantage of this Cruel Weather, does for profit, or pleasure, or vanity, destroy many thousands of them" (3–4). A "sympathetical" reading of the deaths of "many thousands" of "Birds and Fowls" and "Fishes" (4) means, adhering to his logic, that a sweeping destructive force is likewise coming for the human population, "a Fore runner of Mortality amongst Creatures of greater value, and even of men themselves" (4). Cold sympathetically kills in a numerical sense: mortals succumb for the sake of balance, "many thousands" to replace the "many thousands." "Would you know the reason?," he asks, seemingly annoyed. "I told you but now, Universal Nature is Sympathetical" (4).

His query is less rhetorical than that, however, although no less didactic. Despite his outspoken vegetarianism, unpacking species "value" is not his main concern at this moment. Instead, he spotlights the cruelty of "man" and "weather" in order to question the real inequities of said ecological equilibrium. While all living creatures are "endangered" by exposure, some are more susceptible to "great destruction" (4) than others—indeed, for the "innocent" denizens of the skies, they are doubly so. What is the "reason," in fact, that these "thousands" die while others luxuriate in their "vanity"? To ask is to feel (a) cold enveloping humans and nonhumans, to acknowledge that feeling as shared, and to employ the sensation, as is his hope, to advocate for those deprived of "their usual benefits and provisions." It would be too anthropocentric to claim that the death of animals is important only because it foreshadows the death of mankind. Cold brings beings *into* sympathetic relation. Cold is not merely there to harden hearts analogous to the Thames, but rather, by interlacing those bodies and their various "suburbs," it points out the veritable gaps in "charity." Once the ice melts, the care learned by being in discomfort *for* and *with* others should not slip away with it.

At the core of Tryon's "sympathetical" sketches are the considerations cold causes (or fails to incite). Tryon himself admits that "extraordinary" weather events will undoubtedly arrive again, and maybe even become ordinary: "This Extremity of Cold presages many Calamities and Evils to attend Mankind, and the rest of their Fellow-Creatures" (3). By the end of his brief pamphlet, he remains sharply critical of the present. The proclamations made by Charles II directing district officials to dispense money are but one step in the right direction: "Great and truely Royal has our gracious Soveraigns Bounty and Charity show'd it self on this occasion, as well by bestowing a Considerable Summ Himself as Commanding the Officers of every Parish to Importune the Charity of . . . Inhabitants" (5). He calculates that one hundred thousand Londoners foregoing one rich meal a week at the price of three shillings (in addition to the amount saved by avoiding liquor), would easily raise enough for the roughly eighty thousand families in want: "Will you suffer such a Number of Souls to perish, . . . rather than abridge your wanton Palates and Insatiate Paunches of unnecessary, nay pernitious Danities, one only Day in a Week? Look up thou Sottish Epicure that Denyest it, and call thy self Christian hence forwards if thou Darest" (6). Concluding on a contentious note, Tryon's tirade calls out religious hypocrisy and immoderation while outlining a commensal economic policy centered on individual accountability, be it largesse or a healthy diet. His admonishments seem prescient in this regard, as he hails one's neighbors, political leaders, and ultimately the reader. Everyone, by virtue of being touched by cold, is thereby implicated in his disaster recovery plan.

*More just.* "The Poor" and "Poor Tom" struggling in the seventeenth-century snows are the "fore runners" to the February 2021 Texas power crisis, or the "once-in-a-generation" blizzard that struck Buffalo in December 2022. We know these tragedies disproportionately affect the poor;[3] warmth, when denied, has shades of racism to it.[4] Recognizing the historical attention paid to society's most vulnerable, and the accountability people held of the institutions set in place to protect them, leaves us with the motivation to enact similar policies and regimes of change. But it is not enough to simply find inspiration in early modern likenesses. Present-day injustices registered on the skin invite us to reapproach Tryon's advisements, and Shakespeare's as well. The questions asked by these authors are ours to re-ask and are those to which we may respond. "Would you know the reason?" and "Art cold?" interrogate the nature of survival in the Anthropocene: the matter of "sympathetical" aid, what it is, whether or not it is given, and why. It means invoking Lear's shift to cold things, which starts with an act of "unbuttoning." Nearing the final quarter of the book, can you feel it now?

# 4 A Wintering Tale

> Everybody winters at one time or another; some winter over and over again.
>
> —Katherine May, *Wintering*

> Euery time they waded in the Ice, it so gathered about thē that they did seeme like a walking piece of Ice, most lamentable to behold. . . . Thus we seemed to liue in a heape and wildernesse of Snow.
>
> —Thomas James, *The Strange and Dangerous Voyage*

We start with a statue—or something "like a statue" (Shakespeare, *The Winter's Tale,* 5.3 [stage direction]).[1] Or maybe *someone*? "Prepare / to see the life as lively mocked as ever," remarks one witness (5.3.18–19). What was once "warm life . . . now it coldly stands," comments another (5.3.35–36). Its verisimilitude is staggering, and tauntingly so: "I'll draw the curtain," states the former, "my lord's almost so far transported that / He'll think anon it lives" (5.3.67–69). Enter Giovanni Michiel, the Venetian ambassador to England; he too finds it to be "like [a] statu[e]."[2] The scene suddenly widens to a tableau of the questionably vivant. There are "some of them seated in the act of writing, pen still in hand, and the paper before them; others at table, platters in hand and spoon in mouth; others opening a locker, and others in various postures, . . . as if they had been adjusted and placed in these attitudes."[3] Who are these figures? The first passage refers to Hermione's warm reception, or the promise of such, in Shakespeare's *Winter's Tale,* written in 1611, while the second details the literally "cold" stance of Sir Hugh Willoughby (1505/8–1554[?]) and crew in a letter dated November 4, 1555. Sent northeast in 1553 by London merchants who would become the Muscovy Company, Willoughby became separated from his pilot Richard Chancellor, who managed to reach the entrance to the White

Sea. Hugh's two ships eventually set in near the mouth of the Varzina River, close to Vardø, Norway, in September. "In this haven," and "seeing the yeare farre spent, & also very evill wether, as frost, snow, and haile, as though it had beene the deepe of winter, we thought best to winter there."[4] There, he and about sixty mariners perished sometime in January of the following year. Fishermen found the bodies in the summer along with the captain's journal.

The tragedy of one (a narrative) informs the tragicomedy of the other (a play). Heroine mocks hero: Hermione will be resurrected by Paulina's "powers" (5.3.90), Willoughby will not, although his exhumed corpse will cycle through the North Sea. A recovery expedition in 1556 to return the corpses to England failed; both ships succumbed to another storm and sank off Norway's west coast. The English statues' exactness, however, poses a greater problem, and one that, true to romance, thwarts neat resolution. While Paulina can command, "descend. Be stone no more" (5.3.100), the mineralogical and the human refuse to settle on one side or the other outside Vardø. In other words, while metamorphosis may promise completion on the surface (stone to skin, skin to crystal), the gaze remains focused on the swing back and forth *between* states, deep down. What does it mean to freeze to death but seem to be alive? Is motion or warmth (or both) the hallmark of life? Can a cold statue live? An ice statue, stone-like, poses the question of where the human ends, ice begins, and vice versa. When is a frostbitten appendage no longer one's flesh? May it be magically restored, Hermione-style? Pondering this tricky in-betweenness might be behind Paulina's concern for the spectators: "No longer shall you gaze on't, lest your fancy / May think anon it moves" (5.3.60–61).

Far from demonstrating Paulinian artistic prowess, frozen bodies infused with cold posed an ontological conundrum to sixteenth- and seventeenth-century onlookers. Early modern explorers seeking northern passages never set out in winter. Wintering was almost always a last resort for the frigid few; it meant certain death, to physically become winter and its snows. It is no coincidence that the two winterers I opened with bear striking resemblance: literal still lifes whose postures "mock" the life that once was. Perceptive audiences would have connected the figure of one fanciful tale with woeful tales of recent expedition, especially Willoughby's infamous fate. His proved the most haunting, in fact, a "sorrow . . . sore laid on, / Which sixteen winters [could not] blow away" (5.3.49–50). (Or about sixty, in this case.) The company of William Barents returned after their stay on Nova Zembla in the 1590s, in tatters, mauled by bears and bergs alike. Willoughby, as we will see, was a spectral presence in future endeavors. A ghost writer, he is the figure of lethal congelation who will not quite disappear: a corpse caught in the act of writing; a journal pried from cold hands. His intrepid countrymen were all visited in some way by him, and his story was grotesquely reimagined. Richard Hakluyt (1552[?]–1616) made clear that "the companie . . . perished for cold"[5] at the whims of an "evill" north. "Here endeth . . . his note . . . written with his owne hand,"[6] he observed in the margins of *The Principal Navigations* (1598–1600). But the hard story of their wintering endured, even if they did not. It scrawled on without "endeth."

Over the next century and a half, Michiel's haunting image refused to fade from memory. Indeed, the poet-geographer M. Richard Willes (1546–1579[?]) cited Willoughby as one "enforced . . . to end his life for colde, congealed and frozen to death,"[7] and as a reason for England to turn toward the northwest. And to be "congealed" is not simply to die, either. Sir Hugh was contorted into mannequin postures. Henry Lane, perhaps trying to take a bite out of the cold, blamed inexperience for the tragedy in Samuel Purchas's 1625 *Pilgrimes*: "Seventie persons perished, which was for want of experience to have made Caves and Stoves."[8] Chancellor, after all, and later Anthony Jenkinson (1529–1610/11), pushed through to Moscow on behalf of the company. Still, his legacy lingered—and even lay in state. According to Lane, "the dead bodyes of Sir Hugh Willoughbie, and his people . . . remained there in Mosco Agent almost two yeeres."[9] The semithawed man becomes memento mori. While he "and much of the goods and victuals were recovered and saved,"[10] they were ultimately reclaimed by the icescape on that "disastrous voyage" of 1556. John Milton adds a touch of horror to his 1582 *Brief History of Moscovia,* writing that "their breath [was] so congeal'd by the cold, that they fell down as it were stifl'd."[11] Air hardens in the throat; terror spreads. James Thomson's "Winter" from *The Seasons* (1730) speaks of "the Briton's fate . . . shut / By jealous nature with eternal bars . . . Froze into statues; to the cordage glued / The sailor, and the pilot to the helm."[12] Though lost, Hugh habitually reappears: as a caution against hubris; a victim of supernatural asphyxiating force; a model of/for the sublime; a figure to encapsulate the era's desires and fears encircling northern exposure. As the biographer Thomas Fuller generously put it in 1662, his was a worthy sacrifice that typifies the noble spirit of English expedition, and therefore able to resuscitate his nation's geopolitical clout: "Their discoveries did thaw, though their bodies were frozen to death."[13]

## Leads in Winter

So, look again on "like a statue." The fate and flesh of early winterers, and what they reveal for our time as well as theirs, are precisely what my chapter on wintering pursues. It gathers around one corpus in particular: Thomas James's 1633 *The Strange and Dangerous Voyage.* The Welsh captain was a latecomer to the northwestern expeditions that had begun over a century earlier in England. His 1631–1632 voyage from Bristol and that of his competitor, Luke Foxe's from London in 1631, were the nation's last attempts in the seventeenth century, their travels disproving any possible passageway through Hudson Bay. (The impasse eventually led to real riches after the French fur traders Médard des Groseilliers and Pierre-Esprit Radisson spearheaded the formation of the Hudson's Bay Company in 1670. James Knight, its chief factor, tried again for a transoceanic route in 1719 but never returned.) Inauspicious tidal patterns gave James "little hope of a passage."[14] Foxe, author of his own account, *North-West Fox* (1635), was ridiculed for returning to England in 1631. James chose to winter on Charlton Island in the southeastern corner of the bay. Upon arriving home the next summer, he was hailed as a hero: the "worth of a Warrier and Pylot is never discouered but in stormes and skirmishes," wrote his friend Thomas Nash (d. 1648) in an encomium enclosed with the *Strange and Dangerous Voyage* (2:451). In the words of fraternal poets Thomas and Francis Beedome in 1641, his example will make "men . . . rise up with reverence, and keepe / Thy fame from freezing."[15] When confronted with "mounts of solid liquor" and "moving marble, . . . Thou wert above a man, thy zeale like fire / Dissolv'd th'opposing Ice."[16] The hyperbole is significant here: even in confinement, James assumes the super-"man" persona of icebreaker.

To be encircled, as I see it, is to be ensorcelled. As Nash also opined, "let not the cold entertainment you have had in the frozen Seas, freeze up your affections in undertaking other worthy employments" (2:451). There is other ice-speak to be heard within this "cold entertainment" in addition to its martial, capitalist, stylistic, and bookish overtones. James's vivid descriptions of dearth and death on Charlton Island, summed up in a section called simply "The Wintering," is of utmost significance for my purposes here. The ontological, epistemological, and ethical questions therein make his unique amongst sub-Arctic scrawls: they may have been "thawed" over time, but they are not wholly defrosted. Nor are they settled: to conclude her outstanding critical edition, Colleen M. Franklin suggests that *Strange and Dangerous Voyage* "illuminate[s] the roots of such approaches to the literature of the [Canadian] north as the 'garrison mentality' and the nationalist sublime. No longer need the North be strange and dangerous."[17] But without the "strange" and the "dangerous," what does "the North" become? I would like to sit with this ice oddity some more, hunker down only to open up; and while his homeward voyage is "miraculous" and granted by "[God's] preseruation of vs" (2:592), I keep an eye looking backward on the Hudson Bay Lowlands as he departs. My reading of the icescape intentionally mimics the rending, wending, and compression demonstrated by its famously unmanageable, semitransparent materials. As I. S. MacLaren discovered when piecing together poetic responses to the Northwest Passage, "the North in literature exhibits the sort of discontinuous representation that one finds of Canada generally in its literature. Leads in the ice open, but not for long."[18] I espy a four-part journey ahead, with James's grim pronouncements from the epigraph charting my path.

- "Wildernesse of Snow." Departing slightly from the prominence of Willoughby's and Barents's winter camps in the European history of northern exploration,[19] I move to a less-studied location about 5.5 thousand km to the southwest: Hudson Bay, an inland marginal sea of the Arctic Ocean. Broken clocks, statues frozen in time, strained celestial calculations: these were transcontinental phenomena that James and his readers certainly expected. The "intense cold"[20] of Russia would have been anticipated by James, for instance, since Moscow was roughly aligned latitudinally with the middle of the Bay. But the region's harsh "snow" simultaneously adhered to and sharply resisted cartographical projections, since "the climate of North America defied European preconceptions handed down across centuries from classical Greece and Rome."[21] The earliest meteorologists could predict the coldness of North America, but only to a certain extent. The playwright John Marston (1576–1634) puns on the multivalent designation of "degree" as linear space and level of intensity in *The Insatiate Countess* (1613): "I would endure a winter's pilgrimage in the frozen zone—go stark naked through Muscovia, where the climate is nine degrees colder than ice."[22] It is hard to tell what is colder than ice when a "degree" of temperature is ungraspable.

And as the quantitative eludes capture, so does the *klima* of "climate" start to undulate. In his transhistorical study of the word, Thomas H. Ford points out that "climate has meant meaning—meaning in its swerves, silences and unpredictable shifts, in the unanticipated intersections it effects, in its irreducible ambiguities, in its undecidability between literality and metaphor."[23] The tutelage of English clergyman William Watts (ca. 1590–1649) to his students, bound with James's *Strange and Dangerous Voyage,* collapses neat geographical spans: "The place of this *Wintering* was within a [latitudinal] *minute* or two of the *heighth* of our *Cambridge*" (2:627). His lecture on the world's "fiue zones," "temperature and habitation," and the Aristotelian reconciliation of contrary "causes and effects" concludes anticlimactically: "The great and infinite Creator hath so disposed and varied everything . . . [that] it is impossible for mans reason" (2:624). Whether noting its time or its weather, winter on the Bay was wintertime out-of-season, one long winter-long that destabilized four-season stability. Once-discrete locations congeal in winter's whorl-whirl, in the Arctic circle's spin, in the subpolar vortex of James's prose and verse. The *Strange and Dangerous Voyage* warps "climate," illustrating a bewildering of order that *is* "wildernesse."[24]

• "We seemed to liue." While admittedly grave at first glance, the *Strange and Dangerous Voyage* examines the quandaries that freezing posed to transatlantic and Arctic winterers who fortunately lived to tell their tales. In doing so, James pushes what I have been calling "cryocorporeality" and what geographer John Wylie labels "becoming-icy." Comparing the 1910–1913 Antarctic expeditions of Robert Falcon Scott and Roald Amundsen, Wylie argues that "it is through embodied, material practices—through relations of becoming anterior to a duality of discourse and world—that distinctive subjectivities and landscapes are produced."[25] I pick up the material qualities of "icy" to highlight cold's narratological import: namely, the voyage's translation into *Strange and Dangerous Voyage.* And by mapping said "becoming" onto an earlier and northern sphere of elemental influence, I extend the ontological dimensions of "becoming-icy" temporally as well as spatially. We have been introduced to cold's powers already: the "frigorifick" materiality that excites scientific promiscuity (Robert Boyle), and the physics that activates epistemological alternatives to stasis (Gerhardus Mercator and Jodocus Hondius). Foxe, James's grumpy compatriot, coined the word "frigitating" (2:427) to denote the dual functions of freezing—frigidity and agitation—on which wintering depends.[26] Once "snogged" (2:289), or shook, one may try to shake it off.[27] But James pauses here; and, more acutely than his peer, he points up the dangerous and discombobulating blending of embodiment and environment. In his parlance, wintering effects a remarkable chain of events: when shook-up things arrange in shivering line-ups, shake into more-than-human assemblages. It is a contraction into discomforting collectivity, the manifestation of Thomas Dekker's "thrust" and Shakespeare's crowded prince "thronged up with cold" (*Pericles,* 2.1.72): an experience of in/voluntary exposure operating at differing timescales, whether curled-up or no.

James underlines what it means "to liue" *within* metamorphosis: when the human is no longer considered a privileged category, when ice is reconfigured as yourself, both on- and offstage. "Metamorphosis" became a byword for addressing wintry middles where matter "seemed" dead, alive, or both at once. Edward Pelham and seven other whalers marooned in Greenland by mistake in 1630 realized their predicament in *Gods Power and Providence* (1631) thus: "Like men already metamorphosed into the yce of the Country, . . . stood we with the eyes of pittie beholding one another."[28] They were rescued, as if reborn, after "nine months and twelve dayes."[29] To be figuratively "metamorphosed" brushes up against the physical fate of Willoughby, the "yce"-man, which threatened the definition of the human. This physiological uncanniness, or seeing one's self as strange, illustrates the cryobiological concept of "latent life": "the liminal and vague state between life and death; . . . life that is perpetuated indefinitely such that it becomes difficult to assert with confidence that it is not, in fact, death."[30] Becoming-Bay, freezing in/to and somehow out of death, James's *Strange and Dangerous Voyage* renders human–cold relations even stranger, his winter camp resembling a "zone of existence where beings are made to live and are *not allowed to die*."[31] While macabre, James's delicate grasp contains consequential implications for thinking through the fragile conjunctions of season, snow, and bodies. Rather than circumscribe wintry spaces as either malicious or amicable, his tale intensifies vexing issues surrounding climate adaptation, a topic that has become all the more paramount for us in a time of puzzling change.

True, James's experience further evidenced winter's delayed deliverance, insufferable providence, and metamorphosis of the corporeal kind. His was one of ten European winterings that took place in or near the Arctic from 1556 to 1635. Some crews were decimated; other expeditions managed to stay over with few fatalities. Seven Dutch sailors voluntarily wintered in the whaling settlement of Smeerenberg in northwestern Svalbard in 1633–1634 and again in 1634–1635. The first party survived "the insupportable cold and storms,"[32] while the second failed their endurance test. Meanwhile, on the island of Jan Mayen, seven Dutchmen stationed there to defend the island from Basque whalers perished in the winter of 1633–1634. A journal entry from January 8 speaks of the night turning "excessive cold and stormy, whereof we now began to feel the effects in our bodies."[33] Writer's cramp crept in: on April 31, the author's last word was *die* ("that" in Dutch), whereafter he likely "retired to his cabin" and "lived some days after he left off writing; it being very probable, that some might grow sooner stiff, by the excessive cold, than others."[34] When the "very miserable" seven were found on June 4, they were all fully stiff, one with his arm "still extended to his mouth."[35] Keeping up a daily schedule, according to archeologist Louwrens Hacquebord, proved to be a lifesaver: "The wintering group that successfully maintained its diurnal rhythm and remained active during the polar night had the best chance of surviving the polar winter."[36] But wintering also transgressed the illusory line between human and environment. It did not just trouble the shaky protection of warm life from powdery death; it raised the un/comfortable question of keeping up with the pace of polar night, of putting a more tandem "rhythm" into practice. Delving into James's text has the serious question of how to go on "liuing" right now at its heart. In his parlance, winter is not just a test of one's endurance, but a test of endurance itself, of the limits of resilience. Winterers like him wonder if the cold snap will snap, if the world will recoil. His *Strange and Dangerous Voyage* puts pressure on the possibility and even optimism of adaptability and asks, if it happens, how long this flexibility will last, when (or if ever) the *dis*contentment will turn.

- "In a heape." James's story of elemental imbrication is an ongoing one that bears repeating today, particularly in places where winter's very existence is at risk. It provokes questions concerning the Bay's past, present, and future: not only how it is told, but also, given the region's settler-colonialist history in which he participated, who is allowed to tell it. As soon as it was published in 1633, his work sparked a variety of literary, medical, and scientific responses. Instead of automatically shunning this "heape" ecology, though, James's text tempted further collaboration with the strange mass of winter. In a way, he was following creative precedent: far before the fetishization of the fate of John Franklin, Foxe already had enough material in the mid-seventeenth century to compile a two-hundred-page anthology of northwestern travels, half of which was dedicated to his own account. Francis Bacon had previously demonstrated how natural philosophy and travel literature could overlap in "*Calor et Frigus,*" discussing the reactions of Barents's party to drastic temperature drops on Nova Zembla.[37] Robert Burton too connected imprisonment in "continual night" to melancholia.[38] Yet James's enduring connection with a wider audience granted it a unique degree of adaptability. Boyle quoted James several times in his treatise on cold, most notably on the topic "of bodies lasting long unputrified in ice."[39] (He was also an investor in the Hudson's Bay Company.[40]) The strollers' mention in *Blanket-Fair* (1683) of "Admiral James" testifies to his popularity fifty years later. Intertextualities like these prove that not only was the *Strange and Dangerous Voyage* in conversation with empirical and public understandings of cold, but that it was also responsible for advancing them. The stakes of "liuing" in a "heape" are therefore narratological as much as ontological. I will return to this idea of latent communality in conclusion by addressing the world's second-largest bay as an "engine" of imagination (in James's words [2:588]), or "counterarchive" (in those of James L. Smith[41]), where memory, protest, and repair may converge.

- "Lamentable to behold." Ultimately, when talking about James's wintering tale, we are led back to the "heavy matters" of cold beings *being* (*Winter's Tale,* 3.3.102). An oft-noted trouble with "wildernesse" is that it risks emptying the land of precontact cultures.[42] James's account of immense personal hardship—while dismissing traces of Cree and Inuit civilization—helped fuel contemporary debates over the north (and northern America) as an uninhabitable frozen zone, a definition that had become increasingly tenuous for over a century, bothering pithy maxims like that of John Rastell (d. 1536) that, beyond Iceland, "no man may there abyde."[43] Like those who wandered the first fairs while probing the unequal effects of its frosts, the questions of whose life is affected and who is forced to resile, evacuate, and adjust remains at the fore nearly four hundred years later. It is easy to fall back on dependable motifs. Wintering often signals what you are forced to endure: parsed *over* winter, days ticked off a calendar from solstice to equinox, December to March in the northern hemisphere,[44] on into the spring and the springing back to life.[45] Stuck *in,* you must somehow move *through.*[46] "Our men, with this cold, doth begin to hurkle," cried Foxe (2:374n3). A rare word for "to draw the limbs and parts of the body closely together,"[47] "hurkling" is a contraction *against* rather than *for* a community. James had solipsistic reasons to recount the winter of 1631–1632, in that it birthed a best-seller, and yet I believe we can still repurpose his story about self-reliance amidst permeating snow into something else. To be in a "heape" rephrases my project's overarching attention to the topic of uncertain, unfinished shelter. If all this talk of terms seems strange thus far, that has been my intention; it was that of early moderns, too, who reconfigured winter(ing) in more-than-lethal ways.

## Telling Winter Differently

But before we get back on the Bay, I first need to meditate on "winter" itself, eschewing winter as a temporary moment (a period of calendrical time) in favor of a participatory process instead. "[Dwelling] signifies that immersion of beings in the currents of the lifeworld without which such activities as designing, building, and occupation could not take place at all."[48] This would be "winter" in anthropologist Tim Ingold's dialect, an active state of dwelling where human–nonhuman immersive interaction is the prerequisite for building relations. Speaking of "winter" this way unleashes it from its typical connotations: a transitive verb "to provide shelter" (ca. 1440), and most commonly, the intransitive "to protect from," to maintain oneself through the specific season of winter (ca. 1382).[49] These two etymological senses have prevailed, however, stressing intransitive states of endurance through a temporary time period. In each, we imagine the already-built (usually by humans). Yet the "activities" I am after designate what is *to be* built, and early modern authors could stress "winter" as just this active co-construction with the "currents of the lifeworld." While obscure, "winter" marks a "becom[ing] wintery" in 1483; "to be detained by winter weather" in 1555; "to affect like winter, subject to wintry conditions; to make wintry; to chill, freeze" in 1622–1629. It is no coincidence that winter's material agency sprung out of an era of Arctic exploration. Its emphasis on embodiment, in fact, comes from the noun: Old English *winter* (ca. 888), probably a form of the Indo-European base *wed-, wod-, ud-*: "to be wet."

Thus we "liue": if wintering is both a condition and a process, it is imperative that we experiment more often in our conversations with its wetting. James, in fact, left a vocabulary for us, writing in his homage to Charles I that "they were rough elements, which I had to doe withall: and will, with fauour, vouchsafe to pardon, if a Sea-mans style be like what he most conuerseth with" (2:454). Combined with "The Wintering" (to be visited a little later), "winter" indicates how humans "become winter" by and through "wintering." To put it all together, then, and to provide a handy glossary for what comes next: "winter" veers from noun to verb and back again, from fixed season to sluicing slush; it questions how things endure (or do not), rather than reestablishes humanity's eternal fight against rime. It is climatic weather-in-action that challenges temporal compartmentalization (into quad-cameral chronological parts), ontological definition (the "human" subject to wet's piercing cold), allegorical appropriation (that same human's "age"),[50] ethical considerations (whose shelter and for whom), and epistemological assurance (when "heapes" of winter snow are used as evidence for and against global warming). As a noun, it moves from type of weather (wind, snow) to observable pattern (season, climate), albeit an inherently mobile one. There are doings specific to winter that send "season" to its verbal limits, that mark a process, a seasoning of the exposed body, a climate that resists control indoors and outdoors. *The Strange and Dangerous Voyage* is a case study in extreme living, its cold-water baths riskier than what we have seen heretofore, a sojourn into cold of a different continent as opposed to your own.

This urge to reevaluate winter has been taken up recently by cryophilic writers worried about its looming oblivion. "How shall we sing the songs of winter in a warm climate?," Adam Gopnik rhetorically asks in *Winter: Five Windows on the Season.*[51] For him, remembering winter underscores its historical malleability, recalling its various representations under shifting circumstances: "To *make* winter, to distinguish and discriminate against its pleasures and terrors, requires an effort of mind and memory as great as any modern people have attempted."[52] Understanding it as a construction, in addition to a celestial event caused by planetary tilting, helps explain the origin of maxims like "stress makes sweetness," since the planting of seeds during winter (also known as "vernalization") induces blossoming in spring. "Snow and ice," therefore, "are the frosting of loss."[53] He continues: "No effort at naming, discriminating, enduring, explaining, mystifying, fabulizing has been keener than ours with winter over the past two centuries. Even if we were to lose our season, we would not lose all our meanings for it."[54] Early modern winter writers not only anticipate but also contribute to this twenty-first-century condition of seasonal meaning-making *because* their annual cold cycle trended toward accretion instead of loss: the Little Ice Age (LIA), that meteorological eon in which warmth flicked in and out of collective cosmopolitan memory. This is not to say that winterized tropes started with them, obviously, but that their lexicon contained sharp and subtle variances. They saw winter's verboseness as a window into difficult questions about what it makes, unmakes, and comprises. Their musings are incomplete, and thus worth re-posing. At a time in which winter is actively being attenuated, their "efforts" are ours to take up, with all their unusual inflections.

Casting winter as something other than a static backdrop *for* stories and *for* meditations on getting by could be complicated. During this period, winter was most often appropriated for religious purposes. Church authorities helped cement winter's figurative role as a stage for moral combat, a moment when Christian light is pitted against devilish gloom, sapping its material significance in favor of the allegorical. James Anderson's 1614 *Winters-Nicht* epitomizes this function: "But darknesse of our minde it is, / Which hides from us the Heavens blisse."[55] Consequently, it resembled a proving ground for the twinned virtues of piety and charity.[56] John Shower's 1695 *Winter Meditations,* for instance, could commend London's mayor for his largesse, but one-ups him by offering to take care of the poor's souls as well. Citing Psalms, he claims an extreme winter may beneficially "warm" believers' "devotion and Reverence towards God."[57] The polemical sermonizer Cotton Mather (1663–1728) went even further in his 1693 *Meditations* on New England's winters, treating winter as a period of Job-like suffering in which one physically and spiritually toils for redemption. Not only was winter God's work; it was also the time in which God's work was to be done: "For every pinch of Cold, whereto we have Exposed our Bodies, in the Serving of God, all the Winter Long, we shall be Recompenced in our Glorify'd Bodies."[58] Homilies like these promoted real aid; that being said, this recurring metaphor of instructive hardship deserves contextualization within a wider spectrum of seventeenth-century interpretations. Tellingly, Mather's analogies draw from recent discoveries made about winter's "constitution"[59] by familiar names: its genesis from a "store of Corpuscles,"[60] a harshness "as Capt. James found it,"[61] a strength "as Mr Boyl Experienced,"[62] and even whether the "Primum Frigidum" be "a positive Quality, (which I encline to think) or a privative, still 'tis the Breath of God that gives Rise unto it."[63] As his last opinion reveals, cryocurious thinkers could always resort to God's unassailable purpose or power inherent "in the very constitution of the winter itself,"[64] attribute record snowfalls to causation done out of righteous punishment and reward,[65] or establish a divine hierarchy. God "made,"[66] and he rules over, his "Creatures" and "Servants" of snow.[67] Yet there were winterers who were not so quick to explain "accidents"[68] as plan, believer or not. Even the faithful could grapple with scriptural and scripted responses to severe cold spells.[69] James was one who beheld winter as such, a trinity of puzzle, predicament, and potential, and who deepened corporal–spiritual ambiguities rather than resolved them. I now return Bay-side by way of some crucial historical context.

## Bitter Rivalries

The Bay area was the best place to prove one's hot mettle at the time. Only a few years earlier (1626), Purchas hailed those like Thomas Button (ca. 1575–1634) and William Baffin, who sought "to tame Nature, where she is most vnbridled, in those Northeasterly, Northwesterly and Northerly Borders (where she shewes her selfe al Borderer indeed) and to subdue her to that gouernment and subiection."[70] Here, the intrepid polar protagonist repelled "monstrous Icie Ilands, renting themselues with terrour of their owne massines, . . . crashing and splitting their congealed Armours."[71] It was a repeated model: he who entered the "watery Plaines" of "continual ciuill warre" was not expected to skirt these skirmishes, but quiet them. In this case, by merely surviving the "warre," James was saved from disgrace. To reclaim it from disaster, however, the power dynamic had to be flipped. Rather than perceiving his mandatory wintering on the island as an imprisonment—cold's clear victory over the pinioned "warrier-pylet"—his stay was reinterpreted as an act of fortitude, a virtuous choice. Surrounded, his position becomes a site of strength rather than weakness: when the ice presses *in,* the valiant press *out.* His narrative's recuperation depends on making such tenacity readily observable, as readers await the moment when the central human figure powerfully bursts forth from his cold cell, environed no more, with all the chinks in his "armour" on display.

It also helps explain why Foxe's more encyclopedic treatment failed to find an audience. Though briefly intersecting with James in late August (whom he found to be "no Seaman," those hours "the worst spent" of the entire voyage [2:359–60]), the narratives sharply diverged in popular estimation. The sneering Foxe, arguably the more experienced sailor, establisher of "the farthest" (2:393) north at the time (Cape Dorset), was now forced to place apologies at the end of his collection ("some concluding that I have done nothing" [2:408]), and enumerate the "benefit[s] ensuing by my comming home this yeare" (2:415). This capitulation must have particularly stung; he provides nearly two hundred folio pages of English Arctic expedition, an exhaustive history beginning with the conquests of King Arthur, before launching into his own. Despite a few aesthetic flare-ups ("pettiedancers or henbane . . . in the firmament" [2:313], land "the greenest and best . . . I have seene since I came out of the river of Thames" [2:336], an "aurora [that] blusht, as though shee had ushered her Master from some unchast lodging" [2:395]), his spartan prose and penchant for logistical detail predominate. It is what he had promised to the reader, to be fair: "Expect not heere any florishing Phrases or Eloquent tearmes; for this Child of mine, begot in the North-west's cold Clime (where they breed no Schollers), is not able to digest the sweet milke of Rethorick, that's food for them" (1:7). Monotony is his ostensible enemy, one reason for why he omits Henry Hudson's post-mutiny wintering in 1611: "to speake of all the troubles, and of this cold Winter, would be too tedious" (1:134). He also scoffes at the advice to winter, mainly to separate himself from his predecessor while simultaneously establishing a name for himself in an illustrious lineage: "I was not come to do so much as another man, but more [than] any, as I had already done" (2:359).

Foxe's boasting unfortunately backfired, for his "child" proved to be no match for James's riveting tale of wintering. Incredibly, the boredom of a "cold clime" proved to be anything but. As one nineteenth-century scholar tabulated, in James "we hear of ice some 400 times, or five times more than in the six voyages of Frobisher and Davis together."[72] Foxe took to sorting out "this prodigious thing we call ice" (2:288) into two types, bergs and floes; he hypothesized upon the former's formation, "ingendred upon the Winter's snow" (2:292), and treated it grammatically as plural, "where there is few or no Ice" (2:435). His interest in its "unconstant shapes" (2:291) lends him the air of a protoglaciologist,[73] yet he mostly skims over multiplicity. His rival goes further: although the actual voyage was thwarted "in" the "North-west's" place, *Strange and Dangerous Voyage,* on the other hand, was birthed *by* its cold. The icy eloquence that ensued, as we will hear, strangely set up his "fame from freezing" even as he became famous *for* it, circulating the story rather than stultifying it.

If the recuperation of an imperiled human in a prisoning, polar place seems suspicious to the modern reader—a task that relies on recentering the human amidst abominable ice—critics later turned to the book's literary basics, James's imaginative legacy, and the historical significance of the voyage instead. James's text, especially its poetry, has been studied for its literary merits and blend of genres that became synonymous with Arctic adventure. Catastrophe can be creative in this author-explorer sense, although it depends on a certain kind of editorial redemption. Wayne K. D. Davies's assessment sums up this sentiment neatly: "James," he believed, "deliberately used the fear of a hazardous environment to create the tensions that sustained the exploration narrative. In doing so, James transformed a *failure* of exploration into a literary success."[74] Thus, it was his "*narrative, not his voyage and wintering,* that should be seen as his true memorial—one that led to so many other passages of enquiry and representation."[75] Indeed, being "inclosed amongst extraordinary great pieces" of ice (2:575) roundtrip was but one of the seemingly infinite hardships James and his crew suffered, crafting a harrowing picture that proponents of the sublime would later prize: from *Paradise Lost* (1667/1674), to *The Rime of the Ancient Mariner* (1798), to *Frankenstein* (1818).[76] It also reflects the captain's own "hastily written" (2:592) wish for how he wants to be remembered, hapless but not hopeless: "I repent not my selfe, but take a great deale of comfort and joy, in that I am able to giue an account . . . of those parts of the world, which heretofore I was not so well satisfied in" (2:593). John Barrow (1764–1848), Second Secretary of the British Admiralty and Arctic chronicler who helped reinvigorate the search, could mock James's book and touristic tone in 1818 as one of "lamentation and weeping and great mourning. . . . The observations it contains are at this time of no use whatever."[77] Nonetheless, as a survivor, he models how the specter of the gaunt ice-man could be kept at bay, a mental menace resurrected and then banished, proving that the fates of one's predecessors are not prophetic.

It is a cheery recovery project to be sure, but one not quite chilly enough for me. Adriana Craciun, taking in its "orgy of composite inscriptions, images, and performative utterance,"[78] claims James's book acts as "a 'virtual witness' to the extreme Hudson Bay climate," an artifact of "social authorship" that traces "how Arctic exploration was configured within . . . corporate culture, through what material circuits of textual production, readerships, and archiving; according to which temporal scales."[79] Her "line of enquiry" therefore departs from more formal investigations that preoccupy Davies. Her circuitous thinking starts us off. Diverging slightly from these critics' bibliographical emphases, however, I pursue the cold interlocking its rhetoric, the elemental glue that holds the compositional process together and constitutes the "social" as human–nonhuman crystalline conglomerate.

FIGURE 10. Jens Munk, *Navigatio Septentrionalis* (1624), courtesy of the John Carter Brown Library. A burial at center is scarcely discernible amidst the industry attempting to domesticate the Bay.

Separating "voyage" from "narrative," while intentionally generous, sadly sets up a dichotomy in which the Bay's natural environment (the stuff of winter) is pried apart from the forlorn winterer (caught in the cultured act of writing), divorces the Bay's cold contents from the creativity spurred *by,* as the title page pronounces, "miseries indured both going, wintering, returning" (2:449). What I see in the cold quills is not the rescue of the tragically besieged writer, retelling a one-sided story that neglects the role of the "clime" in raising the "child." James cannot shake off the rime from his rhymes; it imbues and bespeaks its mixed-genre, multi-faceted form. Sorting through this polar palimpsest, one that layers substance (ice-snow) and agency (freezing-wintering) with season (wintertime), I propose why its strangeness should be recalled, and for reasons besides recementing its rank in the cold canon of literary history. To return to cold's odd doings, its capacity to snuff lives as well as inspire lines, I argue, is to check human authority and circular centrality at a time when older "discoveries" are physically defrosting and being replaced by new ones. These dangers are impetuses not for reinscribing relations out of fear, but for capaciously reimagining them.

## Have Mercy on Frozen Men

By capitalizing on ostensible failure, James's *Strange and Dangerous Voyage* was "strange" in another sense. Memories of his European predecessors' disastrous outcomes in the area were still fresh. Barely a generation had passed since Hudson's notorious mutiny on his fourth northern voyage (1610–1611), when the crew "exposed [him] and his friends in a boat in the open air."[80] Hudson had ordered that they resume their search for the Northwest Passage after wintering in the part of the Bay that, coincidentally, James would later inhabit (and would be named after him). The prospect of multiple miserable winters exposes one to possible insubordination. And if it could split numbers, it could also reduce them. The Danish explorer Jens Munk, charged by King Christian IV (1577–1648) to find a navigable route, was compelled to winter in the Churchill River estuary (Port Churchill) on the Bay's western side from 1619 to 1620. He and his crew were decimated by frostbite, malnutrition, and disease. The following June, only he and two others out of sixty-five were alive, limping back to Copenhagen. Surrounded by the unburied dead and ridden with scurvy, "at this time commenced my greatest sorrow and misery, and I was then like a wild and lonely bird. . . . Nor had I now anybody to command. . . . I was myself then quite miserable and abandoned by all the world, as everybody may imagine."[81] Even in late spring, "we could not stand any cold, our limbs being paralyzed and, as it were, crushed by the cold."[82] This lament is at odds with the resourceful commotion presented in the picture of *Munkenes Winterhaven* ("Munk's winter harbour"), published in his *Navigatio Septentrionalis* of 1624. The unyielding house, however, is an illusion: the expedition's time on land is short-lived, as the worsening weather sends them back aboard their beached vessel to hunker down. Yet this portrait of the ship placed precariously "on the ground, whatever ice might come"[83] is missing from the plate. Nothing can "remain firm"[84] bayside. Drifting turns one (Hudson) into a berg, yet so does anchoring (Munk): both are results of overexposure to the cold "open." Belonging to their respective bodies of water, corpses freeze, flow, repeat; or, unburied, they lie scattered by "a wind which could move men"[85] and the futile structures they erect. On this Bay, one may only watch and learn what (not) to do.

Button's stay (1612–1613) started to twist this litany of misery into something valorous, even if the trips themselves were of little value. Ordered to find the lost captain and extend his discoveries, if possible, he "endured a sharpe Winter" (1:169) at Port Nelson on the western side, according to Foxe. The first to cross the Bay, and falling ill, he "lost many men" (1:167), although he managed to escape mutiny when the voyage resumed in the spring and he established what he thought to be the northernmost point: *Ne Ultra* ("no further"), or Roes Welcome Sound. It appears that certain "demands" were drawn up during their stay (1:169). The sole surviving account (Foxe's) is threadbare, and Purchas scarcely mentions the expedition.[86] But the Bay still beckoned; its barely drawn maps—like Henry Briggs's in 1625—magnetized others, goading them to disprove Button's pronouncement. (Foxe soon after surpassed it.) There proved to be no end to its icescape,[87] for immediately following Button came his cousin William Gibbons (1614), who was thwarted at the mouth of the Strait and then spent ten weeks icebound off the Labrador coast, a sticky spot that was given the sad name of "Gibbons his hole" (1:201). Button ultimately helped establish a heroic mode, where *ne* ("no") swaps with *plus* ("more"), transforming wintering into a blue badge of honor. In William Vaughan's 1626 *The*

*Golden Fleece,* his "stout pilgrimage" is praised: "Yet they will prize him more, when more they know / How he endur'd a winter deep with' Snow. / For eight moneths space, besides the Icy hills, / Which Natures eares with strange amazeme[n]t fils."[88] The Bay becomes Jason's Black Sea, a laden Colchis, a place that was once, too, considered to be the world's farthest periphery.[89] A cryonaut comparable with the "great Drake"[90] goes in both directions: raising "new pillars . . . like those of Hercules,"[91] he extends the classical edge farther west when he connects to the "new Albion"[92] (California) on the other side. This helped create a logic of success-as-failure: while wintering is a bonus, a "more," it could also be enough for applause on its own. Post-Button, an ice knight who willingly exposed himself to the Bay's baleful cold and suffered the interpersonal consequences for it could be rewarded solely for the tribulation. It is a dis/consolation "prize" that James, who did not supply a pilotable path, profited from. Riffing on Gopnik's "windows," the rest of this chapter peers into four vignettes from his account and "The Wintering" therein. Arranged around the "leads" I previously listed, each reconceives the season as a stirring mode of cohabitation.

## *Ship of Cool*

I begin with the *Henrietta Maria,* the twenty-two crew members' first line of defense and seventy-ton symbolic shield. From the story's onset, "the outward voyage" (4:460), they must deal with "ice that came upon vs with, as it were, with wilfull violence" (2:462). Sentient, it attacks strategically, and tentacularly, with "some of [its] sharp blue corners" reaching underneath them (2:462). Almost "beaten to pieces" (2:466), they struggle to stay nautically and somatically intact. The constant state of alertness threatens to tear them apart. Richard Edwards, the gunner, is caught by a cable; his leg must be "taken off" after it "crush[es] the bone to pieces" and rips "all the flesh" from it (2:486–7). The Hudson Strait is anything but: full of "the most strangest whirlings of the Sea" (2:465), they are "ouer-rackt," like "Ionas in the Whales belly." But there is no deliverance after three days. During their way in, they are frequently "tormented, pestered, and beaten with the Ice, many pieces being higher than our Top-mast-head" (2:464). James likens pesty ice to a plague (Latin *pestis*), to an animal, and even a gendered "him" (2:470). He is awoken one night by "the rutt against a banke of Ice. . . . It made a hollow and a hideous noyse" (2:464). Waves rut (*rugire,* "to roar") upon the shore. He hears it, again, "the rut of the Ice" (2:477). It is a waking nightmare: "The Ice came all driuing againe vpon vs, which put us all to a great extremity" (2:469). And as these pieces splinter, with "a most terrible thundering noyse," it "put vs in a great feare that those about vs would break vs all to pieces" (2:469). The sound registers an anticipated snapping, an echo of human fragility, and a reminder to hold fast in more ways than one. Their entrance cold-conditioned them for a hard journey ahead. By September, "henceforward we were to looke for no other but Winter weather" (2:492)—to be ice-*broken,* not ice-breaker.

It is uncertain how much more the ship, and by extension, the men, can take as their link to Bristol is assaulted. James had ghosts of winterers past from his own country to contend with as he pondered his next move. Fighting his way south to the region where Hudson set up camp, the so-called "East Baye" (2:498n2), "here, Sir Hugh Willoughby came into my mind, who, without a doubt, was driuen out of his Harbour in this manner, and so starued at sea" (2:517). Cold's inability to be overcome, but only briefly barricaded against, understandably troubles the company. Morale drops, murmurs spread, and the first faint whispers of their inextricability (never mind wintering) are recorded. Sometimes, "to put away these cogitations, wee drank a health to his Maiestie on the Ice, . . . boldly [walking] out vpon the Ice to sport and recreate ourselves" (2:478–79). At another point, they all went "vpon a piece of Ice and fell to prayer" (2:468). The conversion of ice to an altar and playground is ineffective, however; to the harassed ship they must inevitably return. The weather inexorably worsens; he feels "colder then euer I felt it in *England* in my life" (2:504). Weighing his options, James decides to winter off Charlton Island in early October, although he doubts his chances at survival, since "euery thing [does] freeze" on ship and he and his men are "disabled with the coldnesse" (2:509, 511). As the snow and temperature fall, as the ice expands, "we did sensibly perceiue withal how wee did daily sinke into more miseries" (2:511). Stunned but still sensing, they chip away the stupefying frost that sticks to everything it touches. The ship's cables, he notes, are especially "wonderfull to behold" (2:513). In short, "the cold did multiply" (2:511). Pesky winter has "come . . . extremely on vpon us" (2:508). The polar parasite finds a way inside their floating home and into them.

Faced with ceaseless perforation, he is eventually forced to look for a more suitable shelter on land. James, glancing longingly back at the *Maria,* recalls that "she did looke like a piece of Ice in the fashion of a Ship, or a Ship resembling a piece of ice" (2:513). Caught up with "tormenting cogitations" (2:513), he reluctantly decides to sink her, intending to build a small house with any pieces they can thaw, and ideally resurrect her in the spring. It is a long farewell. The vessel slowly settles in the water in a matter of hours: "Our men that were ashoare stood looking vpon us, almost dead with cold and sorrowes, to see our misery and their owne. We lookt vpon them againe, and both vpon each other, with woefull hearts" (2:520). But while the cables might be "wonderfull," and the service somber, it is the frozen household (Greek *oikos*) of the ship that is most worrisome, a ruinous winter landscape predating the likes of Caspar David Friedrich's *Das Eismeer* (1823–1824). The true wonder proves to be the home altered from itself, the ship inextricably bound with ice, wintered, rendered foreign, becoming literally strange to the tearful spectators. We can react to this scene differently, though. The purposeful wreck of the *Maria* symbolizes the demolition of any *oikos* of solely human invention, whether culture or nation, an abandoning of the ship of airtight anthropocentricity in an imaginative effort to construct nature-cultures anew, to enter (not exit out of) elemental intimacy, even within catastrophe's brumal "miseries." Scuttling displays the pressure winter puts on any habitation, renders it fluid not frozen, slippery not static, de/constructable, and precious for its precariousness. Letting this object rest for a moment, I will inspect another permeable layer: the skin.

## *Do You Want to Be a Snowman?*

This kaleidoscopic vision of ship as ice and ice as ship extends to their own benumbed bodies. What makes cold uniquely vexing is its powers of fusion as well as fracture. The cold sutures while it distorts the "vs"; as it creeps in, it weirdly conjoins. Despite its synonymousness with all things fleeting, the early modern snowman proved to be an enduring figure for examining the flurried intersections between culture and nature. John Donne (1572–1631) penned an eclogue-epithalamion to commemorate the marriage of Robert Carr, Earl of Somerset, and a favorite of James I, to Frances Howard on December 26, 1613. Donne, however, missed the courtly nuptials, composing the poem months after the ceremony. For his indiscretion, Donne ("Idios") suffers a stern rebuke from Sir Robert Ker ("Allophanes"), his friend who happens to share the same name as the bridegroom: "unseasonable man, statue of ice, / What could to countries solitude entice / Thee, in this yeares cold and decrepit time?"[93] The poet is "unseasonable" in his absence, perhaps, unable or unwilling to join in the jollity of Christmastime. He also seems out of season in that he prefers the company of cold "country" weather over warm royal interiors: "Natures instinct," argues Allophanes, "drawes to the warmer clime / Even small birds. . . . What delicacie can in fields appeare, / Whil'st Flora'herselfe doth a freeze jerkin wear?"[94] Cold on the shoulder and on the inside: no wonder the poet is hailed as a "statue of ice" in the first line. But what if Donne's frigid *faux pas* is reinterpreted within the "unseasonable" time of the LIA, a period of seasons seemingly out of whack? "Man," and not just the rules of etiquette he may or may not have broken, comes under greater scrutiny as a result. For Ker/"Allophanes," to be "seasonable" (and by extension, reasonable) in the winter is to seek heat. Donne/"Idios," on the other hand, is a "statue" precisely because he has been seasoned—"enticed" and touched—by the December cold. He cleverly inverts his accuser's logic by turning the "un-" against him. Indeed, what is more "unseasonable" than to believe that warmth is the factor that constitutes said "man," dictates his behaviors, and drives his desires "in this yeares cold"?

While deeply allegorical, Donne's wintry pun is nonetheless useful for interrogating the tangible bonds between climate and culture that subtended the human. In James's cold hands, the elaborate conceit comes to life. When he and sixteen of his crew take a small boat to reunite with others onshore, ice fashions James and company unrecognizable, a gang of snowmen: "Being arriued vpon the land, we greeted our fellows the best we could, at which time they could not know vs, nor we them, by our habits nor voyces, so frozen all ouer wee were, faces, haire, and apparell" (2:521). This wintering "wonder"-land involves preparations they could not have foreseen: preparing themselves for becoming-wintry; for the changes and not the stasis that freezing entails; for cogitating not just on "Sir Hugh Willoughby" but on peculiar forms of dwelling that incorporate perspectives of both likeness and alterity at once, instances where even your own voice sounds estranged. For many readers, their survival would have been the miracle, yet so are their bodies, mutating in accordance with winter's "three differences of the cold" (2:535): in the house; in the area between the house and the nearby woods; and in the open air across the ice to the boat (for provision), including later to the ship (to be equipped). Just as the house is in perpetual re-makeshift, each spatial station marks an ontological transition in the men: "Euery time they waded in the Ice, it so gathered about thē that they did seeme like a walking piece of Ice, most lamentable to behold" (2:526). Grieving the body's changes as it interacts with degrees of cold throughout their entire insular compound, James exposes the barrier separating humans from ice as nonexistent: not to *look like* ice, but to become it.

At nearly forty, he embodies the metaphor of winter as an old man: "I caused the Chirugion to cut the haire of my head short, and to shaue away all the haire of my face, for that it was become intolerable, and that it would be frozen so great with Ice-sickles" (2:525).[95] Yet personification proves punishing: "No Cloathes were proofe against it; no motion could resist it. It would . . . so freeze the haire on our eye-lids that we could not see; and I verily beleeue that it would haue stifled a man in a very few houres" (2:535–36). The language of melting divides is unnecessary in this case, for freezing in fact reifies the continuum, crystalizes bonds: "Our noses, cheeks, and hands did freeze as white as paper" (2:527). They learn about walking on ice by *being* walking ice. James's humble boast about his crew's humoral temperament attests to this drier style of shape-shifting: "It may be here remembered that, all this Winter, wee had not beene troubled with any rhumes nor flegmaticall diseases" (2:553). Theirs was a transmutation without the usual markings of bodily flow, the mucous excretions of rheum and phlegm. Smeared, blotched, blurred: there are neither hard lines nor "thick rands" (2:477) to either humans or ice here. Winter gets in pores as well as ship panels; it contorts and distorts; it dissembles the macro and the micro at the level of skin.

"In briefe, all this moneth [of March] had beene very cold" (2:537). Nevertheless, James is prolix in his recounting of their squalid conditions over roughly half a year. Perseverance against frosted odds, after all, makes for a suspenseful story, and their "infirmities" are many, whether directly (hypothermia) or indirectly (scurvy) inflicted by the cold (2:534). The threat of "losing one another" (2:528), and of losing one's self, makes for dramatic effect. Cold incapacitates. Snow blinds.

For James, the able body is a working one, one that strives to stay alive and that assists others in doing the same. But when a few men return unsuccessfully from deer hunting, they are "so disabled with cold, which did rise vp in blisters vnder the soales of their feete, and vpon their legges, to the bignesse of Walnuts, that they could not recouer their former estate" (2:537). These snowball-shaped eruptions, or "walnuts," are the symptoms of deep frostbite, where the skin is not just superficially irritated (as with frostnip) but undergoes actual crystallization. Another party tries "their fortune, but they returned worse disabled, and euen more stifled with the cold" (2:537). Their indefinitely stalled "recouery" from sickness to health shores up the idea of wintering as a weariness to be combated. By May, "I verily thought that my feet and legs would haue fallen off, they did so torment me with aking" (2:546). "Walking" or not, James's crippling visions of cryocorporeality resituate the diseased subject amidst the "thicke fogge" of winter (2:528). No peace, and not even relapse—only "pieces."

Writing in hindsight, James can afford to be playful at points: "Since now I have spoken so much of the cold, I hope it will not be too coldly taken if I, in a few words, make it someway to appear vnto our Readers" (2:535). It is a choice pun, in retrospect, an attempt at counteracting the quivering cold with the shuddering of laughter. While he cannot totally defang frost's bite, he can turn it to his advantage, brandish his bare, bruised skin. His dire straits are a rite of passage, a litmus test for life at the limits. "When blood is nipped and ways be foul," sings "Winter" at the tail end of Shakespeare's *Love's Labor's Lost* (5.2.900). James shows us his body's gluey passage-"ways," points to where the blood has been "nipped" (pinched, bitten, or squeezed sharply) by the befouling chill. Fifty years later, John Peter (contra Thomas Tryon's ameliorative views on circulation) will advise against exercise and liquor in cases like his: "For from what parts of our Bodies soever, the Spiritous particles shall be forc'd to with-draw themselves and make a Retreat, they will instantly be supplied with the nimble Particles of Cold, which will congeal our fluid humours, and if suffered to prevail, must certainly put the Spirits to a rout."[96] Indeed, one good wintry blast will "destroy the Ferments" altogether and cause dead men to "[sit] up strait like Statues" on horseback, corroborating the grisly tales he had heard from "Russia, Greenland, Norway, &c"[97] (but not the Bay, conspicuously).

It would be naïve to expect one who has logged "the miserablest frozen that can bee conceiued" (2:528) in "painestaking" detail (2:575) to suddenly "uncover" himself, or "go toward" it, with Serresian swagger. Friendliness occurs only once, perhaps, and flickeringly at that, on a clear night in January in which the stars were more resplendent than he had ever seen "by two thirds" (2:532). Still, I want to pause for a bit and pose a numb question: what, exactly, is the threat of becoming-ice? A crusty death, apparently. No. Wait: the cold cuts deeper than disrupting the able-bodied business of survival. In all, four men perish on the trip. One of them, John Barton, the gunner's mate, is swallowed by the ice, disappeared, lost to the Bay: "It closed vpon him, and we neuer saw him more" (2:511). The injured Edwards succumbs to his wounds on November 22 and is "committed . . . at a good distance from the Ship vnto the Sea" (2:514). Unlike the former, however, he returns while they are refitting the *Maria* six months later, the "plaster" still stuck to his amputated leg. In the middle of May, he is found "fast in the Ice, his head downewards and his heel upward," and, remarkably, "free from noysomenesse" (2:549). Or, at least, he is relatively immune from it: "His flesh would slip vp and downe vpon his bones like a gloue on a man's hand" (2:549). (Boyle was fascinated by this observation.) Cold does not completely preserve, in this instance; even the frost has fluidity to it. The gunner is altered, gelatinized by being (in) the Bay. It is hard to find the humor in this horror. The iced-up bodies of Barton (Willoughby and Hudson, too) are out of sight, even if they remain on James's mind. Here, however, the gunner's slushy skin reflects James's own *in situ*, a direct confrontation from which he cannot conveniently look away. He must face the change, in other words; he must consider what he is turning into, shifting out of.

A key to understanding this terrifying thought-experiment, I believe, lies in the concept of metamorphosis, which means "transform, change shape" in the original Greek.[98] Highlighting "form" (a statue, for instance, or a glove) is essential to understanding the fear, the projected result of one's remolding. But it also must work cooperatively with movement "across," the *trans-*, a preposition that need not signal termination, but an array of further positions that a body may take, a ceaseless shuttling back and forth between "fast" and the "free." To be sure, the reaction to a frozen corpse raises uncanny feelings such as the baffling appearance of being life-like, un/dead, and it may certainly come as a shock to see the natural processes of corruption and decay halted. Mutability, however, does not stop there. Edwards's strange sloughing "vp and downe" is evidence of that: it also draws one's attention to the transfiguration process; asks how snow makes a man (and vice versa); asks whether skin can be floppy and frozen at once; and whether it marks the erasure of the human or the addition to it, the incorporative "and." James not only witnesses but inhabits this middle space, a spectrum, the hyphenated space of ice-man that refuses to settle on either, or pings across (-) in *trans-* potential, muddles beginnings and ends. The "noysomenesse"-less body, purified by the cold, must be treated as but one perceivable shape out of many, as a figuration that is dangerous to idealize. It "slips" out of one's "hand." To freeze, to arrest metamorphosis, is out of the question. His mention is a logical extension of Pericles's chilly self-doubt, a referral to the bathers and philosophers who willfully submersed themselves in baffling in-betweens. A zombie-like Lazarus in the ice sheets; a live-dead man "walking"; a puzzle of missing "pieces" that is non/life. Wintering marks this site of energetic exchange.

## *Give Me Shelter*

Shelter obviously remains paramount amidst the severities of slow transformation. James's haphazard enclosure on the island typifies this struggle. In the cold seventeenth century, one could pull survival tips from a variety of sources. To outlast a winter gale outdoors, advises Johannes Scheffer (1621–1679), the traveler "hath no other remedy but to throw himself on the ground with some garment over him, suffering himself to be quite buried in snow till the storm is past."[99] To live is to temporarily become the "heape." Once inside their makeshift four-hundred-square-foot hut fashioned from parts of the deconstructed *Maria,* they could presumably ride out winter's worst. In lieu of "a Christmas Tale," James describes the construction of the "mansion house" (2:531) for officers, a second house for crew, and a storehouse for provisions in laborious detail. Spread twenty feet apart, their safe placement was top priority: "It is true, we were in a wood, and vnder a South banke too, or otherwise we had all starued [with cold]" (2:538). Lumber for building and firing, like many necessities such as spring and well water, would not come easy: "But I must tell you withall how difficult it was to haue wood in a wood" (2:538). This was the "warmest and conuenientest place" (2:529) in his opinion. For insulation, they used "boughes, . . . spare sayles, and then bedding and clothes" (2:530). The "mayne course" (sail) served as the roof, and boards were laid around the central hearth so "that the cold dampe should not strike vp into us" (2:530). Pathways between buildings were routinely shoveled and tamped to a depth of a "full yard thick" underfoot (2:531). Hearing this holiday tale of tight-fitting architecture, one would not be blamed for feeling snug; statements such as "the one and twentieth [of December] was so cold that we could not goe out of the house" (2:528) sound less alarming. Tellingly, he names the adjoining forest "we did winter in, in memory of that Honourable Knight, Sir John Winter, Winters Forrest" (529). Dedication here acts as another kind of stamping upon a hard land, a terraforming that accentuates humans' highly adaptive forestry skills and downplays habitat as a site of mutual participation.

But the cold, of course, is already inside the boathouse. Lest this luring sense of coziness sink in, James repeatedly highlights the freezing burn of sheltered life. "We now imagined that we were leapt out of the Frying pan into the fire" (2:521). Ensuring that the "dampe" does not "strike" is a futile task. The interior is "frozen & hang with Icesickles" (2:536). Bedsheets are lined "with hoare frost" (2:536) no matter how close to the fire they sleep. Yet instead of shutting off this snow cave of wonders from us, he invites us in: "But . . . come a little neerer to it" (2:536). He intends to "speake miracles of the cold" (2:536), providing his readers with a catalogue of what else unbelievably freezes: the cook's water "Tubs"; the surgeon's "sirrops"; their "vinegar, oyle, and sacke" (2:536). Anything liquid freezes solid, and heat does not guarantee melting. While incredible, "I haue many times both seene and felt, by putting my hand into [a brass kettle], that side which was next the fire was very warme, and the other side an inch frozen" (2:536). The sea remains firm at the beginning of June; the ground will not yield then either. Fire is of no relief. Flesh and clothes are besmirched by turpentine wood and scorched by flame: it "would send forth such a thicke smoke that would make abundance of soote, which made vs all looke as if we had beene free of the Company of Chimney-Sweepers" (2:539). Even time appears to be affected: "As for our Clocke and Watch, notwithstanding we still kept them by the fire's side, in a Chest, wrapt in clothes, yet were they so frozen that they could not goe" (2:535). Altogether, these marvelous anecdotes craft a littler ice age in which the cold and "dampe"—the impersonal "it"—come to be seen as inherited housemates rather than unwanted guests. At the "strike" of cold, he is forced to remember his smoky purgatorial present in which time stands still.

Instead of simply lamenting his fate caused by technological failure or an exterior design flaw, he starts to pay attention to the hydraulic workings around him. In a lengthy section of his wintering account, he stops to "deliuer . . . how this abundance of Ice comes to be ingendered" (2:533). He opines that bay ice is produced by dynamic tidal movements. By late October, snow will settle on the water's surface. Whipped up by the wind, it is "wrought together" (2:534) and freezes up to several inches thick in one night. Then, "being carried with the halfe tyde, [it] meets with some obstacle . . . and . . . it crumples and so runnes vpon itself that, in a few houres, it will be fiue or sixe foote thicke" (2:534). This swift-moving tidal cycle ensures that ice is exponentially accumulative: "By December, it is growne to an infinite multiplication of Ice" (2:534). This multiplying process also explains how "the cold gets the predomination in the Sea," since his men discovered it "more mortifying" to wade through the ice-choked water of June than that of December. James is careful not to be prescriptive ("in all this I freely submit myself vnto the better learned" [2:534]), yet his humble estimation betrays more than just ennui. He epitomizes the slowing down that wintering encourages. He stops to touch snow (April 6), "something moyster and greater than any we had had all this yeere" (2:540); he ponders why the land is never flooded from melted snow, unlike in England: ("It is exhaled vp by the Sunne, and suckt full of holes, like honeycombs" [2:550]); he watches the bay ice crack in May ("then runnes one piece of it vpon another, and so bruises and grinds itself against the shoalds and rocks that it becomes abbreuiated" [2:562]); he fathoms the same ice's maximum depth ("It doth not freeze [naturally] aboue six foot: the rest is by accident" [2:562]); and when snow falls suddenly and heavily in August, he muses upon "the reasons for it" ("Now, of what was exhald from the snowy Ice and cold Sea, could there probably be returned but the like againe" [2:586]). Contrary to what his "watch" might say, James's cryological meditations actually deepen his sense of time by embedding him in the mysterious runnings of the water cycle. Just as the polar "night season" (2:536) would have disoriented his internal diurnal clock rather than halted it, his amateurish interactions grant him the freedom to explore the annual "ingendering" of the winter season, observe its comings and "goe"-ings that point backward and forward at once.

To be unstuck is still destabilizing, however, and James makes sure to enfold his strange new findings in the narrative's manifold dangers. An "vnexpected cold" on May 2 "did so vexe our sicke men that they grew worse and worse" (2:546). It is too hot to work in direct sunlight during the day. The hard freeze at night is likewise intolerable. This "vnnaturalnesse of the season did torment our men" (2:551). Simply put, "the season here in this Climate is most vnnaturall" (2:562). James will partly blame the hot weather for a forest fire caused by one of his men: it "follow[ed] him at hard heeles, . . . bearing a full mile in breadth" (2:560) before it "burnt" their "Towne . . . downe to the ground" (2:561) in an instant. Yet his complaints about the intemperate "season," whether an "vnnaturally" warm winter, cold spring, or a blend of the two, points to a glaring omission in his sheltered thinking: the Indigenous inhabitants of the Bay. The "our" in James's pat phrase "our wintering Iland" (2:561) clearly refers to European overstayers who have claimed the "iland" in Charles I's name. Near the end of his stay in June of 1632, he erects a cross atop "a bare hill of sand" he styles Brandon Hill, named after its counterpart in Bristol, to which he attaches "the Kings and Queenes . . . Pictures, drawn to the life, and doubly wrapt in lead, and so close that no weather could hurt them" (2:558), along with title, currency, and arms. With this emblem of weatherized empire, and "by this ceremony," they "[took] possession of these Territories to his Maiesties vse" (2:559). The question of *whose* shelter is already limited by Anglocentric constraints.

The fact that others winter too often eludes him, and when the thought does cross his mind, it goes no further than pointing out vague traces of an absent presence. Inbound and outbound, he admits that "we found where the Saluages had been" (2:471): on Resolution Island at the mouth of Hudson Strait in June; on Mansel Island, "vtterly barren of all goodnesse" in July (2:476–67); on "The Earle of Danbyes Iland" immediately southeast of their dwelling place in October (2:507); and at Cape Henrietta Maria in July of 1932 (2:572). These are clues that lead nowhere; thus, James enlists the archetype of the spectral "saluage" to harass the unhoused Englishman. Scouting the island's woods, he is afraid of feeling "the winter . . . extremely on vpon us," true (2:508), but he is also scared of finding something else: "I wandered . . . to see if we could discouer any signes of Salvages, that we might the better prouide for our safeties against them" (2:509). He is satisfied only ten days later, when "the cold season was now in that extremity that they could not come to vs if there were any" (2:511). With the mutual assurance of coldness, they "comforted and refreshed ourselues by sleeping the more securely" (2:511). The possibility that the season could not be as extreme as his, again, limits his perspective. His imagination wanders as well: when a reconnaissance boat does not return near the mouth of the Severn in New South Wales, he is far from relieved to espy a signal fire on the shore: "wee thought withall that it had beene the Saluages, who did now triumph in their conquest" (2:588). Without a referent, these pejorative references fit into his larger repertoire of environmental threats used to heighten the story's suspense.

The barest hint of an amicable cross-cultural encounter is, in fact, back at the origin of the devastating fire. Being at a high point, James had converted the area around the "watch-tree" as a site for beacons: "Such fires I had formerly made, to haue knowledge if there were any Saluages on the maine or the Ilands about vs. Had there been any, my purpose was to haue gone to them, to get some intelligence of some Christians or some Ocean Sea thereabouts" (2:559). It is uncertain how such a conversation would have affected the tenor of his survival narrative: whether, for instance, a humble acknowledgement of centuries-long Indigenous habitation in (supposedly) inhospitable wintriness would have minimized his own degree of hardship and therefore detracted from his lauded feat of wintering and returning relatively unscathed. But what is clear is that James's intelligence about shelter is lacking for its "Christian" one-sidedness and his disinterest in traditional ecological lifeways other than his own. Even if establishing a semipermanent winter place was not his explicit intention or directive, his admission nevertheless reflects a pervasive bias at the time that privileged European matters of survivability in high-, low-, and near-Arctic abodes (farther north and west than the more firmly ensconced settlements in Newfoundland and Iceland supported by fishing industries[100]). Before sailing home on the resurrected *Maria*, James gathers wood on Danby Island where he finds two stakes driven into the ground near the waterside as if "they had beene cut sharpe at the ends with a hatchet, or some other good Iron toole" (2:568). Their presence confounds him: "I could not conceiue to what purpose they should be there set, vnlesse it were for some marke for boats. This did augment my desire to speake with the Saluages: for, without doubt, they could haue giuen notice of some Christians with whom they had some commerce" (2:568). The sheltering of non-Europeans is but a passing thought to those bravely traversing the Passage;[101] when their lives are considered, they are treated as signposts that light the way to Christian company and Cathayan commodities. "Saluages" serve as dispensable, interchangeable mediators; historically speaking, James's invisible interlocutors fit squarely into a corporate trajectory leading to the charter of the Hudson's Bay Company in 1670. The im/possibility of settlement around "some Ocean Sea" and its newfound passages was a question to be answered by English imperial eyes only, to the detriment of those whose dwellings they overlooked, intimidated, and eventually displaced.

By now, the concept of shelter—as with the subjects of skin and ship—should seem slippier than when we began. James's monocular perspective may have helped cast non-Indigenous experiences of wintering as involuntary acts of survival, yet it also reveals the contemporary anxieties about dwelling that sponsored those visions. How much winter can a warm-blooded Englishman endure, if not conquer? The environs sharply set this in focus, as understood by historian Sam White: "Climate and climatic change—both as ideas and as physical realities—had a profound impact on the way Europeans encountered the land and people of North America, and shaped the course of the first North American expeditions and colonies."[102] James Hall (d. 1612) was first sent to Greenland in 1605 by the Danish king Christian IV to reestablish contact with tenth-century Scandinavian settlements, and while the crews that accompanied him could scoff at "the noisome cold weather in this waste wilderness,"[103] they were forced to confront the fact that it unsettled white settler colonialist ambitions nonetheless. On his fourth voyage (1612), Hall found "where many of their [Inuit] winter houses had bin."[104] Successful habitation in the short-term (seasonal) and long-term (generational) was achievable, just not by Europeans, and it was sometimes enviable. Baffin, for instance, admired kayakers' agility, and by extension, their self-sufficiency: "The people, all the summer time, vse nothing but fishing, drying their fish and seales flesh vpon the rockes, for their winter prouision. . . . In these boates, they will row so swiftly that it is almost incredible; for no ship in the world is able to keepe way with them."[105] Others, however, saw only their own inadequacy in reflection, and as a result, they lumped together "peoples" who managed to dwell perennially with the Arctic wildlife. The Inuit are more marine mammals than upright Englishmen, wrote Hall, for "they fish being disguised in their Coates of Seale skinnes" and row "making a howling and hideous noise."[106] Inuit layering justified English beliefs in bestiality and underscored unshakable fears about their own vulnerability at the same time. It seems that dressing the right amount for/in the LIA helped "shaped the course" as well. In 1612, Hall "with a dart . . . was slain of one of the salvages,"[107] perhaps in retaliation for the kidnappings that took place seven years before (see chapter 2). Dwelling, in short, becomes a complex act of resistance as well as resilience once other perspectives are incorporated, and not just to the "noisome" weather, but to the climate of colonialism that wreaks havoc on winter(ing).

"We found it not a iot the worse" (2:553), brags James as he retrieves pieces of the *Maria* to be recommissioned. The "iot"-less idea of preservation, like a ship's cable sheltered safely under cold water, is a deep-freeze fantasy that dangerously occludes the changes happening inside and outside bay areas. What is truly miraculous here is not just that they endured winter's strangeness and its dangers that lasted until June, outlining a masculine proving ground ("with this dyet [vetches], and in this manner, did we goe thorow our miseries" [2:545]), but more importantly, that they demonstrate for us how the "thorow" is an endless entrance without exit, a constant passing "thorow" without stable borders and locked-in beings. Here is a mode of dwelling that is as much about winter's potential abilities because of, and not despite, its wet "dampe"-ness and its propensity to disable. To see winter and its lives in a different light, as if refracted: *Strange and Dangerous Voyage* affords an opportunity to choose oscillating winter over impregnable shelter, the latter term too built, too complete, too exclusive, and its scaffolding the airtight protections of guaranteed sustainability. The former recognizes the unpredictability of snowstorms that frustrate stasis and underlying order; it see(k)s shelter as ever-porous and makes plans accordingly for contingent weathering; and it inquires why safety is unequally distributed to different groups, or why the subject is entirely withheld (in James's case, to the ancestors who likely make up the Kashechwean Cree First Nation at present). "The Wintering" bespeaks an enduring interest in cold's material substance, interrogates how to "liue" by and with a "heape" in climatic coexistence: where "shelter" and its definitions are fluid, its harbored bodies busily on the move.

## *I Fall to Pieces*

James's fear of being "starued" with cold, of perishing from it, stems from the word's literal sense we spotted in Salisbury (1685) in the previous chapter. In addition to the word's connotations of hunger and malnourishment, his readers also witness how cold *feeds*. The bulbous blisters plaguing him and his fellow winterers evidence the multiple, malignant growths the human body may experience as it undergoes metamorphosis. Yet there is another area that highlights cold's constructive properties as it interacts with those who dwell within its circles: two "ragged and teared Rimes" penned on the spot, "as I there conceiued them" (2:505). "Literary merits" aside, they have been hailed as historical milestones "for being some of the first—perhaps even the first—composed [in English] in northern Canada."[108] James's pop-up poems are momentous for different reasons, in my opinion: they express winter's literary influence, a slow, cold build-up that spurs artistic creativity. His pun on "rime" with "rhyme" bespeaks an interest in the ways cryocorporeal and textual composition enjoin: a *lingua gelida* in which world and words blend, work, and write together. But unlike most others who delivered their lines in LIA winters, James explores the "lethal limit" through his frostbitten body as well as the "white . . . paper" (2:527) of the blank page.

James's first foray into verse is sponsored by the hazardous gales of late September. His ship spins in the choppy waters of the south Bay: "Which way to turne we knew knew not, but there ride amongst them in extremitie of distresse. All these perils made a most hideous and terrible noyse in the night season" (2:504). Provoked by these night terrors, he crafts a prayer-poem addressed to his battered soul: "Oh, my poore soule, why doest thou grieue to see / So many Deaths muster to murther mee?" (2:505). What ensues is an involute theological metaphor in which the soul's metaphysical voyage resembles Arctic navigation. The compass, as "a rustie wyre, toucht with a little Stone," has fostered their misguided confidence; it has "thought to shun a thousand dangers by / The blind direction of this senselesse flye." Since his instrument is unreliable, piety is the soul's finest compass: "Now thou must Steere *by faith*, a better guide; /'Twill bring thee safe to heauen, against the tyde / Of Satan's malice." He woefully suggests they "doe some penitence / Vnfainedly together" before they depart. The vehicle and tenor of the poem are not entirely new. Claudio in Shakespeare's *Measure for Measure* mimics Hamlet's cool persona as he follows his soul's northward flight: "Ay, but to die, and go we know not where, / To lie in cold obstruction and to rot . . . To bathe in fiery floods or to reside / In thrilling region of thick-ribbèd ice . . . To be imprisoned in the viewless winds / And blown with restless violence round about . . . Imagine howling—'tis too horrible!" (3.1.118–32). The Calvinist firebrand Richard Younge (fl. 1636–1673) will focus his ire on the "frozen soul" in his 1671 *A Spark of Divine Light.*[109] Still, James's remark that "I hope it will not be counted ridiculous if I relate with what meditations I was affected, now and then, amongst my ordinary prayers" (2:504–5) confesses to the cold creeping into his thoughts. Mediation precedes meditation; climatic affect *effects* elegiac lines as much as it imagines a litany of "murthers."

"So many Deaths." James's better-known and arguably more complex poem materializes at the end of his wintering in July of 1632, just before the narrative enters its "homeward voyage" (2:567) and final phase. He and his company solemnly march up Brandon Hill to the cross containing his majesties' pictures. There, surrounded by three crewmembers' graves—John Wardon, master (d. May 6); William Cole, carpenter (d. May 8), and the semiviscid Edwards (reburied May 19)—he delivers his eulogy in rhyme. "Leaning vpon mine arme on one of their Tombes" (2:564), he epitomizes the figure of melancholy. What he "vtters" next is partly performative: "I were vnkind vnlesse that I did shead, / Before I part, some teares vpon our dead; / And, when my eyes be dry, I will not cease / In heart to pray their bones may rest in peace" (2:564). Acting as orator, he affectively taps into national-theological rhetoric to justify their deaths ("seeking Gods glory and their Countries good") and to honor their sacrifice: "So haue they spent themselves; and here they lye, / A famous marke of our Discovery." As the bodies remain at rest in perpetuity, the audience (his crew and his readers) may be assured that these three men did not perish in vain. In fact, James is somewhat envious of their peaceful position: "We that suruiue perchance may end our dayes / In some imployment meriting no praise, / And in a dunghill rot." His self-deprecation speaks to the island's preservative powers.

Unlike a putrefying compost heap, the island's "heapes" of snow help ensure that their figures and fames escape decay. Edwards is firmly emplaced in cold ground; reinterred, his gloopy physique is stilled at last. Being a "solitary place, where none / Will euer come to breathe a sigh or grone," James acts as preserver as well, carrying his "loue" for them back home, committing a heart-felt paean to paper as a dutiful "foster-father" (2:565) should. For these paternal reasons, it is not surprising that Romantic poet Robert Southey applauded in 1812 "the strain of fine and manly feeling . . . breathed in[to]" his lines.[110]

At first glance, James's song about icing up delivers an elaborate conceit: cold fusion reveals a veiled desire to keep the body (like the ship) in shape. In brief, he cannot stand to fall apart. The irony here is that James *needs* "winters" agency in order to think through transmutation's supposed cease. To be exempt from "rot," after all, requires freezing. In a somber way, wintering makes a "good" space for elemental affiliation; it is desired for its "extreme" properties. Materially, it shelters them where they "lye"; metaphorically, it prolongs their memories so that one may "out-liue" the "feare" of being forgotten. Poetry *of* a cold climate, he finds, has its own preservative properties. It is an admittedly strange comment for him to make after enumerating the countless acts that "froze [their] bloud" in excruciating detail. This interdependency is best encapsulated when he pleads on his tears' behalf: "Make these teares, bright pearles: which I would lay, Tomb'd safely with you, till Doomes fatall day." James speaks of bodily fluids ("teares") frozen, a desire for liquid to harden (into "pearles") and then for transformation to halt altogether (to be "Tomb'd safely"). It is impossible to achieve the stasis of "rest" without first moving through the cold "doe"-ings of metamorphosis. Soft tears, in short, must *become* hard pearls. Because of its fluidic and transfigurative valences, James's lament echoes Ariel's tropical song set at *The Tempest*'s lower latitudes:

> Full fathom five thy father lies;
> Of his bones are coral made;
> Those are pearls that were his eyes;
> Nothing of him that doth fade,
> But doth suffer a sea-change
> Into something rich and strange. (1.2.395–400)

But whereas the play's "sea-change" casts doubt on the concept of bodily integrity ("nothing of him that doth fade"), the poem clearly expresses a wish to hold on to *something* that escapes a bay-change. Only "Doomes fatall day" will shatter his men asunder, when their pieces "should return to heauen" to be (presumably) re-composed. James's eschatological assurance offers a modicum of comfort for bodies in *this* world whose skins "slip vp and down," who liquefy in lachrymose fashion in front of their audiences. By permitting the alterations of winter, he can "safely" channel cold for his poetic purposes. Shed a tear, channel its crystallization to prove your point about the perdurance of camaraderie and the eventual repair that awaits the broken-bodied and spirited via salvific congelation; then, captain, you may bid "Farewell" and "neuer put foote more on that Iland" again (2:565).

Interpreted this way, Barrow's snide remark about the story's tedious "lamentation and weeping and great mourning" misses the greater point about what those tears betray: a man in elemental motion. Neither is "manliness" what is truly at stake here, pace Southey, but the notion of what makes said "man": namely, the brumal air "breathed" in, the cold that penetrates the "blood," the weeping that confirms how water-bodies fall, stiffen, fracture, and flow in the severest of seasons. The warm-blooded are quicker than the dead, perhaps, but they are no less susceptible to cold's invasiveness as they step away. True, in the abbreviated version of his stay left for successive voyagers (and reproduced with the full account), James wishes to prolong his words: "I thought it necessary to leaue this testimony of vs and our indeauours, if God should take vs into his heauenly Kingdome, and frustrate our returne into our natiue Countrey" (2:603). But he is a better poet than that; he lingers on "gloue"-like Edwards, turns twice to the absent Barton "who mis-carried in the little Bay" (2:602). Cold's vacillations, not merely its suspensions, are precisely what vexes. James voices the horror of *not* changing, of being cast as a life-like figurine or rendered a snapshot in/of time, in addition to the gruesomeness of dissolution and the promises of refrigeration.

As we have seen, and as he has felt, wintering never conveys stasis, but constitutes a time of metamorphosis. Any entombment (like a ship, a house) that shuts out the material world is fallacious even (or especially) in death. Snow obscures categories as much as it remakes them;

glaciation does not guarantee cohesion. Accompanied by his ice-men above and below ground, James temporarily recognizes his own body in the thickening droplets, scattering his tears like tiny icebergs. It is as poignant as it is passing; yet his poem, like the entire narrative, still manages to capture the multiplicity of wintering by virtue of its kinetic composition. A mélange of the human and hiemal, penned upon white "pages" and tattooed on skin, exhibits a Thoriusian type of cryopoiesis. The lines in winter inaugurate a frenetic, never-frozen mode of dwelling; they versify how things engage in transformative, open-ended processes of cryocorporeal becoming in slow speed, constituting a strange season of warm- and cold-bodied interpenetration. They linger, lastly, in the unsettled and unsettling middle of metamorphosis—bodies not too stiff, not too supple—to raise the possibilities of life in flux, caught amidst unbound "extremes."

## Rime On

"Comming home" (2:567) proves to be just as challenging as leaving it. By mid to late spring, the ice is back to its old tricks. It cracks with "fearefull noyse" (2:551), and, as if parroting *Hamlet*'s shrewd language in the next chapter, it nips the ship "shrowdly" (2:552). Pushing the rehabilitated vessel into deeper water is punishing: "There droue much Ice about vs and within vs" (2:557). Like Pelham had discovered a year before, divine intervention proves necessary when the Bay bites back: "We laboured, flood and ebbe, both with pales and oares, to heaue away and part the Ice from her. But it was God that did protect and preserue vs; for it was past any mans vnderstanding how the Ship could indure it, or we by our labour saue her" (2:559). Once unmoored from their singed shore, however, their troubles only compound: "Ice being all about vs, we knew not which way to turne vs. Now (to avoide telling the same thing 20 times), we were continually, [from July 5] till the 22, so pestered and tormented with Ice that it would seeme incredible to relate it" (2:570). Despite "conceiv[ing] it impertinent to relate every particular dayes passages, which was much alike to vs" (2:572), James makes sure to log his daily battles. Pieces afloat in open water emit "a most fearefull noyse" (2:572). The mid-August heat makes it a most cruel month: "We heard the rut of the Ice ahead of vs, which made the most hideous noyse of any we had heard this voyage" (2:579).

Contending with poop-high icebergs and the people on deck might have seemed tedious to him, but he knew it made for a terrifyingly good read. Gripped by ice makes for a gripping tale, and he rounded his story accordingly. He is careful not to repeat Hudson's fate by listening to the men's "murmur[s] . . . [that] we (say they) are destined to starue vpon a piece of Ice" (2:570). Mutiny looms in the background, but the captain is not ready to cease his search. "Strooke . . . into a dumpe" (2:584), however, his officers enumerate six reasons why they should return home. On August 26, "with a sorrowful heart" (2:585), he consents and sets a course for England. There will be no more wintering that year. "Comming" out, like in, he assumes the mantle of ice-thwarter, and narrowly at that, contra his peers' later panegyrics. "Bowes" and bodies "broken and bruised" (2:592), they reach Bristol on October 22, 1632.

But an astute reader would know by now that one cannot simply flake off the cold. Instead, it hangs on like a life-long leech: "Some took such a cold that they did complaine of it to their dying day" (2:502). Traveling east across the northern Atlantic passage, they have effectively carried the northwestern parasite with/in them. This stowaway should not be surprising; the *Maria,* as we have already seen, represents a mixed-elemental floating (and sometimes sunken) house shared between James's mariners and the brumal matter of the Bay. And despite their protracted "complaints," the sticky nonhuman passenger was occasionally invited in. At the height of his icy drama in mid-August, caught in the "iawes of death" and "never . . . tormented with Ice, as we haue now beene" (2:580), James admits that he has been hauling the toothy stuff aboard since July. Intent on "touching the dissolution or ruining of the Ice" (2:580), he cuts two-foot-square blocks, sets them on a boat in direct sunshine, and monitors their melting: "Notwithstanding the warmth of the Ship (for we kept a good fire), and all our breathings and motions, it would not melt in 8 or 10 dayes" (2:581). Like the hypotheses he made during the wintering (how the bay "ingenders" its ice), he attempts here to complete the cryological cycle by turning to that same ice's disintegration.

His curiosity mirrors Boyle's "promiscuous" mashups: "When we should be two dayes together fast to a piece of Ice, [we] set markes upon it, to see how it did consume; but it yeelded us small hope of dissoluing" (2:581). "Sinking" these slabs does not provide any insight, either, leading him to guess that the ice is "ruined with stormes or consumed with heate" at some unpredictable point (2:581). "Consume" says much about his mindset: from Latin *con-* ("altogether") and *sumere* ("to take up"), James employs the now-obsolete transitive sense, "to cause to evaporate or disappear."[111] Like "heate" to an ice hunk, the verb implicitly speaks to the fear of being consumed "with" (or by) the great white "iawes" as well. Perhaps these impromptu experiments afforded him the chance to play the "tormentor," finally able to torture his f(l)oe as he makes an exit. But it is more accurate to see the ship as a lab in these moments of welcomed, if fleeting, adjacency. Stumped, he must "confesse that these secrets of nature are past my apprehension" (2:581). By letting bioregional "secrets" go unexplained, he leaves gaps in knowledge for future navigators to fill. In taking "such a cold," however, he also underscores the mysterious "nature" of wintering: how a series of phenomena can be "past apprehension" and yet makes its "markes" on dwellers nevertheless.

Tests taken, and homeward bound, James sails through the ice gauntlet triumphant. Once there, he safely disembarks from winter's reconception "within vs"; indeed, his thoughts turn to deliverance: "We went all to Church, and gaue God thankes for his preseruation of vs" (2:592). The prospect of Indigenous societies wintering in harsh climates is similarly abandoned, and his "copie" (2:594) of the letter left on the cross at Charlton makes no mention of first inhabitants, either. But these notions need not be forgotten by "vs." Positively crestfallen at the close of his narrative ("most probable it is that there is no passage" [2:589]), James's concession presciently reveals just how tantalizing polar tales like his truly are: "These hopes haue stirred vp, from time to time, the more actiue spirits of this our Kingdome to research that meerely imaginary passage" (2:588). The Portuguese and Spanish, for example, "write as if they had beene brought home in a dreame or engine" (2:588). To engage this "meerly" dreamy space of human–cold encounter amounts to a quixotic exercise at best: "let vs (by imagination onely) inlarge this Straight, in this Latitude, and free it of Ice; yet what aduantage, in speedy performance, will be gotten by this passage, if the winds be withall considered?" (2:591). James's imagination can only go so far; his readers, however, may let theirs continue to run: "I very well know that what I haue here hastily written will neuer discourage any noble spirit that is minded to bring this so long tryed Action to absolute effect" (2:593).

He was right: wintering went on after him, and his short stay shaded explorers' perceptions of northern coldscapes' in/habitability well into the seventeenth century. The title page of Thomas Allison's (d. in/before 1706) account of his anchorage just shy of Norway's North Cape in 1697–1698 tells "of the Ship and Company Wintering . . . in the Latitude of 71. Their Manner of Living, and what they Suffered by the Extream Cold."[112] It is warmth, however, that turns out to be tortuous. With "frost in their Limbs,"[113] the sight of snowy England upon their return in late April disagrees with him: he prefers "the usual garb of the season"[114] instead. Yet when his wish for "calm and very warm" conditions is granted a few days later, their seasoned bodies start to contort: one man "was so swoln, that we feared he would burst."[115] Even acclimating to one's home can be fatal. Indeed, Allison's final paragraph yearns for the cold: "I and all the rest, perceived ourselves manifestly the worse for the warm weather."[116] Climatic physiological "pains"[117] like his prolonged James's "complaints" of bone-deep winter, and others would use *Strange and Dangerous Voyage*'s example to assess their surroundings' livability. When John Wood resumed England's search for the Northeast Passage in 1676, the prospect of temporary housing on Nova Zembla topped his list of general observations: "Under the superficies of this Earth, about two Foot deep, after we had dug so low, we came to a firm Body of Ice; which, as I think, was never hear of before: so these Men that did imagin, if they were forced to Winter to the Northward, would dig Caves in the Earth to preserve themselves from cold, would find here but very bad Lodging."[118] A morbid fascination with fortitude endured as well. J. G.'s 1684 *Strange News from Plymouth* recounts a grisly tale of cannibalism aboard a Dutch ship bound for Rotterdam from the East Indies. Stuck off the English coast, "from the Severity of the late Season, for the Ice being . . . in very great Flakes,"[119] the last two survivors eventually walked across to safety after lying there for six ghastly days. One strange tale, repurposed, begat tales; putting some to rest, it also prompted others past Hudson's shores.

It is a fitting point for us to circle back to Willoughby, "pen still in hand." If the Anthropocene emphasizes humans' signatures in the geological and glaciological record, what wintering narratives are left for us to inscribe?[120] One story might tell of early modern frozen men writing over the Pleistocene, effectively ushering in a new age of polar exploration-exploitation; another might tell of frozen words lying in wait, as if suspended, not yet spoken. The first relies on what has been written. The second catches us "in the act of writing." "My Books too that stood upon a shelf over my Head, had upon their edges and corners the same ornament [Ice like Enamel]," observed Allison, "a sight I cannot say, whether more pleasant or dismal."[121] Such tomes need not be labeled solely under terror, misfortune, or error, as if confined to the doomed escapades of those who followed thereafter; nor should their fixation on cryocorporeality live on as mere fantasy and not the stuff of real life for northern peoples.

By the southeastern Bay, at least, this reading practice of "revitalization"[122] requires tackling profound transhistorical disquiet: the ravages to regional biodiversity committed by the fur trade; the possession, draining, and damming of Cree and Inuit land by white settlers; and the conversion of rivers into energy and wealth by state-run utility companies like Hydro-Québec. (At minimum.) The ongoing implementation of the James Bay Project, a series of dams first installed in the 1970s by the Canadian government, remains hotly contested.[123] Spikes in mercury levels, diverted animal migration routes, and disrupted water flows underscore Max Liboiron's point that "pollution is best understood as the violence of colonial land relations,"[124] as if *Wînipekw* ("muddy water"), the Cree name for James Bay, expresses the shameful introduction of hydro-colonial impacts. "Sovereign injustice"[125] is a necessary part of this survival story; so are defiance and remedy. As the legal anthropologist Ronald Niezen reminds us, "Cree resistance to large-scale development, the negotiation of regional autonomy, . . . and subsequent adjustments to new administrations provide examples of indigenous activism changing the rules of political engagement with non-native society, responding to social crisis, and trying to accommodate rapid social change with a sense of order and continuity."[126] When talking about wintering, both the "pleasant" and the "dismal" must be spoken in the same breath. In the enterprise that bears his name, we reencounter James's chilling fancy for Indigenous erasure four centuries later. But we also hear Inuit and Anishinaabe voices: "Virtually every mega dam in what's currently known as Canada is within 100 km of an Indigenous community," notes Amy Norman; and "this is what we say, water is life. Me, I call this cultural genocide," adds Lucien Wabanonik.[127]

James Bay was never his to possess, let alone narrate. Its unfolding stories refuse to privilege one perspective over others, or to negate decolonial and anticolonial labor. Pushing back on the configuration of lakes as archives, James L. Smith proposes that we perceive them as "counterarchives" instead, sites "where archival modes and anxieties can be exposed and explored."[128] Bays, too, magnify the perplexities of remembrance and access, and "this is true of all waters."[129] Tracing these controversies and divergences—whose winter is imperiled, exactly?—confronts the historical origins of present-day harms while also offering other possibilities for human–nonhuman impingement. "'Twas vexatious enough to get my Ink ready for use, and no less to keep it so,"[130] bemoans Allison. Seventeenth-century winter tales were never simply about surviving bleak environments far from home. As I have argued, they were about confronting the very vicissitude of dwelling. It is a living arrangement from which we may learn to story alternative winterscapes right now. One finds in winter's keen effects not a resolution between the intimate and the inimical, but the further contemplation of these entwined qualities: a search for even the briefest equanimity, a cold kind of co-flourishing, with chilly substances that have become synonymous with the ephemeral. Contrary to the tone of rehabilitation reflected in the stationers' original entry for *Strange and Dangerous Voyage,* a "miraculous" one,[131] there will be no miracles ahead, just the hard work of wintering. Refashioning Katherine May's metaphorical definition of the term (the self-care concept of "rest and retreat") to grapple with the predicament of weathering "difficult times" is a meditation early modern at its heart: "We must learn to invite the winter in. We may never choose to winter, but we can choose *how.*"[132]

Let us try to keep it just "so." Here is one last (thought) experiment, then, on the final pages of *Strange and Dangerous Voyage.* Like the Passage, James's wintering is an "engine" for the cryological imagination: it offers an organic mode of writing, inhabiting, and dreaming also known as "dwelling." It is an ongoing imagination machine that talks back to its operators, asking how poems are produced, which stories are engineered, and why winter tales must be told amidst warm passageways becoming "free[r] . . . of Ice" (2:480). Wintering is an endurance test that not only pushes at limits, but also expands them. We would do well to imitate Watts's predilection for "the Searche . . . not the finding" (2:620). Wood gauged Nova Zembla's sea-ice to be so thick that it "would have taken some Centuries of Years to Thaw it," and its peaks "covered with Snow, which I believe hath lain there evere since the Creation."[133] In

2019, the Russian navy detected five "new" islands under the defrosting glaciers he thought immovable since time immemorial.[134] Early modern tales allow us to reframe what wintering *is* and *can be* in our warming world, one that augurs winter's very disappearance, while at the same time pointing to ever-present, and sometimes-widening, polar vortices.[135] They help us wonder whether winter can truly afford a time of cohabitation, of humans and nonhumans in pliable partnership, rather than measure the former's fortitude against the latter in increasingly "poletical"[136] arenas of the Anthropocene. They probe the Serresian "limit" of lethality, and of life itself. So, rime on: there is more to piece together with James's "walking" parts. Going "boldly out vpon the Ice to sport and recreate ourselues," we might behold in "cold entertainment" other "affections" and "worthy employments." To live in this "spirit," to winter in this "wildernesse," is to "liue in a heape" of hope at a time of shrinking snow.

# Winterlude

## *Press*

> There you may also this hard Frosty Winter,
> See on the Rocky Ice a Working-Printer.
>
> —Anonymous, *Great Britains Wonder*

Wintertime publishing, just like every other business out on the ice, was risky: "And sure, in former Ages, ne're was found, / A Press to Print, where Men so oft were dround."[1] As we noticed before, novelty drew large crowds: "printing, an Art before ne're publick shown / Upon the Frozen-Flood, to Thousands known."[2] When works like *The True and Exact Representation of the Wonders upon the Water* (1684) boasted of their publication "on the frozen Thames,"[3] they effectively boosted their collectability. These works, cold off the press, have not escaped historians of the book.[4] Yet while instances of printing "on" the ice have been considered for their roles in reconstructing late-seventeenth-century London culture—affecting the realms of memory, social identity, urban space, and so forth—I remain curious about the more-than-human signals they contain. The posturing involved in the proclamatory and prepositional "on the . . . Thames" reminds readers of, and firmly embeds them in, the wider nonhuman ecology of winter. No publishing house is hermetically sealed off from the "frigid blasts" sent south from Boreas's cold kingdoms.[5] By conversing with the elements collaboratively, in "keenest breath,"[6] these self-referential creations, perhaps more so than their offshore counterparts, prompt us to reappraise their crisp atmospheres.

Early modern printers proved savvy in their ruminations about ice's inherent transitoriness and built-in contradictions. They were artistic producers who could muse on solidification and its opposite at once.

A tiny "frost fair mug" on display at the Victoria and Albert Museum boasts the silver-engraved inscription, "bought on ye Thames ice Janu: ye 17 1683/4." Made of glass, its bergy cohesion might seem to mock the "field of glasse" that departed Thomas Dekker's London long ago;[7] more likely, its unknown maker meditated on the delicate comparison between glass (cup) and "glasse" (cold). As the unnamed songwriter of *The Thames Uncas'd* knew in 1684, they "printed your Names / On the River Thames, / While their hands with the cold look'd blue."[8] Made-to-order souvenirs like these were not the answer to cold's capriciousness; instead, they manifested Londoners' attempts to process the fickleness of environmental change and the briskness that they so personally felt. Such purchases made on the ice, whether impressed or engraved, not only memorialize the fair but also commemorate the event (*kairos*) of the object's making. In other words, one witnesses in the souvenir's manufacture the making of time (*chronos*), and in doing so, is permitted to dig deeper into the climatic conditions, especially the matter of frost, that constitute said history.

What would it mean to be caught "blue"-handed in this fashion? Look again into the inkpot that sits on the river's "rocky ice": the prints' very existence demonstrates how cold promoted penmanship as well as curbed it. Far from benumbing one's wits, it sometimes set the "muse to scribble."[9] Pamphlets documenting the specific coldness of 1683–1684 were not passive takings of temperature, but an insight into the shared activity of recording, of bluish human "hands" committing the tactile doings of nonhuman cold to memory. The remembrance here is a reminder of the reciprocal inscriptions that take place between writers and winters. Returning to the point of pressing shows the cooperative component of cryopoiesis at work. When Thamasis, in her *Advice to the Painter,* "out of her watry Bed, amaz'd appears, / And thus the Current of her Language stears,"[10] her anthropomorphosis helps to decolonize language as a privilege (and hallmark) of humans alone. The "current," of course, is a metaphor for the ensuing poem, yet it is also the "River of Thames," the water "on" which the poem was literally re/produced.[11] And quite possibly drafted: as in so many other examples that spoke in "frozen verse," winter cold sparks the flow of the poet's words, stirring and "stearing" her "language," giving it voice across slow-moving streams. The talking Thames advises us to push past the anthropogenic limits of artistic making; she teaches an abiding lesson in cryopoiesis.

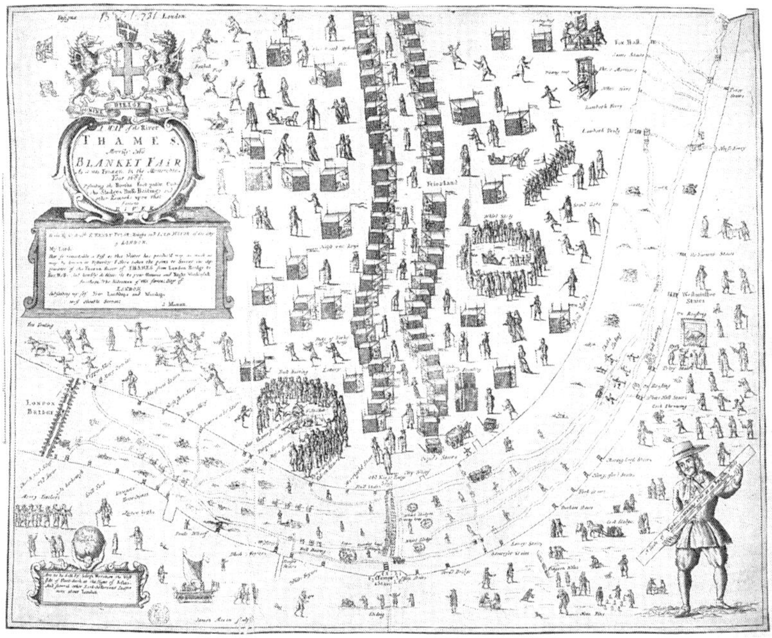


FIGURE 11. Joseph Moxon, *A Map of the River Thames. Merrily Cald Blanket Fair as It Was Frozen in the Memorable-Year 1683/4* (1684), Bodleian Library.

A compressive case in point: the approximately 20×16-inch 1684 *Map of the River Thames* by globemaker Joseph Moxon (1627–1691), dedicated to Henry Tulse, Mayor of London. The "Thames Merrily Cal'd Blanket Fair" could just as well be called "merrily cold."[12] Looking north and west (at bottom and to the right), some of the fun and games like "sliding" and "cock throwing" come with descriptions attached, although not all. The panoply is disorienting. A gigantic citizen dominates the lower right-hand corner, holding out the promise of precise measurement ("a scale of yards"[13]), even though his own body is wildly out of proportion. The activities that appear to take place on land are, upon closer inspection, magnifications of their counterparts upon the ice. Thus, while river entrances ("Temple Stairs") and other notable locations ("London Bridge") are labeled, this map would probably not have been used in a strictly pragmatic sense. More memento than navigational guide, its utility, instead, is in re-creating the joyful aspects of what once was, ensuring that a "remarkable . . . Frost as this Winter had produc'd may as much as may be known to Posterity."[14]

Here, at last, is the "mappe of [the] citie" promised to Dekker's countryman in 1608,[15] albeit distortedly so: the eye is encouraged to follow the fair's waves, streaks, and bends—the river especially is a maze of lines—as if "skate sliding"[16] from point to point on the page before turning (back) again. Even the alley of "Frizeland" gains an undulating asymmetrical motion in Moxon's perspective. His panoramic lens simultaneously zooms in and out, situating the seer in the icy conviviality below. Remarkably, three easy-to-miss vignettes hint at Moxon's interest in more-than-human composition as well as celebration: two printing presses (upper middle), and what appears to be a self-portrait of the sketch artist (upper left). When Moxon's contemporaries illustrated "the printing booth,"[17] they usually curtained its activities. The stall consequently became a "black box" in Bruno Latour's sense, rendering its "scientific and technical work . . . invisible by its own success."[18] Moxon's map, on the contrary, uniquely puts print and its human-nonhuman makers right out in the open, exposing the elements' role in the pressing. It is tempting to see these workers rolling out the map itself, but alas, only its distribution is stated: "Sold . . . on the west side of Fleet ditch at the Signe of Atlas, And Several other Book-Sellers and Stationers about London."[19] But even if cast farther back from the Thames's solid shores, his attention to the printing process establishes a metacommentary about the weight that weather applies to the manual, cold-hand-cranked production of word and picture. If not directly "on," then tangibly *with,* nonetheless, and capable of plummeting the prepositional correspondence to new depths.

Moxon, notably, served as hydrographer to Charles II. The "polar draft" he completed for his king in 1676, looking directly down on "all the discovered Lands about the North Pole," is exactingly detailed.[20] Charted the same year of Captain John Wood's disappointing northeastern expedition, Moxon tacks on a history of adventures from Sir Hugh Willoughby to Thomas James before reiterating that the center of the Arctic Circle was "open Sea."[21] His later map of the Thames loosens up a bit, or is at least a little less imperial. This is the writer who, after all, bequeathed one of the rarest meanings of "winter" to the English language only a year before this map. In his 1683 *Mechanick Exercises,* he calls one of the press's supporting bars "winter": for example, "into this Dustail Mortess is fitted a Dustail Tennant made at each end of the Winter."[22] He was aware of the seasonal connotations, too. The printer should have "a clear, free and pretty loft Light, . . . lest the violence of Winter gain too great advantage."[23] There was a precise term for this accident, in fact: "In Winter when the Paper is Froze, and the Letter Froze, so as the Workmen cannot Work. They say, They are Froze out."[24] Meanwhile, the bracing block of wood required fine tune-ups: "If he doubt the crazy make of the Winter, he will cause two Battens . . . to be nailed close to the outer sides of the Feet of the Press, which will both strengthen the Winter . . . and also hinder the Press from working into a twisting Position."[25]

A polysemous word of uncertain etymology sprang from seasons meeting with publishers' minds: "winter," whose honorific beam buttressed the machine, whose frost braced the lines it manufactured, and whose icy cold, under special circumstances, substantially buoyed both. To be "froze" *in* was an industriously imaginative state; and yet, as Moxon reminds us, the precarious doings of print always bordered on being "frozen out," shut down. Similarly, the "crazy make of . . . Winter" refers to the literal ruptures in the apparatus: *crazy* (ca. 1583), "full of cracks or flaws . . . liable to break or fall to pieces . . . frail, 'shaky,'" derives from Swedish *krasa* ("crunch").[26] Cold can torque too much, take things too far out of proportion; but its fractures, as we have seen, could produce wonderful leads for poets, "painters," and printers to pursue, willingly putting themselves in the crazed "position" of *making*. It is ultimately unnecessary to establish a lexical provenance for the "twists" and turns of Moxon's co-productive labor. His gloss on "winter," just as the substance known as "frozen verse," unlocks the promises of cryopoiesis: a conjunction that bespeaks the congelation of ideas and icescape, embosses in/organic scripts as glassy as the material relations that bore them—and with which they glide.

# 5 *Hamlet* on Ice

> Just as in Shakespeare's original theatre, the audience can enjoy the performance beneath the open sky either as a "groundling" or seated under a roof in an ice box. Cool!
>
> —"Audience Frozen in Their Seats"

> If you intreate him faire in a frostie morning, hee will affoord you whole *Hamlets*, I should say handfuls of Tragicall speeches.
>
> —Thomas Nashe, "Preface to R. Greene's 'Menaphon'"

Meet Murray Hamlet. With his enigmatic stare, trim beard, and relaxed posture, not to mention his colorful dress, this twentieth-century avatar positively resembles a Renaissance courtier. Called upon "to explain the physiological process of becoming cold,"[1] he likens the human body to a house's heating system, with the core, blood, capillaries, and skin standing in for the furnace, heat, ducts, and radiators (respectively). "What piece of work is a / man" (Shakespeare, *Hamlet,* 2.2.264–65),[2] his readers might conclude: the "work" being, ostensibly, the work of multilayered human subjects opposing the frigid forces of the nonhuman environment. The Anthropocene is the time of this "man" who sets his anthropocentrism and androcentrism against an icy "sea of troubles" (3.1.58). "'In offices, the temperature is usually set by males. . . . The men are comfortable, but the women wear sweaters. . . . If you raise the room temperature so all the women are comfortable, then the men would sweat. It's a nuisance.'"[3] Murray's message is clear by the end of his short interview: the cold, without question, is to be kept out and bravely fought off—here is snow country for warm men. While "cold is subjective,"[4] the question of how that "subject" is defined depending on a particular set of ecological circumstances such as weather is unexplored. The business of "becoming cold" is the true "undiscovered country" (3.1.78) of the article; it requires reacting to the unfolding "to be" of cold's distributive agency in which humans *become* via their very corporeality within a wintry world. But the battle over impregnable embodiment has already been settled for us: both in the title of the article (Murray knows "the answer"), and at its conclusion. No one wants "to be" cold; they merely want "to be" told how to resolve the "boot/sock controversy": "Hamlet," indubitably, "slaps the side of the boot and says, 'Now that's a way to stay warm!'"[5] What the title ultimately assumes is that the eponymous prince of *Hamlet* does *not* provide (or cannot reach) any answers, a commonplace reading of the play in popular culture. "*This* Hamlet" (emphasis added), however, has realized how to hermetically seal the human, and he keeps his secrets locked up at the U.S. Army's Cold Research Division, safe from "Soviet"[6] spies who are always eager to steal his findings and potentially shift the cryopolitical stakes of a Cold War almost at its end.

As a member of the Arctic environmental humanities' extended family, I refuse the urge to swaddle Hamlet's (and *Hamlet*'s) "kin" (1.2.65) like so. While it might seem "less than kind" (1.2.65), peeling back the "layers of warmth"[7] magnified in his portrait reveals additional coatings and cryptic questions, underscoring the fact that any perceivable barrier between "skin," "Murray Hamlet," and "snow" is permeable, and that the results of this psychological and physiological overlap are as unpredictable as they are palpable.[8] A cryocorporeal approach to the undisputed pinnacle of early modern drama raises for us, like specters, further questions pertaining to the cold. Climate and culture coldly conjoin; macrocosm and microcosm coolly collapse in both geographical and anatomical space. Daryl W. Palmer views the play in conversation with historic attempts to find the fabled Arctic passages to the northwest and northeast (destinations still very much in vogue at the turn of the seventeenth century, as we have seen), thereby establishing a "nexus of climate and voyaging" for its first audiences.[9] Kristen Poole, citing Margreta de Grazia's insistence that "the language of the play . . . upholds the attachment of persons to land, humans to humus,"[10] associates the play's earthy materiality with contemporary debates over the physical location of purgatory, determined by some authors to be inside Iceland's fiery Mount Hecla. For Poole, the volcano-as-portal motif raises a larger question concerning the legibility of super/natural space; it is a puzzle that leads to "an epistemological understanding

THIS HAMLET HAS THE ANSWER TO THE QUESTION:

TO BE, OR NOT TO BE, COLD

*By Janet Nelson*

"It takes about three years for a paper I've written to show up in Soviet documents," says Murray Hamlet, leaning back in his chair. A Fu Manchu mustache and beard add an air of mystery to his account of Russians borrowing his research.

Hamlet is one of the world's leading authorities on human survival and management in the cold. As the director of the Cold Research Division at the U.S. Army's Institute of Environmental Medicine in Natick, Mass., the Russian episode is all in a day's confrontation.

At the Institute, Hamlet supervises studies of cold, altitude, physical fitness, ergonomics and nutrition—anything that



FIGURE 12. "This Hamlet Has the Answer to the Question: To Be, Or Not to Be, Cold" promises the February 1989 issue of *Snow Country*.

of the environment that does not segregate the natural from the supernatural, or earth from purgatory."[11]

By now, it should be clear that cold provides more than a "whimsical inspiration," in Palmer's parlance,[12] a hypermasculine air that, once followed, entails a "theatrical sense of ruin."[13] His cold open of "I begin with a simple fact: Hamlet, like everyone else in the tragedy is cold"[14] is complicated in reality. While it could be construed as a phenomenal experience in "exoteric" or "outward"[15] terms, cold was not constricted to them; in fact, the categories of interior and exterior can crisply enfold. If "th' cold / ground" (4.2.69–70) is important to this play, it is hard to dig through *Hamlet*'s permafrost. No wonder the "solid" (1.2.129) is called upon to melt. But in a play known for its "worms" (3.6.20), ice too will act as compost. Polar vortices propel the prince's "wild and whirling words, . . . words, words" (1.5.135; 2.2.189). Interrogating English literature's paradigm of introspective inaction, a character who has come to represent both the "human" and Renaissance humanism, I intend to speculate—haptically as much as visually—on the prince's posthumanity[16] and on the interpenetrative nature of cold. I track the environment–embodiment conjunction of becoming cold by examining the characters' recurring cases of cryocorporeality. In a play famous for being/not-being, ice is a prevalent force in the production of selves. If "we must learn to ask the documents interesting questions,"[17] as Erica Fudge recommends, it is convenient that *Hamlet* begins with one: "Who's there?" (1.1.1). Taking up the play's interrogational impulse, I hypothesize: what *is* rimy in the early modern "state of Denmark" (1.4.90), and why might its tactility be important to query today?

## To Put an Arctic Disposition On

I will attempt an answer in four lines of verse: [Francisco] "'tis bitter cold / and I am sick at heart" (1.1.6–7); [Hamlet] "the air bites shrewdly; it is very cold"; and [Horatio] "it is nipping and an eager air" (1.4.1–2). The first part of this chapter probes the grammatically impersonal yet affective "it" behind Hamlet's mundane comment to Horatio on the battlements of Elsinore, a chill first felt by the castle's frostbitten watchman. I argue that the "it" materializes cold's animacy, a creepy tactile presence rather than an absence of heat or an arbitrary number of temperature. The play anticipates, then, Robert Boyle's touching observations that question, but do not conclusively rule out, the Aristotelian theory that bodies freeze from "frigorifick atoms" and "corpuscles." *Hamlet*'s cold occurrences constitute somatic human–nonhuman networks between spectator and landscape, between Danish guard and shrewd "air." The north is a vivified and vivifying place where even ghosts return, its matter vibrant instead of stultifying, its touches tangible. Hamlet (the character) on ice pitches upon the notion that cold is lively.

The question of what cold "is" leads to questions of "its" knowability, how we assign a value to an atmospheric sensation we cannot accurately measure, because we do not completely know "who" or what "it" is, whose "bitter" phenomenological effects travel across variable intensities and affect bodies differently. In addition, the questionable "it" and the various alliances that "it" engenders sponsor both ethico-political and onto-epistemological speculations. Bringing the drama's cryocorporeality into conversation with material ecocriticism highlights, in Stacy Alaimo's words, "insurgent vulnerability—a recognition of our material interconnection with the wider environment that impels ethical and political responses."[18] The potential multispecies and in/organic intimacies afforded by such exposure temper Palmer's insistence that "boreality [is] to be confronted"[19] because it draws one nearer to the shivers of suffering others, predating Lear's realization that "I am cold myself" (*King Lear,* 3.2.69). It is in Shakespeare's earlier and similarly northern play *Hamlet* that cold starts to crawl into spaces between the "self" and the cryosphere. Cold never exists in solitary confinement. Despite its association with soliloquies and "onlyness,"[20] "it" does not act *solus.* These four lines, in sum, serve an important role for us as interlocutors right now: what cold is (and how it becomes); how cold is defined (and how it escapes); and how cold spurs feeling (how it motivates doing). Once we expose ourselves to cold's "bites" that numb as much as mobilize, this piece of early modern art that questions what "it" is ("what art thou[?]" [1.1.45]), and that it is *itself* pierced by cold may help actuate alternative ecological futures at the world's northernmost places.

To help us envision the protests and pleasures that "it" allows, the second part of this chapter pursues the various alliances that *Hamlet*'s "cold" forges via performance, focusing specifically on a three-month-long production staged at the Ice Globe of Jukkasjärvi, Sweden: an Elizabethan replica built entirely from blocks of the Torne River's frozen banks in 2003. That year, the Beaivváš Sámi Našunálateáhter (BST) produced a shortened version of *Hamlet* in the Sámi language. With temperatures hovering around minus 40°C, Hamlet and Horatio's exchange was surely *felt,* and not just seen, by outdoor audiences in attendance. (Speckled throughout are interviews I conducted in situ with Arne Berg, its Art Director, and Yngve Bergqvist, founder of the adjacent Ice Hotel.) These performances banish the romanticized idea of "iceloation"[21] that subtends the suture of body and environment, art and world, play (*poiesis*) and house (*oikos*); instead, they display the ontological "becoming" of in/organic players, advance an epistemological understanding of the Arctic as a nexus of nature–culture impingement, and promote the ethical treatment of its multispecies populations. Gauging these material "airs" of the play and in performance, as well as the polar playhouse's rimy materials, helps to magnify the globe's vanishing snow and the peoples most impacted by it—particularly Indigenous communities like the Sámi. "Environmental ethics and politics can," Alaimo writes, "improvise from within a sense of being embedded, permeable, and profoundly interconnected with climates, landscapes, and nonhuman lives."[22] By "performing exposure" at the Ice Globe, the BST expressly "catalyze[s] that very sense of weathering" she muses on.[23] *Hamlet* (the play) on ice dislodges the "piece of work . . . man" from the center of an anthropocentric and geopolitical Circle, urging us to attend to, in site-specific ways, the quality of cryogenic life contained therein.

## Bitter

I will start with Shakespeare's glassy glossary. "'Tis bitter cold," Francisco complains to his replacement on the night's watch, Barnardo, "and I am sick at heart." Translation: he wants out of the cold; he needs to get the blood flowing again. The Danish air has congealed his humors, sickened his body by sealing up its fluids. (An Aristotelian humoral logic, on the contrary, would mean that the air drew out his cold and dry qualities, leaving him warm and moist instead. But guards, of course, should not be in a sanguine mood.) It is no coincidence that the apparition of King Hamlet appears during a similar interplay between hot and cold physiological and meteorological elements: "Yond same star that's westward from the pole / Had made his course t'illume that part of heaven / Where now it burns" (1.1.35–37). While the ghost is not explicitly linked to cold but to the air ("for it is as the air, invulnerable" [1.1.144]), Horatio "tremble[s] and look[s] pale" at it (1.1.52), a telltale sign of touching cold. And it arrives, as Marcellus notices, benightedly, near the onset of the dark winter solstice: "Some say that ever'gainst that season comes / Wherein our Savior's birth is celebrated" (1.1.157–58). The spirit of Hamlet the older is a supernatural atmospheric occurrence that is connected, crucially, to the local climate, one that "heaven and earth together demonstrated / Unto our climatures and countrymen" (1.1.123–4). "Climature," as we know (chapter 2), was beginning to designate not just a region of the world but also the weather conditions within it. Dressed in "the very armor" (1.1.59) he wore when combating Norway, his costuming begs the question of bodily im/perviousness and the nature of the "invulnerable." (Why else would a ghost wear protection?) It also anticipates the story of penetrability he tells the younger Hamlet four scenes later: death through ear-introduced poison while "sleeping in my orchard" (1.5.35). By pointing to the broader permeability between body and environment to which all humans (armored or not) are susceptible, his shielding ironically portrays "the very" fact of vulnerability.

If we view the icy-hot volcano of Mount Hecla as the purgatorial "prison house" (1.5.14) of fire and frost, the fatherly phantom's ethnography becomes linked to a cold northern plane whose actual weather helped determine somatic traits of temperament, masculinity, and race, from the "pale"-ness of white skin to Hamlet's "solemn black" (1.2.78) melancholy.[24] While a preoccupation with coldness might pretend to fix these terms, it could just as easily frustrate them. To be "coded" black in this play, David Sterling Brown writes, is to exhibit tainted manhood: "Denmark's deterioration" is a corollary to "the decomposition of white masculinity," an affliction that only Fortinbras's hypermasculine arrival can rectify.[25] But cold could undercut as much as abet the logics of white-male cohesiveness, the king's decaying (and graying) corpse a reminder, in his words, "that ideal Danish masculinity no longer has a pulse."[26] (Later, I will unpack how *Hamlet* constructs whiteness via wintry spaces and in relation to internal and external markers of Blackness. Working in tandem with premodern critical race studies, I find that "the play's [cold's] the thing" [2.2.523] for resisting schematics of superior, shatterproof whiteness.) Horatio's manhood requires him to actively wrestle the cold, not just passively "tremble" until dawn. And Francisco never returns to duty: "Give you good night" (1.1.16), he numbingly mutters, and is gone. "Bitter," related to Old English *biter* (from Dutch and German *bitter*), means "bite."[27] Once bitten, we do not know if his cold-sickness is ever cured, although his self-diagnosed heartsickness will haunt what follows. The phenomenological bitterness of cold is also its physical bite with/in flesh. Whereas the bite might emphasize, in Palmer's view, "what is outside the man, namely the biting northern 'air,'"[28] *Hamlet*'s cryocorporeality disturbs inside–outside distinctions while at the same time upending supposedly impenetrable markers of identity. From the curt climatic observation of its very first lines, the play's opening scene troubles the "outside" of the self, and in doing so, crisply delineates a form of subjectivity moving at a glacial, if no less transformative, pace.

## Bites

Cold leaves its (tooth) mark on the susceptible Danes. As Hamlet prepares to meet what he hopes to be his frost-father, he echoes Francisco's earlier declaration—"the air bites shrewdly; it is very cold"—an offhand attempt at small talk, perhaps, to which his longtime friend Horatio agreeably adds: "It is nipping and an eager air." The agency of cold is pronounced slightly differently in this scene: shifting from the adjective of "bitter" to the transitive verb of "bite." While the adverb "shrewdly" carries the action of the verb "bite," the word "shrew" also conveys the animality of cold, the snappy *anima* of its animacy. The simile is strategically employed: rather than forcing two disparate entities to enter into conjunction, it actually bespeaks the biting presence already there. The prince's second line, prefaced by the open-ended semicolon (";"), grasps but does not fully capture this elusive anima, either, presenting an additional, epistemological quandary: how temperature is experienced (felt) and subsequently understood (gauged). Referring to the Second Quarto's (Q2; 1604–1605) spelling of "shroudly" only accentuates this unknowability. Cold arrests facile ways of revealing "itself." Whether or not "it" *is* "cold" depends on who is asking and who is answering. Yet the conversation is already up to the "air"; that is, it is always dependent on the cold and the relations it enshrouds. The editorial crux of which word to provide ("shrewdly" or "shroudly") speaks, therefore, to cold's "subjective" definition. Hamlet's vague modifier of "very" represents the differing degrees of magnitude one individual might feel, but not another, in its "bite." At the same time, it portrays any "bite" as an event of subjective–objective, cryocorporeal enmeshment.

If we watched for this type of interaction on the Danish ramparts, if we truly took its ramifications seriously, we would espy the sinister presence not of the ghost, but of misogyny. "A woman's reliability stands on slippery soles"[29] moralizes the play's Latin source, Saxo Grammaticus's

*Gesta Danorum* (published as *Danorum Regum Heroumque Historiae* in 1514), a text that Shakespeare may or may not have consulted. He might have also recalled a lethal stumble that happened in his home county of Warwickshire on December 17, 1579, when Katherine Hamlett drowned while retrieving water from the Avon. "Standing on the bank," she "suddenly and by accident slipped and fell into the river . . . and not otherwise nor in other fashion came by her death."[30] Such intersections of water and women demonstrate the importance of ascertaining whose bodies are associated with, and are prone to, cold's forces. The zoomorphic adverb attached to the cold, "shrewdly," is glossed as "severely, bitterly" and serves to buttress masculine heroism once more by aligning its annoying "nipping" with hostile female bodies. Palmer hesitates around this point: "An Elizabethan might have wondered whether there was something effeminate in this cold, in its shrewishness."[31] I am less ambivalent than he is, however. Recall Gertrude, the "cold mother" (1.2.77), or Ophelia, the "cold maid" (4.4.170). "Be thou as chaste as ice, as pure as snow, / thou shalt not escape calumny" (3.1.133–34), Hamlet tells the latter, who, "like a creature native and endued / Unto that element" (4.7.178–79) eventually slips underneath "hoary leaves in[to] the glassy stream" (4.7.166). Ice water encapsulates the feminine ideal at the moment of death, literally crystallizes it, even as it retains the fearful "hoar" that must be kept pure (policed) or else purified. In a play about male princely in/action, this damaging conflation that renders women as "slippery" demonstrates an inherent imbalance in agency that must be accounted for if it is to be held accountable. To be a man, one must beat the cold, keeping its "creatures" at bay.[32]

"There's the rub" (3.1.64). It is surprising, then, that Hamlet and Horatio seek the hoary "bite" even as they cannot hope to catch "it" and tame the feminized matter of cold. The men's midnight stroll appears sanctioned at first, due to the martial stature of Hamlet's father, a figure who safely realigns the cold space with patrilineal virtues. But this reasoning not only assumes that the ghost is his father ("I am thy father's spirit. . . . Revenge his foul and most unnatural murder" [1.5.9, 25]); it also supposes that the "it" is vaguely familial, or at least familiar, which "it" is far from. They choose to confront the "it" of Jane Bennett's impersonal, and in this case, inorganic "thing-power" that proffers further speculation *because of* their exposure to it. "Does life only make sense as one side of a life-matter binary," she asks, "or is there such a thing as . . . a life of the it in 'it rains'"?[33] *Hamlet* wonders the same through a different meteorological remark: "It is very cold." Critical ruminations over matter and spirit in the play typically center around the ghost's animacy,[34] but the rimy "it" inherent to a tangible, albeit uncertain, substance deserves greater emphasis for the onto-epistemological predicaments and possibilities it imagines. Spirit-like, neither totally alive nor dead, and up for (troubling) signification by various actors, cold underscores Carla Mazzio's inspired observations on the play's "deinstrumentalizing agency of air," by which she means how Shakespeare "transformed that terrifying unknown into something that might, even or especially in its elusiveness to capture by scientific or theatrical technologies, be absorbed, experienced, and willfully taken in."[35] Truly, "there are more things in heaven and earth, Horatio, / Than are dreamt of in your philosophy" (1.5.168–69). The "nipping" behavior of cold, "its" shrewish "bites" blue in tooth and maw—these are the "things" that may elude, reassess, and amend the central tenets of the most stalwart belief system.

Just briefly, in their brazen decision to wait in the brumal air (a triad of "shrew," "spirit," and "father"), their presumptions about matter, biology, and gender are put to the test. It is baffling that the prince does not "give" the same "good night" to cold *only if* one believes its operations to be rote, its dubiousness resolved, its spaces uncontested. The ghost does "spread his arms" (1.1.127) and "beckon" (1.4.58) his son, to be sure, but Hamlet's response ("it waves me forth again. I'll follow it" [1.4.68]) is remarkable not for his plain desire to fuse with his father's anthropomorphic resemblance, but because of his more parlous choice to expose himself to the wafts, then "waves," of the cold air whipping and "nipping" the ramparts. Respire with care. "This is air from which the oxygen is lacking; it is a cold, sadistic, and impersonal air," warns Steven Swarbrick: "No longer a life-giving breath, as in Genesis, Shakespearean air poses the problem of life's endurance."[36] Horatio's "eager" attribution to the "air" proves to be reciprocal, the atmospheric entrance mutual. These two lines (1.4.1–2) might be dismissed as simple declaratives, notifying an audience watching on a warm sunny afternoon when to conjure a cold dark clime in their minds, or designating differences in class (Marcellus's low learning) by invoking a literal translation ("it is very cold") after a fancier metaphor ("the air bites shrewdly") in one entire line of iambic pentameter. But the "it is" is always more complicated than that, syntactically as well as symbiotically; it demonstrates the meteorological enmeshment of human and nonhuman bodies that takes place whenever "it" "bites" and is "bit" back, the relationality of embodied existence, the dynamism behind becoming brumal. How the chomp-y "it" has been translated through performance is the subject of my chapter's second part, the big and little bites of cold that linger still.

## Snow Globes

The American painter Rockwell Kent (1882–1971), gazing from his house in Illorsuit in western Greenland in 1931–1932, once compared the vista to a playhouse's characteristic features: "One looks out as though upon the stage of a great theatre. Of that stage, the level plain of the sea is the floor, the great circle of the heavens is the proscenium arch, the two headlands are the wings. . . . Despite man's littleness out there, let him just be there, enter on that scene, and as far as the eye can reach all eyes have found him. The speck is the event."[37] The Arctic, like many other landscapes, is often likened to a stage. Theatre, after all, is a visual form of entertainment and thus dependent on sight to a certain extent. (The word derives from the Greek *theasthai,* "behold.") Gretel Ehrlich, who recognizes in Kent's state of transcendental solitude an example of "iceolation," and who excerpts his words in her own 2001 work of elemental mysticism, *This Cold Heaven,* similarly underscores the important role that vision plays in the icescape. When she visited the world's largest island almost sixty-five years later in 1997, she meditated on a single thought: "To see or not to see—that was the only worthwhile question."[38]

The reference to *Hamlet* is dramatic in its delivery, even if hackneyed; yet both Kent's paean to polar theater (he also wintered there in 1929 and 1934–1935) and Ehrlich's prosaic rephrasing reflect the long legacy left by the country's erstwhile colonial possessor: Denmark. The "speck"-as-"him" echoes Hamlet's cynical observation that the earth's "goodly frame" is a "sterile promontory," that its "majestical roof fretted with / golden fire" is "a foul and pestilent congregation of vapors," and that the divinely sanctioned "piece of work" settling it, "man," is nothing but the "quintessence of dust" (2.2.260–69). The human looks very like a "speck" from this perspective. At both Illorsuit and Elsinore, then, one may behold the spectacle of the "speck" brought down rather than held up: man's diminishment and situated seclusion, transgressive in its self-deprivation, and sometimes misanthropic in its desire. The ensuing "event," nevertheless, fixes audience's eyes on a singular small figure on canvas or stage. What is being beheld in both "scenes," captured by Kent's paint and performed by Shakespeare's prince, is the "speck"-"dust" of man performing his "littleness" under the cold heavens of mid-twentieth-century Greenlandic expanse, or beneath the subarctic roof of the Globe Theatre (est. 1599), its boards of starry "fire" stiffening under the chilly climes of London's Little Ice Age (LIA) four centuries earlier.

Ehrlich's mantra is worth returning to, for it invites us to examine *Hamlet*'s current relationship to a precarious northern environment and "the drama endlessly deploying there,"[39] an "Anthropo-scene"[40] threatened by massive anthropogenic harms wrought by the multitudinous "specks" of man no matter how small they may seem at first. Facilitating this conversation risks separating temporal and geographical spheres, however, casting them as two opposing sides barely brought together by one writer's choice of oft-quoted words. The play, despite its rigorous engagement with the bracing cold and a brazen hypermasculinity of the late sixteenth century, is more likely to stress the prince's iconic and "dusty" existentialism than contemplate the fate of the world's ice stores currently melting at the poles at the whims of global warming, especially when viewed from the vantage points of modern-day climate-controlled playhouses. But I do not want to leave my eco-materialist "question" behind. Indeed, what would it mean to perform the play not only indoors within the Arctic,[41] for a cinematic production to place it out in the cold,[42] or for snow to be piled at pivotal moments,[43] but to constitute a dramatic "event" through and with inhuman actors of the physical environment, to not merely liken the landscape to a theatre ("as though"), but to behold the theatre and icescape as co-constitutive shareholders?[44] What happens when the stage's heaven ("the great circle") and earth ("the floor") are cold not just metaphorically but materially, constructed out of the quintessential stuff of the Arctic Circle itself? Is there a *Hamlet,* unlike others, that would not wait for man to "enter" on the wings?

I have another "tale" to "unfold" (1.5.15). The Ice Globe was the brumal brainchild of Swedish actor Rolf Degerlund, "the world's only ice theatre manager,"[45] who suddenly received a vision of a "snowy Globe" while returning from the new Shakespeare's Globe established

FIGURE 13. Snow Globe, Jukkasjärvi, Sweden. Photograph by Alistair Flack, via Alamy Stock Photo.

in 1997 in London.[46] He chose Jukkasjärvi, a town in the municipality of Kiruna located approximately 1200 km north of Stockholm and 200 km north of the Arctic Circle. Formed in three weeks from about fifteen thousand tons of snow and ice, the theater was coupled with Bergqvist's Ice Hotel, a glacial palace resurrected every winter at the cost of seven million Swedish Kroner (SEK). Open-air just like its subarctic twin, the Ice Globe stood roughly two stories high and thirty-five meters across, with a seating capacity of 520 persons. One hundred groundlings could stand directly upon the cold terrace, while the rest sat in the forty or so boxes above the semithrust stage. Everything except the wooden lighting racks was made of ice. "Yea," as if realizing Prospero's prophecy, the Ice Globe and "all which it inherit[ed]" opened on January 24, 2003, and ran for seventy-four days before totally "dissolving" in May—but only to return twice more (*Tempest,* 4.1.154). (*Macbeth,* co-directed by Bo Landin and Alex Scherpf, was filmed in 2004, and an operatic rendition of *Romeo and Juliet* took place the year after that.) The annual reconstitution of the hotel, if not the theater, is assuring as well as lucrative in an era of record-setting high temperatures. Heeding "the circle of ice" and "the rhythm of Torne," as their website advertises, "Icehotel has been reborn in a new guise every year since 1989."[47] But for how long?

Noting the wood shortages England faced at the turn of the seventeenth century, Vin Nardizzi convincingly argues that a stage tree enlisted at the 1599 Globe "proves an active and alive 'star': collectively, these trees comprise the *dramatis arborae* of early modern commercial theatre."[48] The Ice Globe's materials, similarly, are *dramatis glacies* that expose "an array of eco-fantasies and nightmares," the "darker shades of [white]."[49] The material dimensions of the theatre foreground ice's demise, not just its fleetingness, on a global scale.

To the proprietors of the hotel-theater, ice is both figuratively and directly commodified. Human–cold transactions communicate nature's economy: "She [the Torne] generously lends us pristine natural ice as she hibernates on her journey to the coast. In spring, the sun melts artwork and returns our loan."[50] Hosts and guests, one might say, are both borrowers and lenders on the riverbank. In the latter, the goods are literally put up for sale, supporting Jason W. Moore's claim that capitalism acts as an organizing principle: "Almost anything you can imagine in the world of ice, we can turn into reality," their product page boasts, "whether it's stunning art installations, opulent interiors or icy drinking glasses."[51] One may even order an "ice-ogram" with a personalized scratch-on message.[52] This "level[ing] up," ideal for corporate mixers, renders the ice as a telegraphic messenger and less a tale-teller, a block embossed with logos "to help other brands tell their story" and enable exchange from buyer and seller.[53] What seems to evade the logic behind this ice à la carte is the real possibility of dearth in the not-too-distant future. When I met Bergqvist in the comfy hotel lounge in February 2020, he cited the fact that, on average, only eight or nine days from November to March reach temperatures below 25°C (a severe drop from the previous average of thirty days); on the other hand, last winter's temperatures held at negative 25°C for more than thirty days, while the season I was there the river ice formed in October, the earliest in thirty years. I asked whether this flux unnerved him. The "south," he calmly replied, "has been losing snow." Scarcity seems difficult to conceive, let alone confront. (The discussion was practically nonexistent in 2003–2004, he admitted.)

The field of "eco-theatre," fortunately, helps prevent weather from fading out of performance. Like a long exhale crystallizing on a cold night, it works to resituate the substantial presence of air, the breath in and out that lets be "this mortal coil" (3.1.66). Evelyn O'Malley argues that "weather is an important part of the lived theater experience for audiences, highlighting exposure and profoundly affecting how people respond to the plays."[54] Be it collaborated with, mis/appropriated, or suffered through, the actual air that constitutes "open-air Shakespeares"[55] cannot be left out of the ecological–theatrical equation. "Performances of weathering," she says, "comprise lived practices enacted by real bodies in a world and are more material than metaphor."[56] Thinking on cold's "drift" (2.1.37), or the gist of what (weather) is happening, may be more interrogational than instrumental: it queries the nature of being "open" and "in" the air, the current status of Arctic countries that are setting record-high summer temperatures.[57] After polling audiences who "weathered" outdoor productions of Shakespeare across the United Kingdom—like those encircled by "The Willow Globe" in Wales—O'Malley discovered that their "experiences were often tethered to an avant-garde nostalgia that meandered between troubling ahistorical longings for a blurry but better Shakespeare's time and place *and* a progressive desire for a pleasurable and environmentally engaged present."[58] It is precisely this more complicated story that the performances tell, where melancholy (melt) and open-ended uncertainty (climate change) are crystallized in the ice alongside aesthetic enchantment. Here Hamlet and Horatio's mundane conversation in 1.4 gains a unique material purchase, the "it" denoting cold's sharp agency in the play as well as gesturing to the theatre's gelid construction and the pinching "air" of a Scandinavian winter. A *Hamlet* on ice, in short, cannot prevent itself from pointing, ghostlike, to the Ice Globe's (and the globe's) defrosting foundations.

Canny audience members might have also connected the older Globe to its cooler counterpart by recalling that Richard Burbage and Peter Street ordered the dismantling of The Theatre (est. 1576) at the end of December 1598, transporting its snow-pierced lumber to the Thames, where it waited until after the spring thaw to be shipped southward and reassembled as the Globe. Although James Shapiro has debunked the "popular story of the dismantled frame being drawn across or over the Thames" as a "fantasy" for practical and financial reasons,[59] Street's men sliding frozen logs surreptitiously down London's streets to his riverside warehouse adds an icy genesis to the Globe's storied history. Early modern Londoners watching *Hamlet* at the beginning of the seventeenth century would not have experienced the chill of forty below, but they did note unseasonably cold temperatures common to the LIA (chapter 3). In contrast to the reconstituted Shakespeare's Globe, plays were performed during the winter, at least until the acquisition of the Blackfriars Theatre in 1609 allowed the King's Men to close the Globe until summer. (Thus, *The Winter's Tale* would have been better shielded from its eponymous season.) Even without accurate measurements, contemporary reports suggest that the weather surrounding *Hamlet*'s opening was "bitterly cold." According to the chronicler John Stow, the winter of 1597–1598 was particularly bad. The Thames froze for the first ten days of January. The following winter, 1598–1599, the season in which the Chamberlain's Men made their dramatic move, was even worse: "In the moneth of December great frosts, the Thamis nigh ouer frozen at London bridge, but thawed about one weeke before Christmas, began again to freeze on S. Iohns day the 27. and a great snow on the 28. so that the Thamis was againe nigh frozen as before, but on Newyæres day it thawed."[60]

If we set *Hamlet*'s start date somewhere between 1600 and 1601, both years' winters proved similarly dismal, if not unceasing: the river froze again in late January of 1600; on March 23, it "was extreame colde" and snow for a week;[61] "it snowed on the 4. of Aprill, which whole moneth following, with also the moneth of May was colde and dry, frosts euery morning";[62] "very colde frosts [appeared] euery morning" in June of 1601;[63] and the year wrapped up with "lightning and thunder ofentimes before Christmas, and in Christmas holydayes, and an earthquake at London on Christmas œue at noone."[64] Winters at Elsinore were not much better. The traveler Jón Ólafsson, who had escaped "The Torture" (*Píningsvetr*) of an Icelandic winter in 1601–1602, wrote that, in 1619, "so much driving snow fell in the streets . . . that it reached to one's middle, and it lay for a week and a half," hampering peace talks between the kings of Sweden and Denmark.[65] Shortly thereafter, King Christian IV was ferrying west to Elsinore, when "a great-ice-floe came drifting out of the Baltic into [his] course,"[66] pushing him about 5 km northwest to Hellebæk. The storm that sent it suddenly shifted and was now "a violent north-easter with bitter frost."[67] By the time he finally arrived at the castle Kronborg, "he was stiff and much chilled," and, soaked and somewhat chagrined, "would not have a trumpet-peal nor a salute from the guns."[68] Cay Dollerup supplies the conventional wisdom at the time: "The Nordic countries were proverbially cold."[69] Travelers like Fynes Moryson (1566–1630) corroborated this fact. Passing through

Denmark to Danzig in the summer of 1593, he remarked, "though it were the moneth of August, yet the wind blowing strong from the North, and from the Sea, I was very cold, as if it had beene then winter."[70] A land of few, or switched, or prolonged seasons was also that of Londoners. If "Denmarke[,] lying neere the Artick circle, must needs be subject to great cold,"[71] as Moryson casually puts it, England lies closer—an observation that would not be lost on the Globe's patrons.

The play's first audiences in Southwark, while not beset by "driving snow" on Copenhagen Sound, would have surely expected to hear of it, and given the "moneth" of the year, feel its "fell" force in martial terms. Hamlet's father, we are immediately told, "in an angry parle, . . . smote the sledded Polacks on the ice" (1.1.61–62), his maneuver taking a page directly out of Olaus Magnus's *Description of the Northern Peoples*, the eleventh book of which dedicates forty-seven chapters to "wars on the ice."[72] (A snow globe, in this instance, would be a fortress: a defensive "glacis," or gradient, comes from the Latin *glacies*, "ice.") Unsurprisingly, the impetus behind Q2's scripted insertion "it is very cold" is hard to pin down.[73] (Francisco's "bitter"-ness first appears in Q2 as well, but "the air bites" in both.) Ethel Seaton has called the "impress" of "northern myth and story" upon seventeenth-century English literature "not deep . . . diffuse . . . slight." Despite its prolificness, she asserts, it remained a commonplace template for "writers lacking in inspiration."[74] It is curious that, in drama, "there is little indebtedness"[75] to this unlimited smorgasbord of materials, she admits, even when accounting for the possibility of lost evidence. In conclusion, "the very remoteness of the northern countries led to their being used as a literary dumping-ground for tales that merely needed an unusual setting."[76] Yet the exception, of course, was *Hamlet* (and presumably the fabled *Ur-Hamlet*). Shakespeare's debt to his sources is well-documented: Saxo's tale of Amleth, later retold in François de Belleforest's (1530–1583) *Histoires Tragiques* (first French edition 1570). What is intriguing is that these primary texts do not linger on the cold; in fact, they do quite the opposite. Erudite early modern audiences familiar with them would have waited for him to bring the fire. Amleth plies his uncle Fengi's men with alcohol, snares them with a tapestry, and then sets the entire palace aflame: "Every one of its inhabitants [were] cremated, whether they were enjoying deep sleep or vainly struggling to rise."[77] (After which he strikes his stepfather down hotly, without hesitation.)

*Hamlet* is a song of ice, however, not fire. Shakespeare elementally doubled down as he selected and expanded upon his sources. Tapping into northern tropes of incredible cold, he also added a dose of metatheatricality by putting the whole show out in the open. The most well-versed attendees might have shuddered for the warmth he edited out. The chilled lines of the first act fit snugly into this imaginative tradition. Dollerup lists a number of "sources and informants" behind them; yet, while travelers, sailors, other actors, diplomats, Queen Anne, and King James all "were likely to have known of the feature in question," Londoners "may . . . have known," or were "unlikely" to have "cared about it."[78] Small wonder that critics like Gunnar Sjögren have seemed dismissive: "Hamlet's remark . . . as he comes out on the battlements in the middle of the night is surely just a comment on the weather and nothing more."[79] The "Danish background in *Hamlet*" is just that: background, a white stripe of "local color."[80] Sjögren's brush-off points to the larger problem of relegating the physical world to blank backdrops for chilling human drama. To not write it off as "local color," but to take it seriously, to reveal the "more" that is there, is to say otherwise. Shakespeare's lasting contribution to the centuries-long Amleth-Hamlet narrative is to foreground the action of airs upon waters, bodies, and places: watch as they buffet Danish castles, filter through English theaters and populaces. From the time of *Hamlet*'s inception, in sum, frigid meteorological conditions had impacted the construction of the Globe, incited the creation of a play, and influenced the dramaturgical circumstances of performance, detailing a complex northern imagination of borrowing and lending materially linked to early modernity's glacial admixtures.

Within the play text and at either Globe, another "active and alive 'star'" was the cold. Provisions had to be made at the Ice Globe for obvious reasons; "at -38°C it is impossible to stand outside for four hours," Degerlund acknowledged.[81] At negative 35°C the night before opening, dauntless audiences combated the coldness with reindeer skins, infrared heating, and warm drinks from the bar during a number of life-saving intermissions. To protect the bodies of those performing and in attendance from frostbite (or worse), the director, Alex Scherpf, compressed the play into two parts comprising ninety minutes total (Fortinbras, for instance, plus Rosencrantz and Guildenstern were cut), supplementing the production with "elemental drama" and "local colour" (music, drums, clothing) to please both the Sámi and European theatergoers.[82]

FIGURE 14. "The air bites shrewdly; it is very cold." *Isbiten* at the BST's 2003 performance, Jukkasjärvi, Sweden. Photograph by Nick Hanna, via Alamy Stock Photo.

(Hotel guests are close to thirty-five percent British.) Ophelia's corpse is laid on a candlelit sledge, the visiting players arrive at the court on reindeer, King Hamlet builds a snowman before he is poisoned, and the prince smears Gertrude's face with snow while rebuffing her. The production, the first to be performed entirely in Sámi—a Finno-Ugric language spoken by a population of over one hundred thousand people spread throughout northern Russia, Norway, Finland, and Sweden—was also shortened to make the translation more intelligible to native speakers. No subtitles or supertitles were projected for the rest; instead, guests could follow along in a program that presented English, Swedish, and Japanese versions of Shakespeare's lines side by side. "Our company is not a typical English company, beautiful speaking," Scherpf admitted, "they cannot be running around in the snow and talking."[83]

While Scherpf's confession hints at feelings of verbal inadequacy (that guttural Sámi is less aesthetic than mellifluous English), the decision stemmed mainly from his fears for the actors' wellbeing, emphasized by the dynamic and death-defying interpenetrability between bodies and cold happening onstage. This kind of cryocorporeality was exactly what Degerlund wished for and had intended audiences to witness. "What [he] imagined was actors playing *Hamlet* with clouds of frost coming from their mouths."[84] As one reviewer put it, "[Sámi] syllables tend to be expelled from the back of the mouth, so the Danish court spoke like dragons, their lines accompanied by incandescent plumes of carbon-dioxide crystals."[85] (The once-in-a-lifetime opportunity to glimpse *Hamlet* under the aurora borealis was a frequent selling point for Bergqvist and Degerlund's hotel-theater venture, but the light show might have been literally in your face.) As the elements pressed on the bodies who subsequently bore out the drama, they did not always do so to scripted effect: a defrosted cornice of the roof nearly pinned Claudius, and the Gravedigger's coat caught fire while rehearsing King Hamlet's cremation upon a block of ice that opens the show. Overall, by being held "frozen in their seats," audiences are able to behold that, when "the air bites shrewdly," the voice responds *because* "it is very cold." The Ice Globe's lucent innovation is its metatheatrical engagement with the multisensorial cold, drawing onlookers (despite their robes and furred gowns) into a larger climate conversation and continuum among body, environment, and art: a "tale" that "would freeze" (Absolut Vodka-infused) blood young and old, that would linger on the anagrammatic *melt* found in the prince's scrambled name and his "sallied," "sullied," "solid," or slushy "flesh" (1.2.129), and that would deepen humanity's enmeshment with a vanishing cold, a crystalline omen "demonstrated" almost two decades ago in order to be reinterpreted in perpetuity.

The other near-vanishing act on display, regrettably, was the Indigenous culture that the Ice Globe so proudly celebrated. Dangers to Sámi livelihood also took center stage. The BST is a small group based in Kautokeino, Norway. (All but one actor in the 2003 production was Sámi.) One reason for inviting the company, Degerlund hoped, was to cultivate cultural awareness: "As some 80% of the hotel guests come from outside Scandinavia, we thought it would be interesting for them to listen to *Hamlet* in such an exotic language."[86] While "exotic" to his hears, and thus jarring with Scherpf's evaluation (who is German), merely judging the sound of their language misses a serious point involving the historical persecution of the Sámi, a people who are invested in the protection of their forty-thousand-square-km homeland imperiled by industrial development, Sápmi (or the pejorative "Lapland" in English), and who are fighting against the obliteration of their traditional knowledge systems, especially in Sweden.[87]

The BST, in fact, originated from an environmental injustice known as "the Alta controversy." The Alta River was scheduled to be dammed in 1979. Not only would the project disrupt reindeer migration routes (an animal on which the Sámi almost entirely depend), it would also drown the village of Masi. Organized protests by the Sámi Action Group, amongst others, were able to temporarily halt the dam's progress and compel the Norwegian government to establish the Sámi Rights Commission in 1980. (The protesters, unfortunately, were removed in 1981; the dam began operations six years later.) A troupe of activists, who would eventually become the BST, performed a play in 1981 that recounted the injustices they had suffered: *Min Duoddarat* (Our tundra). Their ongoing mission, according to artistic director Haukur J. Gunnarsson, is "to give new expressions to traditional Sámi culture, reflect on the realities of today's Sámi society, make the existence of the Sámi known to the outside world, and build bridges of understanding between cultures."[88] I now turn to constructions of Sámi identity surrounding *Hamlet*'s creation, which requires confronting a long history of racial discrimination, internal colonization, and the multigenerational trauma that ensued and is unbroken. What was made "known" about them helps us understand how a 2003 performance counter-narrated the story of their mandated disappearance, and how it assists in the making "known" (the ushering in) of different stories of Sámi livelihood that are not relegated to strife alone. To brush off the Bard a bit, I will intersperse this part with words from the renowned Sámi poet, Nils-Aslak Valkeapää (1943–2001).

## "Exotic" Lapland

"They came from the end of the world . . . / knew everything / possessed everything / . . . like a white man."[89] True to its namesake, the areas of northeast Europe, like that of Tartary (central Asia), were associated with Tartarus, the realm of perpetual night, or in Marco Polo's words, "the Region of Darkness."[90] There is a clear through line from these earliest sources right up to the preface of Johannes Scheffer's 1673 *Lapponia,* which was translated in 1674 as *History of Lapland* and is considered to be the first comprehensive study of the region. Under the auspices of Queen Christina of Sweden (1626–1689), he was tasked with compiling a volume from the submissions sent to him by clerical authorities. (He himself did not visit there.) "Amidst the barbarity and darkness which reign in Lapland, there appear strictures of light, which will entertain the eie of the most knowing observer."[91]

From this bright view, however, its cultures were often lumped together. As Robert Ralston Cawley points out in his study of Elizabethan voyagers' impacts on the dramatic imagination, "no clear distinction was made among the northern races; Lapps and Swedes, Finns and Norwegians, Goths and Vandals, were all mixed helter-skelter."[92] The Sámi could be branded with the catch-all moniker of "Scythian," with occasional regard for mountain, forest, or coastal heritages, and their ancestral territory moveably tilted "Finmark," "Lappia," or "Lapponia" in lieu of the preferred Sápmi. (The term "Lapp" is considered derogatory by the Sámi; therefore, I will only use it here for purposes of critique and/or when it appears in the original sources.) But this ethnographic disorganization did not preclude attempts at sorting; Giles Fletcher the Elder (1549[?]–1611), author of *The Russe Common Wealth* (1591), is kinder to the "Lapps" than the cannibalistic "Samoyt" (the Indigenous peoples of Siberia).[93] Their deductions, if messy, were uniform in their effect: "The general opinion of them," Cawley bluntly states, "was low."[94] Sunny southern states seized on the fluidity of demographic description ("race" in this case signifying lineage or a group of people), along with the unflattering portrayals of northern peoples, to burnish their enlightened image to the detriment of benighted others. This binary between a barbarous north and a civilized south had to be reinforced over time as the dim Circle and its dark territories gradually began to be filled. Rhetoric around the "exotic" helped perpetuate ideas of an exogenous, alien Arctic, a far-northern backwater belonging to the Sámi and their (slightly) distinguishable neighbors.

While the geographical borders of "Lapland" were being disputed, the appellation "Lapp" remained rife with disparaging overtones. In order to grasp the full extent of the Sámi's historical marginalization, we must contend with the shameful early modern nomenclature used to describe them to others. There are several concepts that readers and theater-goers would have associated with the word "Lapp"[95]: savage skiers[96]; witches in wasteland[97]; uncivilized barbarians[98]; and repellant beasts.[99] By pointing to the print of Christian goodness the diminutive "Sámi" would not take, and by deploring their propensity for backsliding into paganism's ineradicable "remains,"[100] European authors escalated anti-Indigenous sentiment. Thus, the French playwright Jean

François Regnard (1655–1709) could speak of the Sámi as apes without reproach in his travelogue *Voyage en Laponie* (taken 1681, published 1731). The primitive and the primate are inseparable: "generally speaking, it is certain, that all the Laplanders, male and female, are horribly ugly; and very much resemble monkeys."[101] Detailing their facial features and body proportions in a bigoted anthropological blazon, he finishes with "such . . . is the description of this little animal, called a Laplander; and, it may be said, that after the monkey, he approaches the nearest to man. . . . I know not any figure more truly laughable."[102]

It was Scheffer, though, who proved the most damaging by ensuring that these stereotypes were cemented in their respective, reputable intellectual circles throughout Europe. His volume fast became an authoritative manual on "Lapps" and "Lapland," one read by the likes of Regnard and countless others. A self-avowed humanist, his evidence looks scholarly enough: the preface assures that its contents reflect "the faith of authentic records, the testimony of Historians," although he also claims (spuriously) to have heard reports firsthand from "the Discourses of Laplanders themselves, with whom he had ready opportunities of converse."[103] Encompassing his era's entire range of contentious viewpoints, his *Lapponia* represented the apogee of Sámi ethnography. As promised, he leaves few topics untouched: from marriage ceremonies to metals, turns of phrase to tributes paid to powerful kingdoms, shamanic drumming patterns to garment-making. Like his predecessors, he attends to the connection between climate and behavior at length. The air, he says, is "purified by the winds" which are also "violent."[104] There is little space between the extremes of winter and summer, and only the sturdiest may survive: "'Tis not to be endured but by those who have bin bred up in it."[105] At first he seems bent on correcting the low opinions of others: "We see [Laplanders] every day among us," and they are not "Pygmies" or "a deformed People."[106] But their minds are nonetheless susceptible. The reason they are "fearful and mean spirited" is "the cold to which they are condemn'd, and the meanness of their diet, which cannot supply good blood and spirits."[107] It looks as though "Lapland" is doomed to be a prison of malnourishment.

Such passivity in the face of "mean"-making weather might turn the Sámi into sympathetic figures, a people forced to combat an unflagging cold as best they can. Scheffer's estimation becomes more pernicious, however, when he describes how they are "generally dispos'd to idleness" unless "necessity" compels them.[108] Amidst many other "infirmities" that turn them from hard labor, they are, in short, "lovers of sloth."[109] The blame is equal parts genetic ("from their Ancestors the Finlanders") and climatic: "Their cold constitution by reason of the sharpness of the Air in this Country (that it self is sufficient to dispose men to laziness,) as the length of their Nights, and indulgence to much sleep."[110] One of Scheffer's most damning contributions for posterity was diagnosing this pre-"dispos'd" indolence as hereditary (to be passed down) *and* geographic (what the cold brought on). An ambiguous, lazy essence that was both interiorly and exteriorly bred allowed some, but not all, people to be susceptible to the cold's sluggish effects.

Here it helps that Scheffer, hailing from Strasbourg and only in Uppsala at the queen's request, is just southern enough to escape comparison with his objects of study, tirelessly collating his materials in a moderately warmer room. The question for him is not how anyone *can* live in an extreme north, where even diseases are rare, he says, "for the Northern cold easily dissipates the poisonous vapors,"[111] but what it means for a people *to be able to* survive amidst such extremity, or more pointedly, how this endurance poses a threat to hierarchies of dominance. It has been suggested that a major factor for the *History*'s completion was to disprove, once and for all, the rumors that Swedish forces used "Lappish" magic in their recent victories over German armies in The Thirty Years' War (1618–1648). Not only does "sloth" render this intervention impossible (and the charge nets him political points with his benefactors to boot), but it also maintains the delicate balance of power within greater Scandinavia. "Infirm," held back by "laziness" at the end of the world, the Sámi were a mirror for what other northern cultures were not, kept at bay as if exhibits behind glass. Because of, not despite, Scheffer's protestations as a learned, impartial observer, "Lapponia" was seen as a stunted development stuck in infancy, less a cradle of civilization than its collapse.

An insidious consequence of cold's biological and psychological determinism was the denigration of Blackness. Talk of animality enfolded with ideas of inalterable difference and intrinsic superiority based predominantly on skin color, configuring race along physiognomic lines in addition to those of lineage and species. The racial and racist elements of northern anti-Blackness anticipated the pseudoscientific taxonomies of the Enlightenment. Scheffer raises the issue of complexion when he attributes the Sámi's pigmentation to wood smoke: he has seen "clear skin" up close, "to which we may add the length of their frosts, and the bitterness of the Air, against which they neither arm themselves sufficiently with clothes, not know[ing] how to do so: besides the smoak which continually fills their cottages empairs very much their natural complexion, which is the reason why most of the men also are so swarthy."[112] To him, the natural tone is "clear" and white, although he does not specify how the cold impacts skin color. (But he does shortly thereafter say the Sámi are "dark and swarthy"[113] without the aid of smoke.)

Other contemporaries seemed less concerned with explanation and went straight for the "swarthy" castigation. The French physician Pierre Martin de La Martinière (1634–1690) accompanied northbound traders sent by the King of Denmark in 1670. His *Voyage into the Northern Countries* appeared in 1674. The "Laplanders" are foremost witches, he writes; they are "low . . . but strong set . . . tawny . . . their eyes . . . little like Hogs eyes . . . heavy and stupid, without any civility . . . [the women] very lascivious."[114] To the simian zoological tropes he adds the porcine—they sleep "higgledy piggledy" together[115]—and he also equates their "tawny" skin with devilry: "I did and do still think they can be nothing but Devils."[116] His hatred for multicolored hues spreads everywhere: the "Borandines" in nearby Siberia "are as ill-shaped as their Neighbours; . . . they were all of them ugly, little, flat nos'd, and swarthy as Devils."[117] The "Samoides . . . are of a duskish and earthy Complexion."[118] So are the "Islanders . . . swarthy most of them as the Norwegians are."[119] "Barandian" eyes, unlike the "Laponian" variety, are closer to "that which we call the White, being of a Reddish Yealow."[120] But they look perhaps too much like his own: "Their Complexion [is] as swarthy as possible," and "in short they have . . . little more Humanity than Beasts."[121] On Martinière's despicable spectrum, the somatic Blackness of the Sámi reveals an immoral character and a penchant for the occult. ("Swarthy" is derived from German *schwarz,* "black.") Devilry can be read right on the face: no eye exam is necessary.

To Gunnarsson's well-intentioned wish to "build bridges of understanding," this brief and toxic tour I have taken us on of the Sámi's "exotic" mis/perceptions shows multiple authors clearly sabotaging any semblance of intersectionality. Where do we go from this late-seventeenth-century point? Historical attempts to discern the etymology of "Lapp" (not just deciding where "Lapland" was and who was in it) proved no better at erecting transcultural Nordic ties; in fact, seemingly good-natured attempts furthered their estrangement. As a philologist and lawyer, Scheffer launches into numerous hypotheses in his first chapter, "Of the Name of Lapland."[122] Quoting Jacob Ziegler, he notes, "they were named so by the Germans, from the dulness and stupidity of the people, which the word Lappi signifies amongst them."[123] On second thought, "neither are the people so very dull and stupid," for even "[Ziegler] confesses they are good at the needle, and make delicate embroidered clothes."[124] It is also unlikely that their skiing prowess is responsible: "[Hugo] Grotius thinks they are call'd Lapps from running or leaping, but Lœpa, which in the Swedish language signifies to run, is writ with a single P, and the name of this Country with a double one: and these People naturally are no great runners, tho by an art they have of sliding over the frozen snow, they are very swift in their motions."[125] While not conclusive, Scheffer settles on something approaching empathy: "I take Lappi to signify no other than banish't persons, which is the genuine signification of Lapp in the Lapland language; for the Laplanders were originally Finlanders . . . with whom to Lapp signifies to run away: whence the compellation seeming something scandalous, no person of quality to this day will endure to be call'd by it."[126] Lest Scheffer be rehabilitated as an emissary for cultural appreciation or as an advocate for dislocated peoples, we cannot forget how profoundly backhanded his compliments are when put in their proper context. Ziegler, to his partial credit, argued that "owlde" authorities believed them "wilde beastes," either "throwghe ignoraunce" or for "pleasure."[127] Scheffer's preliminary shows of good faith subsequently gave way to some of the most intransigent prejudices against the Sámi. His failings are instructive: if these reprehensible legacies are to be challenged, their labels must be relentlessly interrogated.

Revisiting the "Laplandscapes"[128] envisioned by the travelogues scrutinizes for whom (or to what end) their highly partial blends of "ignoraunce" and "pleasure" serve. What were construed as intercultural exchanges, for example, were actually multispecies kidnappings. The Sámi, like the Inuit, were taken southward in heinous acts done for the "pleasure" of curious onlookers back home. But instead of shattering preconceptions, their novelty shored up the untraversable barriers dividing northern peoples and places. Martinière's party, under orders by the Danish king, seized two Samoyed ("Zemblane") couples and a canoe. He paints a striking picture of one woman: plaited hair, piercings with stones, and blue streaks on her face and chin. "There was never a Barrel better Herring," he says, "one as rich and ill favoured as the other,"[129] presumably pointing to her bald partner's lack of ornament, but also alluding to their capture. "Both [were] little trubs like the Samojedes, Laplanders, Borandians, and Siberians."[130] "Trub," from "truffle," denotes their picking and, eventually, "a little squat woman . . . a slut, sloven."[131] (The king purportedly took them "into his Care"[132] at Copenhagen.)

The Sámi who traveled fared worse. Scheffer, repeating Magnus, tells of six reindeer and their keepers, "a married couple of Laplanders,"[133] who were sent by the Swedish prince Sten Sture the Younger (1493–1520) to Friedrich, Duke of Holstein. Unable to acclimatize, "removed from their native soil, . . . set under the direction of strangers, . . . [and] deprived of the normal, peaceful existence they desired,"[134] all perished soon thereafter in the unaccustomed warmth. The heat, not the sin of original "removal," was to blame. But the aftermath also had the surprising effect of saving others from a similar fate. Regnard, for instance, "should have endeavored to carry some live reindeer along with [him]," but, remembering that "three or four" died in Danzig the year before, "not being able to live such a climate, it being too hot for them," relents.[135] Ten reindeer were sent by Gustav, King of Sweden, into Prussia in 1533, "as an exhibit and for the propagation of the species."[136] "Allowed to run wild,"[137] however, they could not be properly tracked to see if the experiment worked. Efforts like this show at least a minor interest in bioregional lifeways that cut across northern borders, albeit at the expense of their test subjects and the "invariable law of Nature," according to Magnus, that is supposed to prohibit this trafficking. Cold creatures live best "where [they] were born."[138] "Care" or desiccation, reproduction or perishability—"nothing," ominously, "was discovered."[139]

While it seems counterproductive to return to outmoded works interested in cultural differentiation, doing so helps us undermine the historical biases it holds up as truths. Rather than pardoning the aforesaid writers for their outlandish portrayals, it is in the interests of human-rights and environmental-justice movements underway to hold such annals to account. The faint tracks of companion species, the hoof prints and footprints stamped by reindeer and their Sámi handlers, haunt the archives. "Colonialism is not only about the past, . . . but also about the present," Swedish archeologist Carl-Gösta Ojala importantly reminds us, and "current conflicts . . . mark out the field of tension in which the study of the early modern period in Sápmi takes place."[140] We can trace a route from centuries-long mistreatment to present-day abuses and their remediation. Current campaigns, aware of this troubled history, work tirelessly to ensure that the past is not repeated. Any journey into "Lapland" at this time, as I have argued, could have easily cited Regnard's review ("the farther one advances in this country, the misery is the greater"[141]) as its motto, calling on reams of academic and first-hand evidence for support. His line about the Circle is as inexcusable as it is dangerous, for it demonstrates both a paucity of knowledge and a policed ignorance. The Circular edge, in other words, presented an epistemological impasse in addition to a physical border whose lands beyond grew incrementally colder with higher latitudes. The mind may "advance" no further, even if the body tries and takes in "misery" for its efforts.

These authors could not augment the far-northern Arctic imagination because they limited themselves in their ethnographic thinking, desired not to probe past prevailing boundaries, and refused to see themselves in the outlines of not-quite-"white," "tawny," or "reddish-yealow" eyes. To push past binaries, inconceivably, would be to chase after phantasmal reindeer: the idea of Sámi culture and its ability to survive, for instance, or of furred migration (if not assimilation) between climatic zones. Left unresolved, this riddle was employed by settler-based colonialist systems whose fragile sense of white identity depended upon the exploitation of an Arctic alien "exotic," and their methods were sanctioned by what they perceived to be sheer savagery running amok in the old snows north-by-northeast, not just in the icy *incognita* recently encountered on the continent farther to the west. While "the early modern colonial process in northern Sweden was complex, dynamic and multidimensional," Ojala admits, "in [the] narrative of progress and modernization, there was little, or no, space for the Sámi people."[142]

These texts, then, offer up rueful precedents for attempts to unmake the Sámi.[143] The "geopolitical Laplander," as Elena Balzamo puts it, was an awkward fit. Despite Magnus's humanizing influence (certainly when contrasted with Scheffer), "within Sweden the interest in Sámi culture was stimulated both by the needs for internal colonisation (administration and control of these areas) and for propaganda purposes. Both pressures were strong."[144] When King Carl IX of Sweden (1550–1611) was pronounced "King of the Lapps" in 1607, he sought to supersede northern rivals like Denmark and Norway, a goal that required control over trade and markets and the extraction of mineral resources. (Silver was discovered in northern Sweden in 1634, followed by iron in 1642 and copper in the 1650s; metal works and mines opened soon thereafter). The Sámi presence in a newly rich "Swedish America"[145] posed a problem, of course; hence began state-sponsored education programs and church missionary projects aimed at wiping away their unorthodox customs while also enlisting them as an essential labor force to unearth untold spoils. The government-issued *Lappmarksplakat* ("Lapland privileges/freedoms") of 1673 and 1695 officially incentivized the settlement of their land, and the segregated clerical school, Skytte, opened its doors at Lycksele in 1632.

The struggles born in the mid- to late seventeenth century persisted. "But there seemed to be a difference, between existing and not existing," ponders Elsa, the protagonist of Ann-Helén Laestadius's 2021 novel *Stöld* (Stolen).[146] Making the Sámi's existence known (in 2003 and other times) must combat a host of pernicious attempts that strove to eradicate that same existence: either through the erasure of difference (via acculturation or conversion), an enfolding with Nordic nationalities, or a plan of systemic forgetting explicitly mandated by the state. It is for all these reasons that I disagree, ultimately, with Cawley's conclusion: "There is something almost perverse in the Elizabethan's refusal to learn that there was anything except stupidity and cold to be associated with the northern races."[147] The modifier "almost" is unnecessary. What is "perverse" in my view is not just a misstep of cognition or a gap in spatial proximity: it is a precise, deliberate plan put in place to exoticize-otherize non-European northern peoples like the Sámi. To see how the Ice Globe tackled this overtly colonial, transhistorical tendency—with its hegemonies concretized by Scheffer and his ignominious ilk—means looking at (and for) race in *Hamlet*.[148]

## Inky Coat

"Hey hey you great white master / you certainly have not asked permission / ravage forests dam rivers crush mountains."[149] Edward

Belcher (1799–1877) led the British Admiralty's last search party to find John Franklin from 1852 to 1854. On December 21, 1852, the winter solstice and shortest day of the year, the "pioneer tragedians" put on a cold play at sea, *Hamlet,* for the "Queens Arctic Theatre," the converted H.M.S. *Assistance* near the coast of Ilulliq (Melville Island).[150] Sherard Osborn, who captained the H.M.S. *Pioneer,* reviewed the cryo-company's production in *The Queen's Illuminated Magazine and North Cornwall Gazette,* "published in winter quarters, Arctic Regions" from October 28, 1852, to February 12, 1853. He is all adulation: "The truth of the words the air bites shrewdly, it is very cold were never perhaps more thoroughly felt by any auditory."[151] As a grand tragedy instantly recognized around the world, the play seems fitting for those chasing the specter of Franklin that haunts the Passage, the poor captain stuck in a cold purgatory on an undiscovered continent.

What undercuts the poignancy of this production, however, and that links the two productions of *Hamlet* across times, is its engagement with Blackness. Between Shakespeare's play and the next, a comedy named *The Scapegrace,* the "Audience will be entertained," advertises the playbill, by "a highly Pathetic Story, of Negro Love by Mr. J. Reid."[152] Reid, the voyage's navigator, appeared "in full Negro Costume, as being Peculiarly adapted to this Climate."[153] A white man performing as a Black lover is "peculiar" in that such a body does not belong at this "climate," shoring up racial lines with geographic (north and south, equator and pole) and meteorological (hot and cold) ones. But there is also praise in the "peculiar": that Reid, presumably with less clothing to mimic an African persona, could withstand the cold. The white European's versatility asserts nonnegotiable difference ("Negro" people: stay in your zone) while buttressing claims that the Arctic is the region of and for enterprising white men, even if they are lost.[154] Blacking up girds a white, male, intrepid community, one fashioned by counterbalancing it with the "Negro," who cannot take the frost and is all the more "infelicitous"[155] for it.

*Hamlet* has fed into repertoires of whiteness and its makings around the globe, from the steadier stages of early modern London to its better-known shipboard presentation off West African shores in 1607. Consequently, it becomes even more imperative to ascertain not just how whiteness is fashioned by the play in a one-off Victorian performance, but also how race functions in and around the text itself. This an artwork, after all, that is so extreme in its popularity that it almost reached the literal Pole, and the racial thinking it has promoted in its roughly four-hundred-year existence has, tacitly or not, both allowed and endorsed racism. It is not too hard to think that the audience could link Reid's makeshift minstrelsy with the Blackness couched in Hamlet's recounting of "the rugged Pyrrhus" to the traveling players, "he whose sable arms, / Black as his purpose, did the night resemble" (2.2.374–75). Ian Smith's groundbreaking 2022 *Black Shakespeare* unpacks "this dread and black complexion" (2.2.377), arguing that "every soliloquy represents a weak act of performative whiteness in need of blackness-as-action."[156] Put another way, "for Hamlet, agency in the revenge mode devolves into a horrendous stereotype of the Violent Black Man as a form of compensatory will to action."[157] The normalization of this aggression equated with blackness, like calling Claudius a "[blacka]moor" (3.4.67), is appalling for its cultural forgetting, he asserts, with Hamlet's "putting on and taking off the 'inky cloak' of blackface performance" on the English stage serving as "a stark reminder of the superficiality, privilege, and dangers of racial tourism."[158] The preeminent Dane's self-serving allocation of Blackness often goes unseen by critics and audiences today, or at least unquestioned. *Hamlet* is "naïvely loved,"[159] Smith suggests, precisely because of the procedural erasure of race from its critical discussions. Yet Yorick's skull, the epitomic *memento mori,* "also means 'remember the Moor.'"[160] If the "big lie" behind the play, that "white lives have always mattered more than the lives of others," is left unchallenged, it will live on.

Despite its quotable platitudes made to meet any political moment, *Hamlet,* to be clear, is not a solution to systemic racism.[161] As Smith's urging for "racial literacy" in Shakespeare studies indicates, it is unchecked white privilege instead that affords in/action.[162] "In what sense, exactly, do critics share in the racial consciousness and debate that Hamlet exemplifies? Within the project of Shakespeare studies and the canonization of *Hamlet,* this is the pivotal question posed to contemporary scholars and critics."[163] Brown is instructive on this point: "By cloaking rotting, and rotten, white Danish masculinity in literal and figurative blackness, . . . Shakespeare calls attention to the white masculine crisis that is the crux of what 'is rotten in the state of Denmark.'"[164] The remarks by Malcolm X (1925–1965) at an Oxford debate in 1964 on the futility of "moderation" proposed by Hamlet's famous speech "to be or not to be" still resonates: "In my opinion, the young generation of whites, blacks, browns, whatever else there is, you're living at a time of extremism, a time of revolution, a time when there's got to be a change."[165] Have times "changed" for instance, when the press hails Black British actor Adrian Lester's "dreadlocked" look for Peter Brook (2000)?[166] Seen as "indubitably 'Nordic'" by fascists who bent the play's action to their will,[167] *Hamlet*'s unsettling ability to tap into white-supremacist thought lives on the page even before it is given horrendous amplification in performance; it suits the racist stuff of the occultist and Nazi-breeding Thule Society, but also the far-right version of "borealism" in political vogue today, itself owing to the ideology of "Nordicism" that bolstered views of Aryan superiority and gained traction in the late nineteenth and early twentieth centuries.[168] The answer to Peter Erickson's decades-long question of "can we talk about race in *Hamlet*?"[169] is abundantly clear: *Yes.* And furthermore, we may jump beyond the "can" over to the *how* and *why,* into an icy arena that upsets the facile conflation of north and white.[170]

## Remembering the Sámi

"Those / who do not exist / cannot demand / anything."[171] By extending premodern critical race studies' discussions over racial "assemblaging"[172] to the treatment of the Sámi, we are in a better position to grasp the full significance of the Ice Globe's staging. The long arc of *Hamlet*'s production and reception—at points both early (1600–1601) and late (1852) in English empire—was and is complicit in the marginalization of nonwhite others to the benefit of white solidarity. Pushing against this troubling history of fashioning whiteness, the BST's performance is an example of how conversations about race in contemporary cryopolitics can be reshaped by attending to the northscapes of early modern drama. I am not suggesting that the "Lapp" (like the "Moor") is expressly mentioned in the play. But crude depictions of "sledded" northerners and "nipping" air were, and they carried with them the fraught connotations of cold stuff. Just as elaborate images of "Arctic" peoples from Magnus's *Description* and other sources hovered around Shakespeare's stage, so did the pseudo-authorities of Scheffer (et al.) linger in the nightly airs of 2003. Centuries of maltreatment were embodied by the Sámi actors' very presence on stage, translating *Hamlet* into a vital act of communal perseverance.

"Weathering" the "open-air" Ice Globe proffered a commingling of international community: not an Arctic utopia, exactly, but a space of unnerving education in which southern spectators could learn of a population who has suffered dislocation campaigns and assimilation projects tantamount to cultural genocide. In this ice globe of enforced fractures and their discernible scars, the right to Indigenous self-determination is seen as something fought for, not as something formally recognized or ceremoniously gifted by the overseer state. Here, the Sámi move center stage, inverting the map: Europe becomes an adverse edge encroaching upon Sápmi. While difficult to conceive, a paragon of whiteness written by the world's preeminent white male author four hundred years ago actually incites the construction of cold coalitions amidst extreme conditions of climate, justice and race.[173] To witness a hallmark of white Western culture wiped (incompletely) of its "sable" color, and performed by nonwhite actors on a white stage, challenges the centrality of whiteness and the power such ubiquity conveys in the Arctic and elsewhere. In Sámi hands, *Hamlet* refutes the lie of the "Great White North."[174] And by refusing to normalize the "white makings of whiteness,"[175] its "trappings . . . of woe" (1.2.86) may be contested, if not undone.

Even without a direct statement of artistic "intent" from the Sámi players involved, the production was nevertheless entangled in the politics of northern peoples on account of its content, its physical situatedness, and the warming twenty-first-century conditions of performance.[176] If it seems outdated to modern eyes, the horrific legacy of Sámi subjugation lives on in different guises: specifically the rapacity of "new extractivism," a process by which minerals and reindeer are rendered into vendible commodities of metal and meat.[177] Royally decreed conversion, after all, was never wholly spiritual in nature. The Sámi were not just caught up in the whims of counter-Reformation sentiment, even if their so-called paganism played an important part in solidifying Lutheran dogma. The Ice Globe provided a platform for raising awareness about the capitalist logic of resourcism and the disenfranchisement that results, drawing attention to how much Swedish and other Scandinavian powers have gained economically at the Sámi's lived expense then and now, awareness of governments quietly making concessions to mining companies, for example, or justifying environmental abuses as the unfortunate cost of industrial prosperity and so-called "progress." The premodern-sponsored idea of a "pure" Arctic (a pristine space) "purified" by white settler Christianity jars with the metallurgical impurities plaguing the region at present.

There is another contradiction at work, too: a "Lapland" with veins rich in underground wealth yet whose original people are hopelessly impoverished, and at the same time, a land devoid of human civilization that can be redeemed (or made "useful") only with proper technoscientific advancement. Both visions of midcolonial profit have led to socioeconomic inequities that risk turning Sápmi into another "sacrifice zone."[178] In recognition of this transhistorical pattern of injustices, the French anthropologist Christian Meriot gloomily pronounced that the Sámi "were ground under the heel of their more populous and adventurous neighbors," colonialist outsiders whose religion "completed the dismantling of an ancient and traditional society."[179] But the Sámi are not irredeemably broken, despite this crippling assessment. "To acknowledge their aspirations . . . requires more than a simple change of words [from "Lapp" to "Sámi"]"[180] —true, although "words, words, words" (2.2.189) are also edifying to this effect.

To his credit, Degerlund's ancillary aim "was to give Sámi a larger audience, to allow a space for them to be seen and their language heard."[181] Threats to their language are real. While the instruction of Northern Sámi and Lule Sámi has been encouraged in local communities, for example, these dialects are little known by foreigners and Swedes alike. Temperatures in the Arctic are rising at rates double the global average, too, linking the Sámi people's plight to the Inuit and others of the thawing north. Jukkasjärvi, it must be said, sits in Sápmi; its name means "meeting place by the water." Valkeapää makes the analogy between the cruelty of colonialism and the harshness of the climate, only to upset expectations for which is worst: "we knew winter . . . / but this / we did not understand this / not even in our nightmares."[182] Lest the Ice Globe become just another "prison" of capitalism, it taps into an expressive range of creativity, an artistic tradition that spans from the celebration and joy of Indigenous presence to the disapproval of those forces that would see it removed. Addressing the through line of Sámi debasement from yesterday to today, artists like Anders Sunna (2016) literally put (or paint) the issue of disappearance in its proper context: "We are still here!"[183]

It is in accord with the BST's core values to ensure that histories of violence are not willfully ignored and, even more so, that the cultures of its victims are not exoticized through high Anglocentric drama. Indeed, their participation is meant to do the opposite, to enfold *Hamlet* in a centuries-long struggle for a people to be remembered, their rights restored, and their wrongs redressed. "Remember me" (1.5.91), commands the ghost to his bewildered son, the individual ("me") placed above all else. "Remember the Sámi," to repurpose Smith's phrase, is an injunction contrary to the self-serving dichotomies built on race and class that we have seen time and again. It is a motto behind a more polyvocal story of selfhood circa 2003: bodies re-membered and ringed by ice, who told of a heterogenous group of people whose homes cannot be girdled by the given borders of "Lapland," "Fennoscandia," or "Sweden." For these participants in the cool flesh, persons subject to colonization without a *post-* and yet more than its passive victims, "the rest," or what comes next, "is [not] silence" (5.2.336).

The question of audience response remains unanswered: I do not know what spectators coldly contemplated as they retreated to the Ice Bar for a nightcap shortly before sliding down one of the many tunnels chiseled into the hotel's fifty thousand square feet, strolling past galleries commissioned by Berg, finding their splendid art-suite sculpted by architect Åke Larsson (such as "Under the Arctic Skin," "Renaissance," "Ruossut"), and reaching the comfort of their slightly warmer bed. (Although Berg did recall an Englishman next to him exclaiming, "It's negative forty. I'm freezing my balls off. I have no idea what's happening on the stage. But I bloody love it.") Despite the overall impenetrability of the performance, the theater's pricking cold still provided a pleasurable experience. What is more instructive than devising a metric of dis/approval, or pinpointing what people took away once inside its white walls, I believe, is investigating how these now twenty-year-old performances can continue to educate us about ecological life and death and their difficulties up north. To this date, Sweden has not ratified International Labor Organization 169 (1989), a legally binding document upholding the human rights of Indigenous and Tribal peoples. (Although they did vote in favor of the United Nations Declaration on the Rights of Indigenous Peoples in 2007).

The Ice Hotel's marketing campaign appropriates the "exotic" Sámi language in places: "[Here], too, meetings take center stage, . . . between Jukkasjärvi residents and visitors, between different cultures, between people and nature, and between ice and creativity."[184] It is excitingly intersectional, and alluringly so. Underscoring Sweden's deep-seated moral obligation to the environment (as Bergqvist put it, "all people are working [on] climate change"), the hotel unveiled a sustainability plan in 2008 to ultimately become $CO_2$ negative; they retrieve only locally-sourced ice; and they aspire to stay open year-round on solar power alone.[185] As a certified "Sustainable Arctic Destination," it shares in the region's ongoing mission, "where the tourism of Kiruna . . . contribute[s] to improve the social- and financial conditions, and the same time help[s] to preserve the environment, the nature and the cultural treasures."[186] Mention of the Sámi, however, is sparsely made (they "maintai[n] a dialogue with Sami villages and local landowners"), mostly in the form of paid excursions at the Nutti Sámi Siida a mile down the road. When I asked Bergqvist about this line from the hotel's website (now removed), he told me that Sámi rights became mainstream only in 2010. The Kiruna tourism site's definition of the accolade is terse as well: "You can experience three different cultures," it boasts, "Swedish, the Torne valley culture and Sámi culture."[187]

All this of rhetoric affords a space for satisfied guests' highly romanticized accounts of their stay. South African novelist Justin Cartwright (1943–2018) described his experience in exhilarating prose: *Hamlet* was an unmitigated "triumph," the hotel twinkled in "the twilight of the gods."[188] He was entranced by "the intriguing sounds" of Sámi song at one point, roped a reindeer with his "taciturn" guide on a snowmobile the next, and stopped by a tent to try some hearty soup.[189] (He liked it.) Satiated, the illustration that follows is incongruous with the narrative that precedes it: "I went on a trip down Kiruna's iron ore mine, the biggest, the deepest, and possibly the most efficient in the world, . . . worth seeing but not worth going to see."[190] The mine, owned by Swedish company LKAB, is indeed the largest underground site of its kind, producing almost thirty million tons of ore annually. But Cartwright quickly snaps back into the world of the play. Exit, environmental degradation: "From the first moment . . . I was utterly entranced . . . and Horatio's 'Goodnight sweet prince' was spoken under the Northern Lights, which swirled above us in great clouds of pale green luminescence."[191]

Later, the protagonist of *Up against the Night* (2015), Frank McAllister, repeats his author's exuberance almost verbatim: "It was impossible to resist the feeling that we had arrived in a mystical and myth-laden landscape . . . We sat on reindeer skins, in temperatures of minus 30 degrees Celsius [as] the Northern Lights . . . performed their mysterious, swirling rites."[192] Cartwright's casual remark about a massive terraforming scheme taking place only twenty km away from his "glimmering ice palace"[193] is indicative of a larger trend of commercial encroachment that infringes on Sámi rights by determining Indigenous claims to be irrelevant. Since receiving a license in 2006 from the Swedish geological body, Bergsstaten, activists have battled the British mining company, Beowulf, over the unearthing of one of the area's largest iron ore deposits in Gallok, a town only thirty km away from the World Heritage Site of Laponia.[194]

Environmental degradations and their injustices are not exactly out of sight, despite the omnipresent "twilight." The Kiruna iron mine is but twenty km away from the hotel entrance. Regnard went down into the ice-choked copper mines of "Swapavara" (Svappavaara) fifty km south of Kiruna. We can still enter these "hell[s]"[195] just as he did, and Cartwright after him, touring the torn-up pockets that speckle Sámi land. I remember my taxi driver telling me late one night about Kiruna being rebuilt; because of overmining, the city's old foundation is literally crumbling underfoot. I could not imagine relocating something that took up an entire skyline. I also hear in these enterprises the neocolonial echoes of Scheffer and Martinière, learned men who told of a fertile continent closer to Europe. "But here it is indeed, where, rather [than] in America, we have a new World discovered,"[196] promised the former. The latter made a case for their nearer north as the (new) New World by citing the approximately fourth-century-BCE atomistic philosophical trio of Democritus, Epicurus, and Metrodorus, all of "who[m] maintain there are several Worlds" to be scoured: "I do not question but if we had occasion to go farther, we should discover Countries well peopled and inhabited, which we might call new Worlds."[197] Whether the object of protocapitalist or procapitalist desires, Sápmi's wealth resembles a neoliberal New World ripe for plunder.

I fret over rapacious history repeating itself. Yet I do not wish merely to criticize the hotel's green-washing efforts in hues of white; nor do I mean to deflate Cartwright's "life-enhancing experience"[198] by exposing the vacuousness of ecotouristic rapture (of which I was a part);[199] nor is this simply my cynical take on the inescapability of *literally* cool capitalist consumerism, be it carbon-neutral or -negative. Its footprint-reductive endeavors and reframing of industry that seeks a balance between socioeconomic and environmental concerns (by seeing them conjoined) deserve applause in addition to finer scrutiny. The same exercise applies to a 2003 production of *Hamlet* that congeals onstage and offstage cryopolitical issues. As Gunnarsson's optimistic chord of "understanding" suggests, there is plenty of intolerance in the way of multicultural bridge-building. An acuteness of ecological and ethnological critique is needed at a time in which the ugliness of racism has found a prominent stage with far-right Sweden Democrats like Björn Söder, the former deputy speaker of the Swedish parliament who claimed twice (2014 and 2018) that Jewish and Sámi people, and in general those "who belong to other nations," do not help to "create a society with a common identity."[200] Unfortunately, his party, founded in 1988 by a troop of pro-Nazis, could (if they so choose) draw fascistic inspiration from the play's built-in themes of anti-Blackness.

A cold-weather *Hamlet* can numb the extremities, to be sure, but as I have argued, it can sharpen the imagination and fire the senses; it can urge us to be better at thinking, creatively, about the future of nature–culture intersectionality; it can spark our curiosity about the promises of human–nonhuman diversity via the congregation of ice and art briefly held on the banks of a river high above the latitude of Shakespeare's Thames. For all his talk of "solid flesh" going the way of warming things, Hamlet's performance of fragility—the vulnerability of a white body and its white identity—is a disingenuous one:[201] it is too wrapped up with power, its privilege maintained by moody princes and the theatrical plaudits who praise them, its authority reconstituted by black-faced shows and the obfuscation of nonwhite others who threaten to take their place. Melting is too liquefactive, too messy along racialized lines. Brutal hardness is all when it comes to delineating hierarchies and treating incurable white resentment that stems from the perceived "slings and arrows" (3.1.57) of coercive inclusivity. But to really crack this grip, to make less defensible those white protestations of innocence in which ignorance equals exoneration, might just be "to tell [Hamlet's] story" (5.2.327) differently, here, on fragile blocks of white, and by "white Indigenous" players whose "whiteness . . . is ambiguous" by virtue of being on a spectrum of various "shades."[202] As Sámi-Norwegian sociologist Astri Dankertsen writes, "even though Sámi people are often considered white, *this whiteness is socially constructed in everyday life as a different kind of whiteness.*"[203] Exhibiting a color that is not-quite-white denies the Sámi complete access to the systemic rewards of whiteness; at the same time, it puts them in an advantageous position to chip away at whites' core claims to ascendancy over "Lapps" and land, the "assumption of being unmarked racially"[204] and the luxuries that come from it, and the supervision over who can speak of, and back to, the grave offenses committed there.

## Isbiten

"To become a part / of this tundra, these waters / breathe / the northern air."[205] Sitting down for *fika* ("coffee break") in the hotel's borealis-hued restaurant with Berg the day of my departure to ask him about designing the Ice Globe, he introduced me to the delicious Swedish expression *isbiten*: the spontaneous bite of ice that spurs artistic creativity. "Let it lead you," he advised. The Icehotel Creative Experience (ICE), true to this motto, "was born out of the desire for more people to take part in the narrative power of ice as well as its infinite possibilities as a material."[206] So, with a toothy phrase still under my skin, I will close this chapter by riffing on the "power" of icy coauthorship and its "narrative" leads for us to follow. As a text and in (early) modern performance, we are nipped by *Hamlet*'s "air" that crosses temporal as well as spatial and physiological boundaries. As the older Hamlet speaks to the younger, he is worried about passing on his polar plight: "I could a tale unfold whose lightest word / Would harrow up thy soul, freeze thy young blood" (1.5.15–16). It is a truly chilling proposition. Listening entails a cold fusion among father, son, and now the audience, a fusion of "kin" and "kind." Hamlet's response, I have already asserted, is unconventional: "Haste me to know't" (1.5.29). The paradox here is precisely that freezing *imparts* action to Hamlet (never mind how delayed his vengeance is), that the stuff of cold is kinetic anima.

What his welcomed intimacy with "it" would have imparted is hard to predict historically. But by drawing attention to the "bitter" and the "bites," the speaker's mouth and breath are spotlighted, displaying the players' and not just the characters' embodied meteorology. These two words demonstrate the material–metaphorical connection among air, author, and actor that enabled the performance to take place and for the "cold" to be penned, whether the weather in London that day was lovely or intemperate, indoors or outdoors. Cold collaborated with Shakespeare during the LIA to make a play about exposure *in* and *to* northern climes. This climatic capacity for storying is one we might gainfully experiment on, and with, at present. When Hamlet teases Osric in the final scene—"no, believe me, 'tis very cold: the wind is northerly. . . . Methinks it is very sultry and hot" (5.2.81, 83)—we are suspended within the play's climatic confusion, not released from it, and asked to reinterpret both the ontic and phenomenological qualities of temperature. "It is indifferent cold, my lord, indeed" (5.2.82). Our reply, our charge, then, is to "swear" with this cold thrice (1.5.152, 158, 163) and often. Through Hamlet's closing remarks on the cold, we recognize the drastic permutations of climate, one that involves an interest*ed* and interest*ing* (contra the dual meaning of "indifferent") substance that dramatic performance helps us think with. The coldness of indifference (to women, to the weather, to the Sámi) can turn into a passionate care for the cold. Hamlet's philosophy on ice, *Hamlet's* characters literally on top of it: to put a play on ice is not just to preserve its prestige for all time, but to pose abiding questions about how to persevere amidst changing climates with a diverse group of players, all of whom share an ice globe known as our planet.

The fact that two observations of cold that attenuate human–nonhuman difference are placed at various ends of the play (1.4. and 5.2) is not a coincidence. Yet the ideal median (neither too hot nor cold) is misleading, the equilibrium indefinable, illusive, as the ghost himself. Deep freezes still represent the hopes of those who deny climate change, as if one reading of extreme temperature cancels out another. Caring for the cold in and of itself will not necessarily make the world cooler, for the chiastic rise of heat and the fall of cold has already begun, and yet that does not mean that its warming places must meet tragic ends. It means addressing and accommodating change at earth's upper slope, embracing ice for all its shifts. What (not) to be/come remains up for question. Endangered locations bear Shakespeare's impress: from the Arial and Caliban peaks inside Alaska's Gates of the Arctic National Park and Preserve, to Jukkasjärvi post-2003. Shakespeare may have wanted his "climature" to warm rather than cool, but even his opinion cannot preclude the "infinite possibilities" that the matter of ice allows. By the *isbiten* body and its bitter breath, nipped to sundry degrees of dis/comfort and severity of affect, his work calls attention to our own transforming and energetic north, its winds now warmer due to the prosperous petrostate.[207] To "tell [Hamlet's] story" within a shrinking Arctic Circle is to be circumspect of man's warm-blooded and injurious assertions to centric authority. "The question" (3.1.55) turns to how much ice is, and will be, left; how cold becomes harder to find, not just to protect. It is to ask questions with an inquisitive play and wordy interlocutor about material liveliness bound up with death, spirals of thaw and thickness in and around the "loam[y]" (5.1.190) graveyards of a softening Anthropocene. "To be or not to be" (3.1.55) cold is a condition worth reexamining and a decolonial right worth fighting for; it is the cold studies question of *Hamlet*; it is what multiracial and multispecies justice depends on, what allies are made of, and what staying on the ice entails. A snow globe that contains the world but that is also a worlding: what a more-than-human "piece of work" it is, and how much "work" is left to be done. Cool!

# Winterlude

## *Slide*

In 1654, a Dutch whaling captain, Ouwe Kees, landed in the Svalbard archipelago. Taking a crew member named Bommel with him, he started to climb "one of the largest of the so-called Seven Icebergs or glaciers" of Spitsbergen.[1] About a quarter of the way up, Kees suddenly changed direction. Turning to his companion, he said, "I am going back, but I have thought of an easier way to go than walking. I shall just let myself slide." The experience proved terrifying: "Everything shimmered before his eyes and he became like a blind man." Kees dug his heels hurriedly into the snow. Bommel, meanwhile, did not notice anything was amiss; waving his handkerchief over his head and shouting out in a spirit of competitiveness, "I am passing you, captain," he eventually plummeted over the cliff and into the sea.

The narrator, known only by the initials of "P.P.v.S.," claims his fall was double the height of Amsterdam's West Tower (approximately 90 m). Kees carefully descended, unaware, like the spectators below on the boat, of where Bommel had "fallen or flown to." Unsuccessfully searching the surrounding water for his body, they pronounce him dead. But just before sailing away, they hear Bommel's voice: "Here I am, here I am," the survivor being only a "little the worse for his adventure." Martin Conway, who compiled the book *No Man's Land* (1906), in which this anecdote is translated, appears lukewarm in retelling it: "The real fact, I suppose, was that they indulged in a little glissade down a hard frozen snow slope, ending above the sea near one of the Seven Glaciers." "Glissade," from French *glisser,* means "to slip, slide." In calling it an "indulgence," the men's decision to slide becomes sportive, recreational, playful. It is a desire to give up one's self to another's trajectory—"I shall just let myself"—one in which human and ice take off together across uncertain traversals. While "slide" might designate a predetermined,

FIGURE 15. Jan Luyken, *Zeelieden Glijden van een Ijsberg* (1684), Rijksmuseum.

linear course, its inherent "slip" signifies ice's veering potential. Kees lets slip into a slide that leads to additional slips.

As if suggesting this sort of deviating course, the alphabetic letters in the illustration are out of sequential order. Being slipped up is a frightful as well as delightful event all at once; Kees arrests his flight (*B*) as Bommel elongates his, his gleeful glissade unending, his trip effectively suspended in a state of freefall (*E*). The "slide," aloft, bridges both possibilities of life and death: a dismembered human torso lies crumpled along the right margin, a reminder that some tracks do reach a terminus. A poem included in the original publication is admonitory: *laat grootsheid, en sulk wetspul staan . . . Het springen van een hooge kai, / Of brug, of leun, dat is niet frai.* ("Leave grandiose and sulky wet stuff . . . Leaping from a high bay, or bridge, or lean, that's not pretty."[2]) The nonhuman onlookers present (polar bears, a walrus, and a fox) indicate that this slippery capability is not the human's alone; in fact, the fox's gaze toward the slippers and the indeterminate tracks on the mountainside (marking an ascent or a descent) hint that the next attempt could be one in which multiple species take part. What will be (*F*)? Flights of fancy and fracture. Bommel found. Or (*H*)? Further harpooning? Where, onto and into what is the cryosphere sliding?[3] (*S*): an ode to inventiveness, for the slip ups, the mistakes, made along the way.

# Co(l)da

## *Speaking as the North*

Love ice. Not war.

—Alexis Pauline Gumbs, *Undrowned*

Upon realizing her unintended involvement in Desdemona's tragic death, Emilia's next lines burst forth: "'Twill out, 'twill out. I, peace? / No, I will speak as liberal as the north" (5.1.213–14).[1] Editors commonly gloss "the north" as "the north wind" and "liberally" as "freely, without constraint" (ca. 1500), including the additional (now outmoded) connotation of "insolently, licentiously." Iago fatally stabs her shortly thereafter. The broiling, patriarchal violence in Shakespeare's *Othello* demands immediate correction. Emilia, the windy wife, must be silenced by blows from her husband's hand, killed for her cold blood. Ideas of the "north," in this performative case, both gauge and maintain male authority over wintry women and their unruly remonstrations. Impelled by Emilia's example, I will conclude my cold study by speaking a bit more about this blustery line: not only for what it tells us about the relationship among gender, race, and "northern" environments centuries ago, but also for what it can tell us about similar relations today and how we might address—and "liberally," at that—imperiled communities on the upper horizon. Proprietorial slogans like "our owne Nation" (Thomas Dekker in 1608) and "our Northwest passage" (Sir Humphrey Gilbert in 1566 and 1576), as I hear them, can become rallying cries for doing justice with/in the Arctic.

Reflecting on the tense geopolitical climate in which we find ourselves, Michael Byers asks, "who owns the Arctic?"[2] His question, I have suggested, originates in the early modern age of Arctic exploration that peaked in the first decades of the seventeenth century. Claims to cold lands on behalf of the Dutch Republic (William Barents), Kingdom of Denmark (Jens Munk), and English Crown (Thomas James) were both tenuous and tenaciously protected. Disputes over their ownership inflamed European authorities. In an English context, for instance, the mathematician and accused magus John Dee traced jurisdiction back to the legendary figure of King Arthur, who supposedly conquered the north for Britain long before. The "our," in short, raises the controversial matter of dis/possession in addition to the contested policing of ecological access: that is, who is permitted *in* and *out*. In its more common interpretation, "cryopolitics" names the proto/nationalist strategies that regulate participation and undergird structural power, including the absorption of polar persons and places into a territorializing "nation." As many of my chapters have shown, sixteenth- and seventeenth-century monarchial sovereignty and white settler colonialism were predictably dismissive of Indigenous displacement and environmental degradation, two of the most basic components of modern-day climate justice movements. (Dee, it should be noted, was a financial investor in Arctic expeditions.) These troubling types of Arctic interconnection magnify the stakes of the cryopolitical "our" whenever it is mentioned, and they compel us, furthermore, to pry into the "ownership" that encroaching, uninvited governments egregiously believed they were entitled to.

*The Trumpet of Nordland,* written circa 1670–1700 by Norwegian poet and Lutheran priest Petter Dass (1647–1707) and published in 1739, reveals the complex cryocolonial plaitings of race, resource, and rule that many Arctic authors attempted to sort out. The myth of a utopia at the top of the world, for one, proved to be an undying incentive even at the tail end of the century: "For Hyperboreans plead happiness small; / Their treasure has ne'er been discovered at all—/ Saturnus has it in his keeping."[3] Saturn, the Roman equivalent of Cronus, was a gloomy god who symbolized wealth, agriculture, and the Golden Age. But his "treasure," like that in the tropical south, is safe only until it is "discovered" and extracted. The pleasurable zone will not yield its "keepings" without a struggle, however. Dass, like Descartes, describes a southbound cold that pushes back overzealous conquerors: "But now, when Saturnus his orders sends out, / The earth to be punished with frost and with gout, / We take the first blow of the giants."[4] Breezy "blows" inspire martial kinds.

What is more, the lineage of the "giants" intersects with conceptions of race predicated on skin color. Where this hue comes from, he can only guess. When describing the Sámi, he is perplexed: "Now, as to the cause, I have little to say; / It may be the cold, or it may be the way / Of living that makes them so tawny."[5] The Arctic historically furthered and frustrated climactic ideas of race, both resisting and reinforcing hierarchical, ethnonationalist schematics of difference. The "cause" proved crucial; its interrogators had much to say, and subsequently, harm to do. And through it all, unseasonable weather raged. When snow falls in Norwegian summers, Dass defers to the experts: "Who into the earthly foundations have looked? / Let Students of Physics declare what is booked / Concerning the heat and the coldness."[6] Once again, cold is a mystery that the best "students" cannot crack: it brought ideas of race ("tawny" color), physics ("earthly" nature), climate (regional "orders" and their conditions "sent out"), and geography (boreal "happiness") to their breaking points. It was where "booked" theories went to be tested. Borrowing a title to make a less heroic-masochistic point, the Arctic was a "crucible" for cultural encounter.[7] The north is where one went, and what one feverishly examined, to have suppositions reassessed, unlearned, and then "booked" again.

The winds of war: Dass's poem is a prime example of how topical anxieties and aspirations could be contemplated in and as art, proving that cryopoiesis can interrogate the "foundation" of what we know of "our"-selves and of others, and what is (ever) done by the resulting awareness. As Hillary Eklund and Wendy Beth Hyman advise in *Teaching Social Justice through Shakespeare,* "the richness of the past" functions as "a prod to action in the present."[8] It should be clear by this late point that I do not want to let the overheated world go. The reattunement to the Arctic and its cold I am proposing confronts the bigotry and despoliation insinuated by Dass and his peers (like Martinière and Scheffer) that has carried over into the current cryopolitical moment, one in which a president can brag "We need global warming,"[9] where Indigenous histories are too often frozen in the past, and where industrial nations carve passages, plant flags, and drill down in the name of liquefying capital. The wake and waste of colonialist incursions explode the fable of clean, pristine snowscapes Marla Cone dubs the "Arctic Paradox."[10] Deep down, *Arcticologies* contends that early modern characterizations of cold offer critical terms that help advance the aims of climate-change activism in today's Arctic. Throughout, I have tried to underscore how un/familiar descriptions of *norths* pullulating with life amplify ecopostcolonial and environmental-justice efforts that are working to dispel the false idea of a remote, empty region.[11] But I have also underlined where they reveal such life to be under attack and at risk of erasure.[12]

Embodied enmeshment with climate-crossing cold was not always conceived as affirmative; it could be used to divide from, and conquer, the north. Although we do not usually associate Christopher Marlowe with a far-northern imagination, two passing references to boreal regions exist. Orcanes in *Tamburlaine,* part II (1587–1588) boasts:

> Though from the shortest northern parallel,
> Vast Gruntland, compassed with the frozen sea,
> Inhabited with tall and sturdy men,
> Giants as big as hugy Polypheme,
> Millions of soldiers cut the arctic line,
> Bringing the strength of Europe to these arms,
> Our Turkey blades shall glide through all their throats,
> And make the champion mead a bloody fen.[13]

A few years later, in *The Tragical History of Doctor Faustus* (1588–1589), Valdes imagines the world's nations serving the magicians like "Lapland giants trotting by our sides."[14] When Marlowe's mind went to the pole, it envisaged a militarized frozen zone whose "lines" could be crossed, and whose huge war-like citizens, moreover, could be subdued by subarctic civilizations. His "arctic" interests speak to England's nascent imperialist efforts. John Davis had recently returned (1585–1587) from the western coast of Greenland, and Martin Frobisher's (1535[?]–1594) forays into the area were but a decade old. We might not be able to set aright the historical injuries done by his mighty lines, but we are in a position to offset the show of "strength" subtending them, and, in doing so, "champion" different causes instead. As Kathryn Yusoff notes about the Passages' simmering possibilities for collective engagement, "as we witness together the passages opening in the ice, it is our capacity to situate these movements in the world and to understand and respond to that witnessing with acts of responsibility that burn into the future."[15] This mighty Arctic line of coalition strength would show how the north is remade, not won, with a passionate fervor for changing the (political) climate.

The task is a hard one, I admit, since we know that anthropocentric logics were formulated in reaction to humans' cryocorporeal exposure and the feelings of fragility that attended it. Speaking "as" the north could be a physiological action in addition to an elaborate metaphor. Raphael Thorius testifies to how environment and embodiment coalesce when inhaled air (such as "the north") literally becomes one's breath. (Robert Wittie concurs: humans are miniature meteorological systems in constant dis/array.) Conventional readings of "climate" as encapsulated precincts attempted to relieve this vulnerability by predetermining cultural traits around the world. Its stratifications not only compartmentalized the earth but also fed into "geohumoralism": the palpable impacts that climates made on one's temperament, complexion, ethnicity, and other identifying features. As a result, highly generalized connections based on classical authorities were drawn up between a given geography and the type of embodiment it (purportedly) produced. Since the Greek physicians Hippocrates and Galen attributed irascibility to hot and dry airs, nations at the equator were expected to lodge fiery moods, their denizens' choler brought on by an abundance of yellow bile. This system was never truly uniform, however, and its tenets often incurred debate. Contra Hippocrates, Aristotelian adherents held that atmospheres imparted the opposite qualities: chilly airs, some believed, actually drew out sluggish humors (phlegm and black bile) rather than fostered them. Nevertheless, and not surprisingly, geohumoralism developed into a blunt instrument for justifying racist hierarchies that claimed, for instance, that the same burning sun that gave Africans their darker appearance also engendered their impetuous behavior. In the higher latitudes of England, the theory proved "fundamental to . . . conceptions of how their own, more northern, bodies and minds were shaped and influenced by external forces."[16] Over time, colder nations struggled to appropriate geohumoralism for their benefit: how else could hot-headed European seafarers prove so dauntless in their Arctic endeavors? Northern trips into low temperatures demanded constant reediting in order to maintain the semblance of embodied, emotional, and climatically derived equanimity.

Francis Bacon, for instance, leans into this compulsory revision of cold humors in his 1625 essay "Of Vicissitude of Things." "North and South are fixed," he says, for "it hath seldome or neuer been seene, that the farre Southern People have inuaded the Northern, but contrariwise. Whereby it is manifest, that the Northern Tract of the World, is in Nature the more Martiall Region. The Cold of the Northern Parts, . . . without Aid of Discipline, doth make the Bodies hardest, and the Courages warmest."[17] Reframed as a country *for* cold white men, kingdoms of the frigid zone will fall under their "martial" prowess. In this sense, *True Discourse . . . for the Finding of a Passage to Cathaya* (1578) by Arctic seafarer George Best (ca. 1555–1584) could not only "proue all partes of the world habitable," but also show that they were bendable to English power, the calculating and "inuincible mindes of oure Englishe nation."[18] His hypothesis of a warm, occupiable Arctic needs no confirmation beforehand. "Courage," in any case, is the essential ingredient for a successful invasion. Questioning the "habitable" was not the same as recognizing it as already inhabited, of course (chapter 4). But Bacon's plantation mentality simply builds over inferior ways of living. There is no need to worry about the Indigenous peoples of Greenland attacking southward, even if they are farther north than the descendants of the sacking Goths (and certainly the "hard" bodies of Bacon's England). Conveniently, they lack the "aid of discipline." The expansionist George Peckham's (d. 1608) *True Report* (1583) advertises the unrivaled fortitude of *civilized* northern nations. Sir Humphrey Gilbert's possession of Newfoundland—an island originally claimed by John Cabot (ca. 1451–98) for King Henry VII in 1497—is, he argues, "an action tending to the lawfull enlargement of her Maiesties dominions, commodious to the whole Realme in generall, [p]rofitable to the aduenturers in perticuler, beneficial to the Sauages."[19] Such explanations reveal a Global North in the making: stabbing northward, incorporating dominions into its "fixed" position, concealing the violent methods that would betray its swelling stature.

As European author-explorers pursued a passage north-by-northeast and west to Cathay in roughly a century and a half (from John Cabot to René-Robert Cavelier, Sieur de La Salle [1643–1687]), they sought to exalt their country above its continental counterparts. But they also worried about sustaining the body's supposed integrity abroad. Far-northern latitudes, as a result, accrued racial and racist overtones. Visits with, and violence done to, northern Indigenous groups contributed to evolving theories of "darkness" and "Blackness"; concomitantly, the whiteness of Arctic snow and ice assisted in early modern creations of race. Viewed this way, an innocuous comment by Philip Sidney (1554–1586) about his lady's beautifully translucent skin ("thinke now no more to heare of warme fine-odour'd snow") in the fifth song of *Astrophel and Stella* (1591) gains necessary complexity. Just as today's pseudoscientific definitions of "race" try (and fail) to fall back on biological essentialism or genetic codes, the period's cold helps reveal how race is constructed, retained, and weaponized; at the same time, it uncovers the contingency of these racial paradigms and magnifies the abhorrent harms they sanctioned. Northern derogations did not always adhere to physiological markers between white and nonwhite, it should be said, for indigeneity writ large could just as easily serve as a basis for discrimination. The Sámi, "the white Indians of Scandinavia,"[20] have chronically suffered from *vardagsrasism* (Swedish for "everyday racism"), and the merchant Gories Peerse's *Van Yslandt* (1592–1593) belittles "licey" Icelanders of European descent who gorge upon "large amounts of unmelted butter with hair."[21]

These examples, in my opinion, demonstrate the greater need to recognize a multihued early modern Arctic: in particular, how "whiteness" gains its existence, and its power, from those it excludes, how cursory remarks like "the Inhabitants [Inuit] are . . . of a ripe Olive colour, some of them also quite black" become codified.[22] In their introduction to a pivotal cluster of essays on the subject, Kim F. Hall and Peter Erickson compellingly argue for "rereading early modern race": "ignoring or disparaging race will not make it go away as a question for our—or Shakespeare's—time."[23] The indispensable work of Hall, Margo Hendricks, Ayanna Thompson, and many other critical race scholars insists that "race, as an ideology that organizes human difference and power, is always protean and sticky, attaching to a range of ideologies, narratives, and vocabularies in ways both familiar and strange."[24] Thus, confronting the cultivation of race and racism at higher latitudes requires interrogating historical differences rather than simply underlining moments of racial "fluidity"; indeed, the north helped invent and insult darker shades of "otherness," undergirding hegemonic "whiteness" and replaying hurtful dynamics occurring farther to the south and west.

Yet, if the tender traveler's body could be ontologically altered by entering (or being entered by) "sticky," cold environments, its whiteness was likewise at stake. Sequences of Inuit and Sámi encounters unsettled rigid dichotomies and checked the white explorer's eager claims of ethnocentrism. Best could explain the Inuit's darker skin on Baffin

Island only in etiological terms: "This blacknesse procéedeth of some naturall infection of the first inhabitants of that Countrey, and so all the whole progenie of them descended, are still poluted with the same blot of infection."[25] For him, the north puts wholesome whiteness at risk of infection, effectively transforming one's skin color ("blacknesse"), nationality ("countrey"), and even species in the process. (He elsewhere describes the Inuit as "Seales."[26]) The north prompted theories about the matter of whiteness as well. Within the physician Thomas Browne's wide-ranging thoughts on "the Blacknesse of Negroes" in *Pseudodoxia Epidemica* (1646), he notes the propensity for "man" and "animalls," subject to "the effects of cold in Regions far removed from the Sunne" to change color: "many creatures exposed to the ayre, deflect in extremity from their naturall colours, from browne, russet and blacke, receiving the complexion of Winter, and turning perfect white."[27] Whiteness is not merely an a priori, pre-"sunned" state of being, but is physically produced by "deflection." Despite attempts to preserve and protect the porous body and its vanishing white hues, the disease-bearing north refused to remain distant. Strong winds carried penetrating cold as well as Inuit visitors southeastward to European shores, while others were forced to make the transatlantic journey (chapter 2). The first captives, a woman and child from Labrador, were brought to the Netherlands in 1567. Kidnapped "progenie" of the north spoke out, only to be enlisted in southern spectacles of "the Indian."[28] Investigating the charged impingements that the Arctic historically created helps to challenge spatial-racial segregations built on logics of superiorly pure, un-"poluted" whiteness.

Seen through the prism of critical race studies, anti-Indigenous and anti-Black frameworks betray their sinister origins at cold moments of premodern contact. Worse still, their historical problems seem bound to repeat. Some diplomatic exchanges are relatively straightforward, as when John Milton writes in his *Brief History of Moscovia* (1682) of the Russian emperor's annual tradition: every December 12, "5000 Harquebusiers . . . shoot at a bank of Ice till they beat it down."[29] Regal impress is purely destructive, the icebank's demolition a paragon of anthropogenic affront. In more coordinated human–cold maneuvers, city defenders used ice for fortification,[30] and grateful townsfolk blessed glaciers. (They also exorcised them when they crawled too close to municipal limits and cursed them when they went too far. Early "environmental evacuees" knew the dangers of living under glacial shadows.[31]) These political illustrations might seem fantastical, yet they still pertain to the concerns of the eight democracies within the Arctic Council: Canada, the United States, Iceland, Denmark, Norway, Sweden, Finland, and Russia. By resisting the temptation to pull "nature" (illusorily) out of public policy, earlier voices counsel the need for a greater eco- and cryopolitical sense of representation amidst growing riskiness and the advance of "cartographic colonialism."[32]

Taking this opportunity seriously, as "cryoactivist" Jorge Daniel Taillant does, means addressing the hard realities of the "networked north" in which neoliberal brands of globalism (north to south) are impediments rather than catalysts to thriving.[33] The "Arctic Circle" itself, whose line has been arbitrarily set at latitude 66° 33' north, is a flexible boundary that has been likened to a undulating wave rather than a concentric line. Humbly or not, kings, queens, and parliaments knew that their actions had planetary effects that reached into, and beyond, set circles and assigned zones. Analyses about what the "Arctic" is and how it is determined should not mistake its ambiguity, therefore, for a sign to relax. As Arctic environmental historian Adrian Howkins puts it, "engaging with the historical complexity of the interactions between nature and culture is arguably the best approach to the problem of defining the Polar Regions."[34] What is left, in his words, are "geographies of hope and . . . despair."[35] These "complexities," I have shown, emerged from early modern authorities' cryo-, bio-, and geo-political machinations up north. But by mapping cold's transgressive force and its impinging climatic zones, this study has also offered methods to reengage, redress, and resist European nations' "scramble"[36] for Arctic resources and their neo/colonial harms.

There is an infamous anecdote that foregrounds the stakes of the transnational and temporal peace I am visualizing. Meetings between heads of state and the cold could be more complicated than a brute cannonade and yet no less forcefully destructive to the parties involved. "Calichough" and his kin were unfortunate prequels to the unnamed "four naked black youths" who died after dancing in the Norwegian snow for James I's wedding to Anne of Denmark in 1589.[37] His command, whether he intended it to be lethal or not, is enough for condemnation. But this enforced entertainment also constitutes an involuntary experiment in survival conducted exclusively on nonwhite bodies of color. It is not hard to imagine the onlookers in Oslo pondering what will happen to sharp "geohumoral" contrasts suddenly thrust together, and not just for aesthetic reasons. (The fascination lasted until J. Reid's virtuosic performance aboard the H.M.S. *Assistance*, at least.) Their expendable Black lives helped predict what happens to other bodies when exposed to climatic contrasts, a problem, I previously insinuated, that the northern English were trying to figure out about themselves as they sought a northern Atlantic passage through waters and lands argued (inconsistently) to be hospitable. The dance, then, functions at multiple levels: at once symbolic for a king like James who desired a dual hemispherical empire (another marriage, this time planetary), who was also testing *different* humans' physiological endurance based on the scholarly tradition of hot and cold racial dispositions. If so, the performance approximates an example of environmental racism, of literally conditioning (or not) Black bodies to what was assuredly a torturous experience.

Revisiting atrocious scenes like these is painful. Reading (in) the cold archive serves as a "prod," in my view, for pursuing polar relations (pacts, pledges) of political kinds and for arguing why to care. It is imperative that the slippery cause *of* cold leads to righteous causes *for* it. As this chilling vignette illustrates, and as captured kayakers and an embattled icecap evince, more action is required to snap out of circular "doings" of cruelty. I am haunted, too, by a conventional way for disciplining "untrustworthy" servants: "freezing water," Magnus pronounces, "poured drop by drop." But "only negroes shrink from this punishment because their heads are too bare of hair."[38] Since I do not wish to treat "climate justice"—like the Arctic—as monolithic, the equity I have in mind is this: when cold becomes an event of nonhuman–human bonding that acts to free its company from inhumane bondages. Theories of freezing did not merely indicate the mundane process of transforming from an individual liquid into a solid, but of attaching cooperatively to something else. Ice was a connector more so than a divider; as witnessed by Taylor, to be frozen meant to be "conglutinated" by and to the world. There is organizational power, not just horror, within interlocked alignment. "Unmelted"[39] early modern stories and art call us into this sticky *con-* of cold coalitions with others. Slickness is but one part of the dynamic equation, and adhesion and its political opportunities are another.

Much hangs on what happens in the "opening" Arctic. Christian Le Mière and Jeffrey Mazo delineate three governance "zones" that lie ahead of us: "uncertainty," "confrontation," and "cooperation."[40] To their descriptors, I have offered some of my own navigational turns of phrase as well. From portals, to productions, to passages, each chapter's illustration of human–Arctic enfolding is meant to augment our ontological cohesion in more equitable ways. Relearning (c)old words underwrites eco-materialist commitments to decentering the human, fostering just companionships with multispecies company, and devising novel vocabularies and interdisciplinary strategies for a fragile Anthropocene. Refusing to honor the regent's (the state's) hierarchical order, I turn the logic of confrontation against itself. I aim to counter chronic biases, prejudices, and discrimination that still view, for example, vulnerable northern bodies as expendable to climate crises. A better-off Arctic is not one that is hermetically sealed; any "protection" ultimately yields to porosity. I would rather meditate, at last, upon allies and allegiances. My wish is that the words herein (not all of them mine) further empower alternate ways of encountering the cold. This book, I confess, lacks an instrumentalist list of "doings." But its design is purposeful: I humbly propose, invite, and open up "justice" to the voices, agonies, and dreams of others who, like me, are thinking about what is possible and how a friendlier, neighborly Arctic would arise, operate, and start to repair.[41]

Which brings me back, finally, to *Othello*. There remains something powerful in the "no" that Emelia declares; it lingers, still, in the air. I sense it in the story medicine of Madeline Sayet's 2022 *Where We Belong* and in Reneltta Arluk's 2020 *Pawâkan Macbeth*.[42] "Speaking" her "no" resists the chronically racist, nationalist, and androcentric ideologies at present that would claim "the north" for industrialized countries causing "ill" to multispecies societies atop the melting world. The south, in an inversion of Best's logic, leaves the north "poluted" with little risk of reprimand. And yet, it is significantly against this state of cryopolitics that environmentalist women of color and their allies "liberally" speak Emilia's "no." "If we allow the Arctic to melt," argues Sheila Watt-Cloutier, "we lose more than the planet that has nurtured us for all of human history. We lose the wisdom that is required for us to sustain it."[43] An inter-active, inter-Arctic accompl*ice* incorporates the dramatic "will" into their advocacy for climate justice, translates a trenchant outspokenness ("'twill") into ecofeminist practice. In refusing to hold their "peace," cryophiles hold up possibilities for brokering it. Emilia, after all, demands justice. Troublingly, the play fails to deliver a judicious outcome even after the crimes are "out." "The object poisons sight," Lodovico remarks, so "let it be hid" (5.2.357–58). But the Venetian state's official response is a reminder that it always takes more than a single look to recognize, let alone redress, the world's revealed "poisons." Early modern authors spoke of "the north" as wind and place and self: in one breath, they conveyed the precarity and pleasure of Arctic interrelations that remain pressing to this day. Returning to these polar pasts furthers an ongoing commitment in our classrooms and communities[44] to what Leanne Betasamosake Simpson calls a "radically resurgent present,"[45] one in which "speaking" up for "the north" can also mean speaking "as," among, and with its garrulous residents.

# Acknowledgments

In a letter to his sister dated April 17, 1876, John Muir (1838–1914) confessed that "my life these days is like the life of a glacier, one eternal grind."[1] Without these interlocking interlocutors in my life, this book would have ground to a halt:

* My family * Doug Armato * Zenyse Miller * Carla Valadez * Mike Stoffel * Brett Kendall * Shelby Connelly * Steve Mentz * Jesse Oak Taylor * Jeffrey J. Cohen * Sophie Lemercier-Goddard * Sophie Chiari * Julie Van Parys-Rotondi * Brady Feutz * Marilena Zackheos * Kaonashi * Pistachio * Carolyn Dinshaw * Christine Hoffmann * Karen Raber * Holly Dugan * Lara Farina * Julian Yates * Dan Remein * Megan Manas * M Jackson * Todd Borlik * Valerie Fazel * Bernadette Myers * John Ernest * Siobhan Carroll * Kristen Poole * Serenella Iovino * Serpil Oppermann * Robert Edmundson * Jamie Jacobs * Chris Wade * Nic Helms * Will Stockton * Louise Geddes * Courtney Leonard * Tiffany Jo Werth * Ayanna Thompson * Nancy Nowacek * Arne Berg * Yngve Bergqvist * Luca Roncoroni * Samuel Cuisinier-Delorme * Chris Barrett * Viktor Lyagushkin * Annepiet Nouwen * Leon Vosters * Marcus Scarfo * Stephanie Foote * Stacy Alaimo * Moritz Ingwersen * Sophie Morris * Thalia Allington-Wood * Rebecca Zorach * Claudia Swan * Kimberly Williams * Feisal Mohamed * Lisa Smith * Hank Stoklosa * Hillary Eklund * Debapriya Sarkar * Bill Germano * Randall Martin * Rebecca Laroche * Keith Botelho * Délice Williams * Gavin Hollis * Maria Loh * Lia Markey * Leslie Geddes * Pat Keys * AR Siders * Mark Burnett * Dyani Johns Taff * Hsuan L. Hsu * Svenja Engelmann-Kewitz * Amish Trivedi * My students *

"But glaciers, dear friend—ice is only another form of terrestrial love."[2] Muir sent that note to Jeanne C. Smith Carr on December 11, 1871. But I like to imagine that I am speaking to you.

# Notes

## Preface

1. Swimmers disagree over whether San Francisco's Dolphin Club (1877) or Coney Island's Polar Bear Club (1903) held the nation's first U.S. "polar-bear plunge."
2. However, the Harbin Polar Land hotel in China (with rooms overlooking bear pens) and the Cochrane Polar Bear Habitat in Canada (where visitors may swim in a pool separated by shatterproof glass) test this disclaimer.
3. In *The Three Voyages of William Barents to the Arctic Regions,* ed. Koolemans Beynen and Charles T. Beke (London: Hakluyt Society, 1853), 15.
4. Beynen and Beke, 15.
5. Beynen and Beke, 15.
6. Beynen and Beke, 15.
7. Beynen and Beke, 15.
8. Beynen and Beke, clxxv.
9. Beynen and Beke, 197.
10. Vinciane Despret, *What Would Animals Say If We Asked the Right Questions?,* trans. Brett Buchanan (Minneapolis: University of Minnesota Press, 2016).
11. If you are down for it, see my "Exit, Pursued by a Polar Bear (More to Follow)" in *Upstart: A Journal of English Renaissance Studies* (published online by Clemson University Press in 2013). The quantity of tracks I have found deserves a separate book-length study!
12. Ursula K. Heise, *Imagining Extinction: The Cultural Meanings of Endangered Species* (Chicago: University of Chicago Press, 2016), 244.

## Introduction

1. Dolly Jørgensen and Virginia Langum, "Envisioning North from a Premodern Perspective," in *Visions of North in Premodern Europe* (Turnhout, Belgium: Brepols, 2018), 5.
2. Jørgensen and Langum, 3.
3. See Kristinn Schram, "Banking on Borealism: Eating, Smelling, and Performing the North," in *Iceland and Images of the North,* ed. Sumarliði R. Ísleifsson (Québec: Presses de l'Université du Québec, 2011), 305–27.
4. Eleanor Rosamund Barraclough, Danielle Marie Cudmore, and Stefan Donecker, "Introduction," in *Imagining the Supernatural North* (Edmonton: University of Alberta Press, 2016), xv.
5. Peter Davidson, *The Idea of North* (London: Reaktion, 2005), 8.
6. Davidson, 251–52.

7. Gretel Ehrlich, *The Future of Ice: A Journey into Cold* (New York: Vintage, 2004), 178–79.
8. Raphael Thorius, *Cheimonopegnion, Or, A Winter Song* (London: T.N., 1651), 1.
9. John Webster, *The White Devil,* ed. Benedict S. Robinson (London: Bloomsbury, 2019), 90.
10. Quoted in Todd Borlik, *Literature and Nature in the English Renaissance: An Ecocritical Anthology* (Cambridge: Cambridge University Press, 2019), 501.
11. James Howell, *A Winter Dreame* (London, 1648), 13.
12. Margaret Atwood, *Strange Things: The Malevolent North in Canadian Literature* (Oxford: Clarendon, 1995); Anne Cotterill, *Cold Tyranny and the Demonic North of Early Modern England* (Amsterdam: Amsterdam University Press, 2024); Colleen M. Franklin, ed., *The Strange and Dangerous Voyage of Captaine Thomas James: A Critical Edition* (Montreal: McGill-Queen's University Press, 2014), xv.
13. All quotations from Shakespeare refer to *The Norton Shakespeare,* ed. Stephen Greenblatt et al., 3rd ed. (New York: Norton, 2016). References are to act, scene, and line.
14. Dante Alighieri, *Inferno* 34.10–12: "I was by now (I write this verse in fear) / where all the shades in ice were covered up, / transparent as are straws preserved in glass" (trans. Robin Kirkpatrick [London: Penguin, 2006], 305). Cf. Thomas Dekker, *Dekker His Dreame* (London: Nicholas Okes, 1620), sig. D4v–E4r (enlarging on "The Extremities of Cold in Hell").
15. John Milton, *Paradise Lost* 2.587–88 and 2.595, in *Complete Poems and Major Prose,* ed. Merritt Y. Hughes (Indianapolis, Ind.: Odyssey, 1957).
16. Marjorie Hope Nicolson, *Mountain Gloom and Mountain Glory: The Development of the Aesthetics of the Infinite* (Ithaca, N.Y.: Cornell University Press, 1959). The 1695 *Dissertationcula de Montibus Islandiae Chrystallinis* (Short treatise on the ice mountains of Iceland) by Þórður Þorkelsson Vídalín's (1662–1742) "preceded writing on glaciers elsewhere" (Chris Caseldine, *Most Unimaginably Strange: An Eclectic Companion to the Landscape of Iceland* [London: Reaktion, 2021], 164–65).
17. John Evelyn, *The Diary of John Evelyn,* ed. E. S. de Beer, vol. 2 (Oxford: Clarendon, 1955), 514.
18. Nathaniel Lee, *Sophonisba: Or, Hannibal's Overthrow* (London: 1676), 2.
19. As launched by Silje Gaupseth, Marie-Theres Federhofer, and Per Pippin Aspaas, eds., *Travels in the North: A Multidisciplinary Approach to the Long History of Northern Travel Writing* (Hannover: Wehrhahn, 2013). See also Barry Lopez, *Arctic Dreams: Imagination and Desire in a Northern Landscape* (New York: Vintage, 1986); John Moss, *Enduring Dreams: An Exploration of Arctic Landscape* (Toronto: Anansi, 1994); Sara Wheeler, *The Magnetic North: Notes from the Arctic Circle* (New York: North Point, 2011).
20. Gretel Ehrlich, *This Cold Heaven* (New York: Pantheon, 2001), 101.
21. Foxe, for example, likened the Northwest Passage to a "Virgin . . . yet pure and untoucht, either by Christian, Indian, or other nation, although many great dowries have beene spent about her, and some brave Knights have bid faire for her" (*The Voyages of Captain Luke Foxe and Captain Thomas James in Search of*

*a North-West Passage, in 1631–32,* ed. Miller Christy, 2 vols. [London: Hakluyt Society, 1894], 2:423).

22. Stephanie D. Clare, *Earthly Encounters: Sensation, Feminist Theory, and the Anthropocene* (Albany: State University of New York Press, 2019), 1.
23. Lisa Bloom, *Gender on Ice: American Ideologies of Polar Expeditions* (Minneapolis: University of Minnesota Press, 1993), 2, 47.
24. Margaret Cavendish, *The Blazing World and Other Writings,* ed. Kate Lilley (New York: Penguin, 1992), 125–26. See also Delilah Bermudez Brataas, "'Peculiar Circles': The Fluid Utopia at the Northern Pole in Margaret Cavendish's *Blazing World,*" *Utopian Studies* 30, no. 2 [2019]: 214–37.
25. Gina Bloom, *Voice in Motion: Staging Gender, Shaping Sound in Early Modern England* (Philadelphia: University of Pennsylvania Press, 2007).
26. Blair Braverman, *Welcome to the Goddamn Ice Cube: Chasing Fear and Finding Home in the Great White North* (New York: HarperCollins, 2016).
27. Coll Thrush, "Haunt": "'To be haunted' means to be actively entangled in the past, present, and future, seeking traces among the living of what might at first be understood as dead" (in *Veer Ecology: A Companion for Environmental Thinking,* ed. Jeffrey Jerome Cohen and Lowell Duckert [Minneapolis: University of Minnesota Press, 2017], 278).
28. Joscelyn Godwin, *Arktos: The Polar Myth in Science, Symbolism, and Nazi Survival* (Kempton, Ill.: Adventures Unlimited, 1996).
29. Peter Fjågesund, *The Dream of the North: A Cultural History to 1920* (Amsterdam: Rodopi, 2014), 30.
30. A shortlist I consulted while drafting these pages: Shari Fox Gearheard, ed., *The Meaning of Ice: People and Sea Ice in Three Arctic Communities* (Hanover: International Polar Institute, 2017); Zacharias Kunuk, dir., *Qapirangajuq: Inuit Knowledge and Climate Change* (2010); SmartICE, smartice.org; the Inuit Northwest Passage Project, paninuittrails.org/index.html; Devora Neumark's *Letters to the Ice* (2021), devoraneumark.com/works/letters-to-ice/; IsumaTV, isuma.tv; Upper One Games, *Never Alone* (E-Line Media, 2016).
31. Ilan Kelman, "Editorial Introduction," in *Arcticness: Power and Voice from the North* (London: UCL Press, 2017), 1–6.
32. Gail Fondahl, Viktoriya Filippova, and Liza Mack, "Indigenous Peoples in the New Arctic," in *The New Arctic,* ed. Birgitta Evengård, Joan Nymand Larsen, and Øyvind Paasche (Cham, Switzerland: Springer, 2015), 7–22.
33. Zoe Todd, "Indigenizing the Anthropocene," in *Art in the Anthropocene: Encounters Among Aesthetics, Politics, Environment and Epistemology,* ed. Heather Davis and Etienne Turpin (London: Open Humanities, 2015), 241–54. See also "*at least* three key themes" outlined by Kyle Whyte, "Indigenous Climate Change Studies: Indigenizing Futures, Decolonizing the Anthropocene," *English Language Notes* 55, no. 1–2 [2017]: 153–62.
34. Igor Krupnik and Dyanna Jolly, eds., *The Earth Is Faster Now: Indigenous Observations of Arctic Environmental Change* (Fairbanks, Alas.: Arctic Consortium of the United States, 2010), 7.

35. Kim TallBear critiques the failure to recognize Indigenous notions of animism in "Beyond the Life/Not-Life Binary: A Feminist-Indigenous Reading of Cryopreservation, Interspecies Thinking, and the New Materialisms," in *Cryopolitics: Frozen Life in a Melting World,* ed. Joanna Radin and Emma Kowal (Cambridge, Mass.: MIT Press, 2017), 179–202.
36. Sheila Watt-Cloutier, *The Right to Be Cold: One Woman's Fight to Protect the Arctic and Save the Planet from Climate Change* (Minneapolis: University of Minnesota Press, 2015).
37. Watt-Cloutier, 258, 310.
38. Thomas Dekker, *The Great Frost* (London, 1608), sig. A2v.
39. Dekker, sig. A3r.
40. Dekker, sig. A3r.
41. Dekker, sig. A3v–4r.
42. Dekker, sig. A4v.
43. Dekker, sig. A4v.
44. Dekker, sig. A4v.
45. Dekker, sig. A4v–B1r.
46. Dekker, sig. B1r.
47. Dekker, sig. B2r.
48. Dekker, sig. B2v.
49. Dekker, sig. B3r.
50. Dekker, sig. B2v.
51. Dekker, sig. B4r.
52. Dekker, sig. D1r.
53. Dekker, sig. B4v.
54. Thomas Dekker, *The Cold Yeare* (London: W. White, 1615), sig. A1r.
55. Dekker, sig. B3v.
56. Dekker, sig. B2v.
57. Dekker, sig. C2v.
58. Dekker, sig. B1v.
59. Dekker, sig. B1v.
60. Dekker, sig. B2r.
61. Dekker, sig. B1r.
62. Dekker, sig. B1r.
63. Dekker, sig. C1r.
64. Dekker, sig. B4r.
65. Dekker, sig. B4r.
66. Dekker, sig. B4v.
67. Dekker, sig. B4v.
68. Dekker, sig. B4v.
69. Dekker, sig. C3r.
70. Dekker, sig. C3r.
71. Dekker, sig. C3v.
72. Dekker, sig. C3v.

73. Dekker, sig. C4r.
74. Dekker, sig. A1r.
75. Dekker, *Dekker His Dreame,* sig. A4r.
76. Dekker, 37.
77. Dekker, *Cold Yeare,* sig. A3r.
78. Dekker, sig. B1r.
79. Dekker, sig. B1r.
80. Dekker, sig. B1r.
81. Bill Streever, *Cold: Adventures in the World's Frozen Places* (New York: Back Bay, 2009), 164–69.
82. Tom Shachtman, *Absolute Zero and the Conquest of Cold* (New York: Houghton Mifflin, 1999), 125–52.
83. Robert Boyle, *New Experiments and Observations Touching Cold,* in *The Works of Robert Boyle,* ed. Michael Hunter and Edward B. Davis, vol. 4 (London: Routledge, 1999), 293.
84. John Taylor, *The Cold Tearme, Or, the Frozen Age, Or, the Metamorphosis of the Riuer of Thames* (London, 1621).
85. In *Henry Hudson the Navigator: The Original Documents in Which His Career is Recorded,* ed. G. M. Asher (London: Hakluyt Society, 1860), 19.
86. Gino Segrè, *A Matter of Degrees: What Temperature Reveals about the Past and Future of Our Species, Planet, and Universe* (New York: Penguin, 2002), 8–9.
87. Klaus Dodds, *Ice* (London: Reaktion, 2018), 23.
88. In Mariana Gosnell, *Ice: The Nature, the History, and the Uses of an Astonishing Substance* (Chicago: University of Chicago Press, 2005), 473.
89. Jane Bennett, *Vibrant Matter: A Political Ecology of Things* (Durham, N.C.: Duke University Press, 2010), 6.
90. "To become subject to disease attributed to coldness within the body or exposure to low temperatures; to become infected with a cold" dates from 1400[?]–[ca.]1460 (*The Oxford English Dictionary* [*OED*], s.v. *cold* [n.]), P1.a.
91. Pliny the Elder, *The Historie of the World,* trans. Philemon Holland, vol. 1 (London: Adam Islip, 1601), 604.
92. *The Anglo-Saxon Poetic Records: A Collective Edition,* ed. George Philip Krapp and Elliott Van Kirk Dobbie, vol. 3 (New York: Columbia University Press, 1936), 231.
93. See Daniel C. Remein, "Paranormal Prose: 'Para-Narrative' and Ice in the Icelandic Sagas," in *Paranormal Encounters in Iceland 1150–1400,* ed. Ármann Jakobsson and Miriam Mayburd (Boston: Medieval Institute, 2020), 151–71.
94. Gosnell, *Ice,* 407–12. See also Amy Brady, *Ice* (New York: G. P. Putnam's Sons, 2023).
95. Francis Bacon, *Sylua Syluarum* (London: John Haviland and Augustine Mathewes, 1627), 23.
96. Donna J. Haraway, *Staying with the Trouble: Making Kin in the Chthulucene* (Durham, N.C.: Duke University Press, 2016), 58.
97. Boyle, *New Experiments,* 4:355.

98. Roger G. Barry and Thian Yew Gan, *The Global Cryosphere: Past, Present, and Future,* 2nd ed. (Cambridge: Cambridge University Press, 2022), 1.
99. Boyle, *New Experiments,* 4:335.
100. The prefix *κρύος* shares the same Indo-European base as ancient Greek *κρύσταλλος* ("crystal") and classical Latin *crusta* ("crust") (*OED,* s.v. *cryo-* comb. form).
101. See Shawn J. Marshall's accessible tome, *The Cryosphere* (Princeton, N.J.: Princeton University Press, 2012), 1–2.
102. Bjørn Vassnes, *Kingdom of Frost: How the Cryosphere Shapes Life on Earth,* trans. Lucy Moffatt (Vancouver: Greystone, 2020), 6.
103. See Jane Bennett, *The Enchantment of Modern Life: Attachments, Crossings, and Ethics* (Princeton, N.J.: Princeton University Press, 2001).
104. Serenella Iovino and Serpil Oppermann, "Introduction: Stories Come to Matter," in *Material Ecocriticism* (Bloomington: Indiana University Press, 2014), 1–18.
105. I picture "cold studies" augmenting the "Arctic environmental humanities" (AEH), as well as the "ice humanities." See Klaus Dodds and Sverker Sörlin, eds., *Ice Humanities: Living, Working, and Thinking in a Melting World* (Manchester: Manchester University Press, 2022). In that volume, Elizabeth Leane proposes the term "cryonarrative . . . to describe contemporary stories in which ice and humans are closely interconnected" ("Cryonarratives for Warming Times: Icebergs as Planetary Travellers," 251).
106. I use the word *weather* deliberately in the sense outlined by Astrida Neimanis and Jennifer Mae Hamilton: "a particular way of understanding how bodies, places, and the weather are all inter-implicated in our climate-changing world" ("Weathering," *Feminist Review* 118 [2018)]: 80–81).
107. Dagomar Degroot, *The Frigid Golden Age: Climate Change, the Little Ice Age, and the Dutch Republic, 1560–1720* (Cambridge: Cambridge University Press, 2018), 298.
108. Degroot, 298.
109. Anonymous, *Great Britains Wonder: Or, London's Admiration* (London: M. Haly and J. Millet, 1684).
110. Tobias Menely, *Climate and the Making of Worlds: Toward a Geohistorical Poetics* (Chicago: University of Chicago Press, 2021), 214.
111. Menely, 14.
112. Rebecca Laroche and Jennifer Munroe, *Shakespeare and Ecofeminist Theory* (London: Bloomsbury, 2017), 38. See also Vin Nardizzi and Tiffany Jo Werth, "Oecologies: Engaging the World, from Here," in *Premodern Ecologies in the Modern Literary Imagination* (Toronto: University of Toronto Press, 2019), 3–10.
113. In Borlik, *Literature and Nature,* 525–26.
114. Phillip Inman, "Why Does Donald Trump Want to Buy Greenland?," *The Guardian,* August 19, 2019, theguardian.com/us-news/2019/aug/19/why-does-donald-trump-want-to-buy-greenland; Jeffrey Gettleman, "Greenland to

Trump: We're Not for Sale but Let's Talk Business," *New York Times,* January 13, 2025, nytimes.com/2025/01/13/world/europe/greenland-trump-business.html.

115. In Borlik, *Literature and Nature,* 526.
116. Borlik, 506.
117. Richard B. Alley, *The Two-Mile Time Machine: Ice Cores, Abrupt Climate Change, and Our Future* (Princeton, N.J.: Princeton University Press, 2000), 83.
118. Jeffrey J. Cohen, "The Love of Life: Reading *Sir Gawain and the Green Knight* Close to Home," in Nardizzi and Werth, *Premodern Ecologies,* 29.
119. Sophie Chiari, *Shakespeare's Representation of Weather, Climate and Environment: The Early Modern 'Fated' Sky* (Edinburgh: Edinburgh University Press, 2019), 1. According to Porter Fox, "the oldest snowfall records on the planet were kept at a meteorological observatory in Turin beginning in 1675" (*The Last Winter: The Scientists, Adventurers, Journeyman, and Mavericks Trying to Save the World* [New York: Little and Brown, 2021], 176).
120. See Lydia Barnett, *After the Flood: Imagining the Global Environment in Early Modern Europe* (Baltimore, Md.: Johns Hopkins University Press, 2019), 89.
121. Robert Fotherby as quoted in *The Voyages of William Baffin, 1612–1622,* ed. Clements R. Markham (London: Hakluyt Society, 1881), 66.
122. Fotherby, 66.
123. Jon Gertner, for instance, writes that "it seemed likely to me that I could locate the start of Greenland's scientific evolution by returning to a premodern age, . . . the late nineteenth century" (*The Ice at the End of the World: An Epic Journey into Greenland's Buried Past and Our Perilous Future* [New York: Random House, 2019], xxiii).
124. See Alun Anderson, "The Arctic's Revenge," in *After the Ice: Life, Death, and Geopolitics in the New Arctic* (New York: Smithsonian, 2009), 227–44.
125. Andrew Blum, *The Weather Machine: A Journey inside the Forecast* (New York: HarperCollins, 2019).
126. Debapriya Sarkar, "Literary Justice: The Participatory Ethics of Early Modern Possible Worlds," in *Teaching Social Justice through Shakespeare: Why Renaissance Literature Matters Now,* ed. Hillary Eklund and Wendy Beth Hyman (Edinburgh: Edinburgh University Press, 2019), 174–75.
127. Pliny the Elder, *Historie of the World,* 1:554.
128. Tim Ingold, *Being Alive: Essays on Movement, Knowledge, and Description* (New York: Routledge, 2011), 130.
129. Ehrlich, *This Cold Heaven,* 303.
130. In *De Reis van Jan Cornelisz* (The Hague: M. Nijhoff, 1909). Thanks to Claudia Swan for bringing this "ijsblok" to my attention.
131. Maggie M. Cao, "The Entropic History of Ice," in *Ecologies, Agents, Terrains,* ed. Christopher P. Heuer and Rebecca Zorach (New Haven, Conn.: Yale University Press, 2018), 286.
132. Mark A. Cheetham, "Northern Landscape and the Anthropocene: A Long View," in *Artistic Visions of the Anthropocene North: Climate Change and Nature in Art,* ed. Gry Hedin and Ann-Sofie N. Gremaud (New York: Routledge, 2018), 73.

133. Janine Randerson, *Weather as Medium: Toward a Meteorological Art* (Cambridge, Mass.: MIT Press, 2018), 156.
134. John Durham Peters, *The Marvelous Clouds: Toward a Philosophy of Elemental Media* (Chicago: University of Chicago Press, 2015), 2.
135. Peters, 10.
136. Christopher P. Heuer, *Into the White: The Renaissance Arctic and the End of the Image* (New York: Zone, 2019), 190.
137. Christopher P. Heuer, "Arctic Matters in Early America," in *Scale,* ed. Jennifer L. Roberts (Chicago: University of Chicago Press, 2016), 200.
138. Heuer, *Into the White,* 197. Admittedly, he leans farther into the *Lear*-ian "nothing" than I do: "Icy, unpopulated, commodity poor, visually and temporally 'abstract,' the far North . . . offered no clear *stuff* to be seen, mapped, or plundered" (10), adding, "there was almost nothing at which even to wonder" (15). While I am wholly sympathetic to his aim—"to undo the dream of [the Arctic's] otherness" (196)—I move toward this goal in a different way.
139. Eric G. Wilson, *The Spiritual History of Ice: Romanticism, Science, and the Imagination* (New York: Palgrave Macmillan, 2003), 3.
140. Wilson, 4–5.
141. In Henry David Thoreau, *The Portable Thoreau,* ed. Jeffrey S. Cramer (New York: Penguin, 2012), 438.
142. Boyle, *New Experiments,* 4:208.
143. There are several notable exceptions: see Fjågesund's first chapter in *Dream of the North,* "Finding a Footing: The North before 1700" (33–115). Mary C. Fuller's historiographical work on Newfoundland, Iceland, and the "forgotten" roles the Arctic played spurs remembrance of other influential northern areas (*Remembering the Early Modern Voyage: English Narratives in the Age of European Expansion* [New York: Palgrave Macmillan, 2008], 163).
144. Elizabeth Kolbert and Francis Spufford, *The Ends of the Earth: An Anthology of the Finest Writing on the Arctic and the Antarctic* (London: Granta, 2007).
145. Mary Shelley, *Frankenstein* (London: Penguin, 1992), 15.
146. Heidi Hansson and Anka Ryall, eds., *Arctic Modernities: The Environmental, the Exotic and the Everyday* (Newcastle upon Tyne: Cambridge Scholars, 2017); Lill-Ann Körber, Scott MacKenzie, and Anna Westerståhl Stenport, eds., *Arctic Environmental Modernities: From the Age of Polar Exploration to the Era of the Anthropocene* (Cham: Palgrave Macmillan, 2017).
147. Kelman, *Arcticness,* throughout.
148. Gísli Pálsson, "Arcticality: Gender, Race, and Geography in the Writings of Vilhjalmur Stefansson," in *Narrating the Arctic: A Cultural History of Nordic Scientific Practice,* ed. Michael Bravo and Sverker Sörlin (Canton, Mass.: Science History, 2002), 275–309.
149. Douglas Wilkinson, *Arctic Fever: The Search for the Northwest Passage* (Toronto: Clark, Irwin, 1971).
150. Glyndwr Williams, *Voyages of Delusion: The Northwest Passage in the Age of*

*Reason* (London: HarperCollins, 2002); Williams, *Arctic Labyrinth: The Quest for the Northwest Passage* (London: Allen Lane, 2009).

151. Daniel Chartier, "Towards a Grammar of the Idea of North: Nordicity, Winterity," *Nordlit* 11, no. 2 (2007): 35–47.
152. François Rabelais, *Gargantua and Pantagruel,* trans. M. A. Screech (London: Penguin, 2006), 825–30.
153. Robert Macfarlane, *Landmarks* (London: Hamish Hamilton, 2015), 220.
154. Macfarlane, 209.
155. Steve Mentz, *Ocean* (New York: Bloomsbury Academic, 2020), xv–xvi.
156. Mentz, xv–xviii.
157. Melody Jue, *Wild Blue Media: Thinking through Seawater* (Durham, N.C.: Duke University Press, 2020).
158. Jue, 6, 14, 18.
159. Jue, 18.
160. Boyle, *New Experiments,* 4:322, 4:380.
161. See Adriana Craciun, *Writing Arctic Disaster: Authorship and Exploration* (Cambridge: Cambridge University Press, 2016). While her timeline stretches as far back to the establishment of the Hudson's Bay Company in 1670—amassing a collection of "Arctic inscriptions" (26) that amount to an "Arctic archive" (38)—mine begins centuries before the trading post's charter.
162. Hester Blum, *The News at the End of the Earth: The Print Culture of Polar Exploration* (Durham, N.C.: Duke University Press, 2019), 5.
163. See Aida Džiho-Šator, "Cryopoetics in the Political Novel the Damned Yard by Ivo Andrić," *Social Sciences and the Humanities Studies* 2 (2020): 31–44.
164. Blum, *News,* 68, 12, 31.
165. Blum, 4.
166. Blum, 7.
167. Donna J. Haraway, "The Companion Species Manifesto: Dogs, People, and Significant Otherness," in *Manifestly Haraway* (Minneapolis: University of Minnesota Press, 2016), 112.
168. Elizabeth Bradfield, "Notes on Ice in Bowditch," in *Approaching Ice* (New York: Persea, 2010), 71.
169. Thanks to Matthew Schneider-Mayerson and Brent Ryan Bellamy's *An Ecotopian Lexicon* (Minneapolis: University of Minnesota Press, 2019) for its infinite inspiration.
170. Dodds, *Ice,* 83.
171. See my second chapter in *For All Waters: Finding Ourselves in Early Modern Wetscapes* (Minneapolis: University of Minnesota Press, 2017), 97–149.
172. Pierre Berton, *The Arctic Grail: The Quest for the North West Passage and the North Pole, 1818–1909* (New York: Viking, 1988).
173. John McCannon, *A History of the Arctic: Nature, Exploration and Exploitation* (London: Reaktion, 2012), 77–124.
174. Michael F. Robinson, *The Coldest Crucible: Arctic Exploration and American Culture* (Chicago: University of Chicago Press, 2006).

175. Stephen Bocking and Brad Martin, eds., *Ice Blink: Navigating Northern Environmental History* (Calgary: University of Calgary Press, 2017).
176. Such as Sebastian Copeland, dir., *Into the Cold: A Journey of the Soul* (2013), and Anson Fogel, dir., *Cold* (2011).
177. Dahr Jamail, *The End of Ice: Bearing Witness and Finding Meaning in the Path of Climate Disruption* (New York: New Press, 2019).
178. Peter Wadhams, *A Farewell to Ice* (London: Allen Lane, 2016).
179. Henry Pollack, *A World without Ice* (New York: Avery, 2009).
180. Anderson, *After the Ice*, throughout.
181. Doug Macdougall, *Frozen Earth: The Once and Future Story of Ice Ages* (Berkeley: University of California Press, 2004).
182. Charles Emmerson, *The Future History of the Arctic* (New York: PublicAffairs, 2010).
183. Elizabeth Rush, *The Quickening: Creation and Community at the Ends of the Earth* (Minneapolis: Milkweed, 2023), 42.
184. In Emmanuel Le Roy Ladurie, *Times of Feast, Times of Famine: A Climate History since the Year 1000* (Garden City, N.Y.: Doubleday, 1971), 138–39.
185. See Gail Kern Paster, *Humoring the Body: Emotions and the Shakespearean Stage* (Chicago: University of Chicago Press, 2004).
186. Drew Daniel, *The Melancholy Assemblage: Affect and Epistemology in the English Renaissance* (New York: Fordham University Press, 2013), 7 (cf. 230).
187. Donald Anderson, *Below Freezing: Elegy for the Melting Planet* (Albuquerque: University of New Mexico Press, 2018).
188. "Un-Glacier Tour 2019," notokmovie.com.
189. "Un-Glacier Tour 2019."
190. M Jackson, *The Secret Lives of Glaciers* (Brattleboro, Vt.: Green Writers, 2019).
191. See Jackson, 231: "Words about glaciers make glacier stories, and glacier stories make realities and viable futures."
192. Mark C. Serreze, *Brave New Arctic: The Untold Story of the Melting North* (Princeton, N.J.: Princeton University Press, 2018), 27–28.
193. Serreze, 194, 25.
194. Julie Cruikshank, *Do Glaciers Listen? Local Knowledge, Colonial Encounters, and Social Imagination* (Vancouver: University of British Columbia Press, 2005).
195. Thom van Dooren, *Flight Ways: Life and Loss at the Edge of Extinction* (New York: Columbia University Press, 2014), 147.
196. Van Dooren, 46.
197. Van Dooren, 8.
198. Van Dooren, 92.
199. Van Dooren, 137.
200. Van Dooren, 142. I am reminded of the photographer James Balog's tearful reaction to his camera's malfunction in Jeff Orlowski's 2012 documentary *Chasing Ice*: the loss of footage, he feared, meant losing the story of Arctic ice loss.
201. Lauren Berlant, *Cruel Optimism* (Durham, N.C.: Duke University Press, 2011).
202. Berlant, 14.

203. Eben Kirksey, *Emergent Ecologies* (Durham, N.C.: Duke University Press, 2015).
204. Anna Tsing, *The Mushroom at the End of the World: On the Possibility of Life in Capitalist Ruins* (Princeton, N.J.: Princeton University Press, 2015).
205. Tim Smedley, "The Outrageous Plan to Haul Icebergs to Africa," BBC Future, September 21, 2018, bbc.com/future/article/20180918-the-outrageous-plan-to-haul-icebergs-to-africa.
206. Tsing, *Mushroom*, 255.
207. Tsing, 255.
208. Karen Raber, *Shakespeare and Posthumanist Theory* (London: Bloomsbury, 2018), 160.
209. Bruno Latour, *Reassembling the Social: An Introduction to Actor-Network-Theory* (Oxford: Oxford University Press, 2005), 122.
210. Sharon O'Dair, "Growing Pains," *Early Modern Culture* 13 (2018), tigerprints.clemson.edu/emc/vol13/iss1/7/.
211. See Rob Nixon, *Slow Violence and the Environmentalism of the Poor* (Cambridge: Harvard University Press, 2011), 2: "A violence that occurs gradually and out of sight, a violence of delayed destruction that is dispersed across time and space, an attritional violence that is typically not viewed as violence at all."
212. Lutz Koepnick, *On Slowness: Toward an Aesthetic of the Contemporary* (New York: Columbia University Press, 2014).
213. Isabelle Stengers, *Another Science Is Possible: A Manifesto for Slow Science*, trans. Stephen Muecke (Cambridge: Polity, 2018).
214. Maggie Berg and Barbara K. Seeber, *The Slow Professor: Challenging the Culture of Speed in the Academy* (Toronto: University of Toronto Press, 2016).
215. Christine Hoffmann, *Stupid Humanism: Folly as Competence in Early Modern and Twenty-First-Century Culture* (Cham, Switz.: Palgrave Macmillan, 2017).

## Winterlude: *Flake*

1. Johannes Kepler, *The Six-Cornered Snowflake* (Oxford: Oxford University Press, 1966), 23.
2. Kepler, 33.
3. Philip Ball, *Life's Matrix: A Biography of Water* (Berkeley: University of California Press, 2001), 194. See also Mariana Gosnell, *Ice: The Nature, the History, and the Uses of an Astonishing Substance* (Chicago: University of Chicago Press, 2005), 420–24.
4. D.N., *The Figure of Six* (London: 1652, n.p.).
5. Kepler, *Six-Cornered Snowflake*, 39.
6. Kepler, 33.
7. Kepler, 39.
8. See *Oxford English Dictionary*, s.v. *flake* (n.2).
9. Adrian F. Ward, "Winter Wakes up Your Mind—and Warm Weather Makes It Harder to Think Straight," *Scientific American*, February 12, 2013, scientificamerican.com/article/warm-weather-makes-it-hard-think-straight.

10. René Descartes, *Discourse on Method, Optics, Geometry, and Meteorology,* trans. Paul J. Olscamp (Indianapolis, Ind.: Hackett, 2001), 308.
11. Robert Hooke, *Micrographia* (London: Jo. Martyn and Ja. Allestry, 1665), 88.
12. Olaus Magnus, *Description of the Northern Peoples,* trans. Peter Fisher and Humphrey Higgens, ed. Peter Foote, vol. 1 (London: Hakluyt Society, 1996–1998), 52–53.
13. Magnus, 1:52–53.
14. Magnus, 1:52–53.
15. Magnus, 1:52–53.
16. Magnus, 1:52.
17. Hooke, *Micrographia,* 92.
18. You can keep going! The Italian mathematician Donato Rossetti (1633–1686) published *La Figure Della Neve* (The shape of snow) in 1681. I discuss Frederick Martens's (1671) observations on Spitsbergen's weather as well as the American photographer Wilson A. Bentley's (1865–1931) collection of approximately two and a half thousand individual *Snow Crystals* (1931) in *Water and Cognition in Early Modern English Literature,* ed. Nic Helms and Steve Mentz (Amsterdam: Amsterdam University Press, 2024), 179–97.
19. "Snowshoe Artist Simon Beck's Vast Snow Art in Colorado," BBC News, January 17, 2020, bbc.com/news/uk-england-somerset-50972062.

## 1. Finding Frīgus

1. For more on the Wim Hof Method, visit wimhofmethod.com/practice-the-method. Unless specified otherwise, all citations refer to this website.
2. Wim Hof and Koen de Jong, *The Way of the Iceman: How the Wim Hof Method Creates Radiant, Longterm Health—Using the Science and Secrets of Breath Control, Cold-Training and Commitment* (Little Canada, Minn.: Dragon Door, 2016), 17.
3. In Todd Borlik, *Literature and Nature in the English Renaissance: An Ecocritical Anthology* (Cambridge: Cambridge University Press, 2019), 506.
4. Olaus Magnus, *Description of the Northern Peoples,* trans. Peter Fisher and Humphrey Higgens, ed. Peter Foote, vol. 2 (London: Hakluyt Society, 1996–1998), 555–56; Francis Bacon, "Of Custom and Education," in *The Essayes* (London: John Haviland, 1625), 233.
5. Jean Feyens writes in *De Flatibus Humanum Corpus Molestantibus* (1582): "For a hot Country, as the Summer, inflames the spirits, dries the humours, and increaseth Choler, which causeth most acute diseases. But a cold and moist air, as it is in the North, is like the Winter, stupifies the spirits, stops the Pores, and burdens the body with many superfluous humours, and oppresseth the native heat" (trans. William Rowland, *A New and Needful Treatise of Spirits and Wind Offending Mans Body* [London: J. M., 1668], 5–6).
6. Hermann van der Heyden, *Speedy Help for Rich and Poor* (London: James Young, 1653), 52.

7. John Floyer, *An Enquiry into the Right Use and Abuses of Hot, Cold, and Temperate Baths in England* (London: 1697), 77.
8. I am channeling, of course, Stacy Alaimo's influential term: "Imagining human corporeality as trans-corporeality, in which the human is always intermeshed with the more-than-human-world, underlines the extent to which the substance of the human is ultimately inseparable from 'the environment'" (*Bodily Natures: Science, Environment, and the Material Self* [Bloomington: Indiana University Press, 2010], 2).
9. Mary Floyd-Wilson and Garrett A. Sullivan Jr., "Introduction," in *Geographies of Embodiment in Early Modern England* (Oxford: Oxford University Press, 2020), 1–2.
10. In Francis Bacon, *The Oxford Francis Bacon,* ed. Graham Rees and Maria Wakely, vol. 11 (Oxford: Oxford University Press, 2004), 253.
11. Bacon, 11:239.
12. Gino Segrè, *A Matter of Degrees: What Temperature Reveals about the Past and Future of Our Species, Planet, and Universe* (New York: Penguin, 2002), 58. See also Bill Streever, "Preface: A Candle's Flame," in *Heat: Adventures in the World's Fiery Places* (New York: Little and Brown, 2013), xiii–xvii; Steve Mentz, "Phlogiston," in *Elemental Ecocriticism: Thinking with Earth, Air, Water, and Fire,* ed. Jeffrey Jerome Cohen and Lowell Duckert (Minneapolis: University of Minnesota Press, 2015), 55–76.
13. Gustavus Parker, *An Account of a Portable Barometer* (London, 1699), 8, 9, 11.
14. Parker, 18.
15. Anonymous, *Essayes of Natural Experiments Made in the Academie del Cimento* (London, 1684), 69–94; see also Elizabeth David, *Harvest of the Cold Months: The Social History of Ice and Ices,* ed. Jill Norman (New York: Viking, 1995), esp. 55–76 ("Iceman of the Seventeenth Century").
16. See Tom Shachtman, *Absolute Zero and the Conquest of Cold* (New York: Houghton Mifflin, 1999), 1–15, 36–44; Bill Streever, *Cold: Adventures in the World's Frozen Places* (New York: Back Bay, 2009) 161–64. For "coldsploitation" (and "critical temperature studies" more broadly), see Nicole Starosielski, *Media Hot and Cold* (Durham, N.C.: Duke University Press, 2021). I am also a fan of the pocket-sized *Refrigerator* by Jonathan Rees (New York: Bloomsbury, 2015).
17. Giambattista della Porta, *Naturall Magick* (London, 1658), 395, 324.
18. Porta, *Naturall Magick,* 398.
19. Francis Bacon, *Sylua Syluarum* (London: John Haviland and Augustine Mathewes, 1627), 22–24.
20. Bacon, *Oxford Francis Bacon,* 11:263.
21. Bacon, *Sylua Syluarum,* 22–23.
22. Bacon, *Oxford Francis Bacon,* 11:237; see also Francis Bacon, "Instances which Share in the Nature of Heat" (*Oxford Francis Bacon,* 11:217). In general, cold's keenness causes scorching sensations: "And burns indeed the North Wind's piercing cold" (11:219).
23. Bacon, 11:269.

24. Bacon, 11:425.
25. Bacon, 11:429.
26. Bacon, 11:425.
27. Bacon, *Sylua Syluarum,* 23.
28. Bacon, 23.
29. Bacon, 23.
30. "Only let the human race recover that right over nature which belongs to it by divine bequest, and let power be given it; the exercise thereof will be governed by sound reason and true religion" (Francis Bacon, *The Works of Francis Bacon,* ed. James Spedding, Robert Leslie Ellis, and Douglas Denon Heath, 15 vols. [London: Longmans, 1876], 4:115; see Carolyn Merchant, *The Death of Nature: Women, Ecology, and the Scientific Revolution* [New York: HarperCollins, 1980]).
31. Bacon, *Sylua Syluarum,* 101.
32. See "Calor et Frigus," in Bacon, *Works,* 3:641–52.
33. Pierre de la Primaudaye (ca. 1545) admits that "it might seeme . . . [God] hath established some things, principally to take vengeance on the wicked." *The Third Volume of the French Academie,* trans. R. Dolman (London: Eliot's Court, 1601), 208. Others were less hesitant to interpret these verses. John Gore, for example, delivered his 1634 winter sermon during "a time of extraordinary snow and floods" (sig. A1r.). Expatiating upon Ps 147:16–18, his wish was that, "by a kinde of spirituall Antiperistasis, your soules may receive some warmth within, whiles your bodies are encompassed with so much cold without" *Certaine Sermons* ([London: Thomas Cotes, 1635], 1–2).
34. Craig Martin, *Renaissance Meteorology: Pomponazzi to Descartes* (Baltimore, Md.: Johns Hopkins University Press, 2011), 9. The very brief early modern meteorological forecast that follows relies almost entirely on three indispensable studies: Martin's introduction (1–20); the first chapter of Vladimir Janković's *Reading the Skies: A Cultural History of English Weather, 1650–1820* (Chicago: University of Chicago Press, 2000), 14–32; S. K. Heninger Jr.'s *A Handbook of Renaissance Meteorology* (New York: Greenwood, 1968), particularly "Snow" (58–61).
35. "This Region, or middle part of the Air is generally conceived to be vehemently cold and moist by Antiperistasis, and the effects do also prove the same. . . . Frigide Meteors are ingenerated there" (Thomas Willsford, *Natures Secrets* [London, 1658], 48, 51).
36. Martin, *Renaissance Meteorology,* 14.
37. Martin, 1.
38. Martin, 16.
39. William Fulke, *A Goodly Gallerye,* ed. Theodore Hornberger (Philadelphia: American Philosophical Society, 1979), 25.
40. Fulke, 26.
41. Fulke, 98.
42. Poor Robin, *Poor Robin's Book of Knowledge Shewing the Effects of the Planets, and Other Astronomical Constellations* (London: R. Wild, 1688), 92.

43. John Tulley, *An Almanack for the Year of Our Lord, MDCXCIII* (Boston: Benjamin Harris, 1693).
44. Tulley.
45. Fulke, *Goodly Gallerye,* 97.
46. Fulke, 97.
47. Fulke, 99.
48. Descartes, *Discourse on Method, Optics, Geometry, and Meteorology,* trans. Paul J. Olscamp (Indianapolis, Ind.: Hackett, 2001), 264.
49. Descartes, 264.
50. Descartes, 266.
51. Descartes, 267.
52. Descartes, 267.
53. Descartes, 277.
54. Descartes, 266.
55. Thomas Hobbes, *Decameron Physiologicum* (London: J.C., 1678), 63–64.
56. Hobbes, 61.
57. Hobbes, 64.
58. Hobbes, 64.
59. Hobbes, 64.
60. Hobbes, 65.
61. Hobbes, 65.
62. Hobbes, 65.
63. Gilles Deleuze and Félix Guattari write: "The middle is by no means an average; on the contrary, it is where things pick up speed" (*A Thousand Plateaus: Capitalism and Schizophrenia,* vol. 2 of *Capitalism and Schizophrenia,* trans. Brian Massumi [Minneapolis: University of Minnesota Press, 1987], 25). Scientists have shown that molecules in ice, unlike in any other solid, spin up to one million cycles every second; though decelerated, the lattice vibrates, pairing up order's security with disorder's possibility (see Mariana Gosnell, *Ice: The Nature, the History, and the Uses of an Astonishing Substance* [Chicago: University of Chicago Press, 2005], 27–28).
64. Hobbes, *Decameron Physiologicum,* 68.
65. Hobbes, 68–69.
66. See *The Oxford English Dictionary* [*OED*], s.v. *frigid* (adj.), 1.a.
67. Robert Boyle, *New Experiments and Observations Touching Cold,* in *The Works of Robert Boyle,* ed. Michael Hunter and Edward B. Davis, vol. 4 (London: Routledge, 1999), 208. All quotations hereafter refer to this edition and will be cited in text.
68. His comments certainly register the ongoing debate at the time, for example, between vitalists (atomists) and mechanists concerning the nature of matter. For a fuller biography of Boyle and his scientific legacy, see Shachtman, *Absolute Zero,* 23–35, and Steven Shapin, *A Social History of Truth: Civility and Science in Seventeenth-Century England* (Chicago: University of Chicago Press, 1994), 126–92.

69. Anna Tsing, *The Mushroom at the End of the World: On the Possibility of Life in Capitalist Ruins* (Princeton, N.J.: Princeton University Press, 2015), 144. See also Perry Zurn and Arjun Shankar, eds., *Curiosity Studies: A New Ecology of Knowledge* (Minneapolis: University of Minnesota Press, 2020).
70. See *OED,* s.v. *pitch* (v.2), I and II.
71. Bruno Latour, "Foreword: The Scientific Fables of an Empirical La Fontaine," in Vinciane Despret, *What Would Animals Say If We Asked the Right Questions?,* trans. Brett Buchanan (Minneapolis: University of Minnesota Press, 2016), ix.
72. Latour, ix.
73. Bruno Latour, "Why Has Critique Run out of Steam? From Matters of Fact to Matters of Concern," *Critical Inquiry* 30 (2004): 232.
74. All from *OED,* in chronological order: *frigor* (n.), 1599; *frigid* (adj.), 1622; *frigidious* (adj.), 1630; *frigitate* (v.), 1635; *frigidal* (adj.), 1651; *frigorifical* (adj.), 1656; *frigidative* (adj.), 1659; *frigiferous* (adj.), 1664; *frigorific* (adj.), 1668; *frigot* (n.), 1683; and *frigidate* (v.), 1691.
75. *Cryonics* (1966) is defined as "the practice or technique of cryogenically preserving a person's body with the aim of reviving it in the future" (*OED,* s.v. *cryonics* [n.]), whereas *cryogenics* (1899) refers to "the branch of physics which deals with the production of cryogenic temperatures and the effects of such temperatures on matter" (*OED,* s.v. *cryogenics* [n.]). Etymologically, though, *cryogenic* means "cold generating, producing": a cryogenicist studies how cold is produced as well as what it produces.
76. See *OED,* s.v. *promiscuous* (adj.), A.1.a: "Done or applied with no regard for method, order, etc.; random, indiscriminate, unsystematic."
77. Serenella Iovino and Serpil Oppermann, "Introduction: Stories Come to Matter," in *Material Ecocriticism* (Bloomington: Indiana University Press, 2014), 1.
78. It bears mentioning here that curiosity is gendered in his favor. As Donna J. Haraway has argued, Boyle gifted "one of the founding virtues of what we call modernity. This is the virtue that guarantees that the modest witness is the legitimate and authorized ventriloquist for the object world, adding nothing from his mere opinions, from his biasing embodiment." This "modest" style, significantly, was a luxury shared only by male scientists and their colleagues; "women," she asserts, "were invisible in both physical and epistemological senses" (*Modest_Witness@Second_Millennium. FemaleMan© _Meets_OncoMouse™: Feminism and Technoscience,* 2nd ed. [New York: Routledge, 2018], 24, 27).
79. François Villon's famous line from his fifteenth-century poem the *Ballade des Dames du Temps Jadis* ("Ballad of the ladies of times past"): "Mais où sont les neiges d'antan?"
80. Natalie S. Loveless, "The Materiality of Duration: Between Ice Time and Water Time," *Performance Research* 18, no. 6 (2013): 129–36.
81. Nicolás Monardes, *Ioyfull Newes out of the Newfound World* (London: William Norton, 1580), fols. 164r, 172v, 168v.
82. Monardes, fol. 166v.
83. Monardes, fol. 176v.

84. Monardes, fol. 168r.
85. Monardes, fol. 177r.
86. Monardes, fol. 177v.
87. Robert Barclay, *Argenis* (London: G. Purslowe, 1625), 348.
88. Monardes, *Ioyfull Newes,* fol. 180r.
89. Monardes, fol. 181r.
90. Richard James, "An Execration of Hott Water," in *The Poems, Etc., of Richard James, 1592–1638,* ed. Rev. Alexander B. Grosart (London: Chiswick, 1880), 223.
91. Gail Kern Paster, "Becoming the Landscape: The Ecology of the Passions in the Legend of Temperance," in *Environment and Embodiment in Early Modern England,* ed. Mary Floyd-Wilson and Garrett A. Sullivan Jr. (New York: Palgrave Macmillan, 2007), 137–52.
92. Robert Burton, *The Anatomy of Melancholy,* ed. Holbrook Jackson (New York: New York Review of Books, 2001), 239.
93. Floyd-Wilson and Sullivan Jr., "Introduction," 1–2.
94. Burton, *Anatomy of Melancholy,* 239.
95. See R. I. Page, *Lapland Sorcerers* (London: Viking Society for Northern Research, 1963).
96. Burton, *Anatomy of Melancholy,* 239.
97. Joseph Hall, *The Discovery of a New World* (London, 1609), 152.
98. Hall, 153.
99. Bacon, *Works,* 3:650.
100. Bacon, 3:649.
101. Bacon, *Sylua Syluarum,* 32.
102. Bacon, 32.
103. Bacon, 31.
104. Bacon, 1.
105. Robert Wittie, *Scarbrough Spaw* (London, 1660), sig. A4r. All quotations hereafter refer to this edition and will be cited in text.
106. For instance, note Willsford on "the generation of Waters": "There is undoubtedly a continual flux and reflux of waters, both upon the superficies of the *Earth,* and in the channels within it, as you may see by the veins in the bodies of men (a *Microcosmus* in it felt)" (*Natures Secrets,* 64).
107. Mary Floyd-Wilson, *English Ethnicity and Race in Early Modern Drama* (Cambridge: Cambridge University Press, 2003), 2.
108. Willsford, *Natures Secrets,* 143.
109. Floyd-Wilson, *English Ethnicity and Race,* 4.
110. John Peter, *A Philosophical Account of This Hard Frost* (London, 1684), 3, 6.
111. Peter, 6.
112. Peter, 9.
113. Peter, 6.
114. Peter, 9.
115. Levinus Lemnius, *The Secret Miracles of Nature* (London: Jo. Streater, 1658), 288.
116. Lemnius, 289.

117. Lemnius, 290.
118. Lemnius, 290.
119. Lemnius, 289.
120. A homage to Haraway's (2016) insightful phrase for engaging the ecological tensions of the present.
121. Serres, *Biogea,* trans. Randolph Burks (Minneapolis: Univocal, 2012), 175.
122. John Aubrey, *'Brief Lives,' Chiefly of Contemporaries, Set down by John Aubrey, between the Years 1669 and 1696,* ed. Andrew Clark, vol. 1 (Oxford: Clarendon, 1898), 75.
123. Aubrey, 1:75.
124. In Shachtman, *Absolute Zero,* 23.
125. In this vein I am not alone: in *Air Conditioning* (New York: Bloomsbury, 2024), Hsuan L. Hsu reminds us that "our embodied sense of comfort—along with all the ideas and values wrapped up with it—is not innate, but constructed through historical processes, marketing campaigns, and constant recalibration" (142–3). Similarly, Amber Godfrey's architectural projects accent "thermal justice": (koozarch.com/interviews/thermal-justice).
126. Marla Cone, *Silent Snow: The Slow Poisoning of the Arctic* (New York: Grove, 2005), 3.
127. Roy Porter, "Introduction," in *The Medical History of Waters and Spas,* ed. Roy Porter (London: Wellcome Institute for the History of Medicine, 1990), xii.
128. Sheila Watt-Cloutier, *The Right to Be Cold: One Woman's Fight to Protect the Arctic and Save the Planet from Climate Change* (Minneapolis: University of Minnesota Press, 2015), 247.

## Winterlude: *Err*

1. In *Henry Hudson the Navigator: The Original Documents in Which His Career is Recorded,* ed. G. M. Asher (London: Hakluyt Society, 1860), 83, 89.
2. See *The Oxford English Dictionary* [*OED*], s.v. *err* (v.), esp. sense I.1.
3. In Asher, *Henry Hudson the Navigator,* 187.
4. In *The Voyages of Captain Luke Foxe and Captain Thomas James in Search of a North-West Passage, in 1631–32,* ed. Miller Christy, 2 vols. (London: Hakluyt Society, 1894), 1:115.
5. In Edward Butts, *Henry Hudson: New World Voyager* (Toronto: Dundurn, 2009), 30–31.
6. I liken Hudson to Michel Serres' Ulysses: "The Odyssean path is an exodus rather than a method. An exodus in the sense that the path deviates from the path and the track goes off track." *The Five Senses: A Philosophy of Mingled Bodies,* trans. Margaret Sankey and Peter Cowley (New York: Continuum, 2008), 261.
7. Peter C. Mancall puts it plainly: "The historical question—What happened to Hudson?—is easy to ask and difficult to answer" (*Fatal Journey: The Final Expedition of Henry Hudson—A Tale of Mutiny and Murder in the Arctic* [New York: Basic, 2009], 238).

8. Roll up for a crystally tour! See Robert and Johanna Titus, *The Hudson Valley in the Ice Age* (Delmar, N.Y.: Black Dome, 2012).
9. Douglas Hunter follows the river in detail in *Half Moon: Henry Hudson and the Voyage That Redrew the Map of the New World* (New York: Bloomsbury, 2009).
10. Kimiko de Freytas-Tamura, "Snow No-Show in New York City Feels Nice—but Also a Little Unsettling," *New York Times*, January 31, 2023, nytimes.com/2023/01/29/nyregion/snow-nyc.html.
11. In Asher, *Henry Hudson the Navigator*, 12.
12. See *OED*, s.v. *neighbour* (n.); *neighbour* (adj.).
13. In Asher, *Henry Hudson the Navigator*, 91.
14. May Joseph and Sofia Varino, *Aquatopia: Climate Interventions* (New York: Routledge, 2023), 10, and chapter 3.
15. "Theme from *New York, New York*," famously sung by Frank Sinatra (sorry, Ol' Blue Eyes).
16. Corey Sandler's *Henry Hudson: Dreams and Obsession* (New York: Citadel, 2007) is a fitting example, especially "Part V: Deciphering the Hudson Code."

## 2. The North Portals

1. In Albert Hastings Markham, ed., *The Voyages and Works of John Davis, the Navigator* (London: Hakluyt Society, 1880), 5.
2. Samuel Purchas, *Hakluytus Posthumus, or Purchas His Pilgrimes*, vol. 14 (Glasgow: James MacLehose and Sons, 1906), 308.
3. Purchas, 14:321.
4. Olaus Magnus, *Description of the Northern Peoples*, trans. Peter Fisher and Humphrey Higgens, ed. Peter Foote, vol. 1 (London: Hakluyt Society, 1996–1998), 102.
5. In Markham, *The Voyages and Works of John Davis*, 6.
6. Markham, 3–4.
7. Markham, 3–4.
8. Thomas Nashe, *The Terrors of the Night* (London: John Danter, 1594), sig. D3r.
9. Thomas Heywood, *Gynaikeion* (London: Adam Islip, 1624), 417.
10. In Martin Conway, ed., *Early Dutch and English Voyages to Spitsbergen in the Seventeenth Century* (London: Hakluyt Society, 1904), 85.
11. Several writers at the time adumbrated an Arctic utopia: when a spring storm stranded the Venetian merchant Pietro Querini and his crew on the Norwegian island of Røst for three months in 1431, for example, he considered himself to be "in the first circle of Paradise." The French philosopher Guillaume Postel (1510–1581) likewise described a hyperborean heaven in his unpublished manuscript from 1561, *De Paradisi Territstri Loco* (On the location of the terrestrial paradise). And in his *Atland* (1679–1702), the Swedish scientist Olaus Rudbeck (1630–1702) set out to prove that Uppsala was, in fact, Atlantis (for all, see Alessandro Scafi, *Mapping Paradise: A History of Heaven on Earth* [Chicago: University of Chicago Press, 2006], 285).

12. Dithmar Blefkens (1563) described the "Pigmies" of Greenland (Samuel Purchas, *Pilgrimes,* vol. 13 [London, 1625], 513–14), Arngrim Jonas (1609) argued at length that "the first inhabitants of the Northerne World, were of the number of Giants" (13:537–8), while Sir Dudley Digges banished both altogether: "It hath euer been, the Custome of Describers of the World in remote partes, to set downe Land or Sea out of their owne imagination, with Giants, Pigmies, Monsters, and miraculous reportes of fabulous Authors." (*Fata Mihi Totum Mea Sunt Agitanda per Orbem* [London: W. White, 1611], 2). Magnus's multivolume encyclopedia, of course, also ensured the survival of such strange sea tales (1:104–6, and 3:979–80). Cf. Hieronymus Megiser's (1554–1618/19) illustration in *Septentrio Novantiquus: Oder die Newe Nortwelt* (Leipzig: Henning Grossen des Jüngern, 1613), 174–76.
13. See "The booke made by the right worshipful M. Robert Thorne in the yeere 1527": "But it is a generall opinion of all Cosmographers, that passing the seventh clime, the sea is all ice, and the colde so much that none can suffer it. And hitherto they had all the like opinion, that under the line Equinoctiall for much heate the land was unhabitable. Yet since (by experience is proved) no land so much habitable nor more temperate. And to conclude, I thinke the same should be found under the North, if it were experimented" (in Richard Hakluyt, *Principal Navigations,* vol. 2 [Glasgow: MacLehose and Sons, 1903], 178).
14. Jen Hill, *White Horizon: The Arctic in the Nineteenth-Century British Imagination* (Albany: State University of New York Press, 2008), 1–28.
15. Brian Harley, "Silences and Secrecy: The Hidden Agenda of Cartography in Early Modern Europe," *Imago Mundi,* 40 (1988): 57–76.
16. In Adam White, ed., *A Collection of Documents on Spitzbergen and Greenland* (London: Hakluyt Society, 1855), 238.
17. White, 238.
18. White, 186. The entire lines are "*quam circum extremae dextra laevaque trahuntur / caeruleae, glacie concretae atque imbribus atris*" ("Round this, at the world's ends, two [zones] stretch darkling to right and left, set fast in ice and black storms"; in Virgil, *Eclogues; Georgics; Aeneid Books 1–6,* trans. H. Rushton Fairclough [Cambridge, Mass.: Harvard University Press, 1999], 114–15).
19. In White, *Collection of Documents,* 236.
20. White, 236.
21. Virgil, *Eclogues; Georgics; Aeneid Books 1–6,* 452–53.
22. For more on the north's "infernal geography," see Kristen Poole, *Supernatural Environments in Shakespeare's England* (Cambridge: Cambridge University Press, 2011), 95–135.
23. In White, *Collection of Documents,* 236.
24. White, 37.
25. White, 37.
26. White, 35.
27. Donna J. Haraway, *When Species Meet* (Minneapolis: University of Minnesota Press, 2008), 15–19.
28. In White, *Collection of Documents,* 37.

29. All quotations from Shakespeare refer to *The Norton Shakespeare,* ed. Stephen Greenblatt et al., 3rd ed. (New York: Norton, 2016), and are cited by act, scene, and line(s).
30. Rupert Goold's "Arctic" production for the Royal Shakespeare Company (2006) is a well-known departure; see Randall Martin's *Shakespeare and Ecology* (Oxford: Oxford University Press, 2015), 167–71.
31. Giovanni Botero, *Relations of the Most Famous Kingdoms* (London: William Iaggard, 1608), sig. E1r.
32. Sarah Stacke, "See the Amazing, Ethereal Creatures Living Under Arctic Ice," *National Geographic Online,* 12 September 12, 2018, nationalgeographic.com /animals/2018/09/white-sea-arctic-underwater-marine-life.
33. Stacy Alaimo, *Exposed: Environmental Politics and Pleasures in Posthuman Times* (Minneapolis: University of Minnesota Press, 2016), 167; see also "Violet-Black" in *Prismatic Ecology: Ecotheory beyond Green,* ed. Jeffrey Jerome Cohen (Minneapolis: University of Minnesota Press, 2013), 233–51.
34. Patricia Yaeger, "Sea Trash, Dark Pools, and the Tragedy of the Commons," *PMLA* 125, no. 3 (2010): 523–45.
35. Timothy Morton, *The Ecological Thought* (Cambridge, Mass.: Harvard University Press, 2012), 40.
36. Morton, 48.
37. The key phrase here is "more so": narratives of John Narborough's (1640–1688) and Abel Janszoon Tasman's (1603[?]–1659) travels to the "Streights of Magellan, the South Seas, the Vast Tracts of Land beyond Hollandia Nova" may be read in Anonymous, *An Account of Several Late Voyages and Discoveries to the South and North* (London, 1694). Amerigo Vespucci (1454–1512) believed the Antarctic region to be "an earthlye Paradyse"; see Edward Arber, ed., *The First Three English Books on America* (Westminster: Archibald Constable, 1895), 278. And Francis Drake's 1577–1580 circumnavigational voyage neared the southern continent (hence the "Passage" named after him between Cape Horn and Antarctica). Perhaps I will venture south for the next project.
38. Chris Barrett, *Early Modern English Literature and the Poetics of Cartographic Anxiety* (Oxford: Oxford University Press, 2018), 1.
39. Gretel Ehrlich, *This Cold Heaven* (New York: Pantheon, 2001), 157.
40. Joanna Radin and Emma Kowal, eds., "Introduction: The Politics of Low Temperature," in *Cryopolitics: Frozen Life in a Melting World* (Cambridge. Mass.: MIT Press, 2017), 10. The editors' "invocation of 'politics' refers more to the tactics and practices that organize and animate science and technology than," as mine does, "to formal treaties or doctrines that are often the starting point for inquiries into power" (6).
41. Thomas Browne, *Pseudodoxia Epidemica* (London: Thomas Harper, 1646), 62.
42. See Marla Cone, *Silent Snow: The Slow Poisoning of the Arctic* (New York: Grove, 2005), throughout.
43. Bruno Latour, *Down to Earth: Politics in the New Climatic Regime,* trans. Catherine Porter (Cambridge: Polity, 2018), 34–35.
44. Latour, 2.

45. In Arber, *First Three English Books on America,* 295.
46. Arber, 298.
47. Sebastian Münster, *The Description of Swedland, Gotland, and Finland* (London: Iohn Awdely, 1581), sig. A2v.
48. His closest analogue would be the anonymous mid-fourteenth-century *Book of John Mandeville.* For more on the premodern "tradition of *mirabilia,*" "northern marvels," and the Scandinavian supernatural, see Magnus, *Description,* 1:xxxvii–xxxix, xliii–xlv.
49. Magnus, 1:50–51.
50. Magnus, 1:50.
51. Magnus, 1:8.
52. Magnus, 1:126.
53. Magnus, 1:51.
54. Magnus, 1:62; see also 3:1050 ("On a Remarkable Incident on This Frozen Lake").
55. Michael Punke's *The Revenant: A Novel of Revenge* (New York: Picador, 2002) and the subsequent film (dir. Alejandro González Iñárritu, 2015) testify to this lasting combination.
56. Magnus, *Description,* 3:980; see also 3:985–96 ("On Birds Concealed Beneath the Snow").
57. Magnus, 3:980.
58. Robert Burton, *The Anatomy of Melancholy,* ed. Holbrook Jackson (New York: New York Review of Books, 2001), 38.
59. See Astrida Neimanis, *Bodies of Water: Posthuman Feminist Phenomenology* (New York: Bloomsbury, 2017), 97: "Amniotics asserts an aqueous logic that is at once *of, in,* and *between,* while at the same time requiring a force of *becoming.*"
60. Magnus, *Description,* 1:95–96.
61. See Shane McCorristine, *The Spectral Arctic: A History of Dreams and Ghosts in Polar Exploration* (London: UCL Press, 2018), 43: "Ghosts and ghostliness are strangely absent from historical scholarship on the Northwest Passage."
62. Katherine Behar, "Facing Necrophilia, or 'Botox Ethics,'" in *Object Oriented Feminism,* ed. Katherine Behar (Minneapolis: University of Minnesota Press, 2016), 126. See also "Renaissance Posthumanism" ed. Karen Raber and Steven Swarbrick, special issue, *Criticism* 62, no. 3 (2020).
63. Magnus, *Description,* 2:409.
64. Magnus, 2:521–81.
65. Magnus, 1:111; see also 2:563.
66. Magnus, 2:561–62.
67. Magnus, 2:554–55; the editor claims this is misquoted: "In *Spec. his.,* XXVII 127, Vincent connects mortality and hard frost but not in the way suggested by OM; the phrase, 'Nor is it wonderful', does not occur there either. OM's notes were perhaps confused" (2:579).
68. Radin and Kowal, "Introduction," 6.
69. Radin and Kowal, 8.

70. See Fred Schepisi, dir., *Iceman* (1984), *Northern Exposure,* season 3, episode 6 (1991), and Les Mayfield, dir., *Encino Man* (1992).
71. Serpil Oppermann, "Compost": "*To compost* means . . . being part of things that are dead but are in a way undead" (in *Veer Ecology: A Companion for Environmental Thinking,* ed. Jeffrey Jerome Cohen and Lowell Duckert [Minneapolis: University of Minnesota Press, 2017], 136).
72. See *Oxford English Dictionary* [*OED*], s.v. *climate,* (n.1), 1.a.
73. In Richard Henry Major, ed., *The Historie of Travaile into Virginia Britannia* (London: Hakluyt Society, 1849), 179.
74. Robert Boyle, *New Experiments and Observations Touching Cold,* in *The Works of Robert Boyle,* ed. Michael Hunter and Edward B. Davis, vol. 4 (London: Routledge, 1999), 391.
75. René Descartes, *Discourse on Method, Optics, Geometry, and Meteorology,* trans. Paul J. Olscamp (Indianapolis, Ind.: Hackett, 2001), 292.
76. Michael Bravo, *North Pole* (London: Reaktion, 2019), 84–85, 76, 133.
77. A point that cannot be overstated. On "a culture of opposition," see Kenneth Coates, "The Discovery of the North: Towards a Conceptual Framework for the Study of Northern/Remote Regions," *The Northern Review,* 12–13 (1993–1994): 15–43. Peter Stadius argues that "it is . . . the Enlightenment which creates the general pattern of a North-South dichotomy for contemporaneous Europe" in "Southern Perspectives on the North: From Legends and Images to Models and Stereotypes," in *Working Papers of the Baltic Sea Area Studies: Northern Dimension of Europe,* ed. B. Henningsen (Berlin: BaltSeaNet, 2001), 1–27. Peter Fjågesund studies "two . . . frequently overlapping binary pairs, namely that of high versus low culture and that of centre versus periphery" (*The Dream of the North: A Cultural History to 1920* [Amsterdam: Rodopi, 2014], 22).
78. Ursula K. Heise, "Environmentalism, Eco-Cosmopolitanism, and Premodern Thought," in *Premodern Ecologies in the Modern Literary Imagination,* ed. Vin Nardizzi and Tiffany Jo Werth (Toronto: University of Toronto Press, 2019), 285.
79. Raphael Thorius, *Cheimonopegnion, Or, A Winter Song* (London: printed by T. N. for Humphrey Moseley, 1651), 1.
80. Thorius, 2.
81. Thorius, 6.
82. Thorius, 7.
83. Stefan Rahmstorf, in Jon Gertner, *The Ice at the End of the World: An Epic Journey into Greenland's Buried Past and Our Perilous Future* (New York: Random House, 2019), xxii.
84. Dolly Jørgensen and Sverker Sörlin, eds., *Northscapes: History, Technology, and the Making of Northern Environments* (Vancouver: University of British Columbia Press, 2013).
85. Nicola Twilley, "The Coldscape," *Cabinet* 47 (2012), cabinetmagazine.org/issues/47/twilley.php.
86. An unattributed and widely used adage: for example, "Through the Eyes of Satellites, Scientists See Changing Arctic," *National Oceanic and Atmospheric*

*Administration,* April 30, 2015, nesdis.noaa.gov/content/through-eyes-satellites-scientists-see-changing-arctic.

87. Rebecca Totaro, *Meteorology and Physiology in Early Modern Culture: Earthquakes, Human Identity, and Textual Representation* (New York: Routledge, 2018), 2.
88. In Todd Borlik, *Literature and Nature in the English Renaissance: An Ecocritical Anthology* (Cambridge: Cambridge University Press, 2019), 529; also view *The Worldes Hydrographical Discription* (1595), in Markham, *Voyages and Works of John Davis,* 218.
89. Borlik, 529.
90. Borlik, 528; for broader, see 497–530 ("Part VI: Disaster and Resilience in the Little Ice Age").
91. Donna J. Haraway, "Situated Knowledges: The Science Question in Feminism and the Privilege of Partial Perspective," *Feminist Studies* 14, no. 3 (1998): 575–99.
92. Compare Mary Thomas Crane, "Meteorology, Embodiment, and Environment in Shakespeare's *A Midsummer Night's Dream*" in *Geographies of Embodiment in Early Modern England,* ed. Mary Floyd-Wilson and Garrett A. Sullivan Jr. (Oxford: Oxford University Press, 2020), 134–51; Sarah Crover, "Distemperature in *A Midsummer Night's Dream*" in Nardizzi and Werth, *Premodern Ecologies,* 106–20; and Lowell Duckert, "The Climate of Shakespeare: Four (or More) Forecasts," in *Climate and Literature,* ed. Adeline Johns-Putra (Cambridge: Cambridge University Press, 2019), 92–107.
93. See *OED,* s.v. *climate* (n.1), 1.c. and 2.a.
94. John Taylor, *The Cold Tearme, Or, the Frozen Age, Or, the Metamorphosis of the Riuer of Thames* (London, 1621).
95. In Borlik, *Literature and Nature,* 527.
96. Graham Huggan, "From Arctic Dreams to Nightmares (and Back Again): Apocalyptic Thought and Planetary Consciousness in Three Contemporary American Environmentalist Texts," *ISLE* 23, no. 1 (2016): 77.
97. See James S. Romm, "Ultima Thule and Beyond," in *The Edges of the Earth in Ancient Thought: Geography, Exploration, and Fiction* (Princeton, N.J.: Princeton University Press, 1992), 121–71.
98. Dolly Jørgensen and Sverker Sörlin, "Making the Action Visible: Making Environments in Northern Landscapes," in Jørgensen and Sörlin, *Northscapes,* 1–14.
99. Bathsheba Demuth, *Floating Coast: An Environmental History of the Bering Strait* (New York: Norton, 2019), 4.
100. See William E. Glassley, *A Wilder Time: Notes from a Geologist at the Edge of the Greenland Ice* (New York: Bellevue Literary Press, 2018).
101. Lola Sheppard and Mason White, eds., *Many Norths: Spatial Practice in a Polar Territory* (New York: Actar, 2017); see also *What Is North? Imagining the North from Ancient Times to the Present Day,* ed. Oisín Plumb, Alexandra Sanmark, and Donna Heddle (Turnhout, Belgium: Brepols, 2020).
102. In the original: "*Pygmei hic habitant 4 ad summum pedes longi, quem admodum illi quos in Gronlandia Screlinger vocant . . . Haec insula optima est et saluberrimus*

*totius septentri-onis . . . Oceanus 19 ostiis inter has insulas irrumperat. 4 euripos facit quibus indesinenter sub septentrionem fertur: atque ibi in viscera terrae absorbetur.*"

103. E. G. R. Taylor, "A Letter Dated 1577 from Mercator to John Dee," *Imago Mundi* 13 (1956): 60.
104. Taylor, 64.
105. Lucas Jacobsen Debes later proposed magnetism as the cause of the cold in *Færoæ and Færoa Reserata* (London: F.L., 1676), 52.
106. The other famous vortex, of course, was *the* "maelstrom"—from the Dutch *maalen* ("grind, whirl") and *stroom* ("stream")—a mythical whirlpool in northwestern Norway (and a real channel in the Lofoten Islands). Jenkinson mentions the "Malestrand" (Purchas, *Pilgrimes,* 2:415), as does Jacob Aertsz Colom in *The Fierre Sea-Columne* (Amsterdam: 1640), 27.
107. Michel Serres with Bruno Latour, *Conversations on Science, Culture, and Time,* trans. Roxanne Lapidus (Ann Arbor: University of Michigan Press, 1995), 58.
108. Serres, 105.
109. James Shirley, *The Brothers* (London, 1652), 22.
110. "He compares it to a small fire, which is but lighted, and then immediately extinguished" In *Henry Hudson the Navigator: The Original Documents in Which His Career is Recorded,* ed. G. M. Asher (London: Hakluyt Society, 1860), 246–47.
111. Although he faced skepticism during his own time as well: "Sure I am, Gerardus Mercator hath so graced the fancy of this Frier [Nicholas of Lynne], that he made his description of the Countries about the Artick Pole, conformable to this his imaginary discovery, preferring to fill that his Map with a Fiction, then otherwise to leave it altogether empty" (Thomas Fuller, *The History of the Worthies of England* [London: J.G.W.L., 1662], 254–55).
112. Andrea di Robilant, *Irresistible North: From Venice to Greenland on the Trail of the Zen Brothers* (New York: Alfred A. Knopf, 2011), 6, 193.
113. Robert McGhee, *The Last Imaginary Place: A Human History of the Arctic World* (Chicago: University of Chicago Press, 2005). His title, one might object, contributes to the dualist model that configures the Arctic as "a world apart," one that "is not so much a region as a dream: the dream of a unique, unattainable and compellingly attractive world. It is the last imaginary place" (10). He continues: "To most southerners, the Arctic remains what it was to their counterparts centuries and perhaps even millennia ago: the ultimate otherworld" (19). It is precisely this dichotomous logic I am arguing against; to be fair, at the end of his "journey" his (and his readers') views on otherness have been altered: "For the first time we have been given a view of the Arctic as a normal part of the world, a beloved homeland rather than a frightening alien environment. The Arctic is no longer an imaginary place where anything strange and terrible might happen" (273). I raise this point to show just how persistent, even in its deconstruction, the transhistorical trope of the unearthly Arctic has been.
114. Richard Henry Major, ed., *Voyages of the Venetian Brothers, Nicolo and Antonio Zeno* (London: Hakluyt Society, 1873), cii.
115. Major, cii.

116. Derek Hayes, *Historical Atlas of the Arctic* (Seattle: University of Washington Press, 2003), 183.
117. John Gillis, *Islands of the Mind: How the Human Imagination Created the Atlantic World* (New York: Palgrave Macmillan, 2004), 1, 4.
118. Adriana Craciun, *Writing Arctic Disaster: Authorship and Exploration* (Cambridge: Cambridge University Press, 2016), 18–19.
119. Craciun, 18.
120. Latour, *Down to Earth,* 25.
121. John Moss, *Enduring Dreams: An Exploration of Arctic Landscape* (Toronto: Anansi, 1994), 105.
122. Craciun, *Writing Arctic Disaster,* 204, 21, 31.
123. Craciun, 208.
124. Robert J. Mayhew, "Cosmographers, Explorers, Cartographers, Chorographers: Defining, Inscribing and Practicing Early Modern Geography, c. 1450–1850," in *The Wiley Blackwell Companion to Human Geography,* ed. John A. Agnew and James S. Duncan (Chichester, UK: John Wiley & Sons, 2011), 30.
125. Siobhan Carroll, *An Empire of Air and Water: Uncolonizable Space in the British Imagination, 1750–1850* (Philadelphia: University of Pennsylvania Press, 2015).
126. Carroll, 6. While Carroll's focus is the long Romantic period, I share her predilection for "portraying the poles as spaces frequently conflated with the imagination" (14) in a proto-imperialist and settler-colonialist context. The earlier maps suggest that "these spaces were . . . perceived as challenging imperial ambitions by virtue of their intrinsic resistance to cultivation and settlement, and, thus, to territorial appropriation and state control" (6).
127. Purchas, *Pilgrimes,* 14:411, 413.
128. Digges, *Fata,* 9.
129. Purchas, *Pilgrimes,* 14:424.
130. Anonymous, *Account of Several Late Voyages,* 206.
131. Purchas, *Pilgrimes,* 14:107.
132. A neologism inspired by Philip Hayward's "aquapelago"; see "Aquapelagos and Aquapelagic Assemblages: Towards an Integrated Study of Island Societies and Marine Environments," *Shima* 6, no. 1 (2012): 1–11. Nashe, for instance, expresses an arcticpelagic mindset when describing Iceland: "whole Ilands they haue of yce, on which they build and t[r]affique as on the maine land" (*Terrors,* sig. D2v).
133. Pierre Berton, *The Arctic Grail: The Quest for the North West Passage and the North Pole, 1818–1909* (New York: Viking, 1988), throughout.
134. For more on what I mean by this, see 125–29 in my *For All Waters: Finding Ourselves in Early Modern Wetscapes* (Minneapolis: University of Minnesota Press, 2017).
135. These examples are cited in Anonymous, *Account of Several Late Voyages,* 147–48, 182.
136. Purchas, *Pilgrimes,* 14:414.

137. Purchas, 14:415–19.
138. In Arber, *First Three English Books*, 347.
139. Arber, 347.
140. Arber, 286.
141. Humphrey Gilbert, *The Voyages and Colonising Enterprises of Sir Humphrey Gilbert*, vol. 1 (London: Hakluyt Society, 1940), 154.
142. In Miller Christy, ed., *The Voyages of Captain Luke Foxe and Captain Thomas James in Search of a North-West Passage, in 1631–32*, 2 vols. (London: Hakluyt Society, 1894), 2:648.
143. Christy, 2:641.
144. In James A. Williamson, *The Cabot Voyages and Bristol Discovery under Henry VII* (Cambridge: Hakluyt Society, 1962), 229.
145. Jace Weaver, *The Red Atlantic: American Indigenes and the Making of the Modern World, 1000–1927* (Chapel Hill: North Carolina University Press, 2014).
146. One may book a trip to see Greenland's "virgin lands" (*terres vierges*) with Exploris Expeditions and Cruises, exploris.co/fr_FR/taxons/le-groenland.
147. For much more on the history of what follows, see William C. Sturtevant and David B. Quinn, "This New Prey: Eskimos in Europe in 1567, 1576, and 1577," in *Indians and Europe: An Interdisciplinary Collection of Essays*, ed. Christian F. Feest (Lincoln: University of Nebraska Press, 1999), 61–140.
148. In C. C. A. Gosch, ed., *Danish Arctic Expeditions, 1605 to 1620*, vol. 1 (London: Hakluyt Society, 1897), 48.
149. Gosch, 1:70–71.
150. Gosch, 1:70n5.
151. Gosch, 1:111n4.
152. Magnus, *Description*, 1:102.
153. Gosch, *Danish Arctic Expeditions*, xci.
154. In Williamson, *Cabot Voyages*, 220.
155. In Gosch, *Danish Arctic Expeditions*, 2:14.
156. In Martin Conway, *No Man's Land: A History of Spitsbergen from Its Discovery in 1596 to the Beginning of the Scientific Exploration of the Country* (Cambridge: Cambridge University Press, 1906), 104.
157. Gosch, *Danish Arctic Expeditions*, 1:xciii.
158. See H. H. Lamb, *Climate, History and the Modern World*, 2nd ed. (New York: Routledge, 1995), 219; and Dale Idiens, "Eskimos in Scotland, ca. 1682–1924," in Feest, *Indians and Europe*, 161–74.
159. In Robert McGhee, *The Arctic Voyages of Martin Frobisher: An Elizabethan Adventure* (Seattle: University of Washington Press, 2001), 84–85.
160. McGhee, 85.
161. Gosch, *Danish Arctic Expeditions*, 1:xci.
162. Gosch, 1:xcii.
163. In White, *Collection of Documents*, 224.
164. In Gosch, *Danish Arctic Expeditions*, 1:xcii.

165. Gosch, 1:xcii.
166. Gosch, 1:xcii.
167. Gosch, 1:xciii.
168. In White, *Collection of Documents,* 223.
169. White, 225.
170. White, 225.
171. White, 225.
172. White, 225.
173. White, 225.
174. White, 225.
175. White, 226.
176. White, 226.
177. White, 226. That this answer could baffle the Inuit man's interceptors hits on the Eurocentricity of northern exploration I have been probing. Inuit mapmaking and pathfinding have consistently astounded their technoscientific "superiors" (Bravo, *North Pole,* 20–29). Disputing the idea of the Arctic as "otherwordly" and detached from reality, similarly, should not discount Indigenous cosmologies that account for a multiverse of meta/physical planes.
178. In White, *Collection of Documents,* 225.
179. Coll Thrush, *Indigenous London: Native Travelers at the Heart of Empire* (New Haven, Conn.: Yale University Press, 2016), 6.
180. Thrush, 13.
181. Thrush, 23.
182. Thrush, 256.
183. Follow the Inuit Ataqatigiit party in the news: Associated Press, "Greenland's Leftwing Anti-Mine Party Wins Snap Election," *The Guardian,* April 7, 2021, theguardian.com/world/2021/apr/07/greenlands-left-wing-anti-mine-party-wins-snap-election.
184. E. C. H. Keskitalo, *Negotiating the Arctic: The Construction of an International Region* (New York: Routledge, 2003).
185. See Sheila Watt-Cloutier, *The Right to Be Cold: One Woman's Fight to Protect the Arctic and Save the Planet from Climate Change* (Minneapolis: University of Minnesota Press, 2015), xiv: "As the heat (caused, we must never forget, by a series of choices in the rich and settled world) wipes away the ice, so too it is wiping away much of the remarkable civilization of the north" (Watt-Cloutier, *Right,* xiv).
186. Watt-Cloutier, xxi–ii.
187. Watt-Cloutier, 231.
188. Watt-Cloutier, xxi.
189. Watt-Cloutier, 231.
190. Craciun, *Writing Arctic Disaster,* 223.
191. In Christy, *Voyages,* 1:7–8.
192. Anonymous, *A Mirour for Magistrates* (London: Felix Kyngston, 1610), 555.
193. Anonymous, 556.

194. Anonymous, 556.
195. Anonymous, 556.
196. Anonymous, 557.
197. James Howell, *A Winter Dreame* (London, 1648), 1.
198. Howell, 1.
199. Howell, 10.
200. Howell, 16.
201. Howell, 13.
202. Howell, 13.
203. Howell, 17.
204. Howell, 18.
205. Howell, 18.
206. Howell, 10.
207. Howell, 20.
208. For me, a phrase most informed by Toni Morrison's *Playing in the Dark: Whiteness and the Literary Imagination* (Cambridge, Mass.: Harvard University Press, 1992).
209. Craciun, *Writing Arctic Disaster*, 228, 232.
210. For comparison, see Birgitta Evengård, Øyvind Paasche, and Joan Nymand Larsen, "Paths to the New Arctic"; and Heidi Hansson, "Arctopias: The Arctic as No Place and New Place in Fiction" in *The New Arctic*, ed. Birgitta Evengård, Joan Larsen, and Øyvind Paasche (Cham, Switzerland: Springer, 2015), 1–6, 69–77.

## Winterlude: *Ask*

1. All quotations from Shakespeare refer to *The Norton Shakespeare*, ed. Stephen Greenblatt et al., 3rd ed. (New York: Norton, 2016) and are cited by act, scene, and line.
2. From the quarto version (1608); curiously, the folio version (1623) omits "cold."
3. "Edgar I nothing am" (2.3.21).
4. From the Latin verb *confundere* ("mingle together").
5. Simon Palfrey, *Poor Tom: Living "King Lear"* (Chicago: University of Chicago Press, 2014), 13.
6. Palfrey, 71. One of Tom's polyphonous voices is "the brief refrains in which [he] returns to creaturely embodiment."
7. See Laurie Shannon, *The Accommodated Animal: Cosmopolity in Shakespearean Locales* (Chicago: University of Chicago Press, 2013).
8. Palfrey, *Poor Tom*, 83.
9. Randall Jarrell, "90 North," in *The Complete Poems* (New York: Farrar, Straus, and Giroux, 1969), 113–14.
10. See Palfrey, *Poor Tom*, 21: "Repeatedly the part recalls a non- or posthumanist form of living: not machinic, because there is mind and suffering in it, but not returnable to or resolvable in any recognizably humanist contract."

## 3. Slippery Things

1. Reproduced in full in H. H. Lamb, *Weather, Climate, and Human Affairs: A Book of Essays and Other Papers* (London: Routledge, 1988), 112.
2. Lamb, 112.
3. Lamb, 112.
4. Lamb, 112.
5. Lamb, 112.
6. Lamb, 112.
7. Lamb, 112.
8. René Descartes, *Discourse on Method, Optics, Geometry, and Meteorology,* trans. Paul J. Olscamp (Indianapolis, Ind.: Hackett, 2001), 292.
9. John Taylor, *The Cold Tearme, Or, the Frozen Age, Or, the Metamorphosis of the Riuer of Thames* (London, 1621).
10. Rudolf Brázdil, Christian Pfister, Heinz Wanner, Hans von Storch, and Jürg Luterbacher, "Historical Climatology in Europe—The State of the Art," *Climatic Change* 70 (2005): 410.
11. Sverker Sörlin, "Cryo-History: Narratives of Ice and the Emerging Arctic Humanities," in *The New Arctic,* ed. Birgitta Evengård, Joan Larsen, and Øyvind Paasche (Cham, Switzerland: Springer, 2015), throughout.
12. On the first, see Christian Pfister, "Weeping in the Snow: The Second Period of Little Ice Age-type Impacts, 1570–1630," in *Cultural Consequences of the "Little Ice Age,"* ed. Wolfgang Behringer, Hartmut Lehmann, and Christian Pfister (Göttingen: Vandenhoeck and Ruprecht, 2005), 34: "A history of climate should focus on building bridges between micro-weather histories based on record sources and the macro-reconstructions of climatic change." On the rest, see Dagomar Degroot, *The Frigid Golden Age: Climate Change, the Little Ice Age, and the Dutch Republic, 1560–1720* (Cambridge: Cambridge University Press, 2018), 16: "Climate changes led to weather that limited or expanded the choices open to people, but did not determine their actions."
13. I have found Geoffrey Parker's concise outline in *Global Crisis: War, Climate Change and Catastrophe in the Seventeenth Century* (New Haven, Conn.: Yale University Press, 2013), xvi–xvii, helpful for identifying source materials, while, at the same time, I see the line between human and natural less clearly than he. See also Phillip Blom, *Nature's Mutiny: How the Little Ice Age Transformed the West and Shaped the Present* (New York: Liveright, 2019).
14. See Wolfgang Behringer, *A Cultural History of Climate,* trans. Patric Camiller (Cambridge: Polity, 2016), 146–67.
15. Sam White, "The Real Little Ice Age," *Journal of Interdisciplinary History* 44, no. 3 (2014): 345.
16. Robert Boyle, *New Experiments and Observations Touching Cold,* in *The Works of Robert Boyle,* ed. Michael Hunter and Edward B. Davis, vol. 4 (London: Routledge, 1999), 568.
17. Boyle, 4:569.

18. Brian Fagan, *The Little Ice Age: How Climate Made History 1300–1850* (New York: Basic, 2000), 48, xv.
19. Fagan, xiii.
20. Jeffrey J. Cohen and Julian Yates, *Noah's Arkive* (Minneapolis: University of Minnesota Press, 2023), 284.
21. The possibility of economic boon is an important "lesso[n] from ice and gold," Degroot argues, for it asks us to consider "how individuals and communities could endure, adapt to, and exploit changes in the natural world" (*Frigid Golden Age*, 8). See also Sam White's *A Cold Welcome: The Little Ice Age and Europe's Encounter with North America* (Cambridge, Mass.: Harvard University Press, 2017), 250: "The Little Ice Age did not end in 1610. Nor did the challenge of adapting to the climate and environment of North America."
22. White, 6.
23. John Evelyn, *The Diary of John Evelyn*, ed. E. S. de Beer, vol. 3 (Oxford: Clarendon, 1955). 211.
24. L. W., *Strange and True News from Lincoln-shire, Huntinton-shire, Bedford-shire, Northampton-shire, Suffolk, and Norfolk with Wiltshire, and Sommerset shire, and Many Other Places* (London, 1674), 4.
25. L. W., 4.
26. Giovanni Domenico Cassini, *Prognostication Concerning the Frost* (London: 1697), 2.
27. I take up the question of over/wintering and of ontology later; in this chapter, I address the coldly collaborative force of an *in*coming winter and the body politic of London.
28. John Peter, *A Philosophical Account of This Hard Frost* (London, 1684), 9.
29. The "paradice" I paint in this chapter is inspired by Rebecca Solnit's *A Paradise Built in Hell: The Extraordinary Communities that Arise in Disaster* (New York: Penguin, 2009), especially "Falling Together."
30. Gordon Manley, "1684: The Coldest Winter in the English Instrumental Record," *Weather* 66, no. 5 (2011): 133–36.
31. I can provide only a short bibliography here; it is needless to say that the "fairs" have, for centuries, gripped the imagination. In chronological order: G. Davis, *Frostiana: or A History of the River Thames in a Frozen State* (London: G. Davis, 1814) ["As an additional object of curiosity, it may be proper to mention, that a large impression of the Title page of this work, was actually printed on the Ice on the River Thames."]; Edward F. Rimbault, *Old Ballads Illustrating the Great Frost of 1683–4* (London: T. Richards, 1844); William Andrews, *Famous Frosts and Frost Fairs* (London: G. Redway, 1887); Edward Walford, *Frost Fairs on the Thames* (London: C.W.H. Wyman, 1887); Ian Currie, *Frosts, Freezes, and Fairs: Chronicles of the Frozen Thames and Harsh Winters in Britain Since 1000 AD* (Coulsdon, Surrey: Frosted Earth, 1996); Nicholas Reed, *Frost Fairs on the Frozen Thames* (London: Lilburne, 2002); and Helen Humphreys, *The Frozen Thames* (Toronto: McClelland & Stewart, 2007).
32. Evelyn, *Diary*, 4:362.

33. Fagan, *Little Ice Age*, 59.
34. Quaternary scientist Simon L. Lewis and climatologist Mark A. Maslin have proposed that the murder of North American Indigenous peoples ca. 1610—the "Orbis Spike"—initiated a cooling trend, as carbon-sequestering trees were unintentionally left to thrive. See *The Human Planet: How We Created the Anthropocene* (New Haven, Conn.: Yale University Press, 2018).
35. The titular character of Virginia Woolf's novel *Orlando: A Biography* (New York: Harcourt, 1928) watches the "riot and confusion" of "fantastically twisted" icebergs and their wailing inhabitants being swept out to sea at Wapping, an eastern borough of London (62).
36. John Stow, *The Abridgement of the English Chronicle* (London: Edward Allde and Nicholas Okes, 1618), 48.
37. Stow, 103.
38. Stow, 287.
39. Stow, 288.
40. Stow, 329.
41. Stow, 328.
42. Stow, 495–96.
43. See Stow, 544: "By meanes whereof much cattell perished as Calues and Lambes, Déere and Coneys &c. by reason the earth lay long couered with déepe snow, to the great hurt of all manner of cattell, and many were forced to vse new deuices to fadder, this snow brought extreame daunger to all Trauaillers, after this snow thawed there followed Inundations, great and violent which did great spoiles and dammages."
44. Nathaniel Butter, *The Affaires and Generall Businesse of Europe* (London, 1624), 10.
45. Butter, 17.
46. Anonymous, *A True and Perfect Narrative of the Great and Dreadful Damages Susteyned in Several Parts of England, by the Late Extraordinary Snows* (London, 1674), 7.
47. L. W., *Strange and True News*, 8.
48. *A Letter Sent by F.A. Touchyng the Proceedings in a Priuate Quarell and Vnkindnesse betweene Arthur Hall, and Melchisedech Mallerie Gentleman, to His Very Friende L.B. Being in Italie* (London, H. Bynneman, 1576), sig. Fiiv.
49. Anonymous, *True and Perfect Narrative*, 4.
50. Anonymous, 5.
51. Anonymous, 7, 8.
52. Anonymous, *Sad News from Salisbury* (London, 1685).
53. Anonymous.
54. Anonymous, *A True Relation of a Great Number of People Frozen to Death near Salisbury and in Several Other Parts of the West of England* (London: George Larkin, 1685), 2.
55. See *The Oxford English Dictionary* [*OED*], s.v. *starve* (v.), I.1, II.5.a, and I.4.a.
56. See *OED*, s.v. *starve* (v.), III.8.a.
57. Anonymous, *True Relation*, 1.

58. Richard Kirby, *Diurnal Speculum* (London: John Bringhurst, 1684), sig. A1r., 36–37.
59. Kirby, sig. A1r.
60. William Lilly, *Mr. Lilly's New Prophecy* (London, 1678), 4–5.
61. Icedore Frostiface, *An Account of All the Principal Frosts for above an Hundred Years Past* (London: C. Corbett, 1740), sig. B1r.
62. Frostiface, sig. B2r.
63. John Worlidge, *Systema Agriculturae* (London, T. Johnson, 1669), 247.
64. John Flamsteed, *Flemstadts Most Strange and Wonderful Prophecy* (London, 1695), 1.
65. Flamsteed, 4.
66. Flamsteed, 4.
67. Flamsteed, 3.
68. Flamsteed, 5.
69. Flamsteed, 5. Cassini is similarly optimistic: "No sooner shall the Thaw come, but (as an old Witch, a Relation of mine has it) and the Earth become more Beautiful and Productive than ever" (*Prognostication,* 2).
70. Anonymous, *True Account of the Late Extraordinary Frost and Snow and the Great Damages Thereby Sustained in Divers Parts of England* (London, 1676), 3.
71. Anonymous, *Wonders on the Deep* (London: M. H., 1684).
72. A platitude that Thomas Dekker gave, tellingly, to his older "North-Country-Man": "I thinke you haue not seene your Cittie so whited this fourtie yeares" (*The Cold Yeare* [London: W. White, 1615], sig. B1r).
73. Anonymous, *A True Account,* 3, 6.
74. Ibid., 4.
75. Ibid., 3. See also John Tanner's (ca. 1636–1715) extremely detailed list of astrological observations, *Angelus Britannicus,* printed yearly from 1657–1700. Each edition from 1687 (London: E. Horton) counts the years since "the Last great Frost" of 1684 (finally reaching 16) on the title page. Such an "ephemeris" (sig. A1r) was exactly what the author of 1676 was attempting to counter: the projection of astral signs onto recent events. Tanner's type of recounting nonetheless evinces an unsteady baseline. (Indeed, the "great Frosts" of succeeding centuries will be compared to 1683/4.)
76. Anonymous, *True Account,* 4.
77. Anonymous, *Sad News.*
78. Anonymous, *True and Perfect Narrative,* 1.
79. Anonymous, 5.
80. Magnus, *Description,* 2:553.
81. Thomas Dekker, *The Great Frost* (London, 1608), sig. B2v.
82. Dekker, sig. B2r.
83. Dekker, sig. B1r.
84. See Mike Lockwood, Mat Owens, Ed Hawkins, Gareth S. Jones, and Ilya Usoskin, "Frost Fairs, Sunspots and the Little Ice Age," *Astronomy & Geophysics* 58, no. 2 (2017): 2.17–2.23.

85. Anonymous, *True Account,* 6.
86. Anonymous, 7.
87. Anonymous, 7.
88. Anonymous, 7.
89. Raphael Thorius, *Cheimonopegnion, Or, A Winter Song* (London: T.N., 1651), 2.
90. Anonymous, *A Winter Wonder, Or, the Thames Frozen Over* (London, 1684).
91. Anonymous.
92. Dekker, *Great Frost,* sig. B4r.
93. Anonymous, *Winter Wonder.*
94. Anonymous.
95. Anonymous, *Thamasis's Advice to the Painter, from Her Frigid Zone, Or, Wonders upon the Water* (London: G. Croom, 1684).
96. Anonymous, *News from the Thames, Or, The Frozen Thames in Tears* (London: T. Snowden, 1684).
97. Anonymous, *Wonders on the Deep.*
98. Anonymous.
99. Anonymous.
100. Anonymous, *God's Works Is the Worlds Wonder* (London: M.H. and J.M., 1684).
101. Anonymous, *A Wonderfull Fair, Or, a Fair of Wonders* (London: 1684).
102. Anonymous.
103. Joseph P. Ward, "The Taming of the Thames: Reading the River in the Seventeenth Century," *Huntington Library Quarterly* 71, no. 1 (2008): 74.
104. Anonymous, *Winter Wonder.*
105. Anonymous, *Great Britains Wonder* (London: M. Haly and J. Millet, 1684).
106. Anonymous, *Thamasis's Advice to the Painter.*
107. Anonymous, *News from Frost-Fair upon the River of Thames* (London, 1683).
108. Anonymous.
109. Anonymous, *Great Britains Wonder*. See also Anonymous, *Blanket-Fair*: "I'll tell you a Story as true as 'tis rare, / Of a River turn'd into a Bartholmew Fair."
110. See Robert A. Beddard, "The London Frost Fair of 1683–4," *The Guildhall Miscellany* 4, no. 2 (1972): 72–73: "For [stall-holders] the Fair was first and foremost a commercial enterprise; it was there to make money. . . . Few can have been unsuspecting enough to mistake the motive that quickened the Fair's growth: the search for quick profits."
111. Ward, "Taming of the Thames," 74.
112. Alvin Snider, "Hard Frost, 1684," *Journal for Early Modern Cultural Studies* 8, no. 2 (2008): 27.
113. Snider, 9.
114. Anonymous, *Great Britains Wonder.*
115. Anonymous.
116. Dekker, *Great Frost,* sig. B1r.
117. Anonymous, *God's Works Is the Worlds Wonder* (London: M.H. and J.M., 1684).
118. Anonymous, *Great Britains Wonder.*

119. Bruno Latour, *Facing Gaia: Eight Lectures on the New Climatic Regime,* trans. Catherine Porter (Cambridge: Polity, 2017), 3.
120. Christina Rossetti, *Selected Poems,* ed. Dinah Roe (London: Penguin, 2008), 67.
121. Anonymous (London: 1684).
122. Beddard, "London Frost Fair," 80.
123. Beddard, 73.
124. "The Chair sliding in the ring" (Anonymous, *An Exact and Lively Mapp*), for example, or "A Whirling Sledg" (Anonymous, *A Wonderfull Fair*).
125. Anonymous, *Wonders on the Deep.*
126. Anonymous, *News from Frost-Fair.*
127. Anonymous, *A True Description of Blanket Fair upon the River Thames* (London, 1683).
128. Anonymous, *Wonders on the Deep.*
129. Anonymous, *True Description.*
130. Anonymous. See also Anonymous, *Freezland-Fair, Or, the Icey Bear-Garden* (London, 1684).
131. Anonymous, *Blanket-Fair, Or, the History of Temple Street* (London: 1684).
132. Anonymous.
133. Anonymous.
134. Anonymous, *Freezland-Fair.*
135. Anonymous.
136. See *OED,* s.v. *freak* (n.1), 1.
137. See *OED,* s.v. *freak* (v.), 1.
138. See *OED,* s.v. *freak* (n.1), 4.b.
139. Anonymous, *News from Frost-Fair.*
140. Anonymous, *Blanket-Fair.* Expectedly, the compound noun also denoted a moral relapse: "From Heav'n the Scourge is sent us for our pride; / We're plagu'd with Ice, because we do backslide" (Anonymous, *Thamasis's Advice*).
141. Anonymous, *Blanket-Fair.*
142. Anonymous, *Winter Wonder.*
143. Anonymous, *Blanket-Fair.*
144. Elizabeth Bradfield, "Against Solitude," in *Approaching Ice: Poems* (New York: Persea, 2010).
145. See *OED,* s.v. *frig* (v.), 3.b., 3.c., 3.d. in *The Oxford English Dictionary.* Thanks, Vin Nardizzi!
146. See *OED,* s.v. *frike* (v.); and s.v. *frig* (v.), 1, 2.
147. Anonymous, *An Historical Account of the Late Great Frost* (London, 1684), sig. A1r.
148. Anonymous, 28, 9.
149. Anonymous, 54.
150. Anonymous, 61.
151. Anonymous, 96.
152. Anonymous, 141.
153. Anonymous, 8.

154. Anonymous, 30.
155. Anonymous, 31.
156. Anonymous, 31.
157. Anonymous, 37.
158. Anonymous, 39.
159. Anonymous, 40.
160. Anonymous, 40.
161. Anonymous, 41.
162. Anonymous, 43.
163. Anonymous, 41.
164. The subject continues to titillate, although many plots are set around the Regency era (1811–1820) rather than the Restoration. For examples, see Tansy Rayner Roberts, *The Frost Fair Affair* (2020); Tammy Jo Burns, *Love at the Frost Fair* (2019); Edith Layton, *Frost Fair* (2018); Elizabeth Jane Anson, *The Last Frost Fair: A Regency Romance* (2018); Elizabeth Hawksley, *Frost Fair* (2002); and Elizabeth Mansfield, *Frost Fair* (1982). For more period-adjacent works of historical fiction, see Edward Marston's mystery, *The Frost Fair* (2004), and Carol Ann Duffy's illustrated book of poems, *Frost Fair* (2019).
165. Ward, "Taming of the Thames," 75.
166. Anonymous, *True Description of Blanket Fair.*
167. Anonymous, *A Winter Wonder.*
168. Anonymous.
169. Anonymous, *God's Works Is the Worlds Wonder.*
170. Anonymous.
171. Anonymous, *Blanket-Fair.*
172. See R. I. Page, *Lapland Sorcerers,* (London: Viking Society for Northern Research. 1963), throughout; Ernest J. Moyne, *Raising the Wind: The Legend of Lapland and Finland Wizards in Literature,* ed. Wayne R. Kime (Newark: University of Delaware Press, 1981); Ethel Seaton, *Literary Relations of England and Scandinavia in the Seventeenth Century* (Oxford: Clarendon, 1935), 282–87.
173. Anonymous, *The Whigs Hard Hearts* (London, 1684).
174. Anonymous.
175. Anonymous.
176. Anonymous.
177. Anonymous.
178. Thorius, *Cheimonopegnion,* 8.
179. Anonymous, *Londons Wonder* (London, 1685).
180. Anonymous.
181. Anonymous.
182. Taylor, *Cold Tearme.*
183. Taylor.
184. Taylor.
185. Taylor.
186. Taylor.

187. Taylor.
188. See *OED*, s.v. *conglutinate* (v.).
189. See *The Letters of John Chamberlain*, ed. Norman Egbert McClure, vol. 2 (Philadelphia: American Philosophical Society, 1939), 337: "The windes and high tides have so driven the yce on heapes in some places that yt lies like rockes and mounatines and hath a straunge and hideous aspect."
190. Taylor, *Cold Tearme.*
191. Taylor.
192. Taylor.
193. Taylor.
194. Taylor.
195. Taylor.
196. Taylor.
197. Taylor.
198. Taylor.
199. In *News from the Thames,* the waterway is personified as a mistreated woman who likens humans' annoying traffic to settler colonialism: "Over our heads a Colony is come, / That dispossess us both of house and home / Who cross to Natures laws have left the land, / And on my liquid surface firmly stand."
200. Anonymous, *By the Mayor. To the Aldermen of the Ward of . . . Whereas Oftentimes Heretofore, Especially Towards Winter the Evenings Growing Dark* (London, 1654).
201. William Lilly, *Lillie's Invitation* (London, 1668).
202. Rowland Vaughan, *Most Approued, and Long Experienced Water-Workes* (London: George Eld, 1610); Thomas Mace, *Profit, Conveniency, and Pleasure, to the Whole Nation Being a Short Rational Discourse, Lately Presented to His Majesty, Concerning the High-Ways of England* (London, 1675).
203. See Evelyn, *Diary,* 4:357: "It was exceedingly mortal at this time; & the season was unsufferably cold. The Thames frozen, &c"; see also 4:361 and 4:365.
204. Evelyn, 4:364.
205. Anonymous, *God's Works Is the Worlds Wonder.*
206. Narcissus Luttrell, *A Brief Historical Relation of State Affairs from September 1678 to April 1714,* vol. 1 (Oxford: Oxford University Press, 1857), 296. Ward notes that it is hard to verify the amount ("Taming of the Thames," 64n28). For more on the relief efforts, see Beddard, "London Frost Fair of 1683–4," 82–84.
207. Ward, "Taming of the Thames," 69n36.
208. Beddard, "London Frost Fair of 1683–4," 83.
209. William M. Cavert, "Winter and Discontent in Early Modern England," in *Governing the Environment in the Early Modern World: Theory and Practice,* ed. Sara Miglietti and John Morgan (New York: Routledge, 2017), 128.
210. Ward, "Taming of the Thames," 74.
211. Cavert, "Winter and Discontent," 128.
212. Matthew O'Brien, "'Our Frozen Age' and 'Our Destroying Age': The Great Frost of 1608 and the Midland Revolt," in *New Directions in Ecocriticism,* 2010, 8.

213. Anonymous, *A Strange and Wonderfull Relation of Many Remarkable Damages Sustained Both at Sea and Land by the Present Unparraleld Frost* (London, 1684).
214. Anonymous.
215. Sophie Lemercier-Goddard, "Frozen: English Journeys to the End of the World," in *The Experience of Disaster in Early Modern English Literature*, ed. Sophie Chiari (New York: Routledge, 2022), 32.
216. Anonymous, *Strange and Wonderfull Relation.*
217. Anonymous.
218. Anonymous.
219. Anonymous.
220. See *OED*, s.v. *skate* (n.2), 1.a.(a.)ß.
221. Anonymous, *Blanket-Fair.*
222. Samuel Pepys, *The Diary of Samuel Pepys*, ed. Henry B. Wheatley, vol. 2 (London: George Bell & Sons, 1893), 406.
223. Anonymous, *Blanket-Fair.*
224. Anonymous, *Strange and Wonderfull Relation.*
225. The word names more than a predetermined meeting place: "rendezvous" (1556) stems from the French command to "present yourself"; see *OED*, s.v. *rendezvous* (n.), 1.
226. Christopher P. Heuer, *Into the White: The Renaissance Arctic and the End of the Image* (New York: Zone, 2019), 197.
227. Dekker, *Cold Yeare*, sig. A2r.
228. Dekker, sig. B2v.-B3r.
229. Dekker, sig. B3r.-B3v.
230. Anonymous, *Strange and Wonderfull Relation.*
231. Anonymous.
232. Anonymous, *True Account*, 5.
233. Dekker, *Cold Yeare*, sig. B2v.
234. Dekker, sig. B1r.
235. Erica Fudge, *Quick Cattle and Dying Wishes: People and Their Animals in Early Modern England* (Ithaca, N.Y.: Cornell University Press, 2018), 94.
236. Dekker, *Cold Yeare*, sig. B2v.
237. Dekker, *Great Frost*, sig. B4v.
238. See Anonymous, *True Account*, 8: "'Tis certainly under such Circumstances that we ought to open our hands, our purses, and our hearts, to relieve the necessities of our brethren, lest whilst we unchristianly suffer them to starve or perish for Cold, we expose our selves for such unmercifulness to the danger of everlasting burnings."
239. Dekker, *Cold Yeare*, sig. B1r.
240. Dekker, sig. A3r.
241. Quoted in Beddard, "London Frost Fair," 64. Recall how the cold of 1664–1665 "long[ed to] put a stop to the Proceedings of the Press" that manufactured Boyle's seminal work on the topic (*New Experiments and Observations*, 4:206).

Observations like these are legion in missives from the mid- to late seventeenth century.

242. Dekker, *Cold Yeare,* sig. C4r.

## Winterlude: *Sympathize*

1. Thomas Tryon, *Modest Observations on the Present Extraordinary Frost* (London: George Larkin, 1684), n.p. All quotations hereafter refer to this edition and will be cited in text.
2. All quotations from Shakespeare refer to *The Norton Shakespeare,* ed. Stephen Greenblatt et al., 3rd ed. (New York: Norton, 2016). References are to act, scene, and line.
3. For examples, see James Dobbins and Hiroko Tabuchi, "Texas Blackouts Hit Minority Neighborhoods Especially Hard," *New York Times,* February 16, 2021, nytimes.com/2021/02/16/climate/texas-blackout-storm-minorities.html; Brianna Sacks, "Buffalo Blizzard Fuels Racial and Class Divided in Polarized City," *Washington Post,* December 29, 2022, washingtonpost.com/weather/2022/12/29/buffalo-blizzard-storm-race-class.
4. In *Shakespeare on the Shades of Racism* (New York: Routledge, 2021), Ruben Espinosa writes that "both works [*King Lear* and Allen Ginsberg's "Howl"] address systems of oppression. Their cry . . . can be collective when considering the wretched of our day" (144).

## 4. A Wintering Tale

1. All quotations from Shakespeare refer to *The Norton Shakespeare,* ed. Stephen Greenblatt et al., 3rd ed. (New York: Norton, 2016). References are to act, scene, and line.
2. In Eleanora C. Gordon, "The Fate of Sir Hugh Willoughby and His Companions," *The Geographical Journal* 152, no. 2 (1986): 245.
3. Gordon, 245.
4. Richard Hakluyt, *Principal Navigations,* vol. 2 (Glasgow: MacLehose and Sons, 1903), 223.
5. Hakluyt, 2:224.
6. Hakluyt, 2:224.
7. Hakluyt, 7:192.
8. Samuel Purchas, *Hakluytus Posthumus, or Purchas His Pilgrimes,* vol. 12 (Glasgow: MacLehose and Sons, 1906), 50.
9. Purchas, 12:52.
10. Purchas, 12:52.
11. John Milton, *A Brief History of Moscovia* (London: M. Flesher, 1682), 2.
12. James Thomson, *The Seasons: A Poem* (London, 1730), 296.
13. Thomas Fuller, *The History of the Worthies of England* (London: J. G. W. L., 1662), 233–34.

14. In *The Voyages of Captain Luke Foxe and Captain Thomas James in Search of a North-West Passage, in 1631–32,* ed. Miller Christy, 2 vols. (London: Hakluyt Society, 1894), 2:481. All quotations from James's *The Strange and Dangerous Voyage* and Foxe's *North-West Fox* refer to this edition and are hereafter cited in text.
15. In Colleen M. Franklin, ed., *The Strange and Dangerous Voyage of Captaine Thomas James* (Montreal: McGill-Queen's University Press, 2014), xlv–xlvi.
16. Franklin, xlv–xlvi.
17. Franklin, xci.
18. I. S. MacLaren, "Tracing One Discontinuous Line through the Poetry of the Northwest Passage," *Canadian Poetry* 39 (1996): 39; see also "Booking a Northwest Passage: Thomas James and *The Strange and Dangerous Voyage* (1633)" in *The Quest for the Northwest Passage: Knowledge, Nation and Empire, 1576–1806,* ed. Frédéric Regard (London: Pickering and Chatto, 2013), 89–102.
19. Andrea Pitzer's *Icebound: Shipwrecked at the Edge of the World* (New York: Scribner, 2021) is one.
20. Robert Ralston Cawley, *The Voyagers and Elizabethan Drama* (Boston: D. C. Heath, 1938), 255–57.
21. Sam White, *A Cold Welcome: The Little Ice Age and Europe's Encounter with North America* (Cambridge, Mass.: Harvard University Press, 2017), 9.
22. John Marston, *The Insatiate Countess,* in *The Works of John Marston,* ed. A. H. Bullen, vol. 3 (London: John C. Nimmo, 1887), 142.
23. Thomas H. Ford, "Climate Change and Literary History," in *A Cultural History of Climate Change,* ed. Tom Bristow and Thomas H. Ford (New York: Routledge, 2016), 165.
24. See Jamie Lorimer, *Wildlife in the Anthropocene: Conservation after Nature* (Minneapolis: University of Minnesota Press, 2015); David Macauley, "Bewildering Order," in *Elemental Philosophy: Earth, Air, Fire, and Water as Environmental Ideas* (Albany: State University of New York Press, 2010).
25. John Wylie, "Becoming-Icy: Scott and Amundsen's South Polar Voyages, 1910–13," *Cultural Geographies* 9 (2002): 251.
26. See *The Oxford English Dictionary* [*OED*], s.v. *frigitate* (v.).
27. See *OED,* s.v. *snog* (v.1).
28. In Adam White, ed., *A Collection of Documents on Spitzbergen and Greenland* (London: Hakluyt Society, 1855), 265.
29. White, 251. Julie Sanders describes Pelham's "becoming one with the landscape" as a strategy for survival, adding that narratives like his "operated as easily available aids to boost and inform the [Caroline] cultural imaginary of the ocean, an imaginary on which the playhouses were able to depend and which they were certainly able to mobilize to great effect in a dramatic context" (*The Cultural Geography of Early Modern Drama, 1620–1650* [Cambridge: Cambridge University Press, 2011], 59–60).
30. Joanna Radin and Emma Kowal, eds., "Introduction: The Politics of Low Temperature," in *Cryopolitics: Frozen Life in a Melting World* (Cambridge. Mass.: MIT Press, 2017), 8.

31. Radin and Kowal, 6.
32. In John Churchill, *Collection of Voyages,* vol. 2 (London, 1732), 367. The original was published in Dutch in 1635.
33. Churchill, 2:374.
34. Churchill, 2:378.
35. Churchill. 2:378.
36. Louwrens Hacquebord, "Five Early European Winterings in the Atlantic Arctic (1596–1635): A Comparison," *Arctic,* 44, no. 2 (1991): 146.
37. Cawley, *Voyagers,* 242–43.
38. Cawley, 248.
39. Robert Boyle, *New Experiments and Observations Touching Cold,* in *The Works of Robert Boyle,* ed. Michael Hunter and Edward B. Davis, vol. 4 (London: Routledge, 1999), 295.
40. See Steven Shapin, *A Social History of Truth: Civility and Science in Seventeenth-Century England* (Chicago: Chicago University Press, 2011), 251. On Boyle's "circles of gentlemanly learning," see Adriana Craciun, *Writing Arctic Disaster: Authorship and Exploration* (Cambridge: Cambridge University Press, 2016), 140; Franklin, *Strange and Dangerous Voyage,* l–liv.
41. James L. Smith, "Anxieties of Access: Remembering as a Lake," in *Environmental Humanities* 13, no. 1 (2021): 245–63.
42. William Cronon, "The Trouble with Wilderness; or, Getting Back to the Wrong Nature," in *Uncommon Ground: Rethinking the Human Place in Nature,* ed. William Cronon (New York: Norton, 1995), 69–90.
43. John Rastell, *A New Iuterlude and a Mery of the Nature of the .IIII. Element* (London: J. Rastell, 1520[?]), C1r.
44. As seen from a Western perspective. There are at least five seasons in Nunavut: travelnunavut.ca/plan-and-book/visitor-information/weather-climate. Seasons, and "seasons," change.
45. See the anonymous *Debate and Stryfe betwene Somer and Wynter* (London: Laurens Andrew, 1528), one of the earliest examples of what became a popular dispute.
46. It required creative avenues "for the Innocent spending of the . . . Evenings," as Humphrey Crouch put it in his time-wasting book, *England's Jests* (London, 1687). I have identified a score of these recreational titles—ask me about "winter"!
47. See *OED,* s.v. *hurkle* (v.).
48. Tim Ingold, *Being Alive: Essays on Movement, Knowledge, and Description* (New York: Routledge, 2011), 10.
49. For the etymologies of what follows, see *OED,* s.v. *winter* (n.1) and s.v. *winter* (v.).
50. Thomas Willsford provides just one example of this ubiquitous practice: "*winter,* resembling old and decrepit *Age,* being cold and dry" (*Natures Secrets* [London, 1658], 20).
51. Adam Gopnik, *Winter: Five Windows on the Season* (Toronto: House of Anansi, 2011), 179.

52. Gopnik, 183.
53. Gopnik, 181.
54. Gopnik, 209.
55. James Anderson, *Ane Godly Treatis, Callit the First and Second Cumming of Christ, with the Tone of the Winters-Nicht Shewing Brieflie Our Native Blindness* (Edinburgh: Andro Hart, 1614), n.p.
56. Here is only a small sample: the anonymous *Good Christian's Complaint* (London: 1692) comes across Charity "distressed in the bitter Frost and Snow"; it is purely a setting for spiritual dialogue and debate in John Carter's *Winter-Evenings' Communication* (Cambridge, 1628); similarly, John Goodman's three-part *A Winter-Evening Conference* (Edinburgh, 1684) is a two-hundred-page philosophical conversation about religion.
57. John Shower, *Winter Meditations* (London, 1695), 2.
58. Cotton Mather, *Winter Meditations* (Boston: Benjamin Harris, 1693), 67.
59. Mather, 25.
60. Mather, 26.
61. Mather, 42.
62. Mather, 81.
63. Mather. 27.
64. Mather, 25.
65. Mather, 12–13. See Thomas Robins, for whom *The Scholar's Winter Garment* (London, 1667) is "The Garment of Righteousness."
66. Mather, *Winter Meditations*, 26.
67. Mather, 18, 27.
68. Mather, 4.
69. Although no one "knows how soon our halcyon days may be turned into a Tempest," do not "pry boldly into more hidden mysteries" (Benjamin Camfield, *Of God's Almighty Providence Both in the Sending and Dissolving Great Snows and Frosts* [London, 1684], 17, 14).
70. Samuel Purchas, *Purchas His Pilgrimage* (London: William Stansby, 1626), 821.
71. Purchas, 821.
72. Ivor James, in Franklin, *Strange and Dangerous Voyage*, lxxiv.
73. William Coats (d. 1752), explorer-employee of the Hudson's Bay Company, will later divide ice into three "different species . . . (if I may be allowed the expression)" (*The Geography of Hudson Bay*, ed. John Barrow [London: Hakluyt Society, 1852], 19–20).
74. Wayne K. D. Davies, *Writing Geographical Exploration: James and the Northwest Passage 1631–33* (Calgary: University of Calgary Press, 2003), 217.
75. Davies, 297.
76. See Franklin, *Strange and Dangerous Voyage*, xlvii–xlviii, lxxiii–lxxvi, lxxx–lxxxi.
77. John Barrow, *A Chronological History of Voyages into the Arctic Regions* (London: John Murray, 1818), 250.
78. Craciun, *Writing Arctic Disaster*, 183.

79. Craciun, 179, 175.
80. In *Henry Hudson the Navigator: The Original Documents in Which His Career is Recorded,* ed. G. M. Asher (London: Hakluyt Society, 1860), 188.
81. C. C. A. Gosch, ed., *Danish Arctic Expeditions, 1605 to 1620,* vol. 2 (London: Hakluyt Society, 1897), 42, 44.
82. Gosch, 2:46.
83. Gosch, 2:50–51. Gosch elucidates: "There is . . . no illustration on the woodcut of the harbour illustrating the measures taken for the safety of the ship" (2:51n2).
84. Gosch, 2:50.
85. Gosch, 2:56.
86. See Christy, *Voyages,* 1:162n2; Purchas, *Pilgrimes* 14: 412.
87. Gosch lists no less than seventeen voyages from 1576 to 1632 (*Danish Arctic Expeditions,* 2:lxix).
88. William Vaughan, *The Golden Fleece* (London, 1626), 50.
89. Foxe agrees: "Here lyeth the way to *Colcos,* and he that finds the same brings home the *Golden Fleece!*" (2:442).
90. Vaughan, *Golden Fleece,* 50.
91. Vaughan, 51.
92. Vaughan, 51.
93. John Donne, "Ecclogue," in *The Complete English Poems,* ed. C. A. Patrides (London: Dent, 1985), 197.
94. Donne, 197–98.
95. Foxe described the "haire of our faces to be of [Boreas's] hoary colour" (2:403).
96. John Peter, *A Philosophical Account of This Hard Frost* (London, 1684), 7–8.
97. Peter, 8.
98. See *OED,* s.v. *metamorphosis* (n.).
99. Johannes Scheffer, *History of Lapland* (Oxford, 1674), 7.
100. See Mary C. Fuller, "Rebellious Fish," in *Remembering the Early Modern Voyage: English Narratives in the Age of European Expansion* (New York: Palgrave Macmillan, 2008), 117–64.
101. And even to the editors. Christy, for instance, devotes a footnote nearly two pages long to the possibility that Hudson wintered there: "I fail to see that it is by any means impossible that these stakes had been placed there by Hudson and his deserted companions" (*Voyages,* 2:568n1).
102. White, *Cold Welcome,* 6.
103. John Gatonbe, in Gosch, *Danish Arctic Expeditions,* 1:119.
104. William Baffin, in Gosch, 1:126.
105. Gosch, 1:135.
106. In Purchas, *Pilgrimes,* 14:328, 14:330.
107. John Gatonbe, in Gosch, *Danish Arctic Expeditions,* 1:106–7.
108. Davies, *Writing Geographical Exploration,* 239.
109. Richard Younge, *A Spark of Divine Light* (London: J. R., 1671), 1.
110. In Christy, *Voyages,* 1:clxxxix.

111. See *OED,* s.v. *consume* (v.1), I.1.
112. Thomas Allison, *An Account of a Voyage from Archangel in Russia* (London, 1699).
113. Allison, 81.
114. Allison, 111.
115. Allison, 111.
116. Allison, 112.
117. Allison, 81.
118. In Anonymous, *An Account of Several Late Voyages and Discoveries to the South and North* (London, 1694), 193–94.
119. J. G., *Strange News from Plymouth* (London, 1684), 7.
120. I have Erin James's "Anthropocene narrative theory" in mind: "how a clearer look at narrative can help develop our understanding of the Anthropocene, and how a richer exploration of the Anthropocene can enhance our understanding of how narratives do and can work" (*Narrative in the Anthropocene* [Columbus: Ohio State University Press, 2022], 14).
121. Allison, *Account,* 71.
122. "Reading in the Anthropocene is an invariably polyglot, salvage practice in which we employ all of our tools to discover meaning amid the ruins." See Tobias Menely and Jesse Oak Taylor's introduction to *Anthropocene Reading: Literary History in Geologic Times* (University Park: Pennsylvania State University Press, 2017), 20, 13.
123. See Ronald Niezen, *Defending the Land: Sovereignty and Forest Life in James Bay Cree Society,* 2nd ed. (New York: Routledge, 2009), especially chapter 4, "Negotiated Transformations."
124. Max Liboiron, *Pollution Is Colonialism* (Durham, N.C.: Duke University Press, 2021), 6–7.
125. Liboiron, 56.
126. Liboiron, 8. A memoir that explores these sentiments beautifully in a different hydroelectric context—involving the Pimicikamak Cree Nation in Manitoba, Canada—is Kazim Ali's *Northern Light: Power, Land, and the Memory of Water* (Minneapolis: Milkweed Editions, 2021).
127. "Environmental Justice Impacts of Proposed Canadian Hydropower for NYC Highlighted Day before Critical PSC Vote," *Riverkeeper,* April 13, 2022, riverkeeper.org/news-events/news/preserve-river-ecology/environmental-justice-impacts-of-proposed-canadian-hydropower-for-nyc-highlighted-day-before-critical-psc-vote; see also Joel Heath, dir., *People of a Feather* (2011).
128. Smith, "Anxieties of Access," 245.
129. Smith, 245.
130. Allison, *Account,* 60.
131. Christy, *Voyages,* clxxvii.
132. Katherine May, *Wintering: The Power of Rest and Retreat in Difficult Times* (New York: Riverhead, 2020), 13.

133. In Anonymous, *Account of Several Late Voyages and Discoveries,* 186, 194.
134. "Melting Glaciers Reveal Five New Islands in the Arctic," *The Guardian,* October 22, 2019, theguardian.com/environment/2019/oct/22/melting-glaciers-reveal-five-new-islands-in-the-arctic.
135. In fact, I wrote my first conference paper on *The Strange and Dangerous Voyage* from within the belly of winter storm Jonas in January 2016. It might seem paradoxical at first, but warmth is "likely contributing" to the vortex's waviness; see, for example, "Research Links Extreme Cold Weather in the United States to Arctic Warming," *NOAA,* September 7, 2021, cpo.noaa.gov/Divisions-Programs/Communication-Education-and-Engagement/CEENews/ArtMID/8293/ArticleID/2369/Research-Links-Extreme-Cold-Weather-in-the-United-States-to-Arctic-Warming.
136. Jean-Christophe Valtat, *Aurorarama* (New York: Melville House, 2010), 25.

## Winterlude: *Press*

1. Anonymous, *The True and Exact Representation of the Wonders upon the Water* (London: George Croom, 1684).
2. Anonymous, *Wonders on the Deep* (London: M. H., 1684).
3. Anonymous, *True and Exact Representation.*
4. See Joseph Monteyne, *The Printed Image in Early Modern London: Urban Space, Visual Representation, and Social Exchange* (Aldershot, UK: Ashgate, 2007), chapter 5.
5. Anonymous, *A Winter Wonder, Or, the Thames Frozen Over* (London, 1684)
6. Anonymous, *Winter Wonder.*
7. Thomas Dekker, *The Great Frost* (London, 1608), sig. A2v.
8. Anonymous, *The Thames Uncas'd: Or, the Watermans Song upon the Thaw* (London, 1684).
9. Anonymous, *Winter Wonder.*
10. Anonymous, *Thamasis's Advice to the Painter, from Her Frigid Zone, Or, Wonders upon the Water* (London: G. Croom, 1684).
11. Anonymous, *Thamasis's Advice.*
12. Joseph Moxon, *A Map of the River Thames. Merrily Cald Blanket Fair as It Was Frozen in the Memorable-Year 1683/4* (London, 1684).
13. Moxon, *Map of the River Thames.*
14. Moxon.
15. Dekker, *The Great Frost,* sig. B4v.
16. Moxon, *Map of the River Thames.*
17. Anonymous, *An Exact and Lively Mapp*; see also Anonymous, *Wonders on the Deep,* and Anonymous, *True and Exact Representation.*
18. Bruno Latour, *Pandora's Hope: Essays on the Reality of Science Studies* (Cambridge, Mass.: Harvard University Press, 1999), 304.
19. Moxon, *Map of the River Thames.*

20. Joseph Moxon, *A Collection of Some Attempts Made to the North-East, and North-West, for the Finding a Passage to Japan, China, &c.* (London: Joseph Moxon and James Moxon, 1676).
21. Moxon, *Collection of Some Attempts.*
22. Joseph Moxon, *Mechanick Exercises; Or, the Doctrine of Handy-Works Applied to the Art of Printing*, vol. 2 (London, 1683), 39, 43. *The Oxford English Dictionary* [*OED*] cites his work as the first appearance of "winter" applied to printing: s.v. *winter* (n. 3); s.v. *summer* (n. 2), II.4.e. Moxon's legacy lives on, I like to think, in the "glacial indifference" typeset. Thanks, Lara Farina!
23. Moxon, *Mechanick Exercises,* 2:11.
24. Moxon, 2:377.
25. Moxon, 2:273.
26. See *OED*, s.v. *crazy* (adj. 1); s.v. *craze* (v.).

## 5. *Hamlet* on Ice

1. Janet Nelson, "This Hamlet Has the Answer to the Question: To Be, Or Not to Be, Cold," *Snow Country* 2, no. 2 (1989): 60.
2. All quotations from Shakespeare refer to *The Norton Shakespeare,* ed. Stephen Greenblatt et al., 3rd ed. (New York: Norton, 2016). References are to act, scene, and line.
3. Nelson, "This Hamlet," 60.
4. Nelson, 61.
5. Nelson, 61.
6. Nelson, 58.
7. Nelson, 58.
8. For the "psychophysiological reciprocity of self and world," see Gail Kern Paster, *Humoring the Body: Emotions and the Shakespearean Stage* (Chicago: University of Chicago Press, 2004), 50.
9. Daryl W. Palmer, "Hamlet's Northern Lineage: Masculinity, Climate, and the Mechanician in Early Modern Britain," *Renaissance Drama* 35 (2006): 19.
10. Margreta de Grazia, *"Hamlet" without Hamlet* (Cambridge: Cambridge University Press, 2007), 3.
11. Kristen Poole, *Supernatural Environments in Shakespeare's England* (Cambridge: Cambridge University Press, 2011), 98. See especially Sebastian Münster, *A Briefe Collection and Compendious Extract of the Straunge and Memorable Things, Gathered oute of the Cosmographye of Sebastian Münster* (London: Thomas Marshe, 1572), fol. 23v; Thomas Nashe, *The Terrors of the Night* (London: John Danter, 1594), sig. D2r.
12. Palmer, "Hamlet's Northern Lineage," 9.
13. Palmer, 11.
14. Palmer, 16.
15. Palmer, 4.
16. Joseph Campana and Scott Maisano, "Introduction: Renaissance

Posthumanism," in *Renaissance Posthumanism* (New York: Fordham University Press, 2016), 11: "Moments where Renaissance humanism seems to depart and differ from itself." For examples steeped in continental philosophy, see part III of *Posthumanist Shakespeares* ("*Hamlet,* 'Posthumanist'?"), ed. Stefan Herbrechter and Ivan Callus (New York: Palgrave Macmillan, 2012), 179–237.

17. Erica Fudge, "Farmyard Choreographies in Early Modern England," in Campana and Maisano, *Renaissance Posthumanism,* 156.
18. Stacy Alaimo, *Exposed: Environmental Politics and Pleasures in Posthuman Times* (Minneapolis: University of Minnesota Press, 2016), 94.
19. Palmer, "Hamlet's Northern Lineage," 13.
20. Benjamin Newman, *Hamlet and the Snowman: Reflections on Vision and Meaning in Life and Literature* (New York: Peter Lang, 2000), 133.
21. Gretel Ehrlich, *This Cold Heaven* (New York: Pantheon, 2001), 101.
22. Alaimo, *Exposed,* 82.
23. Alaimo, 82. Alaimo's use of "weathering" refers to Astrida Neimanis and Rachel Loewen Walker, "*Weathering*: Climate Change and the 'Thick Time' of Transcorporeality," *Hypatia* 29, no. 3 (2014): 558–75.
24. On the divisive topic of "white melancholy," for example, see Mary Floyd-Wilson, *English Ethnicity and Race in Early Modern Drama* (Cambridge: Cambridge University Press, 2003), 78: "In its representation of a melancholic *Dane,* Shakespeare's play tells the story of an extraordinary northerner—extraordinary because his inward melancholy has estranged him from his native, northern complexion."
25. David Sterling Brown, "Code Black: Whiteness and Unmanliness in *Hamlet,*" in *"Hamlet": The State of Play,* ed. Sonia Massai and Lucy Munro (London: Bloomsbury, 2021), 103.
26. Follow him down: "As we think of what physically remains of Old Hamlet in the grave, we should envision his body as blackened by the decomposition process and we should also imagine it as cold" (Sterling, 116).
27. See *The Oxford English Dictionary* [*OED*], s.v. *bitter* (adj.) and *bitter* (adv.).
28. Palmer, "Hamlet's Northern Lineage," 17.
29. Saxo Grammaticus, *Gesta Danorum,* ed. Karsten Friis-Jensen, trans. Peter Fisher, vol. 1 (Oxford: Clarendon, 2015), 221; see also François de Belleforest: "There is no promise or determination of a woman, but that a very small discommoditie of fortune mollifieth and altereth the same, and which time doeth not pervert" (from an anonymous English translation of *The Hystorie of Hamblet* [London: Richard Bradocke, 1608] in *Narrative and Dramatic Sources of Shakespeare,* ed. Geoffrey Bullough [London: Routledge, 1973], 7:122–23).
30. In Katherine Duncan-Jones, *Ungentle Shakespeare: Scenes from His Life* (London: Thomson Learning, 2001), 152.
31. Palmer, "Hamlet's Northern Lineage," 17.
32. Rebecca Laroche and Jennifer Munroe, concerned over posthumanism's tendency to elide questions of social justice in favor of a broad democratizing approach, state that "ecofeminism [is] a way to theorize the relationship between

human and nonhuman 'things,' but [also to] show how they are intertwined with the matrix of power in early modern England" (*Shakespeare and Ecofeminist Theory* [London: Bloomsbury, 2017], 6–7).

33. Jane Bennett, *Vibrant Matter: A Political Ecology of Things* (Durham, N.C.: Duke University Press, 2010), 53.
34. For example, see Aaron Kitch, "Enchanted Materialism in Paracelsus, Hobbes, and *Hamlet*," in *Enchantment and Dis-Enchantment in Shakespeare and Early Modern Drama: Wonder, the Sacred, and the Supernatural* (New York: Routledge, 2017).
35. Carla Mazzio, "The History of Air: *Hamlet* and the Trouble with Instruments," *South Central Review* 26, no. 1–2 (2009), 185.
36. Steven Swarbrick, "In the Anthropocene Air: Deleuze's Encounter with Shakespeare," *Early Modern Culture* 13 (2018): 110.
37. In Ehrlich, *This Cold Heaven*, 88.
38. Ehrlich, 101, 182.
39. Rockwell Kent, *Salamina* (New York: Harcourt, Brace, 1935), 98.
40. Una Chaudhuri, "Anthropo-Scenes: Theater and Climate Change," *Journal of Contemporary Drama in English* 3, no. 1 (2015): 12–27.
41. Such as the "Globe to Globe" *Hamlet* at the Ystads Teater in Ystad, Sweden, on May 8, 2014.
42. See, for example, Kenneth Branagh, dir., *Hamlet* (1996); Sherwood Hu, dir., *Prince of the Himalayas* (2006).
43. As the Utah Shakespeare Festival did in 2019; see Kathryn Neves, "*Hamlet* Like You've Never Seen It Before," bard.org/news/hamlet-like-youve-never-seen-it-before.
44. A (or the) question similarly asked by Carolyn Philpott, Elizabeth Leane, and Matt Delbridge, eds., *Performing Ice* (Cham, Switzerland: Palgrave Macmillan, 2020), and Anne Hemkendreis and Anna-Sophie Jürgens, eds., *Communicating Ice through Popular Art and Aesthetics* (Cham, Switz.: Palgrave Macmillan, 2024).
45. "This 'Hamlet' May Leave Audiences Ice-Cold," *Los Angeles Times*, January 15, 2003, articles.latimes.com/2003/jan/15/entertainment/et-arctic15.
46. Erlend Clouston, "Get Thee to a Freezer," *The Guardian*, January 30, 2003: theguardian.com/stage/2003/jan/30/theatre.artsfeatures.
47. "The Story of Ice Hotel," ICEHOTEL, accessed April 21, 2021, icehotel.com/art-and-design/art-at-icehotel.
48. Vin Nardizzi, *Wooden Os: Shakespeare's Theatres and England's Trees* (Toronto: University of Toronto Press, 2013), 29.
49. Nardizzi, 136, 28.
50. "Story of Ice Hotel."
51. Jason W. Moore, *Capitalism in the Web of Life: Ecology and the Accumulation of Capital* (Brooklyn, N.Y.: Verso Books, 2015); "The Iceberg Runway—Chanel," ICEHOTEL, accessed April 21, 2021, icehotel.com/iceberg-runway-chanel.
52. "Ice and Design," ICEHOTEL, accessed July 26, 2023, icehotel.com/ice-design#ICE.

53. "Ice and Design."
54. Evelyn O'Malley, *Weathering Shakespeare: Audiences and Open-Air Performance* (London: Bloomsbury, 2021), 2.
55. O'Malley, 5.
56. O'Malley, 19.
57. Lisa Cox, "Nordic Countries Endure Heatwave as Lapland [*sic*] Records Hottest Day since 1914," *The Guardian*, July 6, 2021, theguardian.com/environment/2021/jul/06/heatwave-hits-nordic-countries-lapland-temperature-.
58. Evelyn O'Malley, "'To Weather a Play': Audiences, Outdoor Shakespeares, and Avant-Garde Nostalgia at the Willow Globe," *Shakespeare Bulletin* 36, no. 3 (2018): 422.
59. James Shapiro, *A Year in the Life of William Shakespeare: 1599* (New York: HarperCollins, 2005), 6–7.
60. John Stow, *The Annales of England* (London: Peter Short, Felix Kingston, and George Eld, 1605), 1309.
61. Stow, 1401.
62. Stow, 1401.
63. Stow, 1409.
64. Stow, 1412.
65. In *The Life of the Icelander Jón Ólafsson, Traveller to India*, trans. Sigfús Blöndal, ed. Bertha S. Phillpotts, vol. 1 (London: Hakluyt Society, 1923), 8, 113.
66. *Life of the Icelander Jón Ólafsson*, 1:114.
67. *Life of the Icelander Jón Ólafsson*, 1:114.
68. *Life of the Icelander Jón Ólafsson*, 1:114.
69. Cay Dollerup, *Denmark, "Hamlet," and Shakespeare*, vol. 1 (Salzburg: Institut für Englische Sprache und Literatur, 1975), 120.
70. Fynes Moryson, *An Itinerary* (London: Iohn Beale, 1617), 57.
71. Moryson, 100.
72. Olaus Magnus, *Description of the Northern Peoples*, trans. Peter Fisher and Humphrey Higgens, ed. Peter Foote, vol. 2 (London: Hakluyt Society, 1996–1998), 523.
73. Cherrell Guilfoyle believes the cold opening scene resembles patient shepherds' watching from mystery plays, although this helps narrow the timing of the play (with its echoes of Christian Nativity) rather than highlights the weather's supernatural influence. See *Shakespeare's Play within Play: Medieval Imagery and Scenic Form in "Hamlet," "Othello," and "King Lear"* (Kalamazoo: Medieval Institute, 1990), 21–39 (chapter 2: "The Beginning of *Hamlet*").
74. An opinion slightly contradicted by her own book's sheer number of English–Scandinavian intersections spanning 350 pages (Ethel Seaton, *Literary Relations of England and Scandinavia in the Seventeenth Century* [Oxford: Clarendon, 1935]); her volume remains an unparalleled resource (see esp. 297, 331).
75. Seaton, 320.
76. Seaton, 324; the catalogue she puts together (320–25) is short, indeed. See also Gunnar Sorelius, ed., *Shakespeare and Scandinavia: A Collection of Nordic Studies* (Newark: University of Delaware Press, 2002).

77. Saxo Grammaticus, *Gesta Danorum,* 1:201; see also François de Belleforest, in *Narrative and Dramatic Sources of Shakespeare,* ed. Geoffrey Bullough, 8 vols. (New York: Columbia University Press, 1961–), 7:109.
78. Dollerup, *Denmark,* 2:316, 2:318.
79. Gunnar Sjögren, "The Danish Background in *Hamlet,*" *Shakespeare Studies* 4 (1968): 227.
80. Sjögren, 227.
81. "This 'Hamlet' May Leave Audiences Ice-Cold."
82. Clouston, "Get Thee to a Freezer."
83. Clouston.
84. Barbara Sjoholm, "Macbeth on Ice," *Slate,* February 21, 2004, slate.com /human-interest/2004/02/macbeth-on-ice.html.
85. Clousten, "Get Thee to a Freezer."
86. "Sweden Plans Globe Ice Replica," *BBC News,* January 30, 2002, http://news .bbc.co.uk/2/hi/entertainment/1791169.stm.
87. See Simone Abram, "Jokkmokk: Rapacity and Resistance in Sápmi," in *Postcolonial Perspectives on the European High North: Unscrambling the Arctic,* ed. Graham Huggan and Lars Jensen (London: Palgrave Macmillan, 2016), 67–92.
88. "About the company," accessed August 24, 2023, web.archive.org/web /20070910094816/http://www.beaivvas.no/web/index.php?sladja=25&giella1=eng. Their main website (/beaivvas.no/nb/) is written in Sámi and Norwegian.
89. Nils-Aslak Valkeapää, *The Sun, My Father* (Seattle: University of Washington Press, 1997), 414, 417–18.
90. In Robert Ralston Cawley, *The Voyagers and Elizabethan Drama* (Boston: D. C. Heath, 1938), 238.
91. Johannes Scheffer, *History of Lapland* (Oxford, 1674), n.p.
92. Cawley, *Voyagers,* 238.
93. Giles Fletcher, *Of the Russe Common Wealth* (London: Thomas Dawson, 1591), fol. 75v.
94. Cawley, *Voyagers,* 238.
95. It has been suggested that "Lapp" is related to *lape* in Finnish for "edge, periphery." See Björn Collinder, *The Lapps* (Princeton, N.J.: Princeton University Press, 1949), 205–13; Christian Meriot, "The Saami Peoples from the Time of the Voyage of Ottar to Thomas von Westen," *Arctic* 37, no. 4 (1984): 373–84.
96. Saxo Grammaticus, *Gesta Danorum,* 1:17–19, 1:330–31; see also Magnus, *Description,* 1:57.
97. Cawley, *Voyagers,* 250–52, offers a short review. See Jean François Regnard, in *A General Collection of the Best and Most Interesting Voyages and Travels in All Parts of the World,* ed. John Pinkerton, vol. 1 (London: Longman, Hurst, Rees, and Orme, 1808), 193, 143; and the *Historia Norvegiæ* (ca. 1500), in Fridtjof Nansen, *In Northern Mists,* vol. 1 (London: William Heinemann, 1911), 204.
98. See Peter Heylyn, *Cosmographie* (London, 1652), 143; see also Tacitus, *Agricola; Germania; Dialogue on Oratory,* trans. M. Hutton and W. Peterson (Cambridge, Mass.: Harvard University Press, 1914), 212–13.

99. Peder Claussøn Friis (1545–1614) sums up this pernicious custom in the *Description of Norway* (ca. 1613, pub. 1632): "The Finns [Lapps] . . . are very black and brown on their bodies, and are hasty and evil-tempered folk, as though they had the nature of bears," in Nansen, *In Northern Mists,* 1:227.
100. Scheffer, *History of Lapland,* 34–36.
101. Regnard, in *General Collection,* 1:193.
102. Regnard, 1:163–4.
103. Scheffer, "Preface," in *History of Lapland,* n.p.
104. Scheffer, 7.
105. Scheffer, 8.
106. Scheffer, 13.
107. Scheffer, 13.
108. Scheffer, 107.
109. Scheffer, 107.
110. Scheffer, 107.
111. Scheffer, 124.
112. Scheffer, 12.
113. Scheffer, 15.
114. Pierre Martin de La Martinière, *A New Voyage into the Northern Countries* (London, 1674), 23, 33.
115. Martinière, 34.
116. Martinière, 35. Earlier he associates northern miners with "devils," but this is due to their "black leather" and the pit's analogy to "Hell" (18).
117. Martinière, 79, 85.
118. Martinière, 107.
119. Martinière, 140.
120. Martinière, 71.
121. Martinière, 71–2.
122. Scheffer, *History of Lapland,* 1.
123. Scheffer, 1. He is not far off: it is quite possibly a contemptuous word that comes from the Swedish *Lapp* and comparable to Middle High German *lappe,* "simpleton." See *OED,* s.v. *Lapp* (n. and adj.).
124. Scheffer, 1.
125. Scheffer, 2.
126. Scheffer, 2.
127. In Edward Arber, ed., *The First Three English Books on America* (Westminster: Archibald Constable, 1895) 301.
128. Jan Borm, "'Lavish Lapland': Gender, Primitivism and the Pictorial in Olive Murray Chapman's Travelogue *Across Lapland,*" in *Arctic Modernities: The Environmental, the Exotic and the Everyday,* ed. Heidi Hansson and Anka Ryall (Newcastle upon Tyne: Cambridge Scholars, 2017), 161.
129. Martinière, *New Voyage,* 127.
130. Martinière, 127.
131. See *OED,* s.v. *trub* (n.), 1 and 2.
132. Martinière, *New Voyage,* 145.

133. Scheffer, *History of Lapland,* 13; see also Magnus, *Description,* 3:869.
134. Magnus, *Description,* 3:870. See also Edward Topsell, *The Historie of Foure-Footed Beastes* (London: William Iaggard, 1607), 193.
135. Regnard, *General Collection,* 1:190.
136. Magnus, *Description,* 3:870.
137. Magnus, 3:870.
138. Magnus, 3:841.
139. Magnus, 3:870.
140. Carl-Gösta Ojala, "Encountering 'the Other' in the North: Colonial Histories in Early Modern Northern Sweden," in *Facing Otherness in Early Modern Sweden: Travel, Migration and Material Transformations (1500–1800),* ed. Magdalena Naum and Fredrik Ekengren (Woodbridge, UK: Boydell, 2018).
141. Regnard, *General Collection,* 1:160.
142. Ojala, "Encountering," 222, 216.
143. See Peter Fjågesund, *The Dream of the North: A Cultural History to 1920* (Amsterdam: Rodopi, 2014), 149: "The arrival of the modern world [post-1700] . . . was not necessarily a source of freedom and enlightenment for the Sámi; on the contrary, the scientific and anthropological mapping of new regions was just as frequently a means of subsuming them within administrative regimes that in return for an unsolicited protection would soon be demanding taxes as well as military service."
144. Elena Balzamo, "The Geopolitical Laplander: From Olaus Magnus to Johannes Schefferus," *Journal of Northern Studies* 8, no. 2 (2014): 36.
145. Ojala, "Encountering," 214.
146. Ann-Helén Laestadius, *Stolen: A Novel,* trans. Rachel Willson-Broyles (New York: Scribner, 2023), 42.
147. Cawley, *Voyagers,* 271. What he means by "races" is "Russian," although we have seen that early modern notions of race encompassed more signifiers than that (like skin color and idol worship).
148. As Heidi Hansson and Jan-Erik Lundström write about Sámi spectatorship in a nineteenth-century context, "exhibitions, ethnographic photographs and travel narratives exploit people's fascination for the unknown, but paradoxically, they must be structured according to well-known patterns to be accessible." ("Introduction: Lapland in London and Lapland and Elsewhere," in *Looking North: Representations of Sámi in Visual Arts and Literature,* ed. Heidi Hansson and Jan-Erik Lundström [Umeå, Sweden: Bildmuseet, 2008], 9). A Globe is one such pattern.
149. Nils-Aslak Valkeapää, *Trekways of the Wind* (Tuscon: University of Arizona Press, 1994), n.p.
150. Quotations are from Queens Arctic Theatre, *Hamlet* Playbill, December 21, 1852, in *The Queen's Illuminated Magazine,* fol. 31v. Thanks to Kate Pitt for bringing this to my attention!
151. Queens Arctic Theatre, fol. 32r. The magazine (with illustrations) is held by the British Library (MS 35305). All citations refer to the original page numbers.
152. Queens Arctic Theatre, fol. 31v.

153. Queens Arctic Theatre, fol. 31v.
154. See Ayanna Thompson, *Blackface* (New York: Bloomsbury, 2021), 34: "Performing blackness is the performance property of whites." See also 60.
155. Queens Arctic Theatre, *Hamlet* Playbill, fol. 32v–33r.
156. Ian Smith, *Black Shakespeare: Reading and Misreading Race* (Cambridge: Cambridge University Press, 2022), 140.
157. Smith, 144.
158. Smith, 148.
159. Smith, 118.
160. Smith, 146.
161. Gary Taylor, "What *Hamlet* Can Teach Us about Black Lives Matter," *Tampa Bay Times,* June 14, 2020, tampabay.com/opinion/2020/06/14/what-hamlet-can-teach-us-about-black-lives-matter-column.
162. Smith, *Black Shakespeare,* 14.
163. Smith, 120–21.
164. Brown, "Code Black," 104.
165. See Saladin Ambar, "Justice: 'To Take up Arms against a Sea of Troubles,'" chapter 5 in *Malcolm X at Oxford Union: Racial Politics in a Global Era* (New York: Oxford University Press, 2014).
166. Michael Billington, "Archive Theatre Review: Who Is Hamlet Anyway?," *The Guardian,* December 18, 2008, theguardian.com/stage/2000/dec/02/peter-brook-hamlet-theatre.
167. See Rodney Symington, *The Nazi Appropriation of Shakespeare: Cultural Politics in the Third Reich* (Lewiston, N.Y.: Edwin Mellen, 2005), 187–202.
168. Joscelyn Godwin, *Arktos: The Polar Myth in Science, Symbolism, and Nazi Survival* (Kempton, Ill.: Adventures Unlimited, 1996), 8; see also Chapter 5, "The Thule Society."
169. Peter Erickson, "Can We Talk about Race in *Hamlet*?," in *Hamlet: New Critical Essays,* ed. Arthur F. Kinney (New York: Routledge, 2002), 207–13.
170. Arthur L. Little Jr. puts it plainly: "The *white* melancholic subject . . . one may think of Hamlet . . . becomes the modern subject, abstracted and universalized, the end and the beginning of a *historical,* humanist teleology" ("Re-Historicizing Race, White Melancholia, and the Shakespearean Property," *Shakespeare Quarterly* 67, no. 1 [2016]: 93).
171. Valkeapää, *The Sun, My Father,* 509.
172. See Arthur L. Little Jr., "Is It Possible to Read Shakespeare through Critical White Studies?," in *The Cambridge Companion to Shakespeare and Race,* ed. Ayanna Thompson (Cambridge: Cambridge University Press, 2021), 271: "'White people,' like 'black people,' are not ontologically sui generis, they're made, they're always in the act of being *(re)invented.*"
173. "What are we going to do with Shakespeare's plays?" asks Miles Grier ("Are Shakespeare's Plays Racially Progressive? The Answer Is in Our Hands," in Thompson, *Cambridge Companion to Shakespeare and Race,* 250). "To align Shakespeare with global white supremacy and political or cultural imperialism

is to work with the tide of history. To turn the tide is not impossible, but it also requires reorienting work on economic, material, and ideological fronts—often from what appears to be scratch" (244–245).

174. On "whiteness [as] the standard against which all other races are measured or valued," or "whiteness [as] the norm against which constructed racial differences become meaningful," see Andrew Baldwin, Laura Cameron, and Audrey Kobayashi, "Introduction: Where Is the Great White North? Spatializing History, Historicizing Whiteness," in *Rethinking the Great White North: Race, Nature, and the Historical Geographies of Whiteness in Canada* (Vancouver: University of British Columbia Press, 2011), 5.

175. Richard Dyer, *White* (London: Routledge, 1997), xiii. His point about whites' "placing as norm" is germane: "At the level of racial representation, . . . whites are not of a certain race, they're just the human race" (3).

176. Speaking of the *Macbeth* film directed by Bo Landin and Alex Scherpf in 2004, shot on site, Mark Thornton Burnett argues, "to stage [it] against such a background is to underwrite the play's preoccupation with forms of oppression and to emphasize in Shakespearean language a culturally pertinent cause" (*Shakespeare and World Cinema* [Cambridge: Cambridge University Press, 2013], 181).

177. On the decimation of reindeer populations, the disruption of transspecies migration, and the threats to the *sii'dâ,* see Meriot, "Saami Peoples," 380. See also Peter Sköld, "Perpetual Adaption? Challenges for the Sami and Reindeer Husbandry in Sweden," in *The New Arctic,* ed. Birgitta Evengård, Joan Nymand Larsen, and Øyvind Paasche (Cham, Switzerland: Springer, 2015), 39–55.

178. Rebecca R. Scott defines the "sacrifice zone" as "a place that is written off for environmental destruction in the name of a higher purpose, such as the national interest" (*Removing Mountains: Extracting Nature and Identity in the Appalachian Coalfields* [Minneapolis: University of Minnesota Press, 2010], 31; see also chapter 1).

179. Meriot, "Saami Peoples," 383.

180. Meriot, 383.

181. Sjoholm, "Macbeth on Ice."

182. Valkeapää, *The Sun, My Father,* 511.

183. Viewable at the artist's website: anderssunna.com/work-2016/#!prettyPhoto. In addition to his, the artist-activist voices I draw inspiration from are Mimi Märak, Katarina Pirak Sikku, and Niillas Somby.

184. "Ice Hotel," Magic of Lapland, accessed April 22, 2021, magicoflapland.net/product/icehotel.

185. "Sustainability," ICEHOTEL, accessed April 22, 2021, icehotel.com/about-icehotel/sustainability.

186. "Icehotel Certified Sustainable Arctic Destination," ICEHOTEL, accessed April 22, 2021, icehotel.com/icehotel-certified-sustainable-arctic-destination.

187. "Sustainable Arctic Destination," Kiruna in Swedish Lapland, accessed April 22, 2022, kirunalapland.se/en/see-do/sustainable-arctic-destination.

188. Justin Cartwright, "Sweden: A tale to freeze young blood," *Telegraph,* February 1,

2003, telegraph.co.uk/travel/destinations/europe/sweden/726716/Sweden-A-tale-to-freeze-young-blood.html.

189. Cartwright.
190. Cartwright.
191. Cartwright.
192. Justin Cartwright, *Up against the Night* (New York: Bloomsbury, 2015), 201–2.
193. Cartwright, "Sweden."
194. View updates on the Environmental Justice Atlas, last accessed July 8, 2021, ejatlas.org/conflict/gallok-kallak-iron-mine-sweden; see also the documentary *Gállok,* released in 2018, directed by Truls Andersen.
195. Regnard, *General Collection,* 1:162.
196. Scheffer, "Preface," in *History of Lapland,* n.p.
197. Martinière, *New Voyage,* 153.
198. Cartwright, "Sweden."
199. See Dieter K. Müller, "Issues in Arctic Tourism," in Evengård, Larsen, and Paasche, *New Arctic,* 147–58; Elina Arminen, "Come to Lapland! Changes and Continuities of Lapland Imagery in Finnish and International Travel Posters," in *Visual Representations of the Arctic: Imagining Shimmering Worlds in Culture, Literature and Politics,* ed. Markku Lehtimäki, Arja Rosenholm, and Vlad Strukov (New York: Routledge, 2021), 117–38.
200. David Crouch, "Swedish Far-Right Leader: Jews Must Abandon Religious Identity to Be Swedes," *The Guardian,* December 17, 2014, theguardian.com/world/2014/dec/17/swedish-far-right-leader-jews-swedes.
201. See Dyer, *White,* 40: "The paradoxes and instabilities of whiteness also constitute its flexibility and productivity, . . . its representational power"; instead, "whiteness needs to be made strange" (10).
202. Astri Dankertsen, "I Felt So White: Sámi Racialization, Indigeneity, and Shades of Whiteness," *Native American and Indigenous Studies,* 6, no. 2 (2019): 133. See also 115: "The status of the Sámi as an Indigenous people disrupts and complicates the issue of whiteness in the Sámi context, since being Indigenous is so closely but, at the same time, ambiguously connected to being nonwhite both historically and as understood internationally" (115).
203. Dankertsen, 131.
204. Dankertsen, 131.
205. Valkeapää, *The Sun, My Father,* 544.
206. "Ice and Design."
207. See *the last oil* symposium held at the University of New Mexico, February 21–23, 2018, thelastoil.unm.edu.

## Winterlude: *Slide*

1. In Martin Conway, *No Man's Land: A History of Spitsbergen from Its Discovery in 1596 to the Beginning of the Scientific Exploration of the Country* (Cambridge: Cambridge University Press, 1906), 200. All quotations hereafter refer to this edition.

2. Slide note: when I asked Annepiet Nouwen and Leon Vosters, information specialists at the Rijksmuseum, to translate "wetspul" for me, they were stumped. (Could it be wet "things," or "games," or "law"?) A dictionary of early modern Dutch sayings was of no use. Words, well, *slip away*. See *De Seldsaame en Noit Gehoorde Wal-Vis-Vangst* (Leiden, 1684), 40.
3. One path: Zdenka Sokolíčková's *The Paradox of Svalbard: Climate Change and Globalisation in the Arctic* (London: Pluto, 2023).

## Co(l)da

1. All quotations from Shakespeare refer to *The Norton Shakespeare*, ed. Stephen Greenblatt et al., 3rd ed. (New York: Norton, 2016). References are to act, scene, and line.
2. Michael Byers, *Who Owns the Arctic?: Understanding Sovereignty Disputes in the North* (Vancouver: Douglas & McIntyre, 2009).
3. Petter Dass, *The Trumpet of Nordland*, trans. Theodore Jorgenson (Mosjøen, Norway: Helgeland Museum, 2015), 37. Thanks to the staff of the Petter Dass Museum in Alstahaug, Norway, for sending me a copy overseas.
4. Dass, 45.
5. Dass, 95.
6. Dass, 120.
7. Michael F. Robinson, *The Coldest Crucible: Arctic Exploration and American Culture* (Chicago: University of Chicago Press, 2006), throughout.
8. Hillary Eklund and Wendy Beth Hyman, "Introduction: Making Meaning and Doing Justice with Early Modern Texts," in *Teaching Social Justice through Shakespeare: Why Renaissance Literature Matters Now*, ed. Eklund and Hyman (Edinburgh: Edinburgh University Press), 6.
9. Donald J. Trump, Twitter post of November 7, 2012, twitter.com/realDonald Trump/status/266259787405225984.
10. See Marla Cone, *Silent Snow: The Slow Poisoning of the Arctic* (New York: Grove, 2005), 3: "How could the Arctic, seemingly untouched by contemporary ills, so innocent, so primitive, so natural, be home to the most contaminated people on the planet?"
11. The contributors to Subhankar Banerjee's edited collection *Arctic Voices: Resistance at the Tipping Point* (New York: Seven Stories, 2012) stress the sustained ties between the lifeways of the far north and the earth's overlapping systems.
12. See Klaus Dodds and Jen Rose Smith, "Against Decline? The Geographies and Temporalities of the Arctic Cryosphere," *The Geographical Journal* 00 (2022): 1–11: "Going forward, a task for ice humanities scholars is to be ever mindful of becoming inhumanities in the sense of erasing/dispossessing those who inhabit worlds where there are co-relationalities with ice, multi-species relationships, and multiple spatialities, seasonalities and temporalities that do not pivot

around Euro-American/global framings of time and space, geopolitical worlding and extractive capitalism."

13. Christopher Marlowe, *Tamburlaine,* ed. Anthony B. Dawson (London: Bloomsbury, 2014), 1.1.25–32.
14. Christopher Marlowe, *Doctor Faustus,* ed. Paul Menzer (London: Bloomsbury, 2018), 14.
15. Kathryn Yusoff, "Navigating the Northwest Passage," in *Envisioning Landscapes, Making Worlds: Geography and the Humanities,* ed. Stephen Daniels et al. (New York: Routledge, 2011), 306.
16. Mary Floyd-Wilson, *English Ethnicity and Race in Early Modern Drama* (Cambridge: Cambridge University Press, 2003), 3.
17. Francis Bacon, *The Essayes* (London: Iohn Hauiland, 1625), 335–36. See also Sir Henry Blount's (1602–1682) diametrically opposed climates in *A Voyage into the Levant* (London: Iohn Legat, 1636), 1–2, and Joseph Glanvill's (1636–1680) pseudoscientific connection between "climes" and "mental depravities" in *Scepsis Scientifica* (London: E. Cotes, 1665), 90.
18. George Best, *A True Discourse of the Late Voyages of Discouerie* (London: Henry Bynnyman, 1578), sig. A1r., sig. A4r.
19. George Peckham, *True Report* (London: Iohn Charlewood, 1583), sig. C1r.
20. Harald Gaski, "The Sami People: The 'White Indians' of Scandinavia," *American Indian Culture and Research Journal* 17, no. 1 (1993): 115–28.
21. Gories Peerse, *Van Yslandt,* trans. David Koester, facultysite.sinanewt.on-rev .com/yslandt.pdf.
22. In Anonymous, *An Account of Several Late Voyages and Discoveries* (London, 1694), 201.
23. Kim F. Hall and Peter Erickson, "'A New Scholarly Song': Rereading Early Modern Race," *Shakespeare Quarterly* 67, no. 1 (2016): 3.
24. Hall and Erickson, 12.
25. Best, *True Discourse,* 30.
26. Best, 19.
27. Thomas Browne, *Pseudodoxia Epidemica* (London: Thomas Harper, 1646), 324; see also Boyle's thoughts on whiteness and coldness (Robert Boyle, *New Experiments and Observations Touching Cold,* in *The Works of Robert Boyle,* ed. Michael Hunter and Edward B. Davis, vol. 4 [London: Routledge, 1999], 409).
28. See Peter J. P. Whitehead, "Earliest Extant Painting of Greenlanders," in *Indians and Europe: An Interdisciplinary Collection of Essays,* ed. Christian F. Feest (Lincoln: University of Nebraska Press, 1999), 141–60; Bernadette Andrea, "'Travelling Bodyes': Native Women of the Northeast and Northwest Passage Ventures and English Discourses of Empire" in *Rethinking Feminism in Early Modern Studies: Gender, Race, and Sexuality,* ed. Ania Loomba and Melissa E. Sanchez (London, Routledge, 2016), 135–48.
29. John Milton, *A Brief History of Moscovia* (London: M. Flesher, 1682), 18.

30. Olaus Magnus, *Description of the Northern Peoples,* trans. Peter Fisher and Humphrey Higgens, ed. Peter Foote, vol. 2 (London: Hakluyt Society, 1996–1998), 549–50.
31. See Brian Fagan, *The Little Ice Age: How Climate Made History 1300–1850* (New York: Basic, 2000), 86–90, 113–28; Emmanuel Le Roy Ladurie, *Times of Feast, Times of Famine: A Climate History since the Year 1000* (Garden City, N.Y.: Doubleday, 1971), 129–226.
32. See artist Irene Stracuzzi's 3-D modeling, *The Legal Status of Ice* (2017–2019), irenestracuzzi.com/project/the-legal-status-of-ice.
33. Jorge Daniel Taillant, *Glaciers: The Politics of Ice* (Oxford: Oxford University Press, 2015); Finn Arne Jørgensen, "The Networked North: Thinking about the Past, Present, and Future of Environmental Histories of the North," in *Northscapes: History, Technology, and the Making of Northern Environments,* ed. Dolly Jørgensen and Sverker Sörlin (Vancouver: University of British Columbia Press, 2013), 268–79.
34. Adrian Howkins, *The Polar Regions: An Environmental History* (Cambridge: Polity, 2016), 13.
35. Howkins, 11.
36. Richard Sale and Eugene Potapov, *The Scramble for the Arctic: Ownership, Exploitation, and Conflict in the Far North* (London: Frances Lincoln, 2010); Klaus Dodds and Mark Nuttall, *The Scramble for the Poles* (Cambridge: Polity, 2016).
37. Imtiaz Habib, *Black Lives in the English Archives, 1500–1677: Imprints of the Invisible* (Abingdon, Vt.: Ashgate, 2008), 230, 316.
38. Magnus, *Description,* 2:555–56.
39. Ali Smith, *Winter: A Novel* (New York: Anchor, 2017), 215.
40. Christian Le Mière and Jeffrey Mazo, *Arctic Opening: Insecurity and Opportunity* (New York: Routledge, 2013), 162–68.
41. A title that should be on everyone's (ice) shelf is Lisa E. Bloom's *Climate Change and the New Polar Aesthetics: Artists Reimagine the Arctic and Antarctic* (Durham, N.C.: Duke University Press, 2022). "Friendlier" refers to Vilhjalmur Stefansson's *The Friendly Arctic: The Story of Five Years in Polar Regions* (New York: Macmillan, 1921).
42. Madeline Sayet, *Where We Belong* (London: Bloomsbury, 2022), madelinesayet .com. For more on Arluk's "Cree takeover," visit akpiktheatre.com/pawakan -macbeth. The Scottish play (1606–1607), indeed, is a cold one; see *Shakespeare in the North: Place, Politics, and Performance in England and Scotland,* ed. Adam Hansen (Edinburgh: Edinburgh University Press, 2021).
43. Sheila Watt-Cloutier, *The Right to Be Cold: One Woman's Fight to Protect the Arctic and Save the Planet from Climate Change* (Minneapolis: University of Minnesota Press, 2015), xx.
44. Like the RaceB4Race series run by the Arizona Center for Medieval and Renaissance Studies, acmrs.asu.edu/RaceB4Race. Thanks for everything you do!

45. Leanne Betasamosake Simpson, *As We Have Always Done: Indigenous Freedom through Radical Resistance* (Minneapolis: University of Minnesota Press, 2017), 9.

## Acknowledgments

1. William Frederic Badè, ed., *The Life and Letters of John Muir,* vol. 2 (Boston: Houghton Mifflin, 1924), 60.
2. William Frederic Badè, ed., *The Life and Letters of John Muir,* vol. 1 (Boston: Houghton Mifflin, 1923), 266.

# Index

**Lowell Duckert** is associate professor of English at the University of Delaware. He is coeditor of *Elemental Ecocriticism: Thinking with Earth, Air, Water, and Fire* (2015) and *Veer Ecology: A Companion for Environmental Thinking* (2017) and author of *For All Waters: Finding Ourselves in Early Modern Wetscapes* (2017), all published by the University of Minnesota Press.